BINDING

Vol. VII

The simple border design on this volume is a facsimile of the original on the official German copy of the Versailles Peace Treaty, which was signed by President Ebert and Premier Bauer and deposited in the Archives of the new German Government.

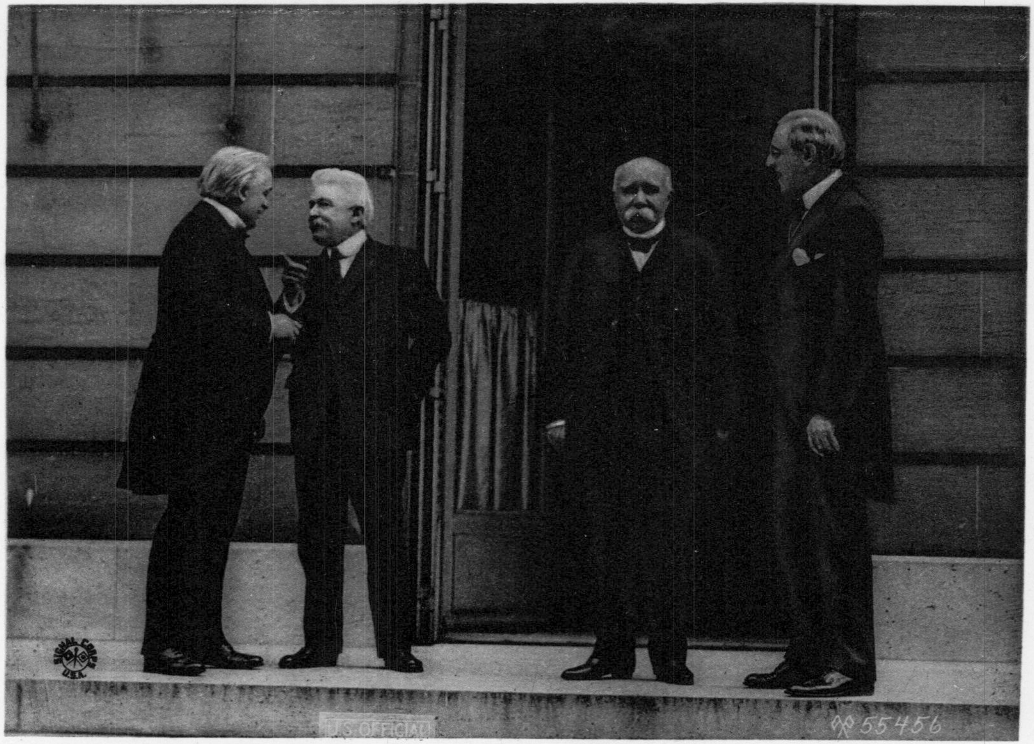
SIGNAL CORPS U.S.A.
U.S. OFFICIAL
55456

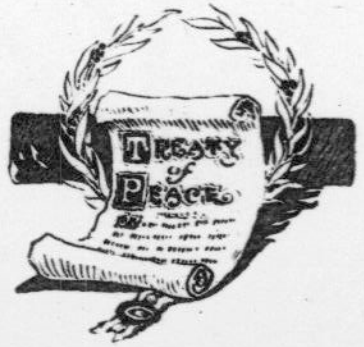
TREATY of PEACE

The Peace Makers
Lloyd-George, Orlando, Clemenceau
and Wilson (from left to right) at
the entrance to the Wilson residence
in the Place des Etats Unis, in Paris

SOURCE RECORDS

OF

THE GREAT WAR

A COMPREHENSIVE AND READABLE SOURCE RECORD OF THE WORLD'S GREAT WAR, EMPHASIZING THE MORE IMPORTANT EVENTS, AND PRESENTING THESE AS COMPLETE NARRATIVES IN THE ACTUAL WORDS OF THE CHIEF OFFICIALS AND MOST EMINENT LEADERS

NON-PARTISAN NON-SECTIONAL NON-SECTARIAN

PRESENTING DOCUMENTS FROM GOVERNMENT ARCHIVES AND OTHER AUTHORITATIVE SOURCES, WITH OUTLINE NARRATIVES, INDICES, CHRONOLOGIES, AND COURSES OF READING ON SOCIOLOGICAL MOVEMENTS AND INDIVIDUAL NATIONAL ACTIVITIES

EDITOR-IN-CHIEF

CHARLES F. HORNE, PH.D.

DIRECTING EDITOR

WALTER F. AUSTIN, LL.M.

With a staff of specialists

VOLUME VII

❧ ❧

National Alumni

9511

COPYRIGHT, 1923, NATIONAL ALUMNI

Printed in U.S.A.

The thanks of the publishers are due for permission to incorporate in this volume the following material: articles by Mme. Grouitch and C. Pergler, Copyright by the American Academy of Political and Social Science: by F. C. Howe, Copyright 1919 by Scribner's Sons: by G. Mason, Copyright 1919 by Outlook Co.: by S. Lauzanne, Copyright by North American Review Corporation: by W. J. Shepard, Copyright and reprinted by permission of American Political Science Review: and extracts from R. S. Baker, Copyright and reprinted by permission of Doubleday, Page & Co.: from E. Borchard, Copyright by Atlantic Monthly Press: from H. Hansen's "Adventures of the Fourteen Points," Copyright by The Century Co.

CONTENTS

VOLUME VII—1918–1919

RECONSTRUCTION AND THE PEACE TREATY

APPENDICES

INDEXES

MAPS AND STATISTICS

ILLUSTRATIONS

VOLUME VII

1918—1919
FROM ARMISTICE TO PEACE TREATY

AN OUTLINE NARRATIVE OF

THE FIRST STEPS IN REBUILDING THE WORLD

BY CHARLES F. HORNE

HUMAN progress moves as with the swing of some vast pendulum, each forward step reversing itself in some sharp reaction. Yet there is progress. Men who have studied that pendulous sweep throughout the ages, have learned to watch its backward swing without despair. They have built for themselves from history the same high and confident faith that spiritual souls have gathered from religion, the faith that every forward step of the human race grows longer and stronger, and that each backward move is shortened, is indeed but the regaining of solid ground from which the divine impulse again sweeps us onward with a larger power. Some such faith we need in dwelling on the days of reaction that followed immediately on the Great War.

On November 11, 1918, the world, or rather the peoples of the Allies, had reached a glory of such exalted spirit as mankind had not known for many centuries. That, at least, the Great War did for our generation. It gave to us a passion of energy, of self-sacrifice, of devotion to a high purpose, of noble thought and noble service, such as no generation had ever reached before, except through the ecstasy of some great religion. The steadfast opposition with which all peoples had defied autocratic savagery, the unyielding "Will to Righteousness" displayed by our men and by our women, on the battle front and in the services of home, had been a revelation of the splendid height to which the universal human spirit can soar, the deeds it can accomplish.

Unfortunately, however, the everyday life of our race holds no such mighty stimulus. That wondrous spirit of the war days faded somewhat, inevitably faded, after the armed victory was won. Those who had saved the world, wanted now to enjoy the world. As the call for love and service to mankind grew less intense, the voice of self-service and self-love grew strong again. Few men have such broad vision that they can see earth as a whole, can realize all the influence of that which happens far in the East upon him who dwells perchance in the farthest West. In the months that followed on the Armistice, the thoughts of each ordinary man centered more and more upon his own nation, his own neighborhood, his own family, his own comfort.

From the universal, therefore, men descended to the particular. The Central Powers of Europe had surrendered. Some disposition of them must be made. They must not be allowed strength ever to disrupt the world again. But on the exact methods by which this was to be done, scarcely any two men agreed, and no two nations were anywhere near agreement. Each studied the future from the viewpoint of its own nationality.

Britain was convinced that the best guarantee of a permanent peace lay in a mighty British Empire spreading a mighty fleet abroad over every ocean. France believed the guarantee should be a greater France extended to the Rhine and holding Germany in thrall by military force. Japan thought the peace path might lead by way of an acknowledgment of complete racial equality; that is, Japanese equality and Japanese supremacy over Chinamen. Italy planned to dominate the Adriatic and the Balkans, and thus, as a wiser Austria, to hold under her control the ever-menacing racial antagonisms of southeastern Europe. Even Bolshevistic Russia had its blinded theory that if only the world were all ignorant and all proletarian it would be all at peace.

In America people had escaped most of these antagonisms through the good fortune of possessing a half empty hemisphere of their own, and a blended ancestry, wise with the sufferings they had endured in every European land. Hence in America there persisted a real strength of purpose toward a broader reconstruction. Men dreamed of a union like that of their already "united states," only on a world-wide basis,

an equal organization of all governments without the enlargement of any one.   But to the crowded eastern hemisphere
this seemed only a dream, or more nearly a nightmare, destructive of what each nation loved the best.

While favorite hopes, and plans for future greatness,
thus swayed each government from its once intense war-
time concentration upon mere survival, all governments occupied themselves mainly with more immediate needs.   Each
studied, in accordance with the special pressure upon each,
to save its people from the exhaustion and misery resultant
from the War. That misery has been sharply impressed upon
the memory of every thinking person, has been stamped hid-
eously and unforgetably upon the vision of all those who
"saw," all those who have endured and have survived their
scars.   Here we need only briefly review the consequences of
the disaster.

During four awful years, a large portion of the world
had been swept by the brutalizing ravage of massacre and
starvation and all the horde of diseases which civilization, in
more prosperous days, had learned to hold in check. A "Black
Death," more deadly than the terrible medieval plague so
named, had once more burst every barrier built up by the
wisdom of scientists and statesmen, had escaped all the chains
slowly wrought by human effort, and had harried the human
race.   What the Horror's toll of lives had been in those
ruined lands which had once rejoiced in the pompous names
of Russian and Turkish Empires we can only guess; and
from those regions as a center its curse had extended in a
destruction but little less deadly over all western Asia and
central Europe.

In its passing, the scourge had not only destroyed human
life and left to the bereaved a lasting and immeasurable grief;
it had also swept away all the garnered store of food and
seed from former years, most of the domestic animals once
counted on for future supplies, and much of that accumulated
treasure of houses and tools and furnishings and clothes
which represented the patient labor of many generations.
Naked almost as Adam, a large portion of the human race
had to recommence its toil in a world less tropically com-

fortable than Eden's garden, and with wants and desires far more complex than those of our primeval parents.

So, while European diplomats discussed the terms of armistice and peace, their governments were far more immediately concerned with questions of food and labor and domestic finance. Many million people had to be carried over the threatening starvation period, until another autumn should bring Nature's harvest once more to the support of man.

In this work of relief America and also Britain gave generous aid. Herbert Hoover, the former director of Belgian relief, was now appointed the United States' commissioner for distributing supplies everywhere. American funds and American food, under his direction, became the chief factor in bringing to all Europe a temporary rescue.

Yet even this last and greatest of the broad charities of the War, fostered misunderstandings and dissensions. Each continental nation was now looking mainly to its own needs; and each asserted its own first claim to aid. In many lands the people were so exhausted both mentally and physically, so drained of hope and energy that they were content just to sit in idleness and be fed. They grew to look upon the supplies as a right; and at length the relief commissioners had to announce everywhere that they would help only such as helped themselves. Even in France, where during the War the gallantry of spirit had been most high and recognition of the service of Britain and America most ready, even there the voice of business sounded louder than the voice of gratitude.

For the first month or so after the Armistice this changing temper of the peoples everywhere was scarcely felt. Vast military supplies had been gathered to support the armies through the coming winter of 1918-19, and it was easy to transfer to the peoples some of these supplies, especially of food and clothes. So November and even December continued to be months of triumph.

By the beginning of 1919, however, the reaction was complete. Only the United States and Britain retained any surplus of power and energy to be turned to other than immediate affairs.   In those lands the plans of reorganization proceeded rapidly and the people still found time to interest themselves in science, in the readjustments of capital and labor, and even in their sports.   Half sporting and half scientific, for example, was the transatlantic flight by air machines.   This was repeatedly attempted, and was first achieved by an American "sea-plane" on May 17th of 1919.

THE TRIUMPH OVER GERMANY

Continental Europe meanwhile was giving all its energies to the primal problem of self-preservation, the saving of civilization from the close approach of Bolshevism and starvation.   Following on the Armistice, the armies of Belgium, Britain, the United States, and France marched eagerly forward into Germany and settled down to that occupation of the Rhine lands which was to be turned by the Peace Treaty into a more permanent tenancy.

To men who still thought along old lines, who recalled the boastful German march through Paris after the War of 1870, this expression of victory over Germany was not a very satisfying form of triumph.   The French indeed strove to give to the investment an air of *"La gloire,"* of soul-satisfying vengeance; but to the other armies this was only the final plodding step in a hard and long extended task.   Everywhere the Ally soldiers found the Germans ready to receive them obediently, almost cordially.   The German people were only too thankful to have escaped armed ravage and plunder, such as they had visited upon other lands.[1]

Hence the investment proved no more than a military parade, followed by the military policing of a region which had indeed been drained bare of all military supplies but had still at command the necessities and most of the comforts of civilian life.   Many of the more ignorant soldiers in the armies of occupation, looking around upon the peace and order and cleanliness that flourished along the Rhine, began even to question if this social organism of Germany were not better than their own.   They failed to realize the crushing

[1] See § I, "Occupation of the Rhine Land," by Hanotaux, Howe, etc.

weight of that autocratic government which had sheltered these lands, failed to see how slavish was the spirit of submission which alone had made such conditions possible. That blind obedience of the German masses had made all Germany's vaunted "organization" inferior, in the end, to the higher spirit of individual independence and initiative in the Frenchman.

Beyond the Rhine, moreover, the German people were in far less happy condition. The revolution of November, which had driven the Kaiser into flight, had left the land without any assured government. The Socialist leaders in Berlin had declared the country a republic, and the old imperial officials had quietly handed over their authority to the newly proclaimed President, "Fritz" Ebert, the Heidelberg "saddle-maker." Thus the revolution had been a most orderly and even dignified affair, many of the former officials continuing their duties under the new authorities.

This very orderliness, however, worked against the suddenly reared republic. Its reality and its sincerity were doubted, both by the Allies abroad and by the discontented and turbulent working-classes at home. The more extreme revolutionists, the "Spartacans," as they called themselves, refused to believe that this was revolution at all. They wanted to go immeasurably further, to set up a government like that of Russia, to establish the "rule of the proletariat," with all the middle and upper classes exterminated or reduced to servitude.

There were tumults everywhere, and fierce uprisings only put down by military force. In January and again in March Berlin was torn by deadly warfare in her streets, and hundreds of the Spartacans were slain. The new government's chief of police, Noske, proved resolute and energetic in crushing each revolt; but he only did so by invoking the very forces which his Socialist comrades had themselves condemned in other days as tyrannous and murderous. The leaders of the Spartacan movement, Dr. Liebknecht and Rosa Luxemburg, were both slain while under arrest by Noske's police. When the whirligig of fortune swings into unexpected power, some tender-hearted proletarian idealist, the form of government which he himself adopts proves usually that of slaughtering his former "beloved brothers" as well as his "brutally tyrannous" opponents, without even the formality of a trial. Few human beings are built so strong as to withstand the temptations that attend upon unlimited power.[1]

Gradually from out the German chaos there emerged a form of order. An election was held by universal suffrage; and on February 6th of 1919 a truly representative "Reichstag" or National Assembly convened. Its members were mainly Socialistic, but by no means impractical. Many had been well-known leaders in former Reichstags, and under their experienced hands the work of reorganization progressed smoothly. President Ebert was by this Assembly confirmed in office; a constitution was prepared for the republic; and a regular democratic government was formed. Twice at least this new government suppressed revolts both by the extreme radicals and by the extreme reactionaries, the latter seeking to restore the military empire. Thus by degrees the Allies came to look upon the German Republic as a reality and as a stability; they began to feel for it a confidence it had not at first inspired. If the new Germany be not perfect, it is at least far more free, far more honest, more democratic, and less vainglorious than the old.[2]

DOWNFALL OF THE "MIDDLE EUROPE EMPIRE"

The other lands from which Germany had hoped to mold her "Empire of Middle Europe" were less swift of reconstruction. Here too, however, the patient watcher of the pendulum will read hope and faith into the future, despite the superficial vision of anarchy and shame. Russia and her former provinces remained deep in misery; but to the other Slavic peoples the giant outcome of the War was freedom, the freeing of all their cowed and "slavish" world from the Teuton yoke of centuries.

That broad belt of submerged races between the Teuton and the Russian centers of power, once coveted and almost

---

[1] See § VI, Germany Crushes Bolshevism," by Matthei, etc.
[2] See § IV, "Germany Begins Republican Government," by Ebert, etc.

wholly devoured by the two great rivals, now lay distracted, lordless, uncontrolled, tossing madly between present starvation and reawakened dreams of nationality and future power. The ill-bound Austrian domain, that merest catspaw and cloak of German expansion toward the southeast, exploded into fragments from within before ever an Ally regiment had crossed its borders.

One dark picture follows there upon another, the horror deepening as we watch. Soldiers shot down their officers, and officers their men. Sailors drowned their captains. Whole divisions of the subject troops refused to advance to the front, and entrenching themselves in armed camps defied their government by force. Hungarian armies were recklessly disbanded by their generals far from their own homes; and they marched across Austria in huge mobs, seizing food and plunder as they went, and leaving behind them strips of desert as bare as where the locust plague had passed of old.

While loyal Austrian troops still stood beyond their outmost former frontier holding back the Serbian army in the Serbian mountains and the Italian army along the Italian rivers, the subject races within the heart of the empire broke into open revolt. The ancient Hapsburg bubble burst as utterly as had that still more swollen bubble of the Hohenzollerns. In the northern Austrian provinces, on October 28, 1918, the people of Prague, the ancient capital of Bohemia, the chief seat of the Czecho-Slavs or north Slavs, turned out their Austrian officials and assumed control of their own government. In the south the leaders of the Jugo-Slavs or south Slavs did the same on October 29th. Hastily gathered committees met at the chief south Slavic cities, at Laibach, at Agram, and at Serajevo, where the War had been begun; and all declared the Austrian dominion was at an end forever.

The Hungarians also sought to escape from sharing the doom of the shattered empire of which they had long been the fiercest and most warlike supporters. On October 31st the Hungarian "Diet" or parliament declared Hungary a wholly independent republic under the liberal democratic leader Count Karolyi. The helpless Hapsburg emperor,

Charles, abdicated early in November; and the new republic hastened to claim from the Allies friendship, alliance, a release from all responsibility for the former empire's misdeeds, and an assurance that the Hungarian sovereignty over the surrounding Slavic races should be perpetuated. When Count Karolyi and the other nobles who had accepted his guidance found this lordly pose ignored by the Allies, they in March resigned office as a protest, appealing to "the peoples of all the world" for "justice."

This was really an appeal to Russia, and a threat to the Allies that Hungary would turn Bolshevist. Indeed, a nominally Bolshevistic government or "dictatorship of the proletariat" was promptly set up in April under the control of Bela Kun, a revolutionary soldier. The Bolshevism of Bela Kun was, however, free from the unreasoning bloodshed and fury against the upper classes which had been displayed in Russia. As dictator he ruled Hungary not unsuccessfully, even conducting an effective military campaign to extend her borders.

Finally, however, Bela Kun ventured to attack Rumania. This brought about the invasion of his country and his own complete defeat. In August of 1919 the Rumanians captured Budapest, the Hungarian capital, and wrung a heavy toll from the entire land. After their withdrawal the wholly disillusioned Hungarian nobles returned to their old trust in the Hapsburgs and chose a member of the royal family, the Archduke Joseph, as their ruler. Him, the Allies ordered out, being resolved that no Hapsburg should again build up an empire. So before the end of 1919 the much changed and changing Hungary was again a so-called republic, but of most reactionary type, dominated by the remnant of its fierce nobility.

A similar anarchy, only made up more of despair and less of arrogance, pervaded Austria itself. Even the long suffering populace of Vienna burst into revolt when the royal armies fled; and on November 10, 1918, Vienna saw a revolution similar to that of Berlin. Driving out the Hapsburgs, the people set up a Socialistic republic, and appealed to all the world for food. The food was slow in coming, and the misery of the city folk of Austria became intense.   In January of 1919 the starving republic voted to unite itself to Germany; but this the Allies forbade, and Vienna still remains in desolation, a capital almost without a country, a great starving city having now little chance and little excuse for drawing its sustenance from the surrounding country.

THE NEW NATIONS OF CENTRAL EUROPE

While the forces of disintegration were thus rending into fragmentary and unreal republics the long planned "Empire of Middle Europe," there were other forces working in the region for reconstruction.   The Bohemians or Czecho-Slovaks, as they now named themselves, had long before built up an army in Russia to fight for the Ally cause.   Of the remarkable exploits of this "army without a country" we have told in a previous volume, as also of the formation of an exile government of Czecho-Slovakia in Paris, under President Masaryk.   The stanch courage of these men now met its reward.   Czecho-Slovakian independence was immediately recognized by the Allies, the Paris government of President Masaryk was transferred to Prague, the Bohemian capital; and a remnant of the wandering army was ultimately restored to its home.[1]

All this northern section of the Austrian Empire thus became a new and important republic, Czecho-Slovakia, a mountain State in the heart of Europe, much larger and stronger than the similar mountain republic of Switzerland. Moreover, Czecho-Slovakia was from the start a democratic State.   Its new president had been accounted a dreamer in the old days, a preacher of impossible extremes of peasant government.   Yet it was upon the support of the Slavic peasantry that Masaryk builded his government.   There was too much work to be done to pause for a general election then; and not until a year and a half later, in May of 1920, did a regularly elected Assembly meet to voice the people's will in Czecho-Slovakia.   Yet when it did meet, it approved practically all that Masaryk and his supporters had done. It renamed him president, it confirmed the laws of the earlier

[1] See § VIII, "The Republic of Czecho-Slovakia," by Masaryk, etc.

irregular Assembly, which had abolished all titles of nobility, and broken up all territorial estates. No proprietor in that resolute democracy can hold more than a square mile of land. On the other hand, the Czecho-Slovak laws are equally resolute against Bolshevism, the attempt to subjugate brain beneath the weight of numbers and of ignorance. The interest in this new and boldly progressive European government, a democracy encircled by every form of tyranny and grasping force, is not confined to Europe.

Far differently moved the forces of reconstruction in the Polish lands. The ancient Kingdom of Poland had been abolished, and its lands divided among neighboring kings more than a century before; but the Polish spirit had never died. The national anthem of the Poles was still sung in secret. It opens with the cry, "Poland yet survives!" During the early years of the War, the regions of Russian and Austrian Poland had been desolated more utterly than any other European land except Serbia. Then in 1917 the exhausted remnant of the populace had obtained shelter under German domination, a peace of suppression and almost of starvation. The German part of Poland was in far better condition; it had suffered but little more than other German lands, had been drained of its young manhood but had not been ravaged. So now, when the Armistice left the Poles to themselves, left them to build anew their ancient and beloved State, it was from the Germanized Poles that their strength chiefly came.

Indeed Germany and Austria had already created from Russian Poland a "Kingdom of Poland" of their own, having it ruled by a "Regency Council" until they could select a proper Teuton princeling to set up as its king. In France the Allies had been supporting a Polish army, made up of exiled Poles who had rallied to the Ally cause from many lands. So the "Council" in Poland now asked for Ally support; and a new Polish Republic was set up, extending over Prussian, Austrian, and much of German Poland. A general election was held in January of 1919; and thus a truly Polish government, elected by the people, came into operation. It requested and promptly received representation at the Peace Conference.[1]

The men elected to the new Polish Assembly were how ever, mainly upper class Poles, representing the ancient aristocratic spirit of the land, rather than the masses of the people. These latter were far too crushed, too enfeebled, to think or act for themselves. Hence the new Polish Republic was set up rather from without than from within. It was the foster child of the Allies, rather than a spontaneous birth from the nation. It was the bulwark which Western Europe sought to build as a defense between anarchistic Russia and militaristic Germany.

Naturally the new Poland showed itself aggressive from the start. Its armies were hurriedly reënforced, received Ally supplies, and began to reach out in all directions, claim- ing all surrounding regions which had once belonged to Po- land, seeking to extend its frontiers at the expense of Russia and of the Ukraine and even of Czecho-Slovakia. There were rumors of military "pogroms," unprevented massacres of Polish Jews, and while investigation proved these charges to have been exaggerated, there remained to them a dark shadow of tragic truth. The new Poland has not pleased all lovers of the human race as has the new Czecho-Slovakia. The former seems only seeking to recreate the Past; the latter to have caught a definite vision of the Future.

RECONSTRUCTION IN SOUTH-EASTERN EUROPE

In south-eastern Europe, the forces of reconstruction cen- tered mainly about Serbia and Rumania. These had been the Allies' champions and the Teutons' victims in the War. To them, or to such of their people as survived, belonged the future, upheld by the Allies.

Few abler, stronger heroes had been brought out by the War than Prince Alexander of Serbia. As regent for his father, the aged, picturesque King Peter, Alexander had won the loyalty and admiration of all his people, and the trust of other nations too. It was to him that the Austrian south Slavs turned. They were chiefly of three kindred Slavic

[1] See § V, "The Rescue of Poland," Paderewski, Hoover, et al.

races, the Slovenes, an agricultural people, the Croats, a
more cultured folk, and the Serbs of Bosnia and Herzegovina, mountaineers, long nominal subjects of the Turks.
When these peoples had declared themselves independent
of Austria, some of them, especially the Slovenes, desired to
set up separate republics like those of their fellow Slavs in
Czecho-Slovakia and Poland. But a large majority voted
to unite themselves with the Serbians, the champions of the
south Slav nationalities throughout the War. So on December 1, 1918, a delegation from the various Austrian south
Slavic peoples came to Prince Alexander in his ruined and
now hastily reëstablished capital of Belgrade, and asked to
be united with his people in a "democratic kingdom" of
all the south or Jugo-Slavs. The new kingdom, promptly
organized, was formally announced to the world on January 3, 1919, as the "Kingdom of the Serbs, Croats and
Slovenes." [1]

Even the Serbs of little Montenegro, the wild mountain
land which had never lost its independence to either Turk
or Teuton, now voted to join the other Serbs in this new
kingdom of "greater Serbia." The Montenegrins deposed
their own aged sovereign, despite his vigorous protests, and
helped to make of all the Serbs a single kingdom, the dominant State of the future Balkan regions.

As for Rumania, having submitted perforce to the Teutons early in 1918, and having received from them a form
of peace, she had been able during the last year of the War
to reorganize a government. This, immediately upon the
Armistice, rallied all its forces and both by diplomacy and
by arms began a vigorous effort for a "greater Rumania,"
as great as circumstances and the Allies might by any possibility allow. Many regions of Rumanian race had been
held subject to Austro-Hungary along its eastern frontier.
Rumania justly claimed all these regions and other similar
adjoining lands in Russia. But in addition to these, which
she was well assured the Allies would restore to her, she
wanted to take from the neighboring Hungarians all she
could. Her armies, as we have already noted, invaded Hun-

See § II, "Union of Greater Serbia," Prince Alexander, etc.

gary and occupied its capital; they refused to withdraw even
when the Allies so commanded. They plundered Hungary
and brought it as near to desolation as their own land had
been, and only withdrew at the Allies' continuous insistance,
when there was nothing left for them to carry off. Rumania
thus achieved a vengeance after the ancient fashion, such as
many of the Allies' peoples had longed to inflict on Germany.

THE PEACE CONFERENCE

While Middle Europe was thus discordantly rearranging
itself, the Allies met in their great Peace Conference at Paris.
Disappointing as the results of this may have seemed to the
sentimentalist who demanded that the conferees should settle every problem of the universe, and each in accord with
the sentimentalist's own pet theories, that Paris Conference
was yet the most important political gathering ever held
among the sons of men. No such assembly had ever shown
before so broad a practical wisdom and so humble and toler-
ant a brotherhood. These leaders were a unit in seeking
some stable readjustment of the nations; but, as we have
seen, each nation viewed this stability from its own angle,
and on matters of detail the Allies were as little in accord
as were their Middle Europe dependants.

In the Conference, the United States delegation held a
unique position, in that they had so much to give and so
little to ask for their country. Hence their leader, President
Wilson, stood out above all the other far-famed leaders of
the Conference. He insisted, more broadly and more securely than any other could, upon a world policy of justice
toward both friend and foe, and of equality for all mankind.
These are noble thoughts, sure always of winning an easy,
superficial approval; but in just what way should these large
ideas be expressed in concrete form? To Woodrow Wilson
they seemed mainly to demand the creation of a League of
Nations; and he fought with unfailing resolution for such
a league.

Many wide-thinking statesmen, chiefly from Great Britain, approved the Wilson purpose of a world-organization. A few idealistic writers in all lands upheld him and

his efforts to the end.   But within the Conference he met most determined opposition.   Moreover, the Congress of his own country afterward repudiated his stand, so that he cannot be said to have had behind him the united voice of his own nation.   His opponents did not question his high intention and sincerity; but European antagonists declared him obstinate and unpractical, while those of his homeland declared him misled by the "keener craft of Europe's diplomats." [1]

Thus the Conference became the struggle of one resolute man with a vision of the future, against a mass of practical statesmen swayed by the immediate desires of the present.   The European leaders were driven by the fears or the ambitions or the hard necessities of their people to make incessant, ever-increasing demands.

In the first flush of peace, after all those long years of agony and ever-darkening FEAR, the peace itself had seemed all that people wished for.   When President Wilson first reached Europe in December of 1918, he was received every-where as the champion and savior of the human race.   It was on his "Fourteen Points" that Germany had surrendered. They contented everybody, since everybody knew that the Allies were themselves to interpret the meaning of the points, and since these included restitution from Germany for the damage she had inflicted.   There were three encouraging impulses in each rejoicing heart: peace was to last forever; Germany was to be the scapegoat who must suffer for all; and every one was to receive back all that he had lost.

Only by degrees did the stunning truth reach out to the mind of the common man, that Germany *could not* pay. Hence there was to be no satisfying restitution.   Destruction is so much easier than creation.   So large a part of the accumulated possessions of the world, its laboriously built up wealth of machinery, of public utilities, of ships and railroads and charities and institutions of learning and resources of every kind had been destroyed in the War that the whole of Germany did not possess and could not restore one-twen-

[1] See § III, "Opening of the Peace Conference," Wilson, Lloyd George, Harden, et al.

tieth part of what had perished. Nay, even if the loss were all charged up as a money debt against her and her children's children forever, and creditors seized all the profits from their toil for generations, the loss would never be made good to any now alive; and if interest were charged against the debt, then through each year the toil of the German peoples thus enslaved would not even pay that interest. Germany must remain a land of serfs forever, held under only by military force, and breeding hatred, poison, and at last universal destruction. Not on such a foundation could the world be recreated.

Of course the leaders of the Allies had long foreknown this. Therefore they hastened to draw the distinction between what Germany had been "justified" in destroying, in accordance with what they regarded as the established international laws of war, and what she had destroyed "illegally," or in defiance of the rules of the game. Also they classed apart such destruction as had been caused by their own armies or governments. But a French farmer, for example, who hoped to have back his little farm with the barns and the stone fences and the herds that he had owned before, had suffered with equal severity whether his cows had been taken legally or no, and his barns destroyed by a French shell or a German mine.

There, then, lay the root difficulty. Germany could not pay! To an American, comparatively little injured by the War, the philosophic conclusion came easily enough. "In that case, let her pay what she can. Cancel the rest." This easy critic was scarce prepared for the fierce European response, "Then, will you pay for her? Will you make good to us from your abundance?" To the American this seemed only another demand for charity, and he had been already largely charitable. The European looked upon the situation in another light. He had suffered to save civilization, which included saving the American. The latter, after long prospering in trade from the War, had only joined it just at the end, and hence had done but a small part of his fair share. It was only just that he should now contribute money where the others had paid so much more heavily in blood. Here came a widening breach between the European and the American. Whatever the latter might do to aid, seemed to the former insufficient. Wherever America insisted on upholding a principle, Europe said, "You have not counted on the cost—to me."

Even the most courageous of Europe's leaders dared not meet their people frankly. The laboring classes, who had borne the main burden of the War, were beginning to demand release from their strenuous effort and privations. They, too, wanted now the pleasure and comfort of life. The shortage of everything was giving increased value to whatever property and stores remained, so prices mounted rapidly; and labor everywhere met this with a demand for higher wages. Then as men began to feel the actual pinch of the world's great poverty, their tempers naturally hardened. If Germany, under the restrictions of the "fourteen points," could not be made to pay, except some small amounts for technically "illegal" damage, then away with the fourteen points.

Instead of the statesmen leading the people now, the people drove the statesmen. Britain's Prime Minister, Lloyd George, returned temporarily from the Paris Conference to direct a British election, and found that his lack of severity toward Germany was likely to lose him his parliamentary control. The gradually changing tone of his speeches during that three weeks' election campaign makes a most interesting study. Before its close, he was pledging himself to exact from Germany a most tremendous indemnity, and to bring to punishment every German "war criminal" from the Kaiser down. Other premiers went through similar or more severe experiences. So little recompense was possible, that in every land the populace were soon vociferously demanding the more than possible. When they failed to obtain it, the fault could always be laid to those "impractical Americans."

And, in simple, saddest truth, the Americans did meet the situation impractically. Not within the Conference, but in their own home land, they ignored the need of harmony among themselves. Forgetting that all agreement must be founded upon compromise, they seemed to think that they were the only victors in the War, that while their President should dictate to none of them at home, they could and should dictate to the other Allies, and to the world, whatever Treaty each American preferred. They argued among themselves over every item of the final document, seeking to turn each to their own pattern and protesting vehemently against points which touched them least. Instead of recognizing that the Treaty was at least far more of American than of European making and a closer approach to democratic ideals than any general organization ever before arranged, they opposed it because it was not wholly and solely what each defined in some different fashion as "American." To attempt to weigh the varying degrees of blame for this confusion, or to discuss how serious were the possible flaws within the Treaty, would be to enter regions of most violent partisanship. The obvious consequence remains. The United States threw away the leadership which might have been hers in the reconstruction of the world organism.

THE OPPOSING DESIRES OF THE POWERS

That is the real story of the Peace Treaty. When the Conference was formally opened on January 18, 1919, President Wilson was still the idol of Europe and the hero of the hour. Over the main point, the German indemnity, there was no real dispute within the Conference. The United States delegates agreed with those of Europe that Germany should pay all she could; and the share of the United States from any such payment would have been so small that she could well afford to resign it to more needy claimants. In this matter, the trouble lay, as we have seen, between the European governments and their hungry peoples.

But as each new point arose by which the various governments tried to snatch some other compensating value from the War, President Wilson found himself opposing each one in turn. He held firmly to the idea upon which the pledge of peace had first been based, that it was to be a "peace of justice" and not a "peace of vengeance." These two catchwords serve as guiding points to all the discussions of the

Conference. Never had delegates come to any such conference with fuller preparedness of information than was here possessed by the United States delegates. For two years past a commission had been gathering and arranging for them every possible item of knowledge on the European situation. As each nation claimed this or that, each found President Wilson fully informed and firmly set for what he accounted justice as opposed to its desires. Each opponent in turn disagreed with him, and blamed him. Soon he had scarce a friendly champion in Europe.

Each step in the long dispute was focused around some popular word by which the world understood or misunderstood it. The first test was that of the "mandatories." The Europeans had found one pleasing way for making Germany pay in part to every government; that was by dividing up among themselves all Germany's colonies. But America here insisted that the "peace of justice" for all peoples obviously required that these colonies should not be held as private property, that they belonged each to its own inhabitants, that only those incapable of self-government should be governed by Europeans, and that even then the "mandatory" ruler should rule only for the colony's own good, and only until its people could learn to rule themselves. This was a severe blow, especially to Britain's empire; and the British long opposed it. They yielded only when the great main purpose of the Conference, the rescue of the world from desolation, made yielding necessary.

There indeed lay the constant reason for the United States' control of the Conference. The other Powers needed her, and she did not need them. They needed her food, her money, her courage. Europe had to have peace quickly, before starvation came, and anarchy. To the United States these daunting specters were still far off and vague. She could dare to delay, to argue; she could even, if antagonism grew too bitter, withdraw from the Conference altogether.[1]

At one time the opposition was so resolute that President Wilson openly threatened to do this, to leave Europe to settle her disputes without American aid. This course, Europe

[1] See § VII, "Problems of the Peace Conference," Borchard, etc.

knew, confronted her with the impossible.   Perhaps what
she needed above all else from America was that very detachment of interest which enabled the American delegates
to weigh without prejudice the bitter problems of the older
hemisphere. So anomalous was the situation that while each
European diplomat disagreed with President Wilson, each
trusted to him to arbitrate among them all, and to him alone.
Thus when he actually ordered his ship and prepared on
April 7th to leave for home, the other leaders accepted his
policies once more.

The "League of Nations" had been on that occasion the
chief theme under dispute, and France was Wilson's main
opponent. Prime Minister Clemenceau had frankly expressed
his lack of faith in any such league; he would have erased
it from the Peace Treaty altogether. Through all his lengthened life the "Tiger of France" had fought the German
menace, and he had won the terrific fight at last. Could such
a man, at such a moment, abandon the very method of his
success! Let peace be maintained by keeping soldiers always in Germany, as Napoleon would once have maintained
it, if he could. As for wars among the European Allies
themselves, their mutual interest in suppressing Germany
would keep them bound together. As for a league to which
everybody belonged, and to which even Germany might some
day be admitted as an equal—the "Tiger" had treated it
with courteous but open scorn.

Still sharper opposition came when President Wilson
championed "Greater Serbia" as against Italy in the "Fiume"
dispute. He insisted that the Serbs must have free access
to the Adriatic, while Italy dreamed of encircling the entire
sea and making it, as ancient Venice once had made it, an
Italian lake. In this dispute the Italian leaders even went
so far as to withdraw from Paris; but when they found
President Wilson was inflexible, they returned to the Conference, accepting, as Britain and France had accepted, the
lesser disappointment for the greater need. They left to
their more irresponsible compatriots, to the poet aviator,
D'Annunzio, and his volunteer army, the seizure of Fiume

by force—a last appeal to the older methods of armed conquest, a definite though feeble voice given to the belief still secretly held in many hearts that the German viewpoint was the true one, after all, that force is the final arbiter, that man's passions are mightier than his wisdom, and that intensity of individual desire will in the end prevail.

The last of all the important controversies of the Peace Conference, and the one in which Wilson yielded most and has perhaps been most sharply blamed, was that with Japan. The Japanese delegates had come to the Conference with three points in view. They hoped to win more island colonies in the Pacific; they planned to confirm their hold upon Shantung, the Chinese region which they had captured from the Germans; and they eagerly desired a declaration of race equality which should place them fully on a level with all Europeans in any diplomatic negotiation of the future. The first point they yielded early in the Conference, when President Wilson's system of "mandatories" was accepted. The point of race equality the President could not grant; he knew that his own people of the western United States would never consent to it. They had a practical dread of being overrun and even crowded from their homes by Japanese immigrants. So here the President had no choice but to accept the will of his own people, just as Lloyd George had bowed to his, and the other European premiers to theirs.

To the Japanese at the Conference there remained, after these two refusals, only their third desire, Shantung. Since they already held it in possession and Germany had held it before during almost twenty years, the continuance of its temporary lease seemed a small concession to make to them. Moreover, the success of the entire Conference might easily have hung upon the refusal; for the strain of many antagonisms was already severe. The Japanese were in the same advantageous position as the Americans, in that they could afford to continue arguing indefinitely; they had no immediate need for peace. So President Wilson yielded as to Shantung; and, except for helplessly protesting China, the Peace Treaty was agreed upon among the Allies.

THE SIGNING OF THE TREATY

Germany was now summoned to receive the treaty, and her commissioners on first reading it were so horrified at its severity, or they so declared themselves, that they refused to sign it. Rather might the Allies march their armies in triumph over helpless Germany and plunder as they would! Fortunately the German parliament took a less defiant view. The governing Socialistic ministry did indeed resign from office; but other Socialists took control, and despite wide public protest, the government declared that it would sign the peace. In doing so the government agreed with every other German in asserting that the details of the peace were practically impossible of fulfillment. Nevertheless, the effort must be made. Other German commissioners were sent to Versailles, and on June 28th the Peace Treaty was signed.[1]

It was quickly ratified by all the European nations concerned. The United States Senate, however, refused its ratification of the Treaty; and so the United States remained nominally, though not actually, at war with Germany through all the period here reviewed. The opposition to the Treaty in the United States was based partly on the Shantung issue, but mainly on that of the League of Nations, several points of which were regarded as favoring Britain unjustly, and several as being likely to involve America unduly in European quarrels.

EFFECTS OF THE TREATY

The signing of the Treaty, and its ratification by at least the European powers, closed the first period of that gradual process of reconstruction which must occupy the world for years. The Treaty did not definitely settle that largest question as to just what Germany shall pay. A "Reparation Committee" was appointed with power to investigate and decide the amount, and the minimum total of this was set below fifteen billion dollars, a sum enormous for enfeebled Germany, but yet not beyond possibility of payment. This sum could only be enlarged by unanimous consent of the

[1] See § IX, "The Peace of Versailles," Clemenceau, Kautsky, et al.

"Reparation Committee" on which the United States had a member and seemed thus able to exercise its disinterested restraint. The American delay in ratifying the peace, however, left this tremendously powerful committee wholly in European hands; and it not only enlarged the minimum of Germany's debt, but by encouraging the hope of huge future payments it served as a means of soothing the impoverished European peoples.

Beyond this perhaps inevitable financial vagueness, the Treaty accomplished important things. It confirmed the existence of three new and wholly independent States, Poland, Czecho-Slovakia, and the Kingdom of the Serbs, Croats and Slovenes. It did not fix the terms of peace for what was left of Austria and Hungary, nor for Bulgaria and Turkey; but it assured the continued existence of these nationalities. Minor details were left for future conference. The treaty with Austria, or rather with the tiny remaining Austrian Republic, was signed on September 20th, and with Bulgaria on November 27th; those with Hungary and Turkey were delayed until the summer of 1920. All positively Bulgarian territory was left to the Bulgarians, and so also with the Austrians and Hungarians. Even the Turks were assured of the independence of regions where there was a clear Turkish majority; though never again were they to be allowed dominion over any Christian region such as Armenia, or indeed over any subject race.

That, at least, the Great War had accomplished. The principle was universally accepted that men everywhere were to be free and self-governing, as soon as they were sufficiently civilized to be capable of self-government. The only anomaly remaining was in the rule of Ireland by the English; and even there the English had accepted at least the principle, and had pledged themselves to the ultimate granting of Irish self-government.

THE LEAGUE OF NATIONS

As to the League of Nations, the other great outcome of the War, it went into immediate partial operation despite the serious crippling of it by the refusal of the United States

to join what her President had created. Much of the subsequent dealings with Germany were carried on through the
machinery of this League. It is not dead; all men must hope
that in some form some such association of the nations will
survive. Whatever the wisdom or unwisdom of this particular league, upon some such union must the future of
the human race depend. If mankind cannot find a means of
larger organization, then mankind must perish. "To divide
is to destroy." So deadly has modern science now made
war, that it is a far other thing than in those older days when
it was lightly called "The Sport of Kings," and when men
could even praise it as a developer of strength and heroism.
It has become to-day the threatening oblivion of mankind.
If not the next war, then some war soon beyond must see the
extermination of our human race. Through long ages we
have at last reached the point where man's destructive
genius can accomplish extermination, and where it will accomplish this, unless man's social genius for constructive
harmony is rearoused and masters the destructive. Without some union, inspired from above and wisely taught and
well-policed, man will inevitably be expunged from the universe, his own universe, as a mis-creation, a being too nar-
rowly selfish, too stupidly contentious, too terribly potent,
to be able to exist.

OCCUPATION OF THE RHINELAND

WESTERN GERMANY BECOMES A SUBJECT LAND

NOV. 23, 1918-JUNE 28, 1919

GABRIEL HANOTAUX   PHILIP GIBBS
FREDERIC C. HOWE   GREGORY MASON

The Armistice of November 11, 1918, arranged for the occupation by the Ally troops of all German territory west of the Rhine. This was to be the great symbol of Ally victory. It was also to make it impossible for Germany to renew her resistance if she objected to the peace terms imposed upon her.

With this in view the Armistice also included in the region of "occupation" three large "bridge-heads," that is, three regions on the east bank of the Rhine covering the chief passages across it. Thus the Rhine remained no longer a German line of defense. The Allies, being already across it, could march into the heart of Germany, with no single fortress, no single natural obstacle, to delay or oppose them. These three bridge-heads were at Cologne, of which the British forces took possession, Coblenz, which the Americans held, and Mainz or Mayence, which France had long possessed in ancient days and now held once again.

The Peace Treaty of June 28, 1919, turned the temporary occupation of these lands into a more extended one. For fifteen years at least, the Allies were to hold the western Rhine-bank, meanwhile giving up the bridge-heads one by one, Cologne first after only five years of occupancy. But the return of these regions to Germany was made conditional on her fulfilling every requirement of the Treaty. If she failed in this, as fail in some details she must, the occupation might extend indefinitely.

The actual entry of the Allies into Germany proper began on December 1st of 1918, on which date the American armies crossed the border near Treves and began their march to Coblenz. The Britons crossed from Belgium on December 3d and were in full possession of Cologne by the 14th. French troops at the time of the Armistice held already some nominally German soil in Alsace, and they occupied Metz, the great stronghold of Lorraine on November 25th. The truly German territory beyond Lorraine was entered on December 2d; and by the 15th the French banners had crossed the Rhine at Mainz.

Everywhere the Germans accepted the occupation quietly, even perhaps thankfully. It saved them from anarchy. When in 1919 the momentary investment was extended over years, it was accepted with equal calm. The Rhine provinces realized that they were fortunate to escape all the tumult and internal war which racked central Germany.

In the following pages the picture of the French entry into Germany is drawn by Gabriel Hanotaux, the most noted of French contemporary historians, specially summoned by his government to see and record the event. Philip Gibbs, most noted of British war-correspondents, depicts his people's entry; and the general government of the Allies is described by the American war correspondent, Gregory Mason. The economic conditions and results are briefly summarized by the noted American economist, Frederic C. Howe.

BY GABRIEL HANOTAUX

A GREAT, a very great leader said to me, "It is fitting that a French historian should witness the crossing of the Rhine by soldiers of France." It was at once an invitation and a command. I took my departure. Thanks to the generous facilities afforded me, I made the difficult voyage. At Metz I found everything ready and Commandant Henri Bordeaux commissioned to be my guide.

We cross the frontier, leaving behind us the desolate scene of war, and arrive in that laughing valley of the Saar which assumes a look of tranquillity and civilization in measure as it recedes from the war zone. We advance towards the Wald, towards the hilly region of Hundsrück. We descend into little valleys, we climb hills. Night falls. The shadows thicken, the horizon closes, we do a hundred kilometers in the dark. The headlights shine ahead on the uninjured street, no more jolts or bounces; on and on goes the motor car.

Now houses begin to come thick and fast, a suburb, factories, chimneys still smoking, ateliers in which we see the silhouettes of men working behind a fire screen, wide streets.

Suddenly we arrive in a square full of light; the gleam of gay shop windows pours forth upon the sidewalks, a crowd gathers about the halted motor. Some are curious, some make advances, some are complacent. In a word, a city full of life, animation, and industry, it is Sarrebrüch; we are having our first contact with war-time Germany. We are frankly surprised. The contrast is too violent; we have left the death of the front behind us and found life once more.

But many kilometers yet remain to be covered before

we shall reach our shelter. The motor car plunges into the night again. Narrow valleys, high hills, barred horizons. Our motor hums. Now we run alongside a huge convoy; now the beams of our lights reveal a poilu hunting for his quarters; then night again, the road, the hills, sentinels at barriers, cities, villages, towns, substantial and calm. A barrier rises before us; suddenly it falls, opens. A town with its lamps turned down. Kaiserlautern. We reach the quarters of the staff. Welcomed with the greatest friendliness by one of the noblest figures of the French army, we may begin immediately to note our first impressions, to ask something about the first contact with the enemy.

Commander-in-chief and poilu give us the same answer —their reception of the French is not hostile; our arrival is rather a relief for them. They were afraid of a revolution. But under their reserve hides a hidden something. Is it hostility? Embarrassment? It is perhaps an attitude of waiting. They are willing enough to have us come, and are, in a fashion, prepared to model their behavior on ours. Listen to the discourse pronounced here this morning by the *bürgermeister.* The discourse is a good one, skillfully *put together,* as they have it, but it is a little too much *put together.* The Mayor says, "We will concern ourselves with giving you satisfaction, although we have suffered greatly." You perceive the system—Solf's system. "Do what you will with us, we are powerless to resist. And in case you ask too much, it will not be our fault if a good, reposeful peace should be swiftly followed by war."

We do not meet with a single threat. We find only a state of resignation, from which complaints and reproaches may rise. There is not the slightest appearance of the revolution. A great fear, an exaggerated fear of some danger to German well-being, to the comfort of the German burgess, to German industry; a good-will measured out drop by drop on the condition that it be profitable. Such is the secret of all one sees, the secret of a significant measure which has just reached our ears, *viz.,* that this municipality, on the very day of the entrance of the French troops, made French a prescribed study in the elementary schools.

On the following day at an early hour we walked about the streets. The factories and the schools were opening. It is then that one best studies the varied aspects of popular life.

Children here, children there, children everywhere. They run towards us on all sides and gather themselves into an extraordinary crowd—well clad, well shod, comfortably bundled up, little rosy faces under crowns of yellow hair, sometimes of brown hair (for brunettes are plentiful in this once Celtic countryside). All these little faces that stare at us, all these familiar, shining-eyed youngsters who throng about our motor car and look at our chauffeurs in uniform, all these children without a single exception are healthy looking. Their faces are full and round; they have not suffered. When I compare them with the poor, pitiful haggard-eyed children of our invaded regions!

There are many, very many workmen, a large number of them being young men. Few women. We see the different elements of a social life still intact, clergymen, schoolmasters, employees of the state and the city. In a word, all those who could decently keep out of the turmoil. All these watch us, wait for our coming. They reply willingly to our requests for information. They go out of their way; some salute. There is a marked but not excessive reserve. Along the streets our placid poilu strolls with his hand in his pockets, stopping before shop windows, asking his way from the girls for the fun of it. In a word, there is nothing particularly striking to this first meeting of Frenchman and foe.

En route! Here we are in the full blaze of daylight hurrying on through the country. We are going to Kreuznach, thence to Mainz by the shortest route along the valley. The city had surprised us a little by its tranquil air of not having suffered, by the "continuity" of its life. In the countryside our surprise was to amount almost to stupefaction.

This countryside is narrow and restricted. It lies along the valley and the road, a long alignment of fields and gardens. To the right and the left the climbing land rises to a double rampart of wooded hills. A stern land this, powerfully molded by Nature for military purposes. History has taught us all this, for we are in the famous lines of Kaiserlautern—that citadel of the Rhenish provinces which dominates all Germany's gates into France and forbids the entry of France into Germany. Who holds this land holds our gates. Alas, the world knows this only too well, for it was simply because of this fact that the negotiators of 1815 gave this territory to Prussia.

In the villages and the towns more children, such a number of children that the chauffeur is forever having to dodge and stop. But here our chauffeur's task grows even more complicated, for he must avoid the barrage of hens. How they flutter and run!

In theory a hen is said to run under a wagon, but what are we to say when there are a thousand hens about? And when we reflect that a hen lives on the same cereals as a human being? Well, we have something to pause over. Horses, attached to wagons, to plows, to agricultural machines are to be seen everywhere on the streets and in the fields. I think of the state to which our French cavalry has been reduced. The fields are well kept and cultivated, not a meter of land has been allowed to lie waste. The vines are cultivated, pruned, and bound, not a twig lies on the ground. The straw lying about is fresh and clean. As far down the valley as the eye can see the squares of green and rose alternate in the fields. The well-rooted wheat shudders in the first chill of winter. I think of our fields, of our best fields, gone to waste and spotted with thistles. Haven't these people been at war?

We advance. A watering place: Kreuznach. Another French staff gives us a second generous welcome. The "Emperor's" dining room, the "Emperor's" office, the "Emperor's" table. He is far away now, the reprobate! We start once more. A new rendezvous. We arrive at dusk in a driving rain. We are at Mainz.

And now approaches the historian's hour. Would that I might reawaken some memories of our history here. Mainz, Cæsar, Napoleon, the siege by the French, the occupation. But the present does not allow us a return to the past.

At first view, the town is scowling, somber, and dark under the rain. They have assigned us quarters in a private house, for they have wished us to have a glimpse of the townsman. A comfortable interior, carpets, carved wood, heavy curtains, richly decorated ceilings, chocolate-colored walls, caramel bric-a-brac, an air of gross and over-abundant bourgeois luxury. And *copper, copper everywhere.* Yet they stole all of ours they could put their hands on, under the pretext that Germany needed copper! And here on a little table are eight copper ash trays, on the mantelpiece are a number of those hideous copper ornaments in which Boche taste delights, little copper wells, little copper clocks. To think, good heavens, of all our lovely chandeliers, all our admirable church candlesticks, our baptismal fonts, our bells, our brass ware melted down to save these *ordures!* But take warning, all this has a symbolic meaning! Germany ended the war to save just these things. She has preserved her well-being. *After having pillaged, she did not care to be sacked.*

I made these reflections while getting into an exceedingly comfortable bed belonging to a rich citizen of Mainz who, in very good French, protested against my intrusion. But I let him understand that I had no ear for his jests and that I had no intention of allowing myself to be put out in the street. "Monsieur, your folk came to my house, drank my wine, raided my cellar, carried off my furniture, my mattresses, my linen, my silver, *my copper,* and then they destroyed my house. This for the time being is my house. Don't worry, however, *for I shall leave it as soon as I possibly can.* For your house, monsieur, is perfectly unspeakable. Mine, in its lovely Louis XVI. delicacy, was a thing of exquisite beauty." He understands French, but I doubt if that penetrated his skull!

Now we must sleep. For to-morrow, at the break of day, General Leconte has said to me, "The earliest hour must find you at the bridge." The St. Quentin regiment, the 287th, will be *the first* to cross the Rhine. We shall be there, *mon Général!*

At dawn we were at the bridge of Mainz. General Leconte's division was to take possession of the other bank at seven o'clock. We decided to go ahead of it and await its coming.

At Mainz the river wears a majestic aspect. It rolled onwards, its gray and hurrying waves under a night-mist still clinging to the valley. Nevertheless, a pale glow strove to pierce its way through the clouds, and finally a rosy light, infinitely delicate, spread through the atmosphere and shone upon our troops drawn up along the bank.

The movement on the long and narrow bridge was already active. That bridge, ornamented with pylons, flanked by four heavy pavilions, and leaping in eight arches across the stream.

The general, accompanied by his staff, arrived on horseback. He dismounted at the entrance to the bridge, walked to the sidewalk and gave orders that the bridge was to be closed to general travel. The crowd being blocked at both ends, the space between swiftly emptied. All awaited in silence the stroke of seven. General Caron and his staff had joined General Leconte.

Seven o'clock! The drums beat, the bugles sound, the defile begins. The 287th regiment of infantry, the St. Quentin Regiment sets foot upon the bridge. In squads of eight, bayonets gleaming, their trampling step causing the great bridge to rumble, the soldiers surge forward towards the general who stands by the illuminating point of the central arch, his standard behind him.

The regiment advanced, the band going first, pounding and blowing for all it was worth. It advanced, disappeared, and soon the whole valley rang with the long echoes of the military march. The two banks awoke, caught up the tune, and replied one to the other. The *Sambre et Meuse* marked the step of our heroes. The soldiers came nearer, the hardy faces could be distinguished. Then came cyclists and men with dogs on a leash. The captain of the first detachment to pass saluted with his sword. The men, their faces turned to the man with the golden visor, passed on, rank after rank. And how many of these masculine figures must have had hidden in his heart under the stern panoply of war, the smile that is born of the dream realized at last!

As the flag was about to pass him, the general, saluting with sword, said in a quiet tone to the surrounding officers, "Gentlemen, let us not forget that our dead also are passing by."

For the dead were at hand. The flag had brought them there in its folds. The immense landscape, of a sudden, seemed swept with light. The bridge itself, having caught the cadence of the passing troops, began to tremble, and soon, marking the passing steps, appeared to dance.

Bayonets gleaming, in ranks of eight, the soldiers passed. The staggering load of the infantryman on campaign bore but lightly that day upon their shoulders. Large and heavily built, they seemed that day to be nimble and alert. The balancing bridge appeared to lift them up. The blue casques grew into a long snake of steel, whose spiny back was formed by myriads of bayonets. Companies succeeded companies; the morning sun poured down on the white faces and black mustaches.

After the infantry came the cannons, the 75's wrapped in their black mantles, and held in leash like hounds. After the cannons the convoy wagons, ambulances, the interminable file of worn wagons drawn by lean-bellied horses, scrubs with long, worn coats; rattling harnesses repaired with rope, all this equipage, covered with the dust and mud of long roads, rumbled on, still laboring to further that sacred task born of so many hopes and desperate efforts.

While this formidable array was crossing from one bank to the other, the crowd assembled at both ends of the bridge remained apparently silent from stupor.

What were they thinking of? What comparisons were struggling in their minds? What overthrown dreams, what sorrows bare of consolation? Or was it the reawakening of a dream? Did they understand? Did they realize? It would seem not. Necks craned forward, with bulging eyes they watched the spectacle. Beneath them the Rhine, majestic and dark, rolled onward the tides of history.

BY PHILIP GIBBS

British report from Malmedy in Germany, December 3, 1918

British troops crossed the Belgian frontier and entered Germany to-day. Here and there some small children, watching from cottage windows or in their mothers' arms, waved their hands with the friendliness of childhood for all men on horses, and they were not rebuked. German schoolboys in peaked caps, with their hands thrust in their pockets, stared without friendliness or unfriendliness. Some girls on a hillside above the winding road laughed and waved their handkerchiefs. There was no sense as yet of passing through a hostile country where we were not wanted.

Round the hairpin turn we came down to Malmedy, lying in a narrow valley with some of its streets and houses climbing up the hillsides. It was a typical little German town, with here and there houses of the châlet style and houses of the modern country type in Germany, with wooden balconies and low-pitched roofs, and beyond very neat and clean-looking factories on the outskirts of the town. The shops were bright, and I saw a display of wooden soldiers and flaxen-haired dolls and toy engines as though for the German Christmas which is coming, and in one little garden there was a figure of the little old gnomelike Rumpelstiltzkin in my old copy of Grimm's "Fairy Tales."

It was surprising to hear that most of the people about one were speaking French. Some of us remembered then that Malmedy was not in Germany until after 1815, and that for a long time it was an independent little town belonging to a Belgian Abbey of great wealth and power before it was destroyed in the French Revolution. The people here were not typically German, and many of them at least had the neutral spirit of people who live close to the frontier and speak two languages, or three, as at Malmedy, where every one is equally familiar with German, French, and Walloon.

At Malmedy there was no sign whatever of hostility except the sullen look on the faces of some men who stared through the windows of a clubhouse and the gravity of other men who turned their heads away when the cavalry passed, as though unaware of them. In many windows was a notice in German, which I read. It was an appeal by Burgomaster Kalpers, reading: "Citizens are earnestly requested to maintain great calm and order on the entry of the Entente troops into our city and to receive them with courtesy and dignity."

That wish was being carried out, and it was with politeness as well as dignity that the strangers were greeted in this first German town across the frontier.

Report From Cologne, December 14th

This morning at 10 o'clock our cavalry passed through the streets of Cologne, crossed the Hohenzollern Bridge, and went beyond the Rhine to take possession of the bridge-heads.

For some days not many British soldiers had been seen in the City of Cologne, the troops being camped in the outskirts, and it was only yesterday afternoon that the British Governor made his entry and established his headquarters in one of the hotels which had been taken over for the purpose. Crowds of German people gathered to see the man who will control their way of life during the British occupation, and were kept back in a hollow square by their own police when the Governor's motor car drove in with an escort of lancers, while a band of Scottish pipers played a greeting.

This morning the passing of the cavalry over the Rhine was an impressive sight for all the people of Cologne, and for the British was another historical episode on the long journey of this war, which has led at last to this river flowing now behind the British lines. To the German people the Rhine is the very river of their life, and down its tide come drifting all the ghost memories of their race, and its water is sacred to them as the fount from which their national legends, their old folk songs, and the sentiment that lies deep in their hearts have come forth in abundance.

In military history the Rhine has been their last line of defense, the moat around the keep of German strength; so to-day when British troops rode across the bridge and passed beyond the Rhine to further outposts it was the supreme sign of victory for them and of German defeat.

BY FREDERIC C. HOWE

The Germany of yesterday, armed, arrogant, imperialistic, is gone; gone, I believe, never to return. The Germany of to-day is broken, faced with bankruptcy, and if work is not found for her vast industrial population, she may, and very probably will, drift quickly into revolution.

Repentant? That is a difficult question. I think it must be answered in the negative. That she believes her ruling caste, Kaiser, Junker, and big industrialists caused the war there seems no doubt. That the Kaiser was the tool, possibly the unwilling tool, of Ludendorff, von Tirpitz, and the Crown Prince is widely held. That Germany will have to pay is accepted as inevitable. That she will come back for the recapture of Alsace-Lorraine and her indemnity is generally assumed by the French high military command. But these admissions do not spell repentance. They merely concede failure.

I have just returned from a fourteen days' motor trip through the occupied territories of South Germany. The tour was organized by the French Government immediately following the armistice. Its purpose was to witness the festivities in connection with the French occupation of Alsace-Lorraine, and to study the economic and industrial conditions of the occupied territory, which is held by the Allied armies as the main gauge of the terms of the armistice. The route was from Nancy to Metz, then along the Rhine to Mayence, thence to Coblenz, where the American army is in occupation, then on to Cologne with the British Expeditionary Force, and then through the whole of Belgium and the devastated regions of northern France, from Ypres to Paris. It included visits to General Pétain, who had just been made a Marshal of France; to General Fayolle, the great French strategist, and, finally, to General Mangin, "the wildcat of the French Army," beloved by all the soldiers and called in for impossible offensives on critical occasions. He is in command of the French advance forces at Mayence on the Rhine.

Along the national road which skirts the Moselle and the borders of France from Nancy to Metz, villages and farmhouses greeted us with French flags, while the people smiled contentedly from their doorways as the caravan of French army motors flashed by.   Metz, the capital city of Lorraine, for nearly fifty years under German occupation, was in gala attire, for Madame Poincaré was holding a Christmas festivity for four thousand school children, who gathered in the town-hall, clad in brilliant red and green Alsatian costumes, with short skirts, gay-colored silk shawls, and little white caps ornamented with the rosette of France.   From the hands of the wife of the president these children received souvenirs of the reunion of Lorraine to France.   Throughout the town of Metz were many signs of French occupation.   German names had been stripped from the streets and German signs had been painted from store windows.   Stores of questionable loyalty bore notices suggesting that the soldiers should not trade there.   On the façade of the cathedral above the market-place we observed a statue of William II., representing David.   His hands had been manacled and below was the inscription: *"Sic Transit Gloria Mundi."*

We were followed from the reception by troops of children.   Chattering in French, they told us how one thirteen-year-old child had been imprisoned for speaking French on the streets.   The girls, who quite naturally repeated the gossip of their parents, complained that American soldiers were fraternizing with German girls; they told us that one officer had eloped with a German girl and that the soldiers accepted wine and food from the German residents.   This story we heard continually in the occupied territory.   But the fraternizing was not confined to Americans.   French officers also danced with German girls in the cafés.   So did the soldiers. Stringent rules have been laid down by the American commanding authorities, but, as one of them said sympathetically, "You can't prevent American boys from playing with children," and this they were doing wherever we went.   The boys had come from the penetrating cold of northern France, they had been living for months without comforts, without a bath, without a home or home surroundings of any kind, and Metz, Mayence, and Coblenz, with their restaurants, theaters, concert-halls, and (most important of all) comfortable billets in well-heated houses, were a joyous relief from the misery of the trenches.

There was in the spirit of the occasion something typical of the attitude of the French, British, and American armies. They were not there to humiliate the people or to emphasize the fact of victory. Rather they were on German soil to see that the war was at an end, that the people were fed, and that the life of the country should flow as freely as was consistent with the terms of the armistice.

One's feeling about war and about the hatreds of peoples was somewhat shaken, it is true, by the relations of the soldiers of all the armies and of the people as well. There were no disturbances of any kind, no clash between the military and civil authorities, no conflicts with the people. One might, in fact, have been in Germany in peace times, so far as the relations of people were concerned. The soldiers were happy that the war was over. The German people accepted the presence of the armies without protest, although there was an almost complete absence of well-to-do persons on the street when the troops went by. The people had a detachment from the whole business of war and peace. Their daily life went on much as it always had. Theaters and opera-houses presented productions of the same high order as before the war. The program of the symphony concerts at Mayence and in the Kursaal at Wiesbaden contained selections from French composers, while Mayence produced the opera, "If I were King," frankly admitting that it was from the French. There were crowds of French soldiers in the theaters and at the concerts, as well as in the shops and cafés, and they were treated with courtesy. They in turn were comporting themselves in a way to make friends for France, for there is a strong demand in the latter country that the frontiers shall be extended to the Rhine, to prevent the possibility of another surprise attack by Germany, and that the territory of the left bank of the Rhine shall be a neutral zone in which no military operations or preparations for war shall be made by either country.

Outside of Alsace-Lorraine the attitude of people seemed despondent. Hotel-keepers and business men said their country had little to look forward to but debt and indemnities.

There were few people in the shops. The formerly busy factories in the Saarbrücken coal districts, as well as along the upper Rhine and at Mayence and Cologne, were empty of workers, although the fields along the highways were cultivated as intensively as they had been before the war. Credit was unorganized, for the banks of Germany radiate out from Berlin, Dresden, and Frankfort, and there is little business communication between the two sides of the Rhine. The great iron deposits of Lorraine which were the source of much of Germany's wealth are now in the possession of France. The life-cord of Germany has been severed by the armistice, as it was by her blockade of the outside world.

Not that Germany seems industrially exhausted. The shops in the cities are filled with all kinds of merchandise, especially such merchandise as Germany can manufacture from iron and steel, from lumber and from those raw materials of which she has an abundance. But there is absolute exhaustion of many raw materials. I did not see a single German automobile in ten days' travel. There is no rubber in the country. It had been stripped for military purposes. Even the bicycles are on steel tires. Copper, too, is gone. To such an extent is this true that manufacturing plants, street-car lines, and other non-essential industries had been stripped of copper for military purposes.

The industrial interdependence of the world is seen in the breakdown of German industry. Mills and factories cannot operate without copper, rubber, cotton, wool, silk, and other raw materials which come only from America, Africa, and Asia. And Germany has none of these. In consequence her industrial life is at a standstill. It can only come to life again when the embargo is lifted and raw materials are permitted to come in. In the meantime German workmen are out of work. They are walking the streets. This is the human material from which the Spartacus movement recruits itself.

The people on the streets seemed healthy and strong. They were well-clothed, although they maintained that the clothes they wore had been bought before the war. Milk is rationed carefully, as it is all over Europe, but the price at the milk stations was lower than in France and seemed adequate for rationing needs.

The market-places, which are the center of every German town, were filled with vegetables of great variety from the rich bottom lands on the left bank of the Rhine, which are still cultivated like a garden. The prices were very low.

The stories of food exhaustion in Germany seem to have been false, at least they have been exaggerated. And if the appearance of the people and the displays in the shops and market-places can be accepted as proof of anything, there is food in abundance for those who can buy. The trouble is not in an absence of food, but in an inability to buy food. The poor are out of work. The answer to the question, "What do people eat?" was always the same—"Potatoes." Potatoes three times a day. There is very little fat. In addition to potatoes, the poor get a little bread and occasionally some meat.

This was the condition in January and on the left bank of the Rhine. Food conditions in Prussia were worse, and German officials asserted that what food there was would be exhausted before spring, and the country would be in a starving condition before the next harvest could be gathered.

Industrial collapse from the embargo on wool, cotton, silk, rubber, copper, and food products, closed the mills and factories. This created destitution and suffering. For Germany, it is to be remembered, is primarily industrial. The supplies in the shops and the industries that were in operation were in those lines in which Germany was self-sufficient, such as iron and steel, machines, cutlery, lumber, and art products.

And this explains, in part at least, the military collapse of Germany. It was not only military, it was civil as well. While Marshal Foch was penetrating the German line and severing its connections the first week in October, the German soldiers in the reserve army and the people were being disrupted by disaffection, and by the activities of the Soldiers' and Workmen's Councils, which everywhere came into existence as a result of hunger and the continued disillusion of the people. And in the days preceding the armistice the soldiers back home refused to fight; they assembled in their barracks and demanded that the officers choose whether they would stand by the people or go with the army. And many of the officers chose the former alternative. Those who did not were permitted to go to the front. The soldiers stacked arms. They laid aside their military uniforms. The people decided that they would fight no longer. This was frankly admitted by people on the left bank of the Rhine.

Every suggestion of militarism in the territories visited was gone. In ten days' time I saw but one officer and not a single soldier in uniform. Even the caps had disappeared. Not a single Iron Cross or other military distinction was to be seen. The people, apparently by common consent, had shed themselves of military trappings and settled down in a kind of despair, waiting for the terms of the armistice to be announced.

Despair is not peculiar to Germany. Despair is universal among the common people. This is true of France, of Italy, of Belgium, and Great Britain. Europe is sitting as at a wake, waiting for politicians to quit talking and set the world to work. But little, if anything, is being done. This is the story that comes from all the countries. The promised indemnities are like a great fund that has poured in upon a community after some devastating flood. The people will not go to work until the fund is exhausted.

There have been ambitious investigations and reports. Plans have been made for placing the returning soldier on the land, for state undertakings on a large scale, for the building of workmen's homes; but the reports are already forgotten. Statesmen in these countries are discussing the terms of peace, when they should first have done their best to set their states in order. The rebuilding of homes, the organization of agriculture, the development of credit to aid the farmer and the shopkeeper, and, most important of all, the demobilization of the army—all these problems are drifting aimlessly. The big problem in Europe is the thirty million men who have to be gotten to work. For revolution is a stomach disease. One needs only to inquire of a policeman, a street-car conductor, a street-cleaner, to hear the same tale in substantially the same

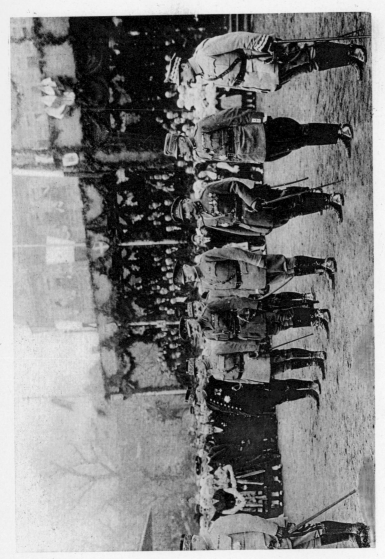

terms. It is a story of potatoes for food, speculative prices, crushing taxes, and a distrust of governments.

BY GREGORY MASON

To disturb existing conditions as little as possible when compatible with the best interest of the general public is the principle which guides the Allies in governing the portions of German territory occupied by their troops under the terms of the armistice. The known admiration of the Germans for intelligence in the adoption of rules and consistency in the application of them has made the Allies proceed very carefully. It would not do, they think, to issue an ordinance in haste and then be obliged to ignore or change its application, for that would mean to lose face before the people they are governing, so potent is the German reputation for the love of logic and efficiency.

Whether the territory occupied is held by French, British, Belgian, or American troops, the administration of it is essentially an inter-Allied matter. Local commanders are allowed a good deal of discretion, but all general principles are determined by reference to an inter-Allied military commission or to Marshal Foch, as the head of the military forces of the Allies. Hence there is a great similarity in the way different sections of occupied Germany are administered, whether they are actually held by French, British, Belgians, or Americans. This unity of control is just as valuable in the administration of quasi-conquered territory as it was valuable in the actual prosecution of battles. For instance, the intention is to make the administration of this territory as humane as possible. The Belgians wanted to apply to the Germans the same harsh regulations which the Germans had used on them, but the inter-Allied directorate wisely blocked Belgium's natural desire to have "an eye for an eye."

This whole work of occupation goes through three phases: first, military occupation; second, the seizure of the means of administration; and, third, economic treatment of the occupied regions.

The military occupation is essentially police work. By whatsoever troops, it is performed in pursuance of rules laid down by Marshal Foch. It has followed the same military zones into which the Germans divided the territory now occupied by the Allies. If Marshal Foch gave the word, the Allied army could advance instantly deep into Germany.

Marshal Foch's police rules are strict but not harsh. They are aimed to protect the people of the occupied zones, and they are softened everywhere as soon as the conduct of the natives justifies such relaxation. For instance, one of the first general rules in all the occupied zones was that the inhabitants must remain indoors from eight o'clock in the evening until six o'clock in the morning, but local commanders were given authority to relax it as they saw fit. When I was in Coblenz, the Americans had already allowed the people an extra hour on the streets in the evening, and at Kaiserlauten the French had postponed curfew until half-past ten. The German *gendarmerie* is purely local in all the occupied zones, and much use has been made of it. Wherever there were German army officers in positions of responsibility in the *gendarmerie,* they were removed, the Allied policy being generally to trust local functionaries and to leave them in office whenever they can be used, but to dismiss all officials who were appointed by Berlin.

At first all use of telephones was forbidden to the inhabitants of occupied towns, but this rule has been relaxed also. In the French zone the natives are allowed telephone calls within their own city; while in Coblenz the Americans allow this and also permit the use of five trunk lines from the occupied territory into Germany proper. Thus a German in Coblenz may talk directly to a German in Berlin. Except in cases of extreme personal necessity, all such calls are supposed to be confined to the transaction of important business, and of course American army censors "listen in" on every call. This privilege was given to the Germans of Coblenz because it was found that the sudden and complete interruption of contact between the two banks of the Rhine caused a great deal of inconvenience and suffering.

The control of mails, like the control of telephones, has been relaxed somewhat already where it seemed safe to do so, and a restricted amount of business correspondence is permitted between the left and right banks of the Rhine.   But there has been no softening of the regulations in regard to the press and public meetings.   A strict censorship against anti-Ally or pro-Bolshevist articles in the press is maintained, and no public meetings of any kind are tolerated without the permission of the local commandant, the sole exception being in the case of the German churches, which are allowed to hold services as usual.   As a matter of fact, through the churches the Germans might carry on not a little propaganda, because the Allies are not so attentive to the utterances of preachers as they might be.   But it is doubtful if they are hurting themselves much by this laxity.   Indeed, a policy of broad toleration toward the German churches is probably wise.   One of the elements most bitter against the French, in particular, has been the German Catholic clergy, who have distrusted the French because of the fame of French liberalism in religious matters and the separation of Church and State in France. In fact, many German Catholic clergymen apparently have thought that all Frenchmen were pagans, and already their press is beginning to express their astonishment at learning that such is not the case.

In approaching the problem of the civil administration of occupied Germany the Allies have, so far as practicable, made use of the existing German civil machinery of government.

The proper judicial and economic measures for occupied Germany are being worked out very carefully.   The French are using a number of special technical advisers—French professors, manufacturers, etc.   These men are working in commissions appointed to study particular subjects, and are also advising France on what her national economic policy ought to be.   Special French economic commissions are with both the Eighth and Tenth French Armies, and are coöperating with a German economic commission.   Subdivisions of these commissions are being established at sub-centers throughout the occupied zones.

A good deal of confusion has been caused by the sudden severance of relations between the left and the right banks of the Rhine.   For instance, the Court of Appeal for Mayence is at Leipzig, which is outside of the zone of occupation.

Therefore the French are arranging to have a special Court of Appeal created to meet this need. Similarly, some of the ecclesiastical authorities for churches on the left bank of the Rhine live on the right bank, and the armistice has thus interrupted German church routine.

That part of the left bank which is held by the French is an industrial district whose chief products are coal and coke, and which produces little of its own food. Deprive this region of transportation and it would starve. The French, therefore, are not only sending in food by army truck trains, but are extending railways and Rhine shipping. This region needs raw materials. The French allow these to be brought across the river from Germany, but they are very careful what they allow to go into Germany from the left bank. All applications for the right to ship goods eastward across the river have to be submitted to an inter-Allied commission, and no manufactured articles are permitted to be bought from Germany proper if the same things can be obtained from Belgium or France.

Politics on the left bank of the Rhine are very amusing. The people have no such strong national feeling as the North Germans. This is partly because of a natural provincialism, and partly the result of history. Remember that all the country up to the Rhine was French for a time under Napoleon I., and that some of the country around Saarlouis and Saarbruck was French for a considerable period. Consequently the thought of being parted from the German Empire is not such a shock to the people of these southern towns as it would be to the people of northern Germany.

It was the Ebert Government with which the Allies concluded the armistice. They have therefore properly refused to deal with any other Government in Germany. They have disbanded the soviets wherever they have found them, and they are not aware that the native population has felt much injured thereby. Before the Allies came into full control various hasty laws were passed by various local German governments. These are disregarded by the Allies, and of the laws and general decrees of the old Imperial Government only those are kept in force which are specifically approved by Foch.

The people of the left bank are waiting on events. They are ready to jump either way. The inhabitants of Saarbruck elected two sets of delegates to the Constituent Assembly. They elected conservative Clerical delegates to represent them in case the French should stay in occupation of their city, and they elected men from the Spartacus or extreme radical wing of Socialism to represent them in case the French should withdraw.

The whole Allied administration of the occupied zones is based on dignity, firmness, and a refusal to fraternize (theoretically at least), coupled with a regard for the best interests of the inhabitants. In fact, so light is the heel of the conqueror on their necks that some Germans do not believe that the Allies are conquerors at all. Their theory is that when the revolution came in Germany the German Government called in the Allies as trustees to care for its interests. As a proof of this some of these inhabitants of occupied Germany point to the easy conditions under which they are allowed to live and say, "No conqueror ever treated the conquered like this."

THE UNION OF "GREATER SERBIA"

FORMING THE KINGDOM OF THE SERBS, CROATS AND SLOVENES

JANUARY 3, JUNE 28, 1919

OFFICIAL ANNOUNCEMENTS

PRINCE ALEXANDER   MADAME GROUITCH

One of the minor peculiarities of the reconstruction period following on the Armistice was that Serbia, which had fought so gallantly throughout the War, took no part in the Peace Conference that followed. That is, she took no part as Serbia. On January 3, 1919, word was sent out from her capital, Belgrade, to all the Allies then assembling at Paris, that Serbia no longer existed under that name but had completed her reorganization as the Kingdom of the Serbs, Croats and Slovenes. Under that name she participated in the Peace Conference; and the Conference, in the Peace Treaty signed on June 28, recognized for all Europe and confirmed the new name and the new kingdom.

What the new name really meant was that little Serbia had at last achieved her dream of the days before the War, by uniting with herself all the Slavic provinces of Austria, a territory larger than her own. She had also been joined by the other Serb State, Montenegro. Of these added Slavic peoples, the race known as the Slovenes were the most northern, centering around the formerly Austrian city of Laibach, which in their language they now call Liubliana. The Croats inhabited the more southerly Austrian region centering on Agram, which they call Zagreb. While south of these again lay the more distinctively Serbian peoples of Bosnia and Herzegovina where the War had started. All of these peoples and the Montenegrins are known in common as the Jugo-Slavs or southern Slavs, and the new kingdom is often loosely called Jugoslavia.

The Jugoslavs began their active movement toward this union by the "Declaration of Corfu," here given. It was signed on July 20, 1917, by the statesman Pashitch, acting leader of the exiled Serbian government at Corfu, and by Dr. Trumbic, the leader of the Austrian Slavs who dwelt in exile in Paris.

As Austria began crumbling to pieces in 1918, her Slavic subjects dared to gather in a convention of their own at Laibach on August 16th. Early in October a committee chosen by this convention proclaimed its intention of working for a free, democratic, united Jugoslav State. Hungarian and Austrian troops offered but little opposition, though there was some sharp fighting in Fiume. Then, on

22

October 29th both at Laibach, now Liubliana, and at Zagreb, these regions were declared independent of Austria and of Hungary.

Meanwhile in Montenegro a similar desire for Jugoslavic unity resulted in decisive action by the Skupshtina or Great National Assembly which was chosen by the people by universal suffrage. This, on December 1st, passed the resolution here given, deposing its own king and seeking union with Serbia. On the same day a commission from the "National Council" of the formerly Austrian Jugoslavs visited Belgrade and presented to the Serbian regent, Prince Alexander, a request voted by their Council on November 24th, asking Serbia for an equal democratic union under the aged hero King Peter of Serbia. Their request and the regent's historic response are given here.

Following promptly upon this memorable meeting, the actual work of organizing the new kingdom was begun. Alexander was, of course, its Regent, and of its Prime Minister also there could be no question; for M. Pashitch, Serbia's Prime Minister, had been one of the great leaders of the War. With him was associated as Vice-Premier the president of the Zagreb Council, Dr. Koroshetz, a Slovene; and the cabinet included a Croatian, a Dalmatian, and afterward a Montenegrin. It was this government which completed the organization of the new union and proclaimed it to the world on January 5th. Some Montenegrins protested through devotion to their king whom the Skupshtina had deposed, and he himself denied their right to depose him. Some of the Austrian Slavs have expressed preference for a republic. But upon the whole the new kingdom, especially since its formal recognition by the Peace Treaty, seems destined to survive.

THE DECLARATION OF CORFU

The first step toward building the new State of Jugoslavia

1. The State of the Serbs, Croats, and Slovenes, who are also known by the name of Southern Slavs or Jugoslavs, will be a free and independent kingdom, with an indivisible territory and unity of power. This State will be a constitutional, democratic, and Parliamentary monarchy, with the Karageorgevich dynasty, which has always shared the ideals and feelings of the nation in placing above everything else the national liberty and will at its head.

2. The name of this State will be the Kingdom of the Serbs, Croats, and Slovenes, and the title of the sovereign will be King of the Serbs, Croats, and Slovenes.

3. This State will have one coat-of-arms, only one flag, and one crown.

4. The four different flags of the Serbs, Croats, and Slovenes will have equal rights, and may be hoisted freely on

all occasions. The same will obtain for the four different coats-of-arms.

5. The three national denominations, the Serbs, Croats, and Slovenes, are equal before the law in all the territory of the kingdom, and each may freely use it on all occasions in public life and before all authorities.

6. The two Cyrillic and Latin alphabets also have the same rights and every one may freely use them in all the territory of the kingdom. The royal and local self-governing authorities have the rights and ought to employ the two alphabets according to the desire of the citizens.

7. All religions are recognized, and may be free and publicly practiced. The Orthodox, Roman Catholic, and Mussulman religions, which are most professed in our country, will be equal, and will enjoy the same rights in relation to the State. In view of these principles, the Legislature will be careful to preserve the religious peace in conformity with the spirit and tradition of our entire nation.

8. The Gregorian calendar will be adopted as soon as possible.

9. The territory of the Serbs, Croats, and Slovenes will comprise all the territory where our nation lives in compact masses and without discontinuity, and where it could not be mutilated without injuring the vital interests of the community. Our nation does not ask for anything which belongs to others, and only claims that which belongs to it. It desires to free itself and establish its unity. That is why it conscientiously and firmly rejects every partial solution of the problem of its freedom from the Austro-Hungarian domination.

10. The Adriatic Sea, in the interests of liberty and equal rights of all nations, is to be free and open to all and each.

11. All citizens throughout the territory of the kingdom are equal, and enjoy the same rights in regard to the State and the law.

12. The election of Deputies to the national representation will take place under universal suffrage, which is to be equal, direct, and secret. The same will apply to the elections in the communes and other administrative institutions. A vote will be taken in each commune.

13. The Constitution to be established after the conclusion of peace by the Constituent Assembly elected by universal, direct, and secret suffrage will serve as a basis for the life of the State. It will be the origin and ultimate end of all the powers and all rights by which the whole national life will be regulated. The Constitution will give the people the opportunity of exercising its particular energies in local autonomies, regulated by natural, social, and economic conditions. The Constitution must be adopted in its entirety by a numerical majority of the Constituent Assembly, and all other laws passed by the Constituent Assembly will not come into force until they have been sanctioned by the King.

Thus the united nation of Serbs, Croatians, and Slovenes will form a State of twelve million inhabitants. This State will be a guarantee of their national independence and of their general national progress and civilization, and a powerful rampart against the pressure of the Germans, and an inseparable ally of all civilized peoples and States. Having proclaimed the principle of right and liberty and of international justice, it will form a worthy part of the new society of nations.

Signed at Corfu, July 20, 1917, by the President of the Council and Minister of Foreign Affairs of the Kingdom of Serbia, Nikola Pashitch, and the President of the Jugoslav Committee, Dr. Anto Trumbic.

DECREE OF THE MONTENEGRIN SKUPSHTINA
Passed on December 1, 1918

Taking into consideration the historical tendencies as well as political and economic interests of Montenegro, the Great Skupshtina, elected by the people of Montenegro and assembled at Podgoritza, has decided:

1. To depose the King, Nicholas Petrovich Niegush;

2. To effect the union of Montenegro with Serbia under the Karageorgevich dynasty and its entrance into the common fatherland of Serbians, Croatians, and Slovenes;

3. To elect a national committee specifically charged with the conduct of the affairs of Montenegro united with Serbia, and

4. To communicate this decision to former King Nicholas and to the Government of the Kingdom of Serbia, as well as to the Governments of the Allied and neutral powers.

ADDRESS FROM THE JUGOSLAV NATIONAL COUNCIL

Sent from the Council at Zagreb on November 24, 1918, and delivered at Belgrade to the Regent of Serbia on December 1st

The National Council desires that a national representation should be established by agreement with the National Council and the popular representatives of the Kingdom of Serbia, and that the Government should be made responsible, according to modern parliamentary principles, to this representation, which would sit in permanence until the Constituent. For the same reasons the former administrative and autonomous institutions would remain in vigor. In this period of transition it is in our opinion necessary to create the conditions for a definite organizaton of one unitary State. With this end in view, the Government should prepare the Constituent, which, according to the proposal of the National Council, would be elected on the basis of secret, universal, and proportional suffrage, and convoked at latest six months after the conclusion of peace.

At this historic moment, when we appear before your Royal Highness as representatives of all the Jugoslav territories of the former Austro-Hungarian Monarchy, we are profoundly grieved to observe that large portions of our national soil are occupied by the troops of the Kingdom of Italy, which is allied with the Entente Powers, with whom we desire to live in friendly relations. But we cannot recognize any contract, not even that of London [the Treaty of April, 1915], by virtue of which, in violation of the principle of nationalities, we should be obliged to surrender part of our nation to other States.

We draw your Royal Highness's attention to the fact that the Italian occupation far exceeds the limits and regions provided even by the clauses of the armistice, which was concluded with the Commander in Chief of the former Austro-Hungarian Army long after these territories had been declared an independent and integral portion of the State of the

Serbs, Croats, and Slovenes. Of this we will furnish proofs
to the Government of your Royal Highness.

In full conscience we express our hope that your Royal
Highness, with our whole nation, will endeavor to secure that
the final frontiers of our State shall be drawn in conformity
with our ethnographic frontiers and with the principles put
forward by President Wilson and the other Entente Powers.
Long live his Majesty King Peter! Long live your Royal
Highness! Long live the nation of Serbs, Croats, and
Slovenes! Long live free and united Jugoslavia!

BY PRINCE ALEXANDER OF SERBIA
His reply to the above Address

It is only by the historic decision which the National Council of Zagreb has reached that we realize finally what was
begun by the best sons of our race of three religions and three
names on either side of the Danube, Save, and Drina, under
the reigns of my grandfather, Prince Alexander, and of
Prince Michael. We thus realize what corresponds to the
wishes and desires of my people, and in the name of King
Peter I proclaim the unity of Serbia with the provinces of the
independent State of Serbs, Croats, and Slovenes, in the Unitary Kingdom of Serbs, Croats, and Slovenes. May this
great historic act be the best reward of all your efforts and of
all who have shaken off the yoke of the foreigner by your
bold revolution.

I assure you that I and my Government and all who represent Serbia will always be guided solely by brotherly love
toward all that is most sacred in the souls of those whom you
represent, and in the sense of the wishes which you have just
expressed—wishes which we accept in their entirety—the
Government will at once take steps to realize all you have said
for the period of transition until the Constituent and for the
elections. Faithful to my father's example, I shall only be
the King of free citizens of the State of the Serbs, Croats,
and Slovenes, and I shall always remain loyal to the great
constitutional, parliamentary, and democratic principles resting upon universal law. I shall therefore ask your collaboration in forming the Government which is to represent our

united country, and this Government will always be in contact with you all at first, and eventually with the national representation. It will work with it and be responsible to it.

With the National Assembly and the whole nation, the Government's first duty will be to endeavor to secure respect for our nation's ethnographic frontiers. Together with you all, I have the right to hope that our great allies will form a just appreciation of our standpoint, for it corresponds to the principles which they themselves have proclaimed and for which they have shed so much blood, and I am sure that the world's hour of liberty will not be stained by placing under a fresh yoke so many of your valiant brothers. I hope also that this standpoint will be admitted by the Government of Italy, which also owes its birth to the same principles that have been so brilliantly interpreted by the pen and acts of its great sons of the last century.

I venture to say that in the respect for these principles and traditions, and in the consciousness of our friendship, the Italian people will find greater well-being and security than in the realization of the Treaty of London, which was signed without you, never recognized on our part, and drawn up in circumstances when the fall of Austria-Hungary was not foreseen.

In this work and in all other respects I hope that our people will remain united and powerful to the end. It will enter the new life, proud and worthy of the greatness and happiness that await it. I beg you to give my royal greeting to all my dear brothers throughout free and united Jugoslavia. Long live the whole people of the Serbs, Croats, and Slovenes! May our kingdom be ever happy and glorious!

BY MADAME SLAVKO GROUITCH

Being an American married to a Serbian and having spent my early years in Europe as a traveler and student, it was as a cosmopolitan that I came to Serbia. Here for the first time in my European wanderings I had the impression of reaching home, so very similar were the conditions of life to those of my native state, West Virginia. The resemblance extended to the atmosphere of the home and to customs of farms and villages, but more particularly to that attitude of mind towards life which we consider peculiarly American, and which I may describe as liberty so great that it is not conscious of laws. The Serbian people have a conception of duty toward the state and a public-spiritedness from choice which I have encountered elsewhere only in Switzerland and the United States. No change was necessary in order to meet the women and men of my adopted country. They knew more about America than America did of them.

I soon learned that the singleness of patriotic purpose which had impressed me in my husband was peculiar to every one I met from King to peasant, from prime minister to goat's herdsman. All were dreaming, as their forefathers had dreamed for centuries, of a united Jugo-Slav kingdom which should include the whole 13,000,000 of their race. As I listened I wondered.

There were barely three and a half million souls in the little Serbia of that day. To the south there was a region spoken of as Old Serbia, because there had arisen the Serbian kingdom of the eleventh century; beyond that was the region we speak of as Macedonia (and which in my mind, until I became Serbian, had not been associated geographically with the Balkans) containing a million and a half inhabitants of pure Serbian race still under Turkish rule. I learned very quickly of loyal little Montenegro—proud of the fact that in the veins of every peasant was the blood of the heroes who had survived from the great battle of Kossovo in 1389, in which the Serbian people had lost their independence, all but that one towering citadel. I learned of Croatia, which I had, in common with most people, always thought of as a province of Austria; of Dalmatia with its republican traditions; of the Adriatic, a kind of Floridian Indian River bordered with pleasure resorts for the opulent Viennese. Very few people had ever realized until lately that this inland sea was as essential to the life of the peoples who bordered upon it as are the Atlantic and Pacific Oceans to the United States.

As I listened to statesmen and people making prophecies of the day when all these would be united to Serbia from that farthest point on the map, called Carinthia, to that extreme point called Monastir—I felt it could happen only a long time after I should have passed away. Nevertheless, within the period of fifteen years I have seen these dreams come true. I myself have witnessed the tragedies—and there have been many—which have brought about the conquest of Old Serbia and of Macedonia, the liberation of Croatia, Bosnia, Herzegovina, Slovenia, and Dalmatia, and also the invasion of Serbia and Montenegro during the war. I have seen the miracle accomplished, and the wonder of it is that it was brought about by impulsions as irresistible as those which "rule the stars and tides." Every little child felt them; every little child contributed; its mother tossed it playfully in the air naming the great Serbian battles in a nursery rhyme; its mother put it to bed in poverty and simplicity, teaching it how to live humbly but to think grandly, sublimely, patriotically.

As the years went by and my diplomatic home was in Russia and afterwards in England—the two countries to which Serbia looked for aid in the achievement of her dream —I came only from time to time to my adopted people. But always their first words were of this wonderful thing that was in the bud, waiting to happen—and yet, so far as I could see, with no preparation for it, any more than there is external action to hasten the coming of spring. In Serbia as well as in all the allied countries at that time there were hopes for arbitration on the questions of liberty of peoples and territorial boundaries. It was the period when the Czar and England made the most intense concessions in settlement of ancient disputes to unite in an Entente with France to prevent war. I watched this accord with a certain fear, because I felt that it surely would mean the buckling in of the aspirations of my adopted people. How were the Jugo-Slavs all to be freed and united if there were an Entente to preserve that present state of injustice?

The Great Entente was made in 1906. Shortly afterward I went home to Serbia. Naturally I talked with every one I met of the new conditions. No one showed depression. The answer invariably was, "It will come about. It is bound to come." I was in England when in 1908 Austria-Hungary, as an act of defiance to the Entente, forcibly annexed the two provinces of Bosnia and Herzegovina. The whole Jugo-Slav nation went into mourning for a deed that seemed to fasten the chains of despotism that much more firmly upon the greater portion of its race, but did not cease to repeat, "The hour of our deliverance will soon be at hand." Then came the war of 1912. I was sent on a mission here to my own country as the representative of the Serbian Red Cross, to ask aid for the sick and wounded soldiers who filled our hospitals. As a child I had heard from American mission-aries of the horrors of the Turkish rule long before I had learned them from the stories of my adopted people who had suffered martyrdom at the hands of the Turks in Macedonia, and therefore I was astonished to find so little understanding of the causes of the Balkan war, so little sympathy for the suffering that was taking place in the Balkans. I believe the United States contributed ten times as much for relief to Turkey at that time as it contributed to any of the Balkan States. Again I asked myself, "Whence the help that is to liberate and unite Jugoslavia, if England, France, Russia, and America combine in the idea that no people shall ever again rise and call out for its own freedom?"

In 1913 there came the terrible tragedy of the Serbian-Bulgarian war, when I saw our Balkan block torn asunder by the agonizing torment of civil war—for war between sister nations is surely civil war. It seemed to me then that the dream of liberty and union for the Jugo-Slavs would fade into yielding, as had been once before the case in Serbian history when the late King Milan declared that Serbia was in the position of a young woman who had a strong affection and inclination for one young suitor—in that case the suitor was Russia—but who must make a *mariage de raison* with Aus-tria. A secret treaty that would afford to Serbia greater eco-nomic prosperity, at the expense of Jugo-Slav freedom, was concluded between the King, his ministers, and the Austro-Hungarian government. The result of that deflection from the dream was that the King had to abdicate, for the Serbian people repudiated a concession that should be for their mate-rial profit, but would enslave further their brethren in Aus-tria-Hungary.

In 1913, looking conditions in the face, I could not see the way out to freedom and union for the Slavs of Austria. The great nations of the Entente had decreed a long era of peace, for which the weak peoples must pay the price in self-restraint, humiliation, and degradation.

Nowhere about me—in our own legation or in the allied countries—had I heard the suggestion that the liberty bells would ring in July, 1914, for Jugoslavia as they had rung in July, 1776, for this country. But the dream began to come true. The first cannon shot across the Danube proclaimed that the hour had come; that the beginning had been made, made by Austria-Hungary herself in an attack on the free peoples of Serbia. The beginning was not made by dreams of freedom, for the enslaved peoples of Austria-Hungary had never descended to plans for ruthless slaughter of women and children, as was done by the bombardment of the Serbian capital before its population could flee towards the interior of the country.

In the months that followed—when three times the Serbian people, though unaided by their allies and with insufficient ammunition for their cannon, resisted the invasion and overthrow of their country; with the dead so close together that I had to step over them in our hospitals to reach the living soldiers lying on straw; without any means of dressing wounds; with disease claiming thousands of victims—how could one hope for victory? And yet I saw hope on every face. No man in authority throughout those terrible months ever within my hearing spoke of a separate peace, of capitulation or surrender. And our splendid old prime minister when asked to capitulate on terms so advantageous to Serbia that it would have seemed at that time wisdom to accept them, replied: "Better to die in glory than to live in shame."

In the month of December, 1914, there happened a real miracle in Serbia, despite the fact that one-third of the country, and that the best of the farming and industrial region, had been invaded by the enemy. With one single railway line from Salonika supplying its economic and military needs, the Serbian army maneuvered its forces until the enemy was routed and driven from its country.

For eight months longer Serbia maintained her own frontiers, Austria being powerless until Germany and Bulgaria joined with her in a fresh attempt at invasion. This time they succeeded in cutting the railway line, encircled our forces, and compelled a general retreat to the Adriatic coast.

For three months, October, November and December, 1915, we tramped over those terrible mountains of Albania without food, without shelter, leaving thousands of dead by the roadside. Day by day I watched the faces of the Serbian statesmen, officers, and soldiers who escorted the diplomatic caravans, in one of which I had been placed. With that curiosity of the American intelligence to probe the very essence of other people's souls I eavesdropped at their minds to know what they were thinking now that their country was invaded, their army forced to retreat, their women and children given over to martyrdom, and all that the army had accomplished in 1912 and 1913 lost by retreat. We were retracing the steps of the victorious army of 1912—retracing them as a defeated army. Where were their hopes of union now? The answer was, "We are bound for Salonika to join our allies and fight for the freedom of Serbia and of Jugoslavia."

With their people scattered, their government living in a borrowed Greek island, it seemed futile to speak of Serbia as a nation. They were reduced to just a little group of men depending upon their allies for money to pay their army, to feed their prisoners of war, and the few thousands of their own people in exile all dependent upon the charity of the allied nations, including America, which, although not as yet an ally, had shown its sympathy and charity. Inside the country the women and children wept under the martyrdom meted out to a conquered people. They were tortured by the Bulgarians, and oppressed in every conceivable way by the Austro-Hungarians, and yet the army and government dreamed and worked for the deliverance, not only of Serbia but of the whole Jugo-Slav nation. The prisoners in German camps, the martyrs under the Bulgarian lash dreamed of Jugo-Slav freedom.

While America played a glorious and noble part in that deliverance, the action on the Western front was, of course, the event that permitted the attack on the South. Was it not the will of Divine Justice, as well as by consent of the great Ally commander to whom we all owe so much, that the Serbian army, a few thousands of men, the remnant of the nation, should aim the first decisive blow of Allied victory? The advance of the Serbian troops over mountains so high that only eagles or aeroplanes could be supposed to cross them struck the final blow for Jugo-Slav liberty, and the blow struck in the Macedonian mountains resounded to the extreme limits of Jugoslavia. "Where are you going?" asked a general of the French army of a Serbian wounded soldier whom he met on the road bleeding from a wound in the head. "That's not the way to the hospital." "I am not going to the hospital— I am going to Serbia and beyond that—I am going home to free Bosnia!" Within a month the face of every soldier of the Jugo-Slav forces was set towards home and the fight still to come for the liberation of the Slav provinces of Austria. There were men from Croatia, Slovenia, Bosnia, and Herzegovina as well as from Serbia fighting in that army— citizens all of a united kingdom of the Serbs, Croats and Slovenes, the national trinity of the Southern Slav race.

They found their country in a terrible condition. There were no roads; the population which came out to meet them was in rags; there was no fire; roofs had been taken off of the houses, floors had been torn up, even windowsills and doorsills had been burned by the enemy. The trees had been cut down in their cemeteries; and in certain sections in an effort to prove that the population was other than Serbian, the very names had been erased from the tombstones. But what did it matter? That for which the Slav peoples had toiled and died throughout a thousand years of conscious history had been accomplished—their complete freedom and union. I, an adopted daughter, have lived this Gethsemane of a people— this apotheosis of a nation—as a Serbian woman; my heart beating with the wonder and the glory of the sacrifice.

Now that this great inspiring gift of freedom and union has come to my adopted people, if we in Jugoslavia may look forward to a century of union and development of our material, ethical, and moral forces, and to the assimilation of whatever foreign elements there may be within our borders, the decisions of our peoples to rule themselves cannot but aid to promote the peace of the world.   The rights of self-determination cannot apply to a single town, or one side of a street; certain minorities must remain even after the wisest alignment of frontiers.   Unhappily one cannot ask for the freedom of all the Jugo-Slavs: there are Serbs, Croats, and Slovenes who must be content with other citizenship, although they have racial rights to be a part of this wonderful Jugoslavia.

The broad lines of the Slav nationality with its openminded religious tolerance offers guarantees to religious liberty: the Orthodox faith under the Patriarch of Constantinople is very like that of our own Episcopal Church.   Among the Catholics of Croatia and Slovenia there exists a feeling of brotherhood towards the other religions of their nationality, as shown by the fact that many dignitaries of the Catholic Church in those states helped loyally to lead the movement for freedom.   In no country in the world does the Jew have greater opportunity and honor than he has in Serbia and than he will have in the whole of the new Jugo-Slav kingdom if he proves himself as good a citizen there as he is in Serbia.   For the Turk I have seen proofs of tolerance in the efforts to preserve Mosques, and Moslem schools, ordered by our Crown Prince.   After the war of 1912 every assistance was given to Turkish women from Macedonia who wanted to go to Turkey to look for their husbands, or for their bodies if dead.

In my travels about Macedonia I have remarked the just treatment of the Serbian authorities towards the other nationalities, Greeks, Turks, Albanians, and Bulgars, and have discussed with them the fact that it is perfectly possible for people of different strains of blood to live together under the same flag and same government, if equal rights of citizenship are accorded to all their citizens.   I believe firmly that we, the Slavs—if aided by America in this difficult hour of our transition when we suffer physically and mentally from the ravages of war—will be able to construct quickly a United States of the Balkans, and that before many years we may yet hold that Educational Peace Conference at Vienna which was interrupted by the Austrian ultimatum.

THE OPENING OF THE PEACE CONFERENCE

THE ALLIES' EFFORT AT THE RECONSTRUCTION OF THE WORLD

JANUARY 18, 1919

PRESIDENT POINCARÉ PRESIDENT WILSON
DAVID LLOYD GEORGE BARON SONNINO
GEORGES CLEMENCEAU SISLEY HUDDLESTON
STEPHANE LAUZANNE MAXIMILIAN HARDEN

The Peace Conference of Paris, which in 1919 began the work of reconstructing the shattered world, was unique in this: it was a conference representing only one party to the War. So complete had been the defeat of the Central Powers that they were given no voice in deciding the terms of peace. They were at the mercy of the Allies. In their surrender they had asked and had been promised that the terms should be based upon President Wilson's "fourteen points"; but the Allies had expressly warned them that the meaning of these points was to be interpreted solely by the Allies. Diplomats have always known, Germany herself knew well, that the words of any document can be so interpreted, so distorted, so misapplied as to mean almost anything. But Germany had no longer any choice. She placed herself wholly in the hands of the nations she had so deeply wronged.

The first formal meeting of the Peace Conference was held in the splendid hall known as the Clock Salon in the great government building of the Quai d'Orsay in Paris. All the peace delegates from all the Ally Powers were there; and the meeting consisted only of the formal addresses here presented, beginning with the welcoming address of Raymond Poincaré, President of France, followed by the brief speeches of the chief representatives of the United States, Britain and Italy naming Premier Clemenceau for President of the Conference, and closing with his speech of acceptance, after the formality of his pre-arranged election.

Following this actual reproduction of the opening words of the Conference, we present the vivid account of its difficulties by the British official observer present, Sisley Huddleston, and also the outline of its purposes by the celebrated French writer, Lauzanne. That Germany, though in no way present, may not be left entirely out of the picture, we close with the characteristic judgment and comment upon the Conference made at the time by that most outspoken of German celebrities, Maximilian Harden.

36

THE OPENING SESSION OF THE PEACE CONFERENCE

President Poincaré's inaugural speech

GENTLEMEN—France greets and welcomes you and thanks you for having unanimously chosen as the seat of your labors the city which, for over four years, the enemy has made his principal military objective and which the valor of the Allied armies has victoriously defended against unceasingly renewed offensives.

Allow me to see in your decision the homage of all the nations that you represent towards a country which, still more than any others, has endured the sufferings of war, of which entire provinces, transformed into vast battlefields, have been systematically wasted by the invader, and which has paid the heaviest tribute to death.

France has borne these enormous sacrifices without having incurred the slightest responsibility for the frightful cataclysm which has overwhelmed the universe, and at the moment when this cycle of horror is ending, all the Powers whose delegates are assembled here may acquit themselves of any share in the crime which has resulted in so unprecedented a disaster. What gives you authority to establish a peace of justice is the fact that none of the peoples of whom you are the delegates has had any part in injustice. Humanity can place confidence in you because you are not among those who have outraged the rights of humanity.

There is no need of further information or for special inquiries into the origin of the drama which has just shaken the world. The truth, bathed in blood, has already escaped from the Imperial archives. The premeditated character of the trap is to-day clearly proved. In the hope of conquering, first, the hegemony of Europe and next the mastery of the world, the Central Empires, bound together by a secret plot, found the most abominable pretexts for trying to crush Serbia and force their way to the East. At the same time they disowned the most solemn undertakings in order to crush Belgium and force their way into the heart of France. These are the two unforgetable outrages which opened the way to aggression. The combined efforts of Great Britain, France, and Russia broke themselves against that mad arrogance.

If, after long vicissitudes, those who wished to reign by the sword have perished by the sword, they have but themselves to blame; they have been destroyed by their own blindness. What could be more significant than the shameful bargains they attempted to offer to Great Britain and France at the end of July, 1914, when to Great Britain they suggested: "Allow us to attack France on land and we will not enter the Channel"; and when they instructed their Ambassador to say to France: "We will only accept a declaration of neutrality on your part if you surrender to us Briey, Toul, and Verdun"? It is in the light of these memories, gentlemen, that all the conclusions you will have to draw from the war will take shape.

Your nations entered the war successively, but came, one and all, to the help of threatened right. Like Germany, Great Britain and France had guaranteed the independence of Belgium. Germany sought to crush Belgium. Great Britain and France both swore to save her. Thus, from the very beginning of hostilities, came into conflict the two ideas which for fifty months were to struggle for the dominion of the world—the idea of sovereign force, which accepts neither control nor check, and the idea of justice, which depends on the sword only to prevent or repress the abuse of strength.

Faithfully supported by her Dominions and Colonies, Great Britain decided that she could not remain aloof from a struggle in which the fate of every country was involved. She has made, and her Dominions and Colonies have made with her, prodigious efforts to prevent the war from ending in the triumph of the spirit of conquest and the destruction of right.

Japan, in her turn, only decided to take up arms out of loyalty to Great Britain, her great Ally, and from the consciousness of the danger in which both Asia and Europe would have stood, for the hegemony of which the Germanic Empires had dreamt.

Italy, who from the first had refused to lend a helping hand to German ambition, rose against an age-long foe only to answer the call of oppressed populations and to destroy at the cost of her blood the artificial political combination which took no account of human liberty.

Rumania resolved to fight only to realize that national unity which was opposed by the same powers of arbitrary force. Abandoned, betrayed, and strangled, she had to submit to an abominable treaty, the revision of which you will exact. Greece, whom the enemy for many months tried to turn from her traditions and destinies, raised an army only to escape attempts at domination, of which she felt the growing threat. Portugal, China, and Siam abandoned neutrality only to escape the strangling pressure of the Central Powers. Thus it was the extent of German ambitions that brought so many peoples, great and small, to form a league against the same adversary.

And what shall I say of the solemn resolution taken by the United States in the spring of 1917 under the auspices of their illustrious President, Mr. Wilson, whom I am happy to greet here in the name of grateful France, and, if you will allow me to say so, gentlemen, in the name of all the nations represented in this room? What shall I say of the many other American Powers which either declared themselves against Germany—Brazil, Cuba, Panama, Guatemala, Nicaragua, Haiti, Honduras—or at least broke off diplomatic relations —Bolivia, Peru, Ecuador, Uruguay? From north to south the New World rose with indignation when it saw the empires of Central Europe, after having let loose the war without provocation and without excuse, carry it on with fire, pillage, and massacre of inoffensive beings.

The intervention of the United States was something more, something greater, than a great political and military event: it was a supreme judgment passed at the bar of history by the lofty conscience of a free people and their Chief Magistrate on the enormous responsibilities incurred in the frightful conflict which was lacerating humanity. It was not only to protect themselves from the audacious aims of German megalomania that the United States equipped fleets and created immense armies, but also, and above all, to defend an ideal of liberty over which they saw the huge shadow of the Imperial Eagle encroaching farther every day. America, the daughter of Europe, crossed the ocean to wrest her mother from the humiliation of thraldom and to save civilization. The American people wished to put an end to the greatest scandal that has ever sullied the annals of mankind.

Autocratic governments, having prepared in the secrecy of the Chancelleries and the General Staff a map program of universal domination, at the time fixed by their genius for intrigue let loose their packs and sounded the horns for the chase, ordering science at the very time when it was beginning to abolish distances, bring men closer, and make life sweeter, to leave the bright sky towards which it was soaring and to place itself submissively at the service of violence, lowering the religious idea to the extent of making God the complacent auxiliary of their passions and the accomplice of their crimes; in short, counting as naught the traditions and wills of peoples, the lives of citizens, the honor of women, and all those principles of public and private morality which we for our part have endeavored to keep unaltered through the war and which neither nations nor individuals can repudiate or disregard with impunity.

While the conflict was gradually extending over the entire surface of the earth the clanking of chains was heard here and there, and captive nationalities from the depths of their age-long jails cried out to us for help. Yet more, they escaped to come to our aid. Poland came to life again and sent us troops. The Czecho-Slovaks won their right to independence in Siberia, in France, and in Italy. The Jugo-Slavs, the Armenians, the Syrians and Lebanese, the Arabs, all the oppressed peoples, all the victims, long helpless or resigned, of great historic deeds of injustice, all the martyrs of the past, all the outraged consciences, all the strangled liberties revived at the clash of our arms, and turned towards us, as their natural defenders. Thus the war gradually attained the fullness of its first significance, and became, in the fullest sense of the term, a crusade of humanity for Right; and if anything can console us in part at least, for the losses we have suffered, it is assuredly the thought that our victory is also the victory of Right.

This victory is complete, for the enemy only asked for

the armistice to escape from an irretrievable military disaster. In the interest of justice and peace it now rests with you to reap from this victory its full fruits in order to carry out this immense task. You have decided to admit, at first, only the Allied or associated Powers, and, in so far as their interests are involved in the debates, the nations which remained neutral. You have thought that the terms of peace ought to be settled among ourselves before they are communicated to those against whom we have together fought the good fight. The solidarity which has united us during the war and has enabled us to win military success ought to remain unimpaired during the negotiations for, and after the signing of, the Treaty.

It is not only governments, but free peoples, who are represented here. Through the test of danger they have learned to know and help one another. They want their intimacy of yesterday to assure the peace of to-morrow. Vainly would our enemies seek to divide us. If they have not yet renounced their customary maneuvers, they will soon find that they are meeting to-day, as during the hostilities, a homogeneous block which nothing will be able to disintegrate. Even before the armistice you placed that necessary unity under the standard of the lofty moral and political truths of which President Wilson has nobly made himself the interpreter.

And in the light of those truths you intend to accomplish your mission. You will, therefore, seek nothing but justice, "justice that has no favorites," justice in territorial problems, justice in financial problems, justice in economic problems. But justice is not inert, it does not submit to injustice. What it demands first, when it has been violated, are restitution and reparation for the peoples and individuals who have been despoiled or maltreated. In formulating this lawful claim, it obeys neither hatred nor an instinctive or thoughtless desire for reprisals. It pursues a twofold object—to render to each his due, and not to encourage crime through leaving it unpunished. What justice also demands, inspired by the same feeling, is the punishment of the guilty and effective guaranties against an active return of the spirit by which they were tempted; and it is logical to demand that these guaranties should be given, above all, to the nations that have been, and might again be most exposed to aggressions or threats, to those who have many times stood in danger of being submerged by the periodic tide of the same invasions.

What justice banishes is the dream of conquest and imperialism, contempt for national will, the arbitrary exchange of provinces between states as though peoples were but articles of furniture or pawns in a game. The time is no more when diplomatists could meet to redraw with authority the map of the empires on the corner of a table. If you are to remake the map of the world it is in the name of the peoples, and on condition that you shall faithfully interpret their thoughts, and respect the right of nations, small and great, to dispose of themselves, and to reconcile it with the right, equally sacred, of ethnical and religious minorities—a formidable task, which science and history, your two advisers, will contribute to illumine and facilitate.

You will naturally strive to secure the material and moral means of subsistence for all those peoples who are constituted or reconstituted into states; for those who wish to unite themselves to their neighbors; for those who divide themselves into separate units; for those who reorganize themselves according to their regained traditions; and, lastly, for all those whose freedom you have already sanctioned or are about to sanction. You will not call them into existence only to sentence them to death immediately. You would like your work in this, as in all other matters, to be fruitful and lasting.

While thus introducing into the world as much harmony as possible, you will, in conformity with the fourteenth of the propositions unanimously adopted by the Great Allied Powers, establish a general League of Nations, which will be a supreme guarantee against any fresh assaults upon the right of peoples. You do not intend this International Association to be directed against anybody in future. It will not of set purpose shut out anybody, but, having been organized by the nations that have sacrificed themselves in defense of Right, it will receive from them its statutes and fundamental rules. It will lay down conditions to which its present or future adherents will submit, and, as it is to have for its essential aim to prevent, as far as possible, the renewal of wars, it will, above all, seek to gain respect for the peace which you will have established, and will find it the less difficult to maintain in proportion as this peace will in itself imply greater realities of justice and safer guaranties of stability.

By establishing this new order of things you will meet the aspiration of humanity, which, after the frightful convulsions of these bloodstained years, ardently wishes to feel itself protected by a union of free peoples against the ever-possible revivals of primitive savagery. An immortal glory will attach to the names of the nations and the men who have desired to coöperate in this grand work in faith and brotherhood, and who have taken pains to eliminate from the future peace causes of disturbance and instability.

This very day forty-eight years ago, on January 18, 1871, the German Empire was proclaimed by an army of invasion in the Château at Versailles. It was consecrated by the theft of two French provinces; it was thus vitiated from its origin and by the fault of the founders; born in injustice, it has ended in opprobrium. You are assembled in order to repair the evil that it has done and to prevent a recurrence of it. You hold in your hands the future of the world. I leave you, gentlemen, to your grave deliberations, and I declare the Conference of Paris open.

President Wilson's Speech Nominating M. Clemenceau as President of the Conference

I have the great honor to propose as definitive president of this conference the French Premier, M. Clemenceau. I do so in conformity with usage. I should do it even if it were only a question of paying homage to the French Republic, but I do it also because I desire, and you certainly desire with me, to pay homage to the man himself. France, as it is, would alone deserve this honor, but we are to-day in her capital, and it is here that this great Conference has met. France, by her sufferings and sacrifices during the war, deserves a special tribute. Moreover, Paris is her ancient and splendid capital, where more than once these great assemblages, on which the fate of the world has depended, have met.

I am happy to think that the meeting which is beginning crowns the series of these meetings. This Conference may be considered in some respects as the final crowning of the diplomatic history of the world up to this day, for never have so many nations been represented at the same time to solve problems which in so high a degree interest the whole world. Moreover, this meeting signifies for us the end of this terrible war, which threatened to destroy civilization and the world itself. It is a delightful sensation for us to feel that we are meeting at a moment when this terrible menace has ceased to exist.

But it is not only to France, it is to the man who is her great servant that we wish to pay homage and to do honor. We have learned, since we have had relations with him, and since he has been at the head of the French Government, to admire the power of his direction and the force and good sense of his actions. But, more than this, those who know him, those who have worked in close connection with him, have acquired for him a real affection. Those who, like ourselves, have seen him work in these recent times know how much he is united with us, and with what ardor he is working for that which we ourselves desire. For we all desire the same thing. We desire before all to lift from the shoulders of humanity the frightful weight which is pressing on them, so that humanity, released from this weight, may at last return joyfully to work. Thus, gentlemen, it is not only to the Premier of the French Republic, it is to M. Clemenceau that I propose you should give the presidency of this assemblage.

Mr. Lloyd George's Speech Seconding the Nomination

Gentlemen, it is not only a pleasure for me, but a real privilege, to support in the name of the British Empire the motion which has been proposed by President Wilson. I shall do it for the reasons which the President has just expressed with so much eloquence. It is homage to a man that we wish to pay before all. When I was at school M. Clemenceau was already one of the moving forces in French politics. Already his renown had spread far. And, were it not for this memory of my childhood, I should be tempted to believe the legend which is commonly spread abroad of the eternal youth of M. Clemenceau. In all the conferences at which we have been present the most alert, the most vigorous, in a word, the youngest man, was always M. Clemenceau. By the freshness of his mind and his indefatigable energy he displayed his youth at every moment. He is indeed "the grand young man" of France. But nothing will give us greater pleasure than to see him take the place which we propose that he should accept. No one is better qualified for that place. We have often had discussions together. We have often been in agreement and sometimes we have disagreed, and in that case we have always been in the habit of expressing our opinions with all the force and vigor which belong to two Celts like ourselves.

I believe that in the debates of this Conference there will at first inevitably be delays, but I guarantee from my knowledge of M. Clemenceau that there will be no time wasted. That is indispensable. The world is thirsting for peace. Millions of men are waiting to return to their normal life, and they will not forgive us too long delays. I am sure that M. Clemenceau will not allow useless delays to occur. He is one of the greatest living orators, but he knows that the finest eloquence is that which gets things done and that the worst is that which delays them. Another reason for congratulating him on occupying the place which we are about to give him is his indomitable courage, of which he has given proof in days of difficulty. In these days his energy and presence of mind have done more than all the acts of us others to ensure victory. There is no man of whom one can say that he has contributed more to surmount those terrible difficulties which were so close to the final triumph. He represents the admirable energy, courage and resource of his great people, and that is why I desire to add my voice to that of President Wilson and to ask for his election to the presidency of the Peace Conference.

Baron Sonnino's Speech Seconding the Nomination

Gentlemen, on behalf of the Italian Delegation, I associate myself cordially with the proposal of President Wilson, supported by Mr. Lloyd George, and I ask you to give the presidency of the Peace Conference to M. Clemenceau. I am happy to be able in these circumstances to testify to my good will and admiration for France and for the eminent statesman who is at the head of her Government.

Opening Address of M. Clemenceau

Gentlemen, you would not understand it if, after listening to the words of the two eminent men who have just spoken, I were to keep silent. I cannot elude the necessity of expressing my lively gratitude, my deep gratitude, both to the illustrious President Wilson and to the Prime Minister of Great Britain, as well as to Baron Sonnino, for the words which they have uttered. In the past, in the days of my youth—long ago now, as Mr. Lloyd George has reminded me—when I traveled over America and England, I used always to hear the French blamed for that excess of politeness which led them beyond the boundaries of the truth. Listening to the American statesman and the British statesman, I asked myself whether in Paris they had not acquired our national vice of flattering urbanity.

It is necessary, gentlemen, to point out that my election is due necessarily to lofty international tradition, and to the time-honored courtesy shown toward the country which has the honor to welcome the Peace Conference in its capital. The proofs of "friendship"—as they will allow me to call it —of President Wilson and Mr. Lloyd George touched me profoundly, because in these proofs may be seen a new force for all three of us which will enable us, with the help of this entire Conference, to carry through the arduous task entrusted to us. I draw new confidence from it for the success of our efforts.

President Wilson has good authority for his remark that we have here for the first time a collection of delegates from all the civilized peoples of the earth. The greater the sanguinary catastrophe which devastated and ruined one of the richest regions of France, the more ample and more splendid should be the reparation—not merely the reparation for material acts, the ordinary reparation, if I may venture to say so, which is due to us—but the nobler and loftier reparation we are going to try to secure, so that the peoples may at last escape from this fatal embrace, which, heaping up ruins and sorrows, terrorizes the populations and prevents them from devoting themselves freely to their work for fear of the enemies who may spring up at any moment. It is a great and noble ambition that has come to us all. We must hope that success will crown our efforts. This can only be if we have our ideas clear-cut and well defined.

I said in the Chamber of Deputies some days ago, and I make a point of repeating the statement here, that success is possible only if we remain firmly united. We have come here as friends. We must pass through that door as brothers. That is the first reflection which I am anxious to express to you. Everything must be subordinated to the necessity for a closer and closer union between the peoples which have taken part in this great war. The Society of Nations has its being here, it has its being in you. It is for you to make it live, and for that there is no sacrifice to which we are not ready to consent. I do not doubt that as you are all of this disposition we shall arrive at this result, but only on condition that we exercise impartial pressure on ourselves to reconcile what in appearance may be opposing interests in the higher view of a greater, happier, and better humanity. That, gentlemen, is what I had to say to you.

I am touched beyond all expression by the proof of confidence and regard which you have been kind enough to give me. The program of the Conference, the aim marked out by President Wilson, is no longer merely peace for the territories, great and small, with which we are directly concerned; it is no longer merely a peace for the continents, it is peace for the peoples. This program speaks for itself; there is nothing to be added to it. Let us try, gentlemen, to do our work speedily and well. I am handing to the Bureau the rules of procedure of the Conference, and these will be distributed to you all.

I come now to the order of the day. The first question is as follows: "The responsibility of the authors of the war." The second is thus expressed: "Penalties for crimes committed during the war." The third is: "International legislation in regard to labor."

The Powers whose interests are only in part involved are also invited to send in memoranda in regard to matters of all kinds—territorial, financial, or economic—which affect them particularly. These memoranda should be addressed to the general secretariat of the Conference. This system is somewhat novel. Our desire in asking you to proceed thus is to save time. All the nations represented here are free to present their claims. You will kindly send in these memoranda as speedily as possible, as we shall then get on with the work which we shall submit for your consideration. You can deal with the third question from the standpoint of the organization of labor.

It is a very vast field. But we beg of you to begin by examining the question as to the responsibility of the authors of the war. I do not need to set forth our reasons for this. If we wish to establish justice in the world we can do so now, for we have won victory and can impose the penalties demanded by justice. We shall insist on the imposition of penalties on the authors of the abominable crimes committed during the war. Has any one any question to ask in regard to this? If not, I would again remind you that every delegation should devote itself to the study of this first question, which has been made the subject of reports by eminent jurists, and of a report which will be sent to you entitled, "An Inquiry into the Criminal Responsibility of the Emperor William II." The perusal of this *brochure* will, without doubt, facilitate your work. In Great Britain and in America studies on this point have also been published. No one having any remark to make, the program is adopted.

It only remains for me to say, gentlemen, that the order of the day for our next sitting will begin with the question of the Society of Nations. Our order of the day, gentlemen, is now brought to an end. Before closing the sitting, I should like to know whether any delegate of the Powers represented has any question to submit to the Bureau. As we must work in complete agreement, it is to be desired that members of the Conference shall submit all the observations they consider necessary. The Bureau will welcome the expression of opinions of all kinds, and will answer all questions addressed to it. No one has anything further to say? The sitting is closed.

BY SISLEY HUDDLESTON

The Peace Conference formally opened on Saturday, January 18th, in the Salle de l'Horloge at the French Foreign Ministry. But for some weeks before there had been a mustering of statesmen from the four corners of the world in Paris, and the French capital, which with its comings and goings of statesmen and generals had for so long been the Capital of the War, was prepared to become the Peace Headquarters.

I think that the strongest criticism that can be made of the Allies is that they permitted two months to slip away before they even proceeded to consider the peace which the armistice promised. There were two things to do, each of which depended on the other. One was to make a temporary treaty which would give us a working relationship with Germany. The other was, not only to make peace in the diplomatic sense, but to pacify Europe. We increased our difficulties with Germany by the long delay. We could in the first flush of victory have imposed our maximum terms almost without protest on the crushed people ; and it would have had an excellent effect to modify them later on. But we muddled, because Clemenceau wanted one sort of peace, Lloyd George another, and Wilson a third. We got in each other's way.

The fact is that the Foreign Offices could not agree. The conflict on the question of admitting Russia was particularly heated between the British and the French. The Quai d'Orsay, which is singularly blind to realities and sometimes allows itself to be maneuvered by foreign reactionaries, declared hotly against Mr. Lloyd George's and Mr. Balfour's views that Lenine should be invited to make peace and send delegates to Paris.

This inability to come to an accord on the most elementary matters pursued the Allies; and it was no wonder that Mr. Wilson, who had been in France for nearly a month, wasting his time, protesting now and again to M. Clemenceau, grew very impatient, and urged an instant beginning. At this time the contradiction between the point of view of the American President and that of the French Premier was flat and flagrant. A deadlock was threatened at the outset. The two men remained courteous, but there was certainly no friendly feeling between them. "If you can persuade me that your plans are better for the peace of the world, I am willing to listen and to learn," said Mr. Wilson. "And if you can persuade me, so much the better," replied M. Clemenceau. "Only—you cannot!"

The scenery, the stage setting, was not very impressive in those rainy days of January, when Paris was drenched in constant showers. There is no season of the year when the city looks more dismal. The leafless boulevards and the wet pavements reflecting faintly at night the feeble illuminations make a picture without color. But in the busy interiors of the buildings that were devoted to the preparations for peace there was an almost feverish activity. The Pressmen from all parts of the world gathered in great clouds ready to swarm down upon any one who could furnish them with the smallest tit-bit of information. Motor-cars dashed to and fro under the leaden skies, stopping at the door of this hotel and at the porch of that Government Department. The last touches were put to the arrangements. The papers stacked in prodigious number were classified. Facts and figures about almost every country in Europe, and statistics about every continent of the world, were available. In short, the supreme moment had arrived when the most immense consultation of Powers and of peoples that the world has ever seen was about to begin.

If you had occasion to come within the shadow of these buildings, whose placid front concealed such prodigious labor and such stupendous compilations, you felt the gravity of the coming events. There were assembled those upon whose wisdom or folly, upon whose vigilance or blindness, upon whose good-will or antipathies, the whole future of the world hung. The fate of mankind was poised by a thread. When you came into the sphere of these proceedings you could not avoid a feeling of awe at the terrible responsibilities shouldered by the statesmen, as they were yesterday shouldered by the captains of the Allies and of their associates.

The British took up their quarters in the Hotel Majestic and in the Hotel Astoria—two huge establishments which are close to the Étoile. The strictest guard was kept, lest there should be a betrayal of secrets. What secrets there were left to betray after the members of the Conference had given away all they knew—except their own quarrels, and those too, wherever it suited them to hint that Mr. So-and-so was preventing an agreement on such-and-such a subject—I really do not know. For my part, I never learnt of anything of any importance through official channels that I had not known before either by personal contact with some member or through the newspapers. There never was such a ridiculous bogy as this fear of publicity, and I am only surprised that the Press did not laugh it to scorn. There were not only men from the Foreign Office but men from Scotland Yard, and the emptying of the waste-paper baskets was a highly important business!

In these buildings the delegates lived and worked and played—for the social side of life was developed by the younger folk at the Hotel Majestic. If it was permissible to dance on the eve of Waterloo it was surely permissible to dance on the eve of Versailles; and the amateur theatricals and the concerts and the dinner parties and the afternoon teas in the Hall of the Hotel Majestic made peace-making a fairly pleasant job, provided you were not too busy.

Nevertheless, it is not at all fair to speak scornfully of this army of officials. They really worked after their fashion exceedingly well. They prepared reports, they put the text of documents in shape, they did the fagging for the British team. Only—the delegates afterwards disregarded what they had done and much of their work was wasted. There was an early outcry about their numbers, but it must be remembered that it was difficult to estimate how large a staff would be required; and, besides, a number came over for only a week or two. A tribute should be paid to the many girl assistants, who in docketing and filing were superior to the men. Responsible positions were given to women. The uniforms of the young girl messengers soon became familiar to Parisians and were celebrated in song.

Most of the decisions with regard to the methods of procedure were taken in the week preceding the Conference proper. It was arranged that the big Powers alone were to lay down the general lines and the smaller States to be called in afterwards, while the enemy Powers were to come in at the end of the deliberations to receive their sentences at Versailles. There was a feeling in some quarters that it would have been better that everybody should have been united in a big conference to agree first on the principles to be applied, and to work out the details in smaller groups. Questions of procedure cannot be regarded as trivial. They have gone very far to make the results of the Conference what they are.

The opening day recalled an event which colored the subsequent history of Europe. It was the anniversary of that day in 1871 when the German Empire was proclaimed by an army of invasion in the Château at Versailles. It was consecrated by the theft of two French provinces, and, as M. Poincaré said, was thus vitiated from its origin by the fault of its founders. Born in injustice, it ended in opprobrium. The scene in the Salon de l'Horloge at the Quai d'Orsay when the seventy delegates met for the first time was an impressive one. The Salle is magnificent, a suitable setting for the drama which was then begun. Looking out on the swollen Seine was M. Bratiano, the Rumanian Premier, in company with M. Pashitch of Serbia. All the Balkan problems which had been hitherto insoluble seemed to be represented by these two men. The picturesque figure of the Emir Feysal, son of the King of the Hedjaz, with his flowing turban falling on his shoulders, reminded one of the tremendous differences of opinion and of interests in the Near East. M. Dmowski and M. Kramarcz, from Poland and from Czecho-Slovakia, evoked the difficulties and the troublous times ahead of the new States. One foresaw the Adriatic quarrel when Baron Sonnino entered. M. Venizelos incarnated Greek aspirations and M. Vandervelde carried us in imagination to suffering Belgium. Marshal Foch, Mr. Wilson, President Poincaré, Mr. Lloyd George and M. Clemenceau formed a group whose points of view it seemed hardly possible to reconcile. After all, when one looked and remembered "so many men, so many minds," it seemed hopeless to expect that they could all be satisfied.

I think in view of the subsequent results it is as well to recall the salient passage of M. Poincaré's speech.

"You will," he said, "seek nothing but justice—justice that has no favorites—justice in territorial problems, justice in financial problems, justice in economic problems.

"The time is no more when diplomatists could meet to redraw with authority the map of the Empires on the corner of a table. If you are to remake the map of the world it is in the name of the peoples and on condition that you shall faithfully interpret their thoughts and respect the right of nations, small and great, to dispose of themselves, provided that they observe the rights equally sacred of ethical and religious minorities.

"While thus introducing into the world as much harmony as possible, you will, in conformity with the fourteenth of the propositions unanimously adopted by the Great Allied Powers, establish a general League of Nations which will be a supreme guarantee against any fresh assaults upon the right of peoples."

How far has this purpose been fulfilled? He would be a bold man who would pretend that the high mission has been carried out without deflection and without conspicuous failures.

The actual representation of the Powers, big and little, was not settled without many protests, and it is now no secret that great discontent was aroused by the allocation of the number of seats to each nation. Mr. Lloyd George soon found an opportunity for his gift of conciliation, since there was indeed much that was arbitrary in the arrangements dictated by material interests. The first intention that Belgium should have fewer representatives than Brazil displeased many commentators. The British delegation was regarded as unfair, since Canada, Australia and India, and other parts of the Empire, helped to strengthen the British point of view. The question of the Dominions was certainly a difficult one, for they are entirely British, and yet could not be assimilated. It was obvious that separate representation was due for their great and gallant part in the war, but the clear-sighted French observed the preponderance of the British element thus given, and asked for (and were refused) representatives from Algeria, Cochin-China and Morocco. The Jugo-Slavs, as such, were not to have a place. The Serbians, who, with their neighbors composing the new nation, were to have so much to say with regard to the Italian claims, had two representatives, and could not therefore speak for three nationalities. The differences among the Asiatic nations were even more fundamental.

BY STÉPHANE LAUZANNE

"I leave you to your weighty deliberations. The Peace Conference is declared open."

M. Raymond Poincaré uttered these words at three o'clock on January 18, 1919, with extraordinary earnestness, and a touch of emotion in his voice which his hearers are not accustomed to find there. And at once a wave of joy seemed to surge through the entire assembly who had listened standing to the opening speech of the President of the Republic, in the great "Salon de l'Horloge" of the Quai d'Orsay.

It was an extraordinary assembly, unlike any other known to history. The sixty-five men present belonged to every race, to every country. Some came from the uttermost ends of the earth, delegates sent by China and Japan. Others from parts little known, vaguely shown on geography maps —for instance, the two representatives of the King of Hedjaz, who arrived at the eleventh hour and were admitted at the last minute. Some were very old—Mr. Pashitch, for one—with his enormous white beard; others, such as the envoys of certain South American Republics, quite young.

From the corner of the hall where I was, my attention never wandered from them all during the half-hour the speech of the President of the Republic lasted, as I tried to read on their faces something of the feelings that were certainly stirring below. But every countenance, whether pale or dark-hued, reflected only pride and joy. And prouder, more joyous perhaps than any of the others, was President Wilson. His smile seemed to dominate and lighten up the entire assembly. When M. Poincaré spoke his closing words: *"I leave you to your weighty deliberations. The Peace Conference is declared open,"* he was the first to spontaneously clap his hands and give the others the signal of applause.

And now the Peace Conference is open and the Allies are trying to rebuild the world.

One question predominates in the vast work to be accomplished: Will the Allies agree, and will they agree to the end? The question has been asked in America more than elsewhere perhaps. Cablegrams, some sensational, others pessimistic, have been sent to the American press on this subject. These cables came from newspapermen whose information was not always as reliable as it was prompt.

Paris is a strange and difficult city for the reporter who does not know it. A city of rumors, of gossip, of talkers and faultfinders. Every one knows all there is to be known without ever having heard anything. The newspaper man who has not understood its psychology is in an unfortunate position! He is at the mercy of any lobbyist of the Palace Bourbon who whispers in his ear an account of the most secret meeting of the Cabinet, and he will take it for history in the making. He is at the mercy of any restaurant waiter who speaks disparagingly of every man in the Government —and he will take it as a true index of the feeling of the Parisian crowd. He sees the moving surface, the lights, women passing in the streets—and he will imagine all of France is before his eyes! Truly, a misguided person the newspaper man who listens too much and does not think enough!

Let us take as an example the question of the League of Nations, which certain American correspondents have striven to describe as one of the main points of divergence among the Allies. It is characteristic of the errors of in-

terpretation which can be made by a newspaper man insufficiently acquainted with France, when he tries to give
an account of French opinion. What has been cabled to
New York, Chicago, Boston and elsewhere? Nine times
out of ten, this: "M. Clemenceau is opposed to the proposed League of Nations of President Wilson, and France
will have none of it." And nine Americans out of ten are
convinced to-day that opposition to the League of Nations
came entirely from France. What is the truth of the matter?

The truth is that French public opinion—that of the
nation, of the people, of the army—has never been opposed to a League of Nations; it is merely skeptical regarding the results of such a League—an entirely different
matter. Skepticism is one thing, opposition is another.
There is not a Frenchman living who would delay by one
hour the dawning of that radiant day when nations will
have the understanding of sisters, and when universal peace
will reign permanently on our earth. But there are many
Frenchmen who believe that day will never dawn as long as
men are men, and cupidity, stupidity, and ill-nature are still
to be found here. So Frenchmen are not antagonistic to the
League; they are simply incredulous about it.

Again, the truth is that M. Clemenceau, who incarnates
every feeling, every fear, every hope of France, shares on
this point, as on many others, the opinion of four-fifths of
the French people. But if, deep down in his heart, M. Clemenceau does not believe in a League of Nations, he is so
little opposed to one that less than a fortnight after he
became Premier of France, in 1917, he appointed a commission for the purpose of preparing the draft of a League of
Nations, and as members of this commission he selected not
only some of the most eminent jurists of France, but also
men who were most in favor of the idea of arbitration among
nations, of peace among peoples, of conciliation among governments. M. Leon Bourgeois, who is the oldest and most
prominent pacifist of France, in the highest and noblest sense
of the word "pacifist," was appointed chairman of the commission.

Further, the truth is that the commission appointed by

M. Clemenceau worked so hard and to such good purpose, for two years, that it had ready an entire series of drafts showing to the last detail the working of such a league, the constitution of international courts of arbitration, the penalties to be resorted to in case of conflict, etc. One part of the work, done by that great authority on international law, Professor André Weiss, even went so far as to give a list of the financial, marine, economic and monetary penalties which could be enforced, if a war were to threaten, against the nation that should be indicated as the author of the trouble. To quote M. Leon Bourgeois: "It is the most marvelous and formidable arsenal that can be imagined: the League will only have to stoop to pick up arms against war."

The day the Peace Conference opened, France was the first country to propose that the League of Nations should be one of the subjects of discussion, and she was the one and only nation to place on the Conference table a concrete and practical draft for such a League.

Other divergences occurred, at the very outset of the Conference, which since have been smoothed away. They deserve to be mentioned here only because they raised questions of principles, and questions of principles are often most difficult.

Among others, there was the question of language and the question of representation of the smaller nations.

The question of language is one that France feels deeply about. The question is in what language the final instrument of the Conference—the peace treaty—shall be drawn up. From time immemorial, international treaties of peace have been drawn up in the French language, and that is what is meant when French is described as the language of diplomacy. Even in 1815, after Waterloo, when France was invaded and crushed by Europe, the peace treaty of Vienna was drawn up in French. Even in 1871, after Sedan, when France was invaded and crushed by Prussia, the Frankfort treaty of peace was drawn up in French. France cannot admit, therefore, that after the Marne and Verdun, the treaty of peace that will be signed in Paris should be in any other tongue than French. Translations may and should be made in every other idiom, but in accordance with a tradition that goes back centuries, the original must be a French original.

The representation of certain smaller nations, whose conduct was so heroic during the war, was a question about which France felt at least as deeply as about the question of language.

In the course of a preliminary meeting, it had first been decided that Belgium and Serbia would have only two delegates at the Conference, whereas at the request of the United States it was decided Brazil should have three. No one in France contests the importance of the services rendered by the noble Brazilian people in the cause of the Allies, but for us who are French, among many precious memories, one will always stand out: the memory of blood shed in common on the battlefield. What has made the friendship of the United States sacred to France is not so much the money lent, the munitions sent, the hospitals built, the ports enlarged, as the two million men who came to her and the fifty thousand boys who sleep their last sleep in our French cemeteries. . . . Belgium and Serbia, too, gave their blood for the cause of civilization. They gave it from the very first day—and they gave it until the very last hour. This makes them in our eyes the equals of the great nations of the earth. This was enough to earn for them five delegates each to the Conference, like France, or England, or America. In no case should it have earned for them fewer delegates than a nation not one of whose soldiers ever suffered in our trenches. At the urgent and pressing request of France, the Conference altered its first decision and assigned three delegates each to Serbia and Belgium. Three is not much, but it is better than two. Would it not have been preferable to have done at once what common fairness made us do later?

All this is slight enough, and simply shows the necessity of examining, and thinking, and taking into consideration the traditions and feelings of the various peoples. Other divergences will occur. What has not been said, telegraphed or written on the subject of France's territorial claims! A great New York paper even went so far as to state that

France and her Government had been carried away "by a spirit of conquest and imperialism which would be the misfortune of France and of the world"! Now, the so-called imperialism and spirit of conquest of France are limited to asking for Alsace-Lorraine, with the frontiers of that province in 1815, that is, with the Saar basin. The Saar basin, in geographical area, only slightly exceeds that of the borough of Manhattan. It was a part of France for nearly two centuries. It was wrested from France in 1815, at the Congress of Vienna, for one reason: because it is rich in coal, and as early as the beginning of the nineteenth century Prussia was busy appropriating everything that had any value, such as iron or coal. France to-day claims that district, first by virtue of right, because it formerly belonged to her, next because it will be compensation for the loss of her Northern coal fields, destroyed or damaged for years and years to come by the Germans, and lastly because it will be a guarantee against any German attack on that side: Germany will be deprived of one of the sinews of war.

And that is the whole story of France's territorial claims. At no hour, at no minute of the war, did France ever dream —I can formally affirm this—of annexing all the left bank of the Rhine. When in secret treaties with Russia, France asked that her hands should not be tied in connection with the left bank of the Rhine, this meant that she wanted—and still wants—to receive proper guarantees in that quarter. France does not want, in the more or less distant future, the Prussian or Bavarian Palatinate to serve as a jump-off from which to attack her or to attack Belgium. So she will ask that there should be no fortifications on the left bank of the Rhine, either temporary or permanent, and no arsenals, no depots of artillery, no garrisons, nothing, in a word, that could be used to repeat the operation of 1914. But the people of that country, provided they do not arm themselves, are free to administer their territory as they see fit, and to annex themselves to Prussia, or Bavaria, or Austria, or to no country at all. Their independence remains absolute. And that is the spirit of conquest of France! It simply con-

sists in taking the proper measures to prevent a renewal of
the attempt to conquer her.

The French are often accused of hatred and of a desire
for revenge where Germany is concerned, because their territory has been ravaged, invaded, set fire to, destroyed by
the Germans. But it is not only the French who are to-day
pronouncing anathemas against Germany, but also the English, who are not hereditary enemies of Germany; the Belgians, who never had the slightest quarrel with Germany,
and the Rumanians, who were in alliance with Germany.

On the very day of the opening of the Conference, I
heard from M. Jean Bratiano, Prime Minister of Rumania, and first delegate of Rumania to the Conference, an
account of the sufferings endured by his country under the
Teuton heel, and I found that this Wallachian from the
far banks of the Danube said the same things as the Walloons
of Belgium or the Picards of France.

"In Rumania," he told me, "there are entire districts with
which there is no communication possible: not even a cart
to go there. We have been despoiled of everything and we
are hungry. There is not a day's reserve of flour in Bucharest. The awful thing about Germany, you see, is not only
that her mentality is that of a savage, but that she has such
a mentality without realizing it. She is cruel instinctively
and without effort. She is cruel with a scientific refinement
that almost amounts to genius."

BY MAXIMILIAN HARDEN

President Wilson, as lately as last autumn known to the
gentlemen in our Foreign Office as "the agent of the plutocracy" (as a matter of fact it was as the antagonist of the
plutocracy that he rose in popular prestige), has now been
admitted into the forecourt of favor. But what can he do
against the flinty heart of his allies in Europe? Almost every
day I get letters asking the same tremulous question, and
proving that the belief in our enemies' "will to annihilate
us" has survived every other product of Nicolai's [1] factory.

[1] Colonel Nicolai was one of Ludendorff's agents for political
propaganda in Germany.

"But do you seriously think that Clemenceau and Lloyd George will ever listen to reason?" I do; seriously. Maybe reason quitted her nest in their heads for a short flight, but has long since returned to roost under the roof of these two Celtic craniums.

Monsieur Georges Clemenceau is a fine spirit (*ein Geistiger*). The classical Jacobin. One suckled on the spirit of Didero—the last man, in all probability, of this stamp. The son of a doctor from La Vendée, he himself after his return from America—to whose free air he was driven by abhorrence of the Empire of the third Napoleon—became a doctor in Montmartre. There he was indefatigable in attending the poor. He is chosen a member of the Paris Municipal Council, then elected to the Chamber, as a follower of Gambetta, from which he is swept away in the year of the malodorous Panama deluge by the inane suspicion of being in England's pay. He fights Gambetta, Ferry, Jaurès, Millerand, Delcassé, Viviani, Briand, overthrows Minister after Minister and, therefore, acquires, as Senator, his nickname "the Tiger." Yet there is nothing of the beast of prey about him, only a great deal of the *batailleur,* the fighting cock *à la* Cyrano. In his struggle for freedom he fights as journalist, as member of Parliament, and, at the age of 66, for the first time, as Minister, to champion the old-style republican's view of right—preferably alone, never in the crowd, and always with the clear weapon of the spirit. Even the opponents of his policy loved him, even his friends dreaded his abruptly veering moods, and did not account him, for all his talents, one of the statesmen upon whom France might rely at the pinch of need. "Great in criticism and destruction only"—that was the stereotyped description. When, in November, 1917, Monsieur Poincaré, cruelly mauled by *L'Homme Enchaîne,* was obliged to offer the old man of 77 the Premiership, I wrote:

"Monsieur Clemenceau already loved his country with the ardent longing, the stormy jealousy of the wooer who is never quite satisfied, when he looked no older than he does in Manet's portrait: And he will certainly strain every pulse, every nerve, every fiber of his will, in the attempt to show to-morrow, at last, before the eyes of all the world, how he can rise to the greatness to which he has always felt himself equal. France will not be the same after him as it was before. He is capable of gaining great things for his country, capable also of running it into gigantic losses."

Greater things than he ever dared to dream has he gained. He secured the unity of command, gave it to General Foch, breathed strong confidence into the war-weary nation, army, citizens, and was for the space of twelve moons all in all. Of the men who protested in Bordeaux against the incorporation of Alsace-Lorraine in the German Empire he is the sole survivor, and to-day he brings back to his country the lost provinces. After a victory which towers far above all hopes, he, who had never seemed to believe rightly in reconciliation, in a League of Nations, in a new world, has not shrunk from confessing his faith in worthier Reason. In November, 1917, he said:

"Only nations who are capable of freeing themselves can found the League of Nations. It is said in this House that Germany herself will break Prussian militarism. Unhappily, instead of breaking it, Germany makes herself its tool. If we win, we shall not be blinded by arrogance. We know the dangers of victory, how easily it leads to an abuse of strength. I am not of such a school; I stick to right. In this respect I have always been true to myself. We want our rights, and we have been compelled to assert them by force."

On the 18th of October, the day which freed Bruges, Douai, Lille, Ostend, Roubaix and Tourcoing, he said: "We have fought for our rights, not for the opportunity to take vengeance. From the liberation of France must arise the liberation of mankind." After the signature of the armistice: "Exhausted Germany had to capitulate; its internal condition was such as to leave no hope of recovery. We must speedily come to its help. Because we have waged war in defense of humanity, not against it."

This man, ennobled by his experience of good fortune, would certainly, now after the death of militarism, be ready to further in the radiance of victory that plan of disarmament, in which King Edward found a consolation of old age, and Mr. Lloyd George a pillar of hope for financial and social reform.

This younger Celt, too, peruse him at close quarters, does not give you the impression of a man for whom the fight which breaks his opponent's ribs is the supreme pleasure. After the death of his parents, who had migrated from Wales to Manchester, he was brought up among Methodists of Kymric speech, well outside the range of England's State Church, in the Welsh county of Carnarvon, which still to-day gives him his seat in the Lower House. He it was who carried the laws which secure the workingman against the ills of age, sickness, and unemployment, and who forced the Upper House to pass the People's Budget, the true stuff of Democracy, which he explained in a speech of almost five hours. It went through although it left industry and the people's food unburdened, and only taxed property, income, and luxuries (among which, it is true, he counted tea). He was always a pacifist, not far removed from the Socialists —those of the sober-minded English brand—and up to the day of Agadir he was wont to speak of Germany—whose system of old-age insurance he had copied, minus the workingman's compulsory contributions—in a tone of the greatest respect. This was not even impaired by his belief that the ordinary German lived on horseflesh and nasty black bread. In every position, as President of the Board of Trade, Chancellor of the Exchequer, Minister for Munitions, Premier, he has stood high above neighbors and predecessors. The well-informed could foresee that Great Britain would not withdraw its favor at the polls from its favorite, the man of vivid temperament, who created its apparatus of war. No one could anywhere be found who loves his homeland as this man does.

"We were never more richly blessed with prosperity than in years after we resolved to care for the poor and the weak. Twelve months ago five mighty countries, Germany, France, Russia, the United States, and our own United Kingdom, groaned under a deficit. England alone has now recovered and is paying for its shipbuilding and covering other expenditure besides from its current annual revenues. What other country on earth can boast of such success? Our country, which some endeavor to intimidate by a well-organized despondency, still offers capital the safest investment."

That is David Lloyd George, "Practical Idealist." The man who wants to make the poorest a strong member in the body of the State, who is saddened when he sees in the Welsh mountains a stream rushing impetuously over a precipice and then, in the valley, turning some worn and rusty mill-wheel, but never serving to bring light into the dark hovels of the poor.

Such a stream would be a fit parable of the German people, were the will, which you are supposed in this country to embody, to become the law of the world. All too long it has been just like such a stream. No one, save a man blinded with rage, can deny that the performance of this people during the war has been marvelous. Enthusiasm for a duty, devotion to a duty whose fulfillment was represented as necessary for the Fatherland, quiet accommodation to the hardships of privation, joy in self-sacrifice—there was a grandeur in this storm of will-power! And it is no vain self-admiration which prompts the question whether any other among the peoples softened by civilization would have carried for so long a stretch the dreary daily burden of such misery. Shameful, therefore despicable, calumny, is the talk which taxes the home country with having rotted and poisoned the army at the front. We were beaten in the military way; army was defeated by army; General Ludendorff by General Foch; poison gas by tank. An army nourished only on the certainty of victory, drilled only for that event, could not but flag when the hope of victory faded, when in every resting-time they witnessed the impudent indulgences on the lines of communication, and in front, in the firing line, learned to realize that no technical apparatus, neither U-boats nor heavy guns, nor long-range guns, nor poison-bombs, nor even the gigantic imposing gas-bags of Zeppelins, could effect anything permanent against the might of an Idea, a Faith. The home country did more and suffered more than was hitherto thought possible for human power, for men in the mass. But all their pains could not avail to bring mankind one single step forward. Dost thou still swirl, stream of national energy, down mossy slopes and precipices, dost thou still swell high in eager passion, and leap the crag to a new bed of stones, in order to turn in the valley a mill-wheel half rusted away, at least half rusted away? The question often flashes through one's head. And to-morrow must the German energy of purpose still spend itself fruitlessly, be compelled to do at the beck of the conquerer what up till yesterday appeared to the blinded people the work of its own free will? Germany, who has no longer any companion to take a share of the burden, is to "indemnify" all the hostile peoples (except the United States); without Alsace-Lorraine, the Saar region, North Schleswig, Posen, Upper Silesia, without gold, copper, oil, oversea trade, is it to create anew by the labor of its own hands all that its enemies have lost by the war? Such a task would last for scores of years and grind no bread-corn, warm no hearth, light no home, for the people chained to its enforced labor.

Let the eye of your soul, chief man of Britain, look away from the electoral contest in whose sunshine you now stand, victor at home as over the foreign foe—let it glance back into the dust of the contest fought twelve years ago. Then Lord Milner, to-day your Minister for War, heard from a thousand throats an angry cry; that, in order to glut the greed of the mine-owners, he should allow forced labor to be imposed on the Chinese in the Transvaal, was an outrage which the free Britons' sense of honor must make good instantly. The demand for the full costs of the war would compel the Germans, a whole nation of Europeans, to undergo the lot of coolies. In shaft and smelting furnace, in the weaver's stool and at the smith's anvil, in the furrowed plowland, the workshop, the machinery shed, the merchant's office, men would sweat, gnashing their teeth, to furnish the tribute. What Virgil says of oxen and of bees—that they draw the plow and make honey for others—would be true of a whole human nation. With a national debt of 200,-000,000,000, municipalities disorganized, industrial bodies crippled, nothing but what was barely necessary for sustaining life would be left them on this little planet; everything produced over and above that would have to be given over to the foreigner. Not the patience of the most patient could submit to such a yoke for long.

I do not believe that men whose being has been tinged with Western civilization desire the enslavement of a nation; that they think, in the quietness of peace, just as our militarists thought in the turmoil of battle, when they tossed the worldly goods of Austrians, Hungarians, Bulgarians, Turks into the pans of their field-kitchens. The German who groans, saying that the throng of victors wants to murder him, to ruin his country's future, is given his answer: "Since it was you who devised murder and destruction, you have no right to ask that we, after the huge agonies and sacrifices of a long-drawn-out defense, should take upon us in addition losses for which reparation can be made, should saddle our children and grandchildren with this heavy burden." The murmur of complaint dies away; no gracious echo would be awakened by the trumpet tone if the Three upon the seat of judgment were indeed such as fear, the mother of hatred, paints them:

"It is our wish that Germany should turn aside from schemes of military domination and devote all her strength to the great beneficent tasks of the world."—*Lloyd George.*

"Only a diplomacy informed by a new spirit can make peace secure. He who wants to build a new house, must not use old, worn stones, antiquated rules of building."—*Clemenceau.*

"Loud resounds, inaccessible only to the deaf, the cry for humanity, for the triumphant dominion of justice over all the world; and our most immediate duty appears to me to be to devote ourselves in friendship to mankind."—*Wilson.*

The Three do not dream of shutting up the German people to the bitter condition of helots. Their eyes (so it seems to me) are turned upon this people, would like to discern clearly toward what new aim its will is bent, would gladly be convinced that the German soul has changed. And their eye strains, puzzles to make out whether the stream is not still wasting its torrent force to turn the rusty wheel.

GERMANY BEGINS REPUBLICAN GOVERNMENT

PROGRESS OF THE GERMAN REVOLUTION

FEBRUARY 6, 1919

WALTER JAMES SHEPARD   GENERAL LUDENDORFF
GEORGE SAUNDERS   SEÑOR AZHEITUAS
PRESIDENT FREDERICK EBERT

The first "Ruling" Assembly ever known to Germany, that is, the first that ever held real control of the country without being overshadowed by kings or other rulers more powerful than itself, was the Assembly which gathered at 3 p. m. on February 6th, not in Berlin but in Weimar, the ancient capital of one of the smaller German states. Under this Assembly, Germany became a really self-governing constitutional state.

From the time of the revolution of November, 1918, the country had been governed by Frederick Ebert, the Heidelburg leather-worker and socialist. Nominally he had been at first Chancellor and then temporary President. He had suppressed all disorder, compelled an election of an Assembly by universal suffrage, and now that Assembly was met as the true representative of the people to organize a constitutional government.

Almost the first act of the Assembly was to elect Ebert to a more regular presidency. Then they prepared a permanent constitution which, after careful discussion of detail, was declared established in the following August. So Germany joined the ever-growing list of self-governing peoples.

The picture of the gathering of this profoundly important Assembly is here sketched by the American economist, Professor Walter James Shepard of the University of Missouri. The actual labors of the Assembly are outlined by a British eye-witness, the special representative of the London *Times*, Mr. Saunders. He looks to the meaning and the probable future of this new government. So also, but from a neutral standpoint, does Señor Azheituas, a Spanish economist. Then finally we let Germany speak for herself, by giving first the bitter almost frenzied denunciation of the new régime by Ludendorff, the last leader of the old. Then follows the speech with which President Ebert welcomed the new Assembly. The marked interruptions to the speech show the temper of the men who listened to it. In their hands lay the destiny of the German nation.

BY WALTER JAMES SHEPARD

THE revolution in Germany strikes the observer as different in essential respects from revolutions which have taken place in other countries. One looks, in such events, for a few short days of blood and battle; for power wrested by force from the grip of those who have held it; for popular turmoil, the citizenry waging conflict behind street barricades against the disciplined but gradually disintegrating and increasingly disaffected troops of the established government—in short, for a *journée* in which the overturn is speedily accomplished and the new régime quickly set up. But the German revolution affords no such spectacle. There has been, to be sure, street-fighting and bloodshed, but they have been incident to the attempt of the extremists to overthrow the revolutionary government or to compel it to undertake a more radical program. The revolution itself was bloodless, and the establishment of the provisional government under Ebert was only the last step in a crumbling process which had been evident during the latter part of the administration of Count von Hertling and the whole of that of Prince Max. Not only were a number of radically liberal measures inaugurated during this period, but the ministry of Prince Max included three Socialists, one of them being Philip Scheidemann, later to become prime minister of the new republic.

Friedrich Ebert's accession to the chancellorship was proclaimed by his predecessor, and the personnel of administration, even in the higher posts, was changed but little. Except for the abdication of the Kaiser and the lesser monarchs, the renunciation of his rights by the crown prince, and the announcement that the government was provisional, pending the convening of a national assembly for the purpose of forming a new constitution for Germany, the events might easily have been brought within the category of orderly legal development. It is true there had been mutinies among the sailors at Kiel and soldiers' and workmen's councils were established in a number of places; but it can scarcely be said that the government was unable to cope with these sporadic disturbances. On the whole the people were quiet and remained so for some time. It was a revolution which was not at all a revolution, and therein lies the key to the events of the succeeding months.

In order to understand the complex situation in Germany during this period it is necessary to review briefly the political forces which contended among themselves for power. Soon after the revolution all the political parties were reorganized, adopting new names, though they remained essentially unchanged in character and principles. The old Conservative (Junker) party and its minor allies were reconstituted under the name of the German National People's party, with Count Westarp and Baron von Gamp as its leaders. Frankly Pan-Germanists, conservative, militarist and monarchist in principle, this party awaited a favorable moment for inaugurating the counter-revolution.

Most of the old National Liberal party joined the German People's party, under the leadership of Dr. Stresemann, whose real program is hidden behind vague promises of peace, freedom, order and bread. They are, in fact, very little changed. While declaring themselves ready to collaborate with the republic they are, in truth, attached to the old times. They understand the futility of a counter-revolution, as the Hohenzollerns have made themselves impossible forever in Germany; but they have no enthusiasm for a republic. Indeed the leader late in April announced adherence to the monarchical principle. Representing the great industrial and commercial elements in the country, their attitude on most political questions differs only from that of the German National People's party in being somewhat less outspoken.

The old Catholic Center was rechristened the Christian People's party, and acknowledged the leadership of Dr. Spahn and Herr Erzberger. It made a not very successful effort to attract adherents of other faiths to its banner. It is considerably less intransigeant than the other two parties of the Right, has not refused to support the government on occasion, and in the person of its leader Erzberger shared in governmental councils.

These three parties of the Right are capitalistic, though occasionally admitting the principle of socialization in vague terms and with many restrictions. Their hatred of England is still bitter, and they can scarcely hide their hope of revenge. They maintain that it is the Entente's intention to allow the Bolsheviki to overrun Germany, and they use the Bolshevist menace to private property as a means to secure votes. They have all opposed the measure of the Prussian minister of education for separation of church and state, and the government's order against officers wearing distinctions of rank and swords. They have adopted the motto, "March separately, fight together," and while there is no formal alliance, there appears to be sufficient unity of action among them.

On the Left, a new German Democratic party has been formed out of the old Progressive People's party and a part of the National Liberals, under the leadership of a group of very able men, including Herren Fischbeck, Conrad Haussman, Theodor Wolff and Professor Hugo Preuss. This party is out and out republican, in favor of gradual socialization, at least of natural monopolies, with few reservations, but decidedly opposed to spoliatory legislation. They favor free trade, the separation of church and state, and are strongly attached to the principle of the League of Nations. Although predominantly *bourgeois* in character, they are collaborating whole-heartedly with the Majority Socialists and share with that party the control of the government. Among their ranks are a large number of men of high technical training and ability, whose assistance is indispensable at this time. Their leaders are inclined to take a rather sanguine view of the situation. They believe that Germany will develop sufficient strength to check Bolshevism and will recover from the present crisis in a reasonable time.

The Social Democratic party of the early years of the war eventually split on the question of voting war credits. The dissenting minority seceded and formed the Independent Socialist party. The Majority Socialists continued to support the war until the defeats on the western front in the summer and autumn of 1918 made it clear to the world that the German cause was hopeless. Led by Ebert and Scheidemann, it is this party that has been chiefly in control of the government since events culminated in the abdication of the Kaiser. Their program included gradual socialization, popular election of judges and officials, a steeply graduated income tax and the separation of church and state. They, of course, are republican and favor a League of Nations. In principles they differ but little from the German Democratic party; their membership is, however, chiefly proletarian, instead of *bourgeois*. *Vorwärts* is their mouthpiece.

The Independent Socialists are led by Herr Haase. They opposed the war during the last two years of its course. They support all proposals of political reform. They stand firmly on the Socialist Erfurt program of 1891; and demand immediate socialization, without restrictions or reservations. They favor the conclusion of immediate peace on the Allied terms. At first inclined to collaborate with the Majority Socialists and to support the government, they have drifted more and more into opposition as the government has tended more and more toward the Right. The Independent Socialists are, in fact, divided into two wings: the Right, which has on the whole supported the government, and may be ultimately absorbed by the Majority Socialists; while the Left, which appears now to be the stronger, approaches the Spartacists, and may eventually be amalgamated with them.

Finally on the extreme Left are the Spartacists, or Communists. In general purpose and principle they are closely affiliated with the Russian Bolsheviki, from whom, moreover, they have received constant and considerable financial support. There has been a well-organized Russian Bolshevist propaganda in Germany, four hundred propagandists who were trained by Schomel, a Bolshevist missionary, at his propagandist school in Moscow, having been sent to Berlin some time before the armistice. Later a similar school was started in Germany. It is said that a daily courier service is maintained through the lines between the Russian agents in Berlin and Moscow. The Spartacists are the German Bolsheviki. They are ultra-internationalists, being avowed enemies of the capitalist and *bourgeois* state. They would deny all share in the government to the capitalist and *bourgeois* classes; abolish all public offices in the civil service and the army, as well as taxes and national debts; and substitute a workmen's militia for the army. They are not so numerous as one might think from the noise and confusion they are causing, but they make up in fanaticism. They were opposed to, and did all in their power to prevent, the convening of the constituent national assembly. Direct action, not elections, is the weapon on which they rely. It is this group which is responsible for the almost continuous series of strikes, some of which have assumed the proportions of general strikes, which have so greatly increased the economic distress of the country. It is they also who have opposed the government by force, attempting its overthrow and the establishment of a soviet republic on the Russian model.

Successful for a time in various cities, and notably in Munich, they have eventually in every instance been defeated. They wished to prevent the signing of peace and to force the Entente to undertake the military occupation of Germany, which they believed would result in a world-wide spread of Bolshevism, the overthrow of the capitalist régime and the establishment of international socialism. Drawn for the most part from the industrial proletariat, their membership also includes a considerable number of younger peasants who have returned from the army. Their leaders have been Karl Liebknecht and Rosa Luxemburg (both killed on January 15th under circumstances of official savagery), Ledebour, Levien and Eichhorn.

The provisional government, established under the chancellorship of Friedrich Ebert on November 9, 1918, was composed of three Majority and three Independent Socialists, though most of the high officials of the previous régime were retained in office. It accepted the armistice on November 11th and announced a policy of concluding peace at the earliest possible moment, of immediately inaugurating measures for economic reconstruction, and the convening of a constituent national assembly to be elected on the broadest possible suffrage. In December the date of the election for this body was announced as January 19, 1919. On November 28th the former Kaiser's abdication, in which he renounced for himself for all time his rights to both the imperial and the Prussian thrones, and a similar renunciation by the crown prince were published. On December 28th disagreements between the two sections of the cabinet, growing out of the Spartacist disturbances in Berlin on Christmas Eve, led to the retirement of the Independents, Herren Barth, Haase and Dittman, leaving the Majority Socialists in entire control. With no legal support for the power which they were exercising, and mindful of the fact that, in any case, they represented but one party in the country, they could only pursue a temporizing policy until the meeting of the national assembly. They were bitterly accused of weakness by the parties of the Right for not dealing more rigorously with the Spartacist outbreaks.

Elections for the national assembly were held under the law of November 30th, which provided for universal manhood and womanhood suffrage for all citizens over the age of twenty. On the basis of the population before the war this would give an electorate of 39,000,000 (21,000,000 women and 18,000,000 men). However, elections were forbidden in Alsace-Lorraine, and the vote in the Polish provinces was light. Excluding these, a very heavy vote was polled, approximately 90 per cent. of the eligible voters participating. A great flood of election pamphlets and posters, and numerous canvassing processions had aroused a tremendous popular interest. Even the sick and crippled were carried to the polls. This heavy vote proves that the Ebert government was able to afford adequate protection to the voters, in the face of determined efforts by the Spartacists to prevent the election of a national assembly. It also proves that women participated quite generally; and that the people understood the importance of the decision which they were called upon to render.

The result of the election was as follows: The Majority Socialists secured 165 seats; the Christian People's party (Center), 91; the German Democratic party (Progressives), 75; the German National People's party (Conservatives), 38; the German People's party (National Liberals), 22; the

Independent Socialists, 22; and various other sectional and minor parties, 8.

As compared with the composition of the last Reichstag (which it must be remembered had only 397 members), the Majority Socialists have gained greatly, now holding 39 per cent. of the seats as against 27.5 per cent. held by both branches of the party in the old body. The Conservatives have lost equally heavily, dropping from 17.9 per cent. to 9 per cent. The strength of the Center has not been greatly altered, there being a slight loss from 22.2 per cent. to 20.7 per cent. The National Liberals have decreased in strength from 11.3 per cent. to 5.2 per cent. The Democratic (Progressive) party has gained from 11.6 per cent. to 18 per cent.

It will thus be seen that there has been a heavy movement toward the Left. This can largely be accounted for by the fact that the old negative gerrymander resulting from a failure since 1870 to redistrict the country has now been eliminated; and partly by the system of proportional representation now used for the first time. While there has been some shifting in opinion, it has been less than might have been expected. No party has an absolute majority in the Chamber, and what had been expected now became quite evident, viz., that any ministry which might command the confidence of this body would have to be coalition in character. The election, however, did much to clear the situation and to strengthen the Ebert government. It is of interest to observe that twenty-four women secured seats in the new assembly.

The government announced the convening of the national assembly for February 6th, at Weimar, the continual strikes and the constant Spartacist disturbance making Berlin an undesirable place. This decision was, however, bitterly assailed by the Independent Socialists. As the day approached the Spartacists became increasingly turbulent and there was serious doubt whether the assembly would be permitted to meet. The leaders of the soldiers' and workmen's councils called a general congress of these councils in Berlin for the same date, in order to indicate their lack of confidence in the government, and to confuse the situation as much as possible. The government, however, was able to afford ample protection and the assembly convened without incident. The orderliness of the assembly made a good impression. The body displayed a high degree of coherence, and except for the Independent Socialists who had desired to postpone its meeting and now would have, if possible, frustrated its efforts, there was no disturbing element. The opening address by Herr Ebert was largely devoted to a vehement protest against the terms which the Allies had submitted for a renewal of the armistice. He asserted Germany's right to enter the League of Nations on equal terms, and demanded that German Austria be permitted to join the republic. Dr. David David, a Majority Socialist, was chosen president of the assembly, but on his entering the cabinet this post was filled by Herr Fehrenbach, the former Centrist president of the Reichstag. The voting for president and vice-president of the assembly indicated that a working understanding had been reached among the three major parties.

An executive was organized by electing Herr Ebert as President of the republic. He announced that as president he would not be a party man but maintain the two principles of his career, viz., pacifism and a stout adherence to the principles of a League of Nations. His first official act was to ask Herr Scheidemann to form a ministry. In this cabinet, consisting of fourteen members, the Majority Socialists had seven seats, the Democrats three and the Center three. Count von Brockdorff-Rantzau, whose politics are uncertain, held the post of minister of foreign affairs. The new chancellor announced the task of the government in the immediate future to be: (1) The maintenance of the unity of the state by means of a strong central authority; (2) the immediate conclusion of peace; (3) adherence to President Wilson's program; (4) rejection of any peace of violence; (5) restoration of Germany's colonial territories; (6) immediate repatriation of German prisoners; (7) admission of Germany into the League of Nations with equal rights; (8) general and reciprocal disarmament; (9) the constitution of general arbitration courts; (10) the abolition of secret diplomacy.

The national assembly and the new government appear to have started with as large a degree of popular confidence as was possible in the circumstances. By many the assembly was looked upon as a sort of cure-all for the ills from which the state was suffering. The Majority Socialist-Democratic-Centrist *bloc* represented 77 per cent. of the assembly, and might expect to command the active support of an equal proportion of the people. It is true that the personalities of Ebert, Scheidemann and Erzberger did not arouse enthusiasm, but this was a democratic régime, and doubtless the change from the aloofness and pomp of royal courts and aristocratic ministers to these simple burghers was a welcome one to many.

It required only a short time, however, to show that neither the assembly nor the executive could command the respect of the nation. The former lost itself in interminable debate. There is none of the rapid cross-fire of questions and interruptions which give the proceedings of the House of Commons a never-failing interest. Rather do long-winded party-hacks indulge in what appear to be copybook speeches. One remembers that it was this same tendency to speech-making that contributed largely to the futility of the Frankfort Parliament in 1848. Furthermore, in spite of the new basis of election, it developed that most of the leaders of the Reichstag were returned to the assembly, and the membership in general was much the same. Where new men of ability were elected they have been regarded as political upstarts and deprived of influence by the traditionalized and hidebound fogeys who were in control. They have not been appointed to important positions on the committees or given a chance to be heard. Within two months of its convening the assembly was being generally criticized in the press as having completely failed to rise to the occasion, and by June it had almost ceased to attract any attention.

Nor has the experience of the government been much happier. Inclining more and more to the Right in its policy, it aroused increasingly bitter opposition from the Independent Socialists and Spartacists. A considerable number of Majority Socialists, indeed, became disgusted at what appeared to be its lukewarmness in the cause of socialization. The difficulties in the way of economic reconstruction were doubtless insuperable; but the fact remains that it has accomplished nothing, indeed attempted almost nothing, toward the rehabilitation of the country. It is clear to every one that it is largely controlled by the bureaucracy, which has changed but little. The root of the whole trouble is that the men who are at the helm, whether in governmental or administrative posts, are the same who were responsible for the war. A few of the loftiest personages have been retired, but, on the whole, the old figures and the old methods are in the ascendancy. A real revolution would have brought Maximilian Harden to the fore. He has had the courage to denounce the hypocrisy of a republic whose promoters have immediately appointed monarchists to the highest posts; who say that Germany was not defeated and threaten Bolshevism if the peace terms are not to their liking.

On the other hand, the parties of the Right have found ample cause to criticize the government's weakness and condemn its opportunism. It continued to exist merely because there was no one else to take its place. It was generally predicted that it would fall on the question of the peace treaty, whether it decided to accept the treaty or not. One man alone has thus far risen into a commanding prominence which forecasts for him the possibility of a career of more than a few short weeks. That is Herr Noske, Minister of National Defense. He is described as an imperialist Socialist, who supported the war throughout, expressing at times chauvinistic sentiments which would do credit to von Tirpitz or Bernhardi. He is a believer in force, and has known how to use the volunteer military units, which were recruited ostensibly for the campaign against the Poles on the Eastern border, effectively against the Spartacists. It is believed that had he a free hand he would give short shrift to the Bolsheviki.

Alongside the regularly constituted, albeit at first provisional, government, there has existed a second government, or set of governments, which have displayed in many respects more strength, vitality and initiative. This is the system of workmen's and soldiers' councils, or *Asrats* as they have come to be called from the initials (*Arbeiter und Soldaten Rat*). As a phase of the revolution, and coincident with the establishment of the provisional governments for the nation and the several states, self-constituted councils of workmen and soldiers seized control of the government in many of the principal cities, including Berlin. These bodies sprang up like mushrooms and quickly secured an authority which the provisional governments could not gainsay. They appear generally to have permitted the city officials, even the *Bürgermeisters,* to remain in office, confining themselves to a general supervision except for taking over the police function. The Berlin council, pending the establishment of a central executive council representing all the councils of the country, assumed to act as such. Eventually congresses of representatives from the several local councils were held and a central executive council set up. Gradually, too, the basis of their authority has been more clearly defined, though varying in different cities. In Berlin all workers, twenty years of age, whose earnings do not exceed 1000 marks, are eligible to elect, and to be elected, to the workmen's council; while in Hamburg workers are defined as including "owners, directors, managers," etc., as well as wage earners. Their party composition has also varied a great deal. The Berlin council in the earlier period consisted of seven Majority Socialists, seven Independent Socialists and two Democrats. The tendency has been, however, for them to become predominantly Independent and Spartacist. They are not to be held responsible for the Spartacist uprisings, though these have in many instances had for their purpose the strengthening of the councils.

BY GENERAL LUDENDORFF

The power of the state failed, as nobody can doubt, because in its external and internal policy, before and during the war, it had not recognized the exigencies of the struggle for existence in which Germany has always been involved. It had demonstrated its inability to understand that politics is war and war is politics.

The situation into which the German Empire drifted was not attributable to its constitution—the same constitution which existed in the days of Bismarck—but was caused by the members of the state themselves. They understood neither history nor the signs of the times, nor could they, prepossessed, as they were, in favor of international and pacifist ideas, begin to realize that, in view of the turn of mind of other nations, power in the hand of a strong government is the only means of securing the liberty and well-being of a people; that only the power of the state can prevent criminal confusion within and guard against slavery imposed from without.

Our executive government deserved its fate. But what was done intensified the misfortune. An innovation would have been justified if the leaders of the majorities, supported by the confidence of the Reichstag, had really created a new and strong government aiming at the national defense—something that the former government had neglected to do. This purpose was expressed, but deeds were lacking. The majorities undertook nothing to secure the power of the state against aggression from without in the last hour. On the contrary, they occupied themselves with interior affairs, for the purpose of increasing their own power. They did not tell themselves that the possession of power imposes duties; and when they came to the top they soon proved even more inefficient than had been the previous government. Finally it may be said that it could not have been otherwise. The parties and men who now held the reins of government belonged to those who, previously in peace times, had labored to bring about the internal weakening of Germany. They were the parties and men ever ready for peace with their destructive, unstable mode of thinking, the men who doubted the power of the people of their own nation. They endeavored, in their external policy, to effect a peace based on compromise, which lay beyond the realm of possibility; within, they sought to introduce the parliamentary form of government, which would break the power of the Emperor and the princes of the land, so that they might put it into their own hands.

This ambition went hand in hand with the desire of pleasing Wilson and thus facilitating a peace. They did not tell themselves that what an enemy wants can only be bad for ourselves. They were strong alone in the fervor with which they believed in the mission of the President of the United States to establish the happiness of the whole world, and in the eagerness with which, in consequence of the attitude of the government till then in power, they lent faith to the delusive representation that the high command had trodden underfoot the aims at peace of the Imperial Chancellor.

The belief in the human reconciliation, personified in the adoration of Wilson, the servile fear of aggravating the enemy by inflaming him and the feeling, correct in itself, of obtaining and maintaining full power within the country itself through a bad peace—these, together with a consideration of the independent social democracy, were in the following days to gain the victory in the Cabinet.

Government and Reichstag left the army in the lurch, and the political leadership did the same for the military commanders.

When the terrible conditions of Versailles became known in May, 1919, the democratic deputy, Conrad Haussman, who, in the session of October 17, 1918, as Secretary of State, had considered possible a continuation of the struggle and who, like his associate von Payer, had probably foreseen the disastrous consequences of a Wilson peace, gave expression to the following opinion: "Had our army had our workmen, on the 5th and 9th of November, known that peace would have looked that way, the army would not have laid down its arms; it would have held out."

The military command had warned the political leaders against disarmament, because, in its instinctive knowledge of the nature power and mode of thinking of the enemy, it had gauged with correctness what was to come. Not our brave army, which scorns the accusation, laid down its arms; it was forced to do so by our political leadership.

The people followed their bad leaders—and "misleaders"—and rushed blindly to their fate. They could and would not, even now, understand the aims of the military leaders, who had correctly gauged the will of the enemy but also knew his weaknesses, and who had demanded, as the only possible measure, the utmost resolution and exertions of a united people.

When the Reichstag's majority had attained its goal as regarded the internal policy of the country, had robbed the Kaiser and the princes of the confederation of all power, and had strengthened their own, the government, in its fourth note to Wilson, consummated the political capitulation before the enemy. In a spirit of abject servility they fawningly styled the prospective peace of annihilation a "peace of justice."

Finally the political leadership disarmed the unconquered army and delivered over Germany to the destructive will of the enemy in order that it might carry through the revolution in Germany unhindered. That was the climax in the betrayal of the German people.

Thus was perpetrated the crime against the German nation. No political régime has ever committed anything worse. Not the enemy, but our political leadership broke down the power of our military command, and consequently of the nation—that power which was embodied in the officers' corps and in the army.

BY GEORGE SAUNDERS

It must be acknowledged that the German Government and National Assembly proceeded in an expeditious and businesslike manner to give the empire a new constitution. The National Assembly, elected by universal male and female suffrage, met on February 6th, at Weimar, and within four days enacted a provisional constitution, in accordance with which it chose a provisional president of the new empire (Herr Ebert) and set up a Council of States to take the place provisionally of the old Federal Council. The president appointed a ministry of the empire, which proceeded to draw up the scheme of a definite constitution. This measure, after having been materially revised by a special committee of the Assembly and by the Assembly itself in plenary session, passed the third reading on July 31st, and was promulgated on August 11th.

As compared with the constitution under which the late German Empire existed, the new arrangements exhibit one feature which is of fundamental importance. The old imperial constitution of 1871, like that of the North German Confederation on which it was built, was essentially a treaty between the rulers of the different German states. The constitution of August, 1919, is the expression of the will of the sovereign German people expressed through its representatives in the National or Constituent Assembly, which alone and without the coöperation of the president or the Committee of States enacted the new arrangements.

Under the old constitution Bavaria and, in a lesser degree, Württemberg and Saxony, retained a certain independence in the organization of their military forces. They had War Ministers of their own, and Bavaria had separate army estimates. All this has been abolished by Article 79, which enacts that the organization of the national defenses is to be arranged on a unified basis, though some regard is to be paid to local peculiarities. In accordance with this provision, Noske, the Minister of Imperial Defense, has assumed supreme control of all the German forces.

The new German Army (*Reichswehr*) has been divided into four main groups or commands, with headquarters at Berlin, Kassel, Stettin and Munich. Subordinate to the Berlin command is Dresden, and to the Kassel command, Stuttgart and Hanover. These arrangements suffice to show how radical are the constitutional changes in the sphere of the army when they come to be carried out in detail.

Of still more vital significance for the unification of the empire is the centralization of the finances. This is not explicitly enacted in the new constitution, but Article 84 gives the empire legislative power with regard to the management of taxation in the separate territories (states) "so fas as the unified and uniform execution of the imperial taxation laws demands." The empire, moreover, can institute the authorities who are to be entrusted in the states with the collection of imperial taxation and can define their powers. Direct taxation, until the date of the levy for the imperial defenses the year before the war, had been the prerogative of the separate states. The scheme of taxation recently announced by Herr Erzberger, the Imperial Minister of Finance, shows that this preserve of the separate states will now be formally invaded by the empire, with the probable result that the states will more and more lose the basis for their separate political existence.

One of the new institutions which marks the supersession of some of the old state rights is the Reichsrat or Council of Empire. It forms the definitive substitute for the old Federal Council, but its position is very different. Under the old régime all legislation was initiated in the Federal Council, where the supremacy of Prussia, and with it the personal supremacy of the King of Prussia, the German Emperor, was practically secured. The larger states will be represented in the Reichsrat by one vote for each million inhabitants, and each state will have at least one vote. No state is to, have more than two-fifths of the votes (Article 61). Roughly speaking, the new council of the empire will be composed of about 60 to 65 members, of which Prussia will appoint 24 to 26. These delegates will be chosen from the members of the governments of the separate states. In the case of Prussia, however, it is enacted (Article 63) that the half of its representatives on the council must be supplied by the Prussian *provincial* administrations in a manner which a future Prussian law is to decide. This provision is manifestly intended as a sop to the partitionists, who desired the division of Prussia into several smaller states, and who, if Professor Preuss's first draft of the constitution had been adopted, would have carried their point.

Under the old régime the Federal Council was supreme, although, as already mentioned, that supremacy was in practice exercised by the King of Prussia through the chancellor. The Imperial Secretaries of state were mere organs of the Imperial Chancellor. Now there is an Imperial Government with ministers who in all essentials are independent of the Council of Empire (Reichsrat). The members of the Imperial Government have the right to attend the sittings of the Reichsrat, over which one of them is to preside. The sessions of the Reichsrat, unlike those of the old Federal Council must as a rule be public. The Reichsrat, it is true, can initiate legislation, for the Imperial Government is bound to submit its legislative proposals to the Reichstag.

The popular assembly, the Reichstag, also has the power of legislative initiative, and so has the electorate itself. In the case of the electorate, the demand for a legislative measure (which must first be formally drafted) must be supported by at least one-tenth of the registered electors. If the Reichstag thereupon passes the measure without alteration, no further plebiscite is required. Otherwise, it would appear (Article 73, section 3), a general plebiscite on the measure has to be taken.

The Reichsrat may hold up a measure which has been passed by the Reichstag. In that case the measure goes back to the Reichstag and, if no agreement is attained, the president of the empire may within three months order a plebiscite. If he does not decide to take this course the measure lapses. If, however, a two-thirds majority of the Reichstag maintains the bill, the president must either within three months promulgate the measure as law or must ordain a plebiscite (Article 74). These arrangements, it will be seen, represent a great curtailment of the powers of the state governments in the initiation and control of legislation.

The only other points in the constitution which space permits to be dealt with here are the articles which define the position and powers of the president. President Ebert was elected by the National or Constituent Assembly. The constitution provides that the president shall be chosen by the whole German electorate, but a law has first to be passed in order to regulate the mode of election. The president takes in the new constitution the place which the German Emperor occupied under the old régime, but his powers are, naturally, much more limited. He is to be elected for seven years, but may be reëlected—how often the constitution does not say. Before the expiration of his period of office he may be deposed by a plebiscite on the initiative of a two-thirds majority of the Reichstag (Article 43). If the plebiscite results in the rejection of the proposal for deposition, the president is to be regarded as reëlected for another seven years. Like the emperor under the old régime, the president is to be the representative of the empire in its international relations, but, unlike the emperor, he is subject to the decision of the Reichstag in the matters of the declaration of war and the conclusion of peace (Article 45). He has the supreme command of the armed forces of the empire, and he appoints and dismisses the officials of the empire and the officers of the army and, presumably, of the navy, although, by the way, there is no mention of a navy in the whole constitution. All dispositions and ordinances of the president, including his control of the army and of military appointments, require the signature of the Imperial Chancellor or of the minister whose department they concern. These ministers thereby take responsibility for the president's acts, a responsibility which does not merely, as under the old régime, necessitate the delivery of a speech in the Reichstag but entails the minister's resignation, if the Reichstag expresses its want of confidence in him (Article 54).

The president of the empire, the chancellor, and the ministers can be impeached at the instance of the Reichstag before the future State Court of Justice. But, as has been pointed out by German critics, and as, indeed, the constitution expressly states, they can be brought to trial only on the charge of having "culpably infringed the constitution or a law of the empire." The Bülows, the Bethmann-Hollwegs, and the Michaelises would have got off scot free. It was their acts of policy, not breaches of the constitution or of the laws, that wrought the damage.

In examining the prerogatives of the German President it is interesting to speculate upon the loopholes which the constitution might afford for establishing a dictatorship or restoring the monarchy. In this connection it is important to note that after having, on the second reading, adopted an article proposed by the Independent Socialists for the permanent exclusion of all members of the former ruling families from candidature for the presidency, the National Assembly on the third reading rejected this article—by 198 votes to 141. Unfortunately, there is no adequate report of either of the debates available. There must have been some interesting discussion of the possibility of a restoration. The decision of the Reichstag was probably dictated by the consideration that all Germans are in future to be equal before the law, and that the exclusion of the princes would establish an inequality. The ex-Emperor's sons and grandchildren, as is well known, are allowed to live in Germany without incurring any disabilities.

The president's control of the army, it has been noted, is subject to the responsibility of the chancellor or the war minister, expressed in their counter-signature of his ordinances. But, in the event of civil disorder, he can apparently act at once on his own initiative, "if necessary with the help of the armed forces" (Article 48). He can also, in the same emergency, suspend a number of articles of the constitution which guarantee the liberties of the citizen and freedom of speech, writing and public meeting. It is true that he must "without delay" inform the Reichstag of the exceptional measures which he has adopted, and that the Reichstag may demand that these measures should be abandoned. Yet it is conceivable that, if a president secretly cherished reactionary aims and were supported by the bulk of the army, he might go far in achieving his object before the Reichstag could intervene. A German MacMahon, or Louis Napoleon, might wrest the constitution to his own ends.

BY SEÑOR AZHEITUAS

The revolution is being conducted in an orderly manner, and the fights between groups of officers and the Red Guard were merely insignificant skirmishes, that is to say, if the radical transformation of the country is taken into account. Order is maintained chiefly through the indifference of the public at large. People regard the red flags waving over public buildings as no concern of theirs, since, although the restoration of the Empire is not contemplated, no one believes in the permanence of the Social Republic. The organizers of the revolution know that, in order to find favor with the law-abiding public, they must prove that not only do they not intend to disturb the public peace, but that they will use every means in their power to maintain it. Hence the continual proclamations and speeches by the revolutionary leaders enjoining the maintenance of order. These proclamations clearly reveal the fear that disorganization may bring the whole revolutionary fabric to the ground. The public indifference is the chief factor in the maintenance of the public services. The service of food supplies is the object of special zeal since, in view of the present shortage, a hitch would mean famine, and famine would mean revolt.

The old Imperial organizations coöperate in the consolidation of the Social Republic since they consider it a crime to disturb the citizens, their women and children. Without the aid of the State officials of all ranks the Soldiers' and Workmen's Committees would be helpless. It is their love of order and of their neighbor which is the salvation of the German people in this fateful hour. The authorities appointed by the Empire desire to save the people further suffering after four years of war and privation.

Until quite recently there was still a danger of conflict between the two Socialist groups, but the Soldiers' Council has imposed harmony. The Independent Socialists desired communism and the exclusion of the middle class, whereas the followers of Ebert were adverse to communism, and considered the assistance of the middle class essential to the building of the new State. The majority of the Independents have fallen into line and only the Spartacus group of Liebknecht remains outside the revolutionary organization. The Germans have confined themselves to imitation of the Russians; the Soldiers' and Workmen's Committees are a copy of the invention of Lenine and Trotsky, and all the literature published has already appeared in Russian. The German genius is adaptive rather than creative, and the men at the head of the movement show gifts of organization and of adaptation of theories and inventions from abroad, but a total absence of original ideas. The German revolution is an imitation of the Russian revolution, but without its violence, since the German character will not permit disorder.

BY PRESIDENT EBERT

Address delivered to the German Assembly at its opening session of
February 7th

The Imperial Government welcomes through me the Constituent Assembly of the German nation.   With a special
warmth I greet the women who for the first time appear in
the Imperial Parliament with equal rights.   The Provisional
Government owes its mandate to the revolution.   It will return it into the hands of the National Assembly.   In the
revolution, the German people rose against an obsolete col-
lapsing tyranny.   (Hisses from the Right.)   As soon as the
right of the Germans to self-determination is assured, it
returns to the road of legality.   Only on the broad highway
of Parliamentary discussion and decision can the urgent
changes in the economic and social spheres be progressively
achieved without destroying the Empire and its economic
position.   ("Hear, hear.")   Therefore the Government welcomes in this National Assembly the supreme and single sovereign in Germany.   (Applause.)   We have done forever
with the old kings and princes by the grace of God.   (Loud
applause on the Left; hisses on the Right: renewed loud applause on the Left; cries from the Right, "Wait!")   We
deny no one his sentimental memories, but as surely as this
National Assembly has a great Republican majority, so
surely is the old God-given dependence abolished forever.
The German people is free, remains free, and governs itself
for all the future.   (Cries from the Independent Socialists,
"With Noske.")   This freedom is the one hope which remains to the German people—the one way by which it can
work itself out of the bloody morass of war and defeat.
We have lost the war; this is not the consequence of the
revolution.   (Cries from the Right, "Oh, oh!"   Cries from
the Left, "No, never!")   Ladies and gentlemen, it was the
Imperial Government of Prince Max of Baden which began
the armistice which made us defenseless.   After the collapse
of our allies, and in view of the military and economic situation, there was nothing else for it to do.   ("Hear, hear.")
The revolution declines the responsibility for the misery into

which the evils of the old autocracy, and the arrogance of
the military threw the German people. ("Hear, hear."
Loud applause from the Socialists; protests from the Right.)
It is also not responsible for our serious shortage of food.
("Hear, hear." Protests, and a cry of "Soldiers' Councils.")
The fact that by the hunger blockade we have lost many
hundreds of thousands of human lives—that hundreds of
thousands of men, women, children, and aged people have
fallen victims to it—disposes of the story that we could have
managed with our food supplies if the revolution had not
come. Defeat and food shortage have handed us over to the
enemy Powers. But not only we, but also our enemies, have
been terribly exhausted by the war, and the feeling of exhaustion among our enemies springs from their effort to
indemnify themselves at the cost of the German people, and
the idea of exploitation is brought into the work of peace.
These plans of revenge and oppression called for the sharp-
est protest. (Loud applause from all sides.) The German
people cannot be made the wage slaves of other nations for
twenty, forty, or sixty years. (Loud applause.) The fear-
ful disaster of the war for all Europe can only be repaired
if the peoples go hand in hand. (Applause.) In view of
the misery of the masses of the peoples; in view of the mass
misery on every side, the question of guilt seems almost small.
Still, the German people is resolved itself to call to judgment
all against whom deliberate guilt or deliberate baseness can
be proved. But those ought not to be punished who themselves were victims—victims of the war, victims of our former lack of freedom. ("Hear, hear," from the Socialists.)
To what end, on their own witness, did our enemies fight?
To annihilate Kaiserism. Kaiserism exists no more. It is
abolished forever. The very fact of this National Assembly
proves it. They fought "to destroy militarism." It lies in
ruins, and will never rise again. (Cries from the Independent
Socialists, "You are setting it up again.") According to
their solemn proclamation, our enemies fought "for justice,
freedom, and a permanent peace," but so far the armistice
conditions have been of unprecedented severity and have
been pitilessly carried through. Without more ado, Alsace

is treated as French territory. The elections to the National Assembly prescribed by us have been illegally prevented. ("Shame!") The Germans have been driven out of the country—("Shame!")—and their properties sequestrated. The occupied territory on the left of the Rhine has been cut off from the rest of Germany. The attempt is being made monstrously to extend the provision of the armistice agreement that no public property is to be made away with, and to turn it into a general financial enslavement of the German people. Though we have long been in no condition to renew the war, our eight hundred thousand prisoners of war are still kept back and most seriously threatened by psychological collapse and the hardship of forced labor. ("Shame!") In this act of Might policy, there is no trace of the spirit of reconciliation. The armistice conditions are explained on the ground that they were imposed on the old Hohenzollern régime. What justification is there for continually intensifying them against the young Socialist Republic, in spite of the fact that we do our very utmost to satisfy the very heavy obligations laid upon us? We warn the enemy not to drive us to extremities. Any German Government may one day be compelled, like General Winterfeldt, to renounce all further participation in the peace negotiations and thrust upon the enemy the whole burden of the responsibility until the new order of the world! Let them not place before us the dangerous choice between starvation and disgrace. Even a Socialist People's Government, and this one above all others, must hold fast to its principle that it would rather suffer the extremity of want than be dishonored. (Loud applause.) If to the millions who have lost everything in the war and fear to lose nothing more were added also those who believe that Germany has nothing to lose, then tactics of desperation would irresistibly prevail. Germany laid down her arms in confidence, trusting in the principles of President Wilson. Now let them give us a Wilson peace, to which' we have a claim. (Applause.) Our free People's Republic —the whole German people—aims at nothing other than to enter with equal rights into the League of Nations, and there win for itself a position of respect by industry and probity.

(General applause.)   Germany can still do the world many
services.   It was a German who gave the workers of the
world scientific Socialism.   We are on the way to leading
the world once again in Socialism, since we serve that Socialism which alone can be permanent, which increases the
prosperity and the *Kultur* of the people—Socialism in process
of realization.   Once more we turn to all the peoples in the
world with the urgent appeal to see that justice is done to
the German people—not to permit the annihilation of our
hopeful beginnings by the oppression of our people and our
economic life.   The German people has won its right to self-
determination at home.   It cannot sacrifice that right abroad.
We cannot renounce uniting the whole German nation in the
frame-work of a single Empire.   (Applause.)

Our German-Austrian brothers as far back as November
12th last in their National Assembly declared themselves
to be part of the great German Republic.   (Applause.)
Now the German-Austrian National Assembly has again,
amid storms of enthusiasm, sent us its greeting and given
expression to the hope that our National Assembly and theirs
will succeed in again uniting the bonds which violence tore
asunder in 1866.   (Applause.)   German-Austria must be
united with the Motherland for all time.   (Applause.)   I
am sure that I am speaking for the whole National Assembly
when I welcome this historic manifestation sincerely and
joyfully, and reply to it with heartfelt fraternity.   (Loud
applause.)   The brothers of our blood and destiny can be
assured that we will welcome them with open arms and
hearts in the new Empire of the German nation.   (Applause.)   They belong to us and we belong to them.   (Applause.)   I may also express the hope that the National Assembly will empower the future Imperial Government to
negotiate as soon as possible with the German-Austrian free
State concerning the final union.   (Applause.)   Then there
will be no more frontier posts between us.   Then we shall
really be a single people of brothers.   (Loud applause.)
Germany must not again fall into the old misery of disintegration and confinement.   It is true that history and the
past stand in the way of the creation of a strongly centralized

unitary State, but the different tribes and tongues must be harmonized into a single nation with a single speech. (Applause.) Only a great united possibility of developing our economic life—a politically capable, strong, single Germany —can secure the future of our people. (Applause.) The Provisional Government has entered into a very evil heritage. We were the liquidators of the old régime. ("Hear, hear," from the Left; protests from the Right; applause on the Left.) We, with the support and at the request of the Central Council of the German Workmen's and Soldiers' Councils have applied all our strength to overcoming the danger and misery of the transition period. We have done everything to set economic life in motion again. (Protests from the Right.) These continued interruptions (turning to the Right) prove truly that in the hard days which Germany has passed through in the last few weeks and months you have learned little indeed. (Storms of applause from the Left.) If the success of our work has not corresponded with our desires, the reasons must be rightly appreciated. Many employers, accustomed to the high secured profits which the war economy in the old monarchical and protectionist State created for them, have neglected to display the necessary initiative. Therefore, we address to the employers the urgent appeal to help with all their strength the restoration of production. (Applause.) On the other side we call to the workers to employ all their strength in work, which alone can save us. ("Hear, hear.") We understand the psychology of those who, after an undue expenditure of strength in time of war, now seek relaxation. We know how difficult it must be for those who have lived for years on the battlefield to settle down to peaceful work; but it must be. We must work and create values, otherwise we collapse. ("Hear, hear.")

Socialism means organization, order, and solidarity, not high-handedness, perversity, and destruction. There must no longer be room for private monopolies and capitalist profit without effort in time of national emergency. Therefore, profit is to be methodically obviated where economic development has made a trade ripe for socialization.

The future looms before us full of anxiety. In spite of all that, we trust in the indestructible creative power of the German nation. ("Hear, hear.") The old foundations of the German position based on force are forever destroyed. The Prussian hegemony, the Hohenzollern army, the policy of the shining armor have been made impossible among us for all fuutre. As November 9, 1918, follows on March 18, 1848, so must we here in Weimar complete the change from Imperialism to Idealism, from world power to spiritual greatness. ("Hear, hear.") Now must the spirit of Weimar, the spirit of the great philosophers and poets, again fill our life, fill it with the spirit described in *Faust* and in *Wilhelm Meister's Wanderjahre*. Not roaming in the interminable and losing one's self in the theoretical, not hesitating and wavering, but with clear vision and firm hand taking a firm hold on practical life.

So will we set to work with our great goal clear before our eyes. To maintain the right of the German people, to anchor firmly in Germany a strong democracy and to fill it with true social spirit and Socialist character. ("Hear, hear.") So shall we create an Empire of right and of righteousness, founded on the equality of everything that wears the form of mankind.

President Ebert's address of February 11th, after his election by the Assembly, to be Provisional State President of Germany

I will administer my office not as the leader of a single party, but I belong to the Socialist Party and cannot forget my origin and training. The privileges of birth already have been eliminated from politics and are being eliminated from social life.

We shall combat domination by force to the utmost from whatever direction it may come. We wish to found our State only on the basis of right and on our freedom to shape our destinies at home and abroad. However harsh may be the lot threatening the German people, we do not despair of Germany's vital forces.

THE RESCUE OF POLAND

THE FIRST MEETING OF A POLISH NATIONAL ASSEMBLY AND RECONSTRUCTION OF THE ANCIENT COUNTRY

FEBRUARY 10, 1919

ALEXANDER KAKOWSKI   JOSEPH PILSUDSKI
IGNACE PADEREWSKI   HERBERT HOOVER

On February 10, 1919, the newly constructed Republic of Poland came into formal existence through the first sitting of a National Assembly elected by the people, as that of Germany had just been, and having for its purpose the organizing of a constitutional government. This date thus marked the end of the period of confusion and of tumultuous disorganization from which the Poles had been suffering all through the War.

Russia's breakdown had left Russian Poland, as well as the German Polish regions, in Germany's hands; and Germany had placed in nominal command a "Regency Council" of Poles, sitting at Warsaw, the ancient capital. Of course this Council was compelled to rule under Germany's dictation, and its most noted member, General Joseph Pilsudski, soon resigned and began working for a more real independence. He was imprisoned by the German authorities.

With the breakdown of the Central Powers in the fall of 1918, the Regency Council was able to assume a genuine control of Poland, including also the Austrian Polish provinces. The reunion of all these lands, remaking ancient Poland, was afterward approved and decreed by the Peace Conference at Paris, and made part of the final Peace Treaty. On June 28th, the day of the signing of the general Treaty, the Allies also signed a special treaty with Poland, thus completing the formal recognition of her independence.

Meanwhile there had long existed in Paris a committee of Polish exiles working in harmony with the Allies for Poland's independence, raising Polish armies in the Ally lands. At the head of these exiles stood M. Dmowski, a Polish statesman of the old Russian government, who was accepted as Poland's representative at the Peace Conference and most ably handled her cause.

The Regency Council in October of 1918 summoned the Paris committee to join it in forming a temporary Polish government; but the somewhat aristocratic government thus formed proved to have such little influence over the Polish masses that it soon formally dismissed itself. General Pilsudski was just then released from his German prison. He was the popular idol of the people, and the Regency Council at once requested him to assume a Dictatorship over the distracted and starving land, until a regular election could be held and a representative government formed.

Pilsudski promptly accepted; and being himself most interested in the military defense of the land against all the foreign foes environing it, he entrusted the civil government to the patriot who had been most active in bringing foreign aid to Poland, the celebrated musician, Ignace Paderewski. With Paderewski as Prime Minister and Pilsudski as Military President or Dictator, a general election was held on January 26, 1919; and the elected delegates gathered in Warsaw. On Sunday, February 9th, a solemn religious service of consecration was held in the great Roman Catholic cathedral at Warsaw; and on the next day the Assembly held its first formal meeting to begin its work of building the new Poland. Both Pilsudski and Paderewski promptly resigned their power, and both were thereupon authorized in their positions by the Assembly, and were requested to continue their services through Poland's days of trouble.

The dangers which the new Poland faced are here described by both its leaders, as also by the great American leader, Herbert Hoover. The latter visited Poland in his official capacity as head of the American reconstruction organization which saved eastern Europe from starvation in 1919. In addition to starvation, Poland's chief foes were: the Germans, seeking to retain as much of German Poland as they could; the Bolshevists, seeking to unite the entire land to Russia; and on the south, Ukraine and Czecho-Slovakia each seeking to make its own boundaries as broad as possible at the expense of the Poles. Against all of these Pilsudski and his hastily gathered armies fought in turn.

BY ALEXANDER KAKOWSKI

Statement of the Polish temporary "Regency Council," issued on November 11, 1918

IN view of the threatening dangers from within and without, and in order to unify all military action and preserve order in the country, the Regency Council intrusts military authority over and the chief command of the Polish Armies to Brig. Gen. Joseph Pilsudski.

After the National Government has been organized, the Regency Council will, in accordance with its former declaration, transfer to it the sovereign power of the State, and by countersigning the manifesto, General Pilsudski binds himself likewise to surrender to it his military powers, which are a part of the sovereignty of the State.

Decree of November 14, 1918

To General Joseph Pilsudski, the Commander-in-Chief of the Polish Armies:

The temporary division of the sovereign power of the

State created by the decree of November 11, 1918, cannot last without harm to the nascent Polish State. This power should be indivisible. In view of that and in the best interest of the country, we decree to dissolve the Regency Council, and from this moment we place in your hands, Sir, all our duties and responsibilities before the Polish Nation for the transference of them to the National Government.

(Signed) ALEXANDER KAKOWSKI,
ZDZISLAV LUBOMIRSKI,
JOSEPH OSTROWSKI.

BY GENERAL JOSEPH PILSUDSKI

Statement issued November 14, 1918, on accepting the Dictatorship over Poland

Upon my return from German imprisonment I found the country in a most chaotic state in the face of exceedingly difficult tasks, for the performance of which the nation must reveal its best organizing abilities. In my conversations with the representatives of almost all political parties in Poland, I found to my delight that the great majority share my opinion that the new Government should not only rest on democratic foundations, but be composed in a considerable proportion of representatives of the rural and urban masses. The difficult life conditions of the people have not allowed very many among them to attain professional expertness, which is in such great demand throughout the country. Realizing this, I have requested that in the interest of the highest efficiency the President of the Government appoint to the Cabinet recognized experts without any reference to their political affiliations.

By the nature of the situation, the character of the Government, pending the convocation of the Constituent Assembly, is purely provisional and precludes the enactment of any thoroughgoing social changes, which only the Representative Assembly can undertake.

Considering the peculiar legal position of the nation, I have requested the President of the Cabinet to submit to me the plan for the creation of the provisional supreme representative authority of the Polish Republic, embracing all three parts of Poland.

BY CHARLES BONNEFON
Interview with General Pilsudski by a French news-correspondent in February, 1919

WARSAW.

Poland has placed at the head of its government the man who suffered most for its cause—a man who was a prisoner in Siberia, who was immured by the Germans in the fortress of Magdeburg, who was arrested for conspiracy in 1887, 1900, and 1917.

Joseph Pilsudski is a Socialist and a soldier. In 1894 he founded *The Workman,* which was printed secretly in Vilna. He organized the Polish Socialist party, and in 1904 started the uprising that drove the Cossacks from part of Warsaw. But this Lithuanian and son of a great landed proprietor, has devoted himself first and foremost to arousing the national sentiment of the working classes, and no one knows whether his Socialism is a means or an end.

In 1914 Pilsudski fought Russia at the head of a Polish legion, but when the Germans began to win, he changed his camp. His legion, which had already mutinied once, just before the Brusiloff offensive, refused to take the oath of allegiance to Germany. On July 21, 1917, Pilsudski was arrested with his faithful companion, Sosukovski, who is now Assistant Minister of War. On November 10, 1918, after the civil population of Poland had disarmed thirty thousand German soldiers, Pilsudski reëntered Warsaw in triumph.

Since that date he has held the reins of power firmly with that pliable tenacity which is characteristic of him. He likes to employ a sudden change of tactics to defeat his opponents, and even his most intimate friends cannot read his thoughts.

Two cavalrymen with drawn sabers guard the foot of the staircase leading to his apartments. When he presents himself on public occasions, or before the assembled diplomatic corps, a herald precedes him, shouting: "Every one

uncover and stand silent before the War Lord of the Most
Serene Republic!" Carefully chosen *aides-de-camp* throw
into relief by their brilliant uniforms and glittering deco-
rations the sober gray garb of the head of the government.

His enemies murmur that he imitates Bonaparte. His
friends insist that he emulates Kosciuszko. One of his boy-
hood companions said to me: "I place him in the same
group with Clemenceau and Foch. He will be the greatest
man of reborn Poland." Others mutter that he is an ad-
venturer, an undetected conspirator, a demagogue supporting
himself upon the mob.

But while he appears to some people a Louis XI., sus-
picious and cunning, always on the alert for defense and
attack, and to others a charming conversationalist, a profound thinker, a brilliant genius, all agree that he is a man
of the highest intellectual ability, with a will of iron.

You can well imagine that my curiosity was piqued by
all these characterizations. When I saw him my precon-
ceptions were overthrown in an instant.

He is a large man, at first glance severe in aspect, with
eyebrows that overhang his deepset and piercing eyes like
heavy mustaches. His nose is long, and the nostrils are
sensitive and mobile. His general aspect inspires you with
an impression of honesty and sincerity.

General Joseph Pilsudski is the most genial and good-
humored head of a government that I ever met. His conversation overflows with humor and is punctuated by great
roars of laughter.

He said to me: "You have come, sir, at a moment unusually serious and decisive for Poland. There are questions which, as the head of the government, I cannot answer just now. For instance, I am unwilling to say what
the attitude of Poland will be if the Entente decides either to
make peace with the Bolsheviki or to continue the war.

"What I want to state first and most emphatically is
that Poland needs to have the decision, whatever it may be,
made immediately. The great evil afflicting our country is
the fact that the Allies have no clear and definite program.
We are left to face this big Eastern question all alone, because

Europe does not know what it wants. France and England
can afford to wait and make combinations, and see what is
going to happen. Possibly that is to their advantage. We
Poles are next-door neighbors to Russia. Our success or
failure depends on our acting promptly. We have got to
decide 'yes' or 'no,' peace or war. We cannot wait any
longer."

"Do you think," I inquired, "that a protracted war would
ruin Poland?"

Poland's master answered: "What weighs upon us even
more heavily than a war is the suffering of the last five years
and the accumulation of distress they have brought. Our
present military operations are not a serious drain upon us,
as we have not been forced to mobilize as many men as
would be required in a serious campaign. Our factories and
our farms have plenty of labor. We have every confidence
in our army. Last winter we were able to test the morale
of our soldiers. Lacking equipment, munitions, and almost
destitute of supplies for days at a time, they nevertheless
fought admirably.

"We are facing a military organization very inferior
to yours. Modern equipment does not play a decisive rôle in
our campaign. We have accomplished all that was necessary up to the present by simple maneuvering. What we
lack particularly is railway supplies, so as to concentrate and
maneuver our troops more rapidly.

"My long experience with the Bolsheviki makes me confident of the future. Their soldiers are poorly commanded,
poorly led, and irresolute. Some small advance parties will
fight well. The great bulk of the troops behind them are
hardly soldiers at all.

"I have studied carefully the tactics and strategy of the
Bolsheviki. This is the result of my experiences so far:
When upon the defensive the Bolsheviki will fight until
evening; when night comes they light out. In attacking they
will hold out only a few hours. Then their morale is exhausted and they relax their efforts. Their troops are very
poor in maneuvering. So, in all honesty, I do not consider
these forces formidable, although German officers are in-

structing them and draw up the plans of their general staff."

"But how about Kolchak?" I objected.

A loud burst of laughter was my answer. "Kolchak was still worse. His army was made up of officers without soldiers, or mercenaries without patriotism. Over and above that, it was miserably organized. His advance guard fought well, but the rank and file of his forces were even worse than the Bolsheviki.

"Neither do I fear the Germans just at present. A little later they will be a terrible danger. I was greatly disturbed over the German concentration in Courland. I know that their troops were well armed, well organized, and provided with everything. But these forces lacked confidence and enthusiasm. So we saw the Letts, poorly equipped, scantily provided with munitions, with no artillery except two little batteries, successfully resist and defeat these great warriors. That is inexplicable, unless you assume that the Germans lack morale. They have been defeated. The oppression of defeat still weighs them down. And, with all due respect to Ludendorff and Hofmann, and all those gentlemen who hope to restore the monarchy in their own country by restoring the monarchy in Russia, I am convinced that the Germans will not fight the Bolsheviki. They are thoroughly war weary. They would lie down under the task."

"You have just come from Vilna, General. Would you tell me your impression of the trip?"

The face of Poland's chief magistrate became fairly radiant: "Oh, as for me, I am a child of that country. Every one has known me all his life, and is fond of me. I am their local pride out there. They received me at Vilna like the leading local citizen, who has been the honor of the city."

"Are there as many Jews in Vilna as they say?"

"Their number is greatly diminished. Before the war Vilna contained 200,000 inhabitants. Since then they have joined all the suburban districts to the city proper. In spite of this extension it has not more than 120,000 people to-day. Many Jews have gone away."

"What is your policy toward White Russia, Lithuania, and the Ukraine?"

"I am a practical man, without preconceived plans and theories. I confine myself to figuring out the means at my disposal in advance, and applying them to the best of my ability to the purpose I seek. The wishes of the people in the territories we have occupied are, in my mind, the only rule to go on. I would not for all the world encourage Poland's occupying great regions filled with people at heart hostile. History has taught us Poles that in the long run such agglomerations of discordant elements are dangerous. Look at western Russia! When a country like Poland is in the process of restoration we must not load ourselves with costly embarrassments.

"We have carried liberty to these unhappy countries at the point of the bayonet. It is a liberty without conditions. I know perfectly well that many Poles do not agree with me. They interpret the opposition which certain of our neighbors show to becoming Poles to their "mental errors and their evil hearts." Some of our patriots say these people are Poles without knowing it. That is just what the Russians and the Germans used to say about us. They used to ascribe our Polish hatred of Russia and Germany to our 'stupid brains and our evil hearts.'

"I shall esteem it my greatest honor as a statesman and a soldier to have brought liberty to the peoples who are our neighbors. I know the historical ties that unite them with us. I know these ties were broken in places by the partition of Poland; but it is my first wish to efface every trace of that partition by liberating these oppressed nations. However, attach them to Poland by force? Never in the world! That would be to substitute the violence of to-day for the violence of yesterday."

BY SECRETARY LANSING

United States message to Poland, published January 29, 1919, recognizing the Paderewski government

The President of the United States directs me to extend to you, as Foreign Minister and Secretary of Foreign Affairs of the Provisional Polish Government, its sincere wishes for your success in the high office which you have assumed and his earnest hope that the Government of which you are a part will bring prosperity to the Republic of Poland.

It is my privilege to extend to you at this time my personal greetings and officially to assure you that it will be a source of gratification to enter into official relations with you at the earliest opportunity. To render to your country such aid as is possible at this time, as it enters upon a new cycle of independent life, will be in due accord with that spirit of friendliness which has in the past animated the American people in their relations with your countrymen.

BY IGNACE PADEREWSKI
Address made in May, 1919

The Polish nation is to-day living through solemn moments. I suppose that in its eventual history there was never a time more solemn, more fateful than the present. The fate of our country is at stake; powerful people holding in their hands the destiny of the world, are building a framework for our independent existence, are deciding the frontiers of our State, and soon will pronounce a final sentence, from which, no doubt for long years, there will be no appeal, perhaps for many generations. Violent bursts of hope and of joy and anxiety are strongly shaking our national spirit. From every side, from every corner of our former commonwealth, people are coming here to Warsaw and going there to Paris, in frock coats and smock frocks, in old-fashioned country dress, in mountaineer costume, and they cry aloud and implore that their distant provinces should be united to the Polish state. The Polish eagle does not seem to be a bird of prey, since people are gathering themselves under its wings.

What will Poland be like? What will be her frontiers? Will they give us everything we should have? These are the questions that every Pole is asking. I am here to answer, as far as I am able, all these questions. I have taken part in the work of the Polish Delegation to the Peace Conference, and I am here to report on this work to the Seym, and I ask for attention. I will begin with what has been done. The Conference has only dealt as yet with one of their defeated

adversaries, the Germans.   Conditions have been dictated
to them, though they are not yet signed, which give us considerable advantages on the west frontier.   We are not all
satisfied with our frontier.   I admit freely that I belong to
the unsatisfied ones; but have we really a right to complain?
The Conference tried to decide justly according to the rule on
ethnographical and national majority as regards all territorial
questions.   They applied this rule to our territory, and we
have obtained considerable advantages from it on the west.
But not everything was decided according to this principle.
Thus, for example, our Polish population in the Sycowski
and Namyzlowski district and in some parts of the locality
of Posen has distinctly been wronged.   The Polish Peace
Delegation will do their best to have this remedied.

The press has already published the chief points of the
Peace Treaty.   I will, however, remark in passing that by
this Treaty we are to receive more than 5,000,000 of population.   This territory may yet be increased if the plebiscite in
other districts formerly Polish has results favorable to us.
The Peace Conference has not yet given us Warmia, Prussian
Masuria, part of the Malborg district, also the Stzumsan,
Kwidzynsan, and Suski districts, through which passes the
railway line from Gdansk (Danzig) to Warsaw by way of
the Mlava.   The Peace Conference has given us the Keszybski
coast, the Silesian mines, and the unlimited use of the port of
Gdansk, also complete control over our Vistula, and a protectorate over the town of Gdansk under almost the same conditions as we had it in the most glorious days of our Commonwealth.

These conditions are different only in so far as present-
day life is different from the life of that time.   The area of
the free town has been considerably increased.   In the course
of 126 years of Prussian oppression and systematic Ger-
manization many Poles have forgotten their native tongue,
and there are many real Germans settled in Gdansk.   However, the former will soon remember Polish, and the others
will soon learn it.   Gradually Gdansk will tend to become
what we wish it to become, if we show seriousness and common sense, enterprise, and political understanding.   All

Polish State property is returned to Poland absolutely, without any burdens or expenses. On the whole, I consider that Poland may be grateful for the verdict. If we are not obliged to shed more of our blood, I say that this is a great and fine gift from God.

For about two weeks the affairs of the Austro-Hungarian Monarchy have been under consideration. Naturally, our affairs there are extremely important. Already the matter has been eagerly discussed, and has been the subject of passionate and violent interpellations in this House, and of certain painful reproaches. Fortunately, this affair has taken a good turn. Our dispute with the Bohemians was not settled offhand. Time has calmed passion, and to-day, without renouncing our rights, we are quietly considering these matters, and the Bohemians are doing the same. The Peace Conference wishes that we should settle our quarrel with the Bohemians in a conciliatory manner among ourselves. Mr. Lansing expressed this wish in the name of the American delegation. I have had many conferences with Mr. Benes, the Bohemian Minister for Foreign Affairs, and with the most important representatives of Silesia, and I am glad to say that in my opinion the matter is on the right road.

If Parliament honors me with its confidence, I shall see President Masaryk in Prague to-morrow or the day after to settle the preliminaries of the agreement with him. I want to have the conference on our territory in Silesia, with the co-operation of delegates of the Polish Government, representatives of the General Military Staff, members of the National Council, also specialists, engineers, and lawyers. Yesterday I had the following reply to a question addressed to Mr. Masaryk, which I translate: "Thank you for your kind telegram. I shall be very happy to welcome you on a day to be named by yourself, only please give me immediate information as to the day of your arrival. I agree to the plan of a conference, and I expect we shall be able to lay a firm foundation for it. With most sincere good feeling for you and your people." (Signed) "Masaryk."

I come to other affairs. True to the national spirit, we shall never wage a war of conquest or gain. We sacrifice

our lives in defense of the lives and property of our countrymen, and in the conviction that our great sacrifice will insure
the preservation of order and will protect Europe from the
threatened ruin of the world's civilization.   In defending the
borders of our former Commonwealth, the life and property
of the inhabitants, without discrimination between religion
or language, we are at the same time protecting the west from
the invasion of the east.   We are doing the same as our an-
cestors did 700 years ago.   We are not seeking new glory for
the Polish arms.   We are not boasting of our victories; but
we cannot shut our eyes to the chivalrous virtue and civic
merits of our incomparable soldiers.   We express our admiration and gratitude to the commanding chief for the
liberation of Lida, Swiencian, and Oilno from the Bolshevik
hordes, for the liberation of Sambor, Drohobycz, Boryslav,
Strye, Izolkiew, Brody, and Zloczow from the demoralized,
merciless, and cruel Ukrainian troops.   We express our
warmest thanks and highest recognition to our heroic, brave,
and devoted army.

The foreign press and different political parties abroad
sometimes accuse Poland of having an imperialistic policy.
One of our most prominent Deputies eloquently stated a few
days ago that there is a general prejudice abroad against
Poland, and, at the same time, said that the responsibility
for this falls upon certain classes of our community.   I do
not go so far.   I cannot blame any party for this.   I must,
however, remark that this prejudice actually exists, and is
even spreading.   The reproach of imperialism was made
against us very long ago by the very three Empires that
robbed us and divided us.   To-day this reproach is made by
just those people who are stretching out their greedy hands
for Polish territory and its wealth.   Though it is much easier
to break down a hundred fortresses and reduce a thousand
towns to dust than to overcome one prejudice, I consider that
the moment is come for a great, powerful, and distinct voice,
the voice of the Polish people, to make a declaration in this
House which will confute all these unfounded foreign reproaches.

We never conducted a war of conquest, and we have no

intention of doing so. We do not want what belongs to others; we do not want to conquer anybody else's territory. Poland does not deny the right of Lithuania and Ukrainia to be independent, nor the right of the White Ruthenian people to individual development. Poland is ready to help them heartily and effectively. Food always follows the Polish soldier. We are sharing with the border peoples the supplies we get from America. In order to establish autonomy in these border countries, without prejudice to the future declarations of the Conference, we should immediately institute a plebiscite in these northeast territories. Let all the local populations declare their will freely and boldly. The result of the plebiscite will greatly facilitate the work of the Paris Conference.

I come to still more pressing matters. As you know, we have recognized the authority and dignity of the Peace Conference, as all other civilized nations have done, and we wait for its verdict. Up to the present its verdicts have been favorable to us. We voted here an alliance with the Entente, that is, with France, England, and Italy, who are continually sending us the help which is absolutely necessary to us in present circumstances. We have very much to be grateful for from America and its President. Without the powerful support of President Wilson, whose heart the best friend of the Polish cause, Colonel House, was able to win for us, Poland would no doubt have remained an internal question for Germany and Russia, at best confined within those frontiers which were assigned to her by the Germans in the Act of November 5, 1916. America is giving us food, America is giving us clothes, boots, linen, and munitions of war, and other supplies, on very easy terms, and with long credit.

Just before my departure from Paris, I received a letter from Mr. Hoover, promising Poland effective financial and economic help. That is the beginning of a very important help for us. Yesterday I learned that 2,000 tons of cotton would arrive at Gdansk in a few days, and that the Ministry of Finance in Washington were considering the question of granting Poland a considerable loan. Gentlemen, the Peace Conference, and especially England and America, with President Wilson at the head, while recognizing the necessity of our defending ourselves against the Bolsheviki, does not wish for further war on any front. Mr. Wilson expressed this wish repeatedly and very firmly. Could a Polish Prime Minister, director of the Polish Government, a man upon whose shoulders falls the really dreadful responsibility for the fate of his people in the near future, could such a man wave aside such demands? I did as my conscience prompted me. I acted as my love for my country and my honor as a Pole demanded. I said that I would do all I could to satisfy these demands, and I have kept my word.

An armistice was demanded. I agreed in principle to that. It was demanded that Haller's army should not fight against the Ukrainians. It was withdrawn from the Ukraine front, and finally it was required that the offensive should be stopped. Although the Ukrainians in their telegram of May 11th asked for the cessation of hostilities, on the 12th, at noon, they attacked us treacherously near Ustrzyk, bombarding the town of Sanok from aeroplanes. In the face of this criminal attack no force could stop the elemental impulse of our young soldiers. Like a whirlwind they threw themselves upon the enemy, and with lightning swiftness took Sambor, Drohobycz, Boryslav, Strye, Izolkiew, Sokl, Brody, and Zloczow, being joyfully greeted everywhere as saviors by the Polish and Ukrainian population. To-day our soldiers are probably approaching Stanislavow. But from Podwoloczysk and from Husiatyn a strong Soviet army has entered unhappy Galicia, or rather, Ruthenia. Haller's army will probably be obliged to fight on the Ukraine front, but not against the Ukrainians, only against the Bolsheviki, and perhaps it is fighting to-day.

On May 14th I broke off by telegraph all negotiations for an armistice, as I considered that after the way the Ukrainians had behaved themselves an armistice was absolutely impossible. The oppression, violence, cruelty, and crimes committed by them are without parallel. Wounded soldiers were buried alive in a wood near Lwow. Yesterday news came which brought mourning to our ministerial colleague, Linde. His wife's sister was murdered in Kolomia.

Gentlemen, I am far from blaming the Ukrainian people

for such crimes. It was not they who made such an army. Other people made it for them. But speaking of the Ukrainians, I must state that people who do such monstrous deeds cannot be treated as an army. Thus our Polish expedition into East Galicia is not a war, but a punitive expedition against bandits from whose oppression both the Polish and the Ruthenian population must be set free before law and order can be set up on this immemorially Polish territory. Law and order will quickly be introduced there by every possible means. We are, at least for the moment, strong there, but we shall not abuse this strength. None of us think of retaliation or revenge, nor would Polish sentiment ever permit such a thing. There should be liberty, equality, and justice for everybody. And in this spirit and with this wish I ask the honorable Seym to vote in favor of autonomy for East Galicia, and at the same time I ask for powers for the Polish Government to open peace negotiations with any Government in Ukrainia that shows moral strength and inspires confidence. I have finished.

Public Statement by M. Paderewski, September 18, 1919

From a Polish point of view, our one hope of future security as a State lies in the League of Nations. Upon it, and I fear upon it alone, depend the liberty of the Polish people and the successful development of democratic and liberal government in Poland. Standing, as we are, between Germany on one side and Russia on the other, we cannot hope to maintain our integrity during these years, while we build up the strength of our people, unless we have the protection of the League.

Poland at the present moment has 500,000 men under arms. Our people are short of food supplies, short of clothing, short of many of the necessaries of life. We are compelled to make every sacrifice to sustain the army, and this, with our population needing its resources for the upbuilding of the nation, in order that we may protect ourselves from encroachment.

To-day we are defending 1,500 miles of front against

Bolshevist forces, and in so doing, we stand as the front line in Europe against Bolshevist invasion from the east.

We are endeavoring to maintain this front line and at the same time to achieve an economic stability, to recuperate our people from the effects of repeated invasions of German and Russian armies. The task is a terrible one. The tax upon our strength will be too great unless we can have the assurance that there will be a body in the world to whom we can appeal for aid in the righting of our wrongs.

Poland has set up a democracy under the inspiration of the American people. Had it not been for American intervention in Europe we might possibly have had some semblance of independent Government under an autocratic overrule, but with American intervention and American help we have sought to establish not only the independence of the State, but also the internal liberty of our people, through the difficult road of democracy.

The pressure is upon us on all sides through military action and through Bolshevist propaganda and an intense propaganda from Germany. Unless we have a protective power in the world, under whose strength we can secure an opportunity for peaceful development and the solution of our internal problems, free from distracting and antagonistic influences, I fear for the safety of our democracy.

The great power and the support which it may furnish need not be military, its moral and economic force is all that we ask, and that power is the League of Nations.

BY HERBERT HOOVER

Statement made August 19, 1919, after visiting Poland

As a result of seven invasions by different armies the country has largely been denuded of buildings. The estates of the larger landowners have been destroyed, and while the peasants are cultivating approximately enough foodstuffs for their own supplies, these regions, which in normal times export large quantities of food, mostly from the large estates, are four-fifths uncultivated.

In normal times the town populations exist by exchanging manufactured goods to the peasants and landowners for food.

There has been virtually no import of manufactured goods for years, and the supplies of foodstuffs having vanished, the town populations are left entirely without support or employment. As there have been no manufactured goods to exchange, and as the currency no longer has any purchasing value in goods and the peasants do not care to exchange foodstuffs for it, there has been a total breakdown of the economic cycle.

In addition to the destruction and robbery which accompanied the repeated invasion of rival armies, these areas have been, of course, through a caldron of Bolshevist revolution and the intellectual classes either fled from the country or to a considerable extent were imprisoned. Some were executed. The Ruthenian peasants have been stirred up against the great landowners, which accounts for the destruction of the equipment of the large landed properties. It appears to us that it will require years for this region to recover, for animals must be provided, agricultural implements imported and the whole agricultural production restarted.

GERMANY CRUSHES BOLSHEVISM

THE MARCH GENERAL STRIKE AND SPARTACIST REVOLT

MARCH 3-10

F. S. DELMER
 GEORGE YOUNG
L. E. MATTHEI

The new "Socialistic Republic" government of Germany had no easy time maintaining itself. The people cried out against their Socialist leaders each time that the latter yielded perforce to one Ally demand after another. The militarists constantly plotted to regain the reins of government. And, most dangerous of all, the more reckless Germans insisted that revolution had by no means gone far enough. These "Spartacists," as they called themselves from the fiery appeals signed "Spartacus" by their leader Liebknecht, made every effort to carry the overthrow of monarchy onward to complete communism, sovetism and even Russian bolshevism. The Russian envoy, Radek, had at least equal weight with Liebknecht in their councils, and Russian gold was freely lavished in their cause.

Their first effort at revolution by force was made in Berlin in January under Liebknecht and Rosa Luxemburg. The uprising failed, and both the leaders were seized and slain by their captors in the streets. Then came the second and more dangerous Spartacist effort. The great mass of the toilers of Berlin were already so dissatisfied with their Socialist leaders as to join in a "general strike" which was begun on March 3rd. It was soon broken by vague government promises of better conditions. Meanwhile, however, the Spartacists had seized the opportunity for an uprising, hoping to draw all the strikers after them. Again the revolt failed; and this time it was stamped out by the "Governor of the City," Gustav Noske, with far more bloody severity than in January. For a week Berlin continued a bewildered battlefield. Its buildings were torn and battered by artillery from either side, and hundreds of non-combatants were slain. By March 15th the Spartacists were crushed completely. Revolts afterwards arose in other cities and with other aims; but the menace of German bolshevism was broken by Noske in those March days in Berlin.

We give here the picture first of the parliamentary struggle between the extreme Socialists or Independents and their more moderate opponents, as this was seen by an Englishman in Berlin, the well-known economist, F. Sefton Delmer. Then George Young, an English radical, who had been a prisoner of war in Germany, sketches with a sympathetic pen the actual uprisings as he saw them. Then the well-known Teuton economist, Matthei, explains the "general strike" and the real movement which underlay all the tumult.

III

BY F. S. DELMER

THE salient fact in the Berlin Revolution was the skill-ful maneuvering by which Scheidemann and his party, to the unspeakable annoyance of the Independent Socialists, pushed themselves forward as protagonists and directors of the movement. Already, on the forenoon of the 9th of November, Scheidemann, calling from the steps of the Reichstag across the Atlantic to President Wilson, took it upon himself to proclaim the Republic *urbei et orbi,* as if America would be likely to mistake for republican idealism this pancaking device by which the Nationalist Socialists tried at the last moment to save the crash. The plaudits of the endless masses of factory workers filled the immense space between the Reichstag and the Tiergarten. Above the crowd towered the eclectic glories of the parvenu Reichstag, and further off the vulgar Column of Victory and the three gigantic statues that stood as eloquent symbols of the rise and fall of the Blood and Iron period—the bronze Bismarck, the marble Moltke, and the wooden, thrice wooden Hindenburg.

Between twelve and one o'clock on the same day, Herr Haussman, a democratic Under-Secretary of State in Prince Max's Government, accompanied by Herr Ebert and Herr Scheidemann, the leaders of the Social Demo-crats—who may be called Nationalists in contradistinction to the Independent Socialists, who were Internationalists—hastened from the Reichstag meeting to the Chancery in the Wilhelm Strasse. In answer to a question from von Payer, the Vice-Chancellor, as to whether he was taking over the Government on the basis of the Constitution or on behalf of the Workmen's and Soldiers' Councils, Ebert declared "On the basis of the Constitution."

After a brief conference with the Cabinet, Prince Max decided to hand the reins of government over to Ebert. Ebert thereupon requested Haussman to continue in office as a Secretary of State, thus indicating that he intended to form a democratic and not an exclusively Social-Demo-cratic Government.

The Independents, when also invited to join in forming a provisional government, from the very beginning
made their consent conditional on the exclusion of the
bourgeoisie parties from the Ministry, objecting oven to
Haussman. They thus insisted that they would be satisfied with nothing short of the dictatorship of the proletariat. In this matter they had their way, for at the great
meeting of the delegates of the Workmen's and Soldiers'
Councils, held on Sunday afternoon, the second day of the
Revolution, three Nationalist Socialists, Ebert, Scheidemann and Landsberg, and three Independents, Haase, Ditt-
mann and Barth, were elected to act as an Executive Council (*Vollzugsrat*), on behalf of the W. and S. Councils,
Haussman and all non-Socialists being excluded. This
Executive Council came to be somewhat irreverently called
the "Six-headed Chancellor." The Coalition proved, however, to be of short duration, the Independents quitting the
Government on the 29th of December, 1918. .

It soon turned out that the Independents, as a body,
were determined to direct the Revolution along Russian
lines, even identifying themselves, to a considerable extent,
with Liebknecht and his Spartacist friends. When I got
to Berlin on the 15th of December, 1918, the quarrel between the official Socialists and the "whole-hog" followers
of Liebknecht was already in full swing. They would hear
nothing of the proposed National Constituent Assembly
which was to decide, on the basis of an election by the entire nation, Germany's future form of government. They
insisted that a Soviet Government was the only panacea.
"All power, political and economic, must be given into the
hands of the W. and S. Councils." This was the one question eternally debated at the street corners and argued by
stump orators on every square up till the 6th of January.
Under my window, at the corner of Friedrich Strasse and
Unter den Linden, I could hear them disputing, debating
and wrangling as I lay in bed, sometimes till half-past one
in the morning.

Liebknecht had already begun his appeal to the street,
seeking to incite the populace by means of long processions

of factory workers and unemployed through the main thoroughfares of the city. He himself, sitting well back with eyes gleaming in the shadow of his motor car, looking like an animal at the mouth of a cave, drove through the town at the head of his scores of thousands of gaunt and grimy disciples, made and female. "His long imprisonment has fanaticized him. He is no longer the same man," his friend, Frau Dr. C., said to me. On the top of his car was mounted a machine-gun bearing a placard with the words, "To be used only in self defense." At various notable points en route the car would halt and Liebknecht from the top of it would deliver his inexhaustible harangues in denunciation of Scheidemann and Ebert. Sometimes, from some great house before which he had halted, a hand would put aside the blind and a face peep out for an instant, only to withdraw in terror when threatened with the fists of women below and cries of "String them up to the lamp-posts!"

As Liebknecht's opponents also took to organizing street demonstrations, it was clear that sooner or later there must be a collision. The Lebknecht danger hung like a nightmare over the city, and, whether from policy or powerlessness, the government at that time did little to check it. As the crowds marched through the streets, they from time to time shouted in chorus their hoarse eternal "Nieder mit Scheidemann! Nieder! Nieder! Nieder!" Those three last long-drawn Nieders, with a pause after each, still sound in my ears like the bellow of some Stygian sea. It was quite a natural progression for this sound to change to machine-gun fire on Christmas eve, and then at the beginning of January to fill Berlin with civil war and street fighting. Politically the experience of that week's wild chaos and murder broke the chances of Communism in Berlin, and with Communism fell the cause of the Indepent Socialists, which was more or less associated with it.

BY GEORGE YOUNG

The first result of the failure of German Liberalism and of the Weimar Assembly in February was that revolution and reaction came into active collision with each other in the provincial capitals.

These two conflicts ran concurrently, and collision in the provinces was a necessary consequence of collision in the capital. Moreover, when the revolution had failed twice to assert itself by force in Berlin, it stood little chance of surviving in Bavaria, Brunswick, or Bremen. Such spontaneous and sporadic appeals to force met by organized police measure and prosecutions only prevented the Socialist party from reuniting, and forced German politics into a duel between the propertied classes and the proletariat, in which the latter had no prospect of success.

This duel started in Berlin in the December and January conflicts which were settled in favor of the government, and its subsequent continuance in the provinces had the same result. The outbreaks in the coast ports and the coal districts of Westphalia were remote, and their unexpectedly easy repression by flying columns only confirmed the Government in a policy of coercion. The outbreaks in Munich and the south were outside the political orbit in which the government was moving. If the spread of the general strike from the west to Saxony, which broke Germany in two and cut Berlin off from Weimar, was more serious, yet the Maerker column soon succeeded in removing any danger to Weimar and in reopening communications with Berlin. These outbreaks were not formidable enough to force the Government to depart from its policy of suppressing not only revolts, but the revolution.

But the general strike and street fighting in Eastern Berlin during March, although it was intentionally exaggerated so as to impress Paris with the Bolshevist danger, did for a few days imperil not only the Scheidemann Government, but the whole Parliamentary system. Both were consequences of the coalition which by giving the government a class basis had made it quite incapable of going half way to meet the revolutionary demands for recognition of the Council System and for socialization. At first party ties had held the moderate mass of the Social-Democratic workmen; but as time passed and the middle class mentality of the men in power became more and more marked, dissatisfaction with the government and defections to the Opposition grew rapidly. Even *Vorwärts* admitted there was cause of complaint.

In vain did the government poster the streets with pathetic protests that "socialization is already here," and issued manifestoes pointing to its legislative achievements —Eight-Hour Day, Unemployment Benefit, Land Settlement, what we should call "Whitley Councils" in coal mining districts, War Pensions and Repeal of War Measures. These had already been put in force provisionally by the previous government, and did not amount to much any way. In vain did the government profess its intention of pushing through the two bills approving, in principle, nationalization of coal mines and potash deposits; for no one wanted nationalization except as a step to socialization. The workmen felt that the government was, as one put it to me, "a revolution profiteer." It had perverted the purposes and pocketed the profits of the revolution. They felt that Weimar, as another one expressed it, was only a "soviet of profiteers" and would produce no socialist legislation.

The revolutionary opponents of the Coalition saw their opportunity, but their leaders could secure no combination or concerted action. Nothing, indeed, was more surprising than the incapacity of the Germans to associate and organize for a political purpose.

The general impression one got was that Germans had so grown to look on political responsibility as the function of a specialized class that they never could consider anyone outside that class as capable of replacing any member of it. We see something of the same sort of helplessness growing up in England, where it is becoming increasingly difficult for the man in the street to conceive a Cabinet formed from outside a small clique of the ruling class. And the German revolutionaries of the Opposition showed themselves as incapable of making use of their opportunities as did their Liberal opponents in the government. The game was in the revolutionaries' hands in the early months of the year if they could have combined. But the different disturbed districts declared war on the government at just such intervals of time as allowed them to be conveniently beaten in detail by very small forces. Each district again was divided into all manner of dissentient organizations in different stages of development. In some the Councils were really representative, in others they had co-opted themselves; while there were as many kinds of revolutionary corps as of Councils.

In Berlin alone there were some ten different corps. A leader of one of the last insurgent parties to hold out, told me, during an attack by the government troops, that it was not the great disparity of numbers and munitions that had defeated him, but the difficulty of getting the revolutionaries to work together.

Moreover, the issue between reaction and revolution in Berlin was fought out in two different and quite distinct conflicts, that were invariably confused by the foreign press. One took the form of strikes, the other of street fighting. The general strike was the resistance of the Workmen's Council organizations to suppression by the middle class Ministry. The street fighting was the resistance of the remains of the old revolutionary forces to suppression by the new Frei-Corps "mercenaries" of the reaction. The two developed concurrently though with little connection.

The strikes that were always breaking out everywhere for no apparent reason, culminated in the Berlin general strike of March. This general strike was forced on the reluctant Majority Socialists by the Independents, themselves propelled by the Communists. For these two latter controlled the Executive Committee of the Berlin Councils. But though the Majority Socialists did not oppose the general strike, they did their best to make it a failure, and when, after three days, the Communists pressed for its extension to water, gas, electricity and food supply in order to support the fighting Spartacists, the Majoritarians withdrew, and by the end of the week the strike was declared off. The Majority Socialists' proposal for unconditional surrender was rejected, that of the Independents for surrender on conditions of amnesty accepted, and the conditions were agreed to by the government. Thereupon the Left of the Communists, including the brilliant Clara Zietken, took the opportunity of this crisis and of the party caucus (Parteitag) then sitting in Berlin to secede to the Spartacists.

The loss of their left wing was, however, more than compensated to the Independents by the movement leftward in the ranks of the Social-Democrats, the supporters of the government. And this leftward trend was accentuated by disapproval of the action of the government in bombarding whole quarters of Berlin and in shooting wholesale its political opponents. This rapid response of the Council system to a trend in public opinion was in strong contrast to the irresponsive inertia of the Weimar Assembly, which remained representative only of a nationalist mood, and remote from the whole Socialist movement.

The Ministry had to give way to the political pressure. Already before the strike it indicated concessions as to industrial socialization and constitutional sanction of the Councils, and these were elaborated and established by negotiations at Weimar with missions sent from the Central and Executive Councils. These concessions were in principle very considerable, and much more than could ever have been imposed in practical application on the Centrum supporters of the government. The result of this crisis was therefore to prepare the way for a reconstruction of the government on a moderate Socialist basis, between a Centrum-Conservative opposition to the right and a Communist to the left. This would have represented the true balance of political power at the time; and the fact that it would not have had a majority at Weimar would have been only a formal difficulty.

But this, the natural, solution was made impossible by the extraordinary severity with which the armed resistance to the government was punished. For this severity made it impossible for even the most moderate Independents to join the government. And this fighting was not a development of the strike, but of the campaign carried on by the government with volunteer flying columns against the revolutionary corps throughout Germany.

Of these corps, of which there were many in Berlin, the most important were the Republican Guard and the Marine Division. The former had from the first supported the government, while the Marine Division of Kiel sailors had already been in collision with it in December. The other corps were all more or less in opposition, and some were mere camouflage for bad characters. Until these corps were dispersed the constitutional government had no complete control of Berlin apart from their "Council" rival, the Executive Committee. A first step was made towards their suppression by the arrest of sixty ring leaders; whereupon the Marine Division and the other corps prepared for resistance, with the assistance of the Spartacist irregulars and a rabble of roughs and rascals. These were joined later by about half the Republican Guard, which had come into collision with the Frei-Corps—the government volunteer contingents. The strikers, however, took no part in the fighting.

The strike was declared on a Monday; Tuesday passed in preparations by the regulars and plunderings by the rabble, and on Wednesday the garrisons of government buildings in the east central district of Berlin were attacked and besieged. They were hard pressed, but held out, being supplied by aeroplane until relieved by an offensive of the government's troops on Thursday afternoon. For some hours a tremendous bombardment was carried on round the Alexanderplatz and neighboring streets, but the damage to property, though considerable, could only have been as little as it was if at least half the "hows" and "minnies" had been firing blank; for the benefit rather of the correspondents than of the insurgents. The insurgents' positions were eventually made untenable by aeroplane observation and bombing. During the following days they were driven, with terrific fusillades and some fighting, through the east end into the suburbs, where the bombardments were continued for no obvious reason for several days.

Berlin will long remember these Ides of March. So shall I, not because of Thursday's fighting—you could generally get your fill of such fighting in Germany those days —but because on that Thursday I got a real lunch. It was given me by a banker, and cost just about four shillings a mouthful. I know, because I counted them. And in the cellars of the same house were families living on 5 lbs. of bad potatoes and 5 lbs. of black bread a week.

The banker and I were enemies, and I was nominally and nationally engaged in starving him; though, as members of our respective Independent Labor Parties we were politically working in the same cause. And a few streets away men of one race and one class were killing each other respectively in the names of Law and Liberty. Such was European civilization in the year of Our Lord 1919.

But probably you are more interested in the fighting; so, if you like, I will take you two excursions through it. We will start the first on Thursday afternoon, when the insurgent soldiers and Spartacists were trying to force their way westward from their base in the east end, across the Spree, past the Schloss, to the Linden, and the Government troops were trying to drive them eastward. The main battleground was the Alexanderplatz, from which radiate the main thoroughfares leading east.

At the west end of the Linden all is much as usual. Instead of the omnibuses laid up by the general strike long German farm carts drawn by ponies are carrying passengers perched on planks resting on packing-cases. Lorries with mounted machine-guns patrol up and down, and machine-gun pickets guard all important buildings. As we go east the roadway empties and the traffic on the pavements thickens into hesitating groups all facing eastward, or knots encircling some political discussion. Further on the roadway is blocked by artillery of the Lüttwitz Volunteer Corps going into action—field-guns, trench mortars and minenwerfer, the latter towed behind lorries loaded with the missiles, great brown conical cylinders four feet high.

A soldier with a rifle at the ready comes down the middle of the empty street scanning the windows. "Window shut," he shouts, aiming at one. A red poster proclaims that anyone loitering will be shot at. We are now in the danger zone. A lorry hurries forward, the bottom spread with brown-stained mattresses. The noise becomes bewildering— the *crack* of roof snipers and the *rap* of the machine-guns are incessant. A field-gun is banging away round the corner, and that heavy boom is a minenwerfer shelling the Alexanderplatz.

The main struggle has already passed into the roads radiating eastward, which the insurgents are barricading hastily, while others on tugs retreat south down the Spree. But of this fight we can only see the aeroplanes swooping a few hundred feet over the roofs and bombing the machine-gun nests. An insurgent plane engages for a few minutes, but retires outnumbered. The battle is over; though fighting will go on for days as the troops drive the insurgents from one street to another through the eastern quarter out into the suburbs.

And now it is the following Tuesday, and I will take you for our second excursion into the insurgent camp at Lichtenberg—the most easterly suburb of Berlin, where the main body still holds out. This morning's government bulletin has told us that the victorious government troops have cleared the whole East End, except Lichtenberg, which is encircled with a "ring of steel." That several thousand insurgents have barricaded all approaches and are sweeping them with field-guns. That they have destroyed hundreds of tons of flour. That they have short sixty—a hundred —two hundred prisoners. That others have been torn in pieces by the mob, which has taken wounded from the ambulances and clubbed them to death. That no one in a decent coat can venture on the street without being murdered. That in consequence of these "bestial atrocities" anyone found with arms will be shot. But we've read war bulletins before!

On our way we pass a convoy of prisoners, hands handcuffed behind their backs, armed motor-cars before and behind. A young soldier blazes off several shots to scatter the crowd, at which a well-dressed woman remonstrates, but she is at once arrested and put with the convoy.

Here we are at the Warschauer Brücke over the Spree, where there is an imposing concourse of steel-helmeted troops and guns, and a cordon.   We pass this after being searched for arms, and across the bridge come on a lot of guns and machine-guns firing fiercely down the Warschauer Strasse, though there is no audible reply or visible reason. After watching the shells holing houses, we start working our way round to the south through empty streets, keeping close to the house-fronts and taking cover when bullets whisper a warning.   At last crowded streets again, and through them to a broad avenue crossed by shallow trenches and ramshackle barricades — the much-bulletined Frankfurter Allee.   Here an insurgent picket takes charge of us and undertakes to bring us to the secret headquarters.

"But where are your field-guns?" we ask.

"Field-guns? We haven't any," they say, surprised.

"And how do you keep the troops in check?"

"Oh, those boys! Two of us take machine-guns, charge with them down each side of the street, and they run."

"And how many of you are there?"

"Some two or three hundred perhaps—it varies, but we're all old soldiers—we allow no boys to fight for us."

"And have you shot the sixty policemen you took in the Lichtenberg station?"

"Sixty policemen?   There aren't that number in all Lichtenberg. Two got shot defending the station, but after they surrendered to a quarter of their number we let them all go home. You can go and see any of them."

It is impossible not to believe these intelligent, even intellectual and eminently honest faces.   So the sixty policemen follow the field-guns and the "ring of steel" into the limbo of "White" lies.

We pass a railway goods yard where plundered flour is being carried away in sacks.

"Where is that going?" we ask.

"To the bakers and afterwards to be distributed gratis to the crowd."

We see later women with red crosses distributing loaves from a cart to women and children.   We reach our destination, only to be warned by a woman just in time that it is now occupied by troops—a narrow escape that so shakes the nerve of our guide that he takes refuge in a dressing station improvised in a shop. Here are "neutral" doctors and nurses, very angry at the bombardment of crowded tenement houses and the reckless shooting by the young volunteers. They run great risks, as robbers have so often misused the Red Cross that it is now no protection against the government troops. Here are many wounded, mostly women and children, and but a few fighters. The latter all indignantly deny having shot prisoners, though they know the other side are doing it. And then at last to the evasive headquarters, where the leaders tell us of what they hope to achieve by this desperate resistance of a few hundred men armed with rifles and bombs against as many thousands armed with all the machinery of modern war.

"Noske," they say, "is only a puppet in the hands of Majors Gilsa and Hammerstein, and they are agents of the Eden Hotel, the headquarters of the Cavalry Guard and the center of reaction. The old story again of Bethmann-Hollweg, Ludendorff and the General Staff, militarism and monarchism is what all this bombardment means, for they want to convince the Entente that they must have a large standing army. They have just raised the pay and doubled the rations of these young mercenaries. Why don't the Entente abolish them and insist on a Swiss militia here?

"If this White Guard goes on we shall organize a Red Guard, and we shall win. But that will mean Bolshevism. We are not Bolsheviks, but Socialists to-day. We have offered to keep order in Berlin and here, with a militia representing all parties, but they go on bombarding. It is the old Prussian terrorism again. They have learnt nothing from the war."

And so in the twilight, back the way we came, wondering at the working of moral laws that have now subjected Berlin to a self-inflicted punishment of bombardments and bombing worse than any of those it inflicted on other cities.

The behavior of the government can only be explained by their having left the whole matter to Noske, who, in turn, left it to his military advisers, Majors Gilsa, Pabst and Hammerstein, who again were agents only of the militarist reactionary faction. This faction intended to exploit the crisis by killing two birds with one stone—the anti-Bolshevists at Paris and the pro-Bolshevists at Berlin. Their policy was to make an excuse for raising a large professional army with which to suppress the revolution, and, if the gods were kind, to restore Germany's ancient *régime* and its racial frontiers. For this purpose atrocities were invented as a pretext for reprisals and for recruiting and raising the pay of the Frei-Corps. The government could have kept order of a sort through the revolutionary corps if it had kept in touch with the revolutionary councils; but it fought the corps with flying columns of undertrained over-armed boys, and it fought the councils with its patched-up majority of old parliamentary hands and party hacks.

In the resultant civil war that raged, and still rages, all over Germany one may distinguish certain combats more decisive than the others. There were the conflicts in Berlin—of December against the Marine Division, of January against the Spartacists, and of March against the Republican Guard and other corps. In the provinces, the expeditions against Bremen, Halle, Brunswick and Munich. And with each of these failures ended some distinctive element of the German revolution.

BY L. E. MATTHEI

In Germany, as in so many places, there is a struggle going on between the old ideas of political democracy and the idea of the Soviet or industrial democratic system which is connected with the Bolshevik Revolution in Russia. The strikes and bloodshed which took place in Germany during the week March 1st-8th, subsequent events, and the proposals for the "socialization of industry," can only be properly understood in the light of this conflict.

The Revolution in Germany brought into existence two groups of bodies claiming authority:

(1) *Political Democratic Bodies of the Old Type.*—The most important of these is the Central Government for the whole empire of Germany, with Ebert as President and Scheidemann as Premier. It derives its authority from the National Assembly, elected by universal equal suffrage. It is supported by the various states' governments, *e. g.,* Prussia and Saxony.

(2) *Industrial or Soviet Bodies.*—Workers' Councils or Soviets were formed all over Germany in the early days of the Revolution, in imitation of the Bolshevik system. These Soviets are grouped in a National, Central or Pan-German, Congress of Soviets. The Soviets of Berlin are grouped in a special Congress of their own, which has assumed a more than local authority.

The struggle between the political government and the Soviets began very early. Attempts were made to play off the Congress of Soviets against the National Assembly. The attempt collapsed at the Congress held on December 16th, when the majority voted for the holding of a National Assembly, and an Executive Committee, consisting of Majority Socialists, was elected to work with the government. But the conflict was not over. The "Spartacists," or, as they are more properly called, the Communists, continued to demand the "dictatorship of the proletariat" and a "Soviet Republic."

The course of the struggle showed a gradual weakening of the Central Government and the Majority Socialists before the violent tactics of the Spartacists. At first the Majority relegated the Soviets to purely "social tasks," and denied them any political functions. They replied to the new ideas only with the unimpeachable but, to the Spartacists, well worn doctrine of democracy, which they interpret as government by simple majority, resting on equal and universal franchise. Having struggled desperately for seventy years to obtain democracy, they, not unnaturally, think there must be something in it. Thus a certain amount of emotion goes into their argument. But democracy is what the Spartacists scorn. Accordingly, the two sides have been simply arguing over each others' heads. There

has not been a single article in *Vorwärts* dealing with the
new idea of the right of "the conscious and active" minority to direct the unconscious mass.   In Germany, as everywhere else, there has been a refusal to try to understand
the new point of view on its merits, and the Soviet system,
as such, has been condemned, owing to the terrible methods
used by those who proposed to put it into practice.

Thus in the project for a Constitution, elaborated with
such care by Hugo Preuss on behalf of the government,
the Soviet was not mentioned.   At the opening of the
National Assembly on January 26th, neither Ebert nor
Scheidemann gave a word to the new institutions; and in
the columns of *Vorwärts*, Friedrich Stampfer, quite the
best Majority Socialist leader-writer, and not a particularly narrow-minded man, relegated the Soviets to functions of a mild trade unionism.

The first attack of the Spartacists upon the government
was in January.   It was a failure.   The attitude of the government towards the Soviets and the new ideas remained
the same right up to the outbreak of March 1st-8th.   But
there is evidence that the Soviet idea had by no means been
killed.   At Munich, after the murder of Eisner, the pure
"Soviet Republic" was immediately declared.   And even
among the Majority Socialist supporters of the Central
Government, there were signs of a movement for recognizing and utilizing the Councils as "social political" bodies.

The position at the end of February, therefore, was
that the Soviet idea had made considerable headway, and
that the demand for some kind of "recognition" of the
Workers' Councils was widespread.   The government still
resisted the demand.   The General Strike which led to the
Spartacist outbreak began on March 3rd.   The Central
Government, on March 1st, when it was too late, attempted
to prevent the outbreak by a half concession to the Soviet
idea.   A manifesto was issued on March 1st at Weimar,
and afterwards placarded all over Berlin.   In this the government, after announcing that it would "stand or fall on
the principles of democracy," and that "political power belongs solely to the freely chosen representatives of the peo-

ple and the government who enjoy their confidence," goes on to promise the development of "the organizations which belong to industrial democracy."

On the same day on which this manifesto was issued (Saturday, March 1st), the Berlin Soviets met under the chairmanship of Herman Müller, a foolish and incompetent man, who seemed quite incapable of maintaining order in these huge and unruly meetings. The speaking was, as usual, very confused. Suddenly a "deputation" from Hennigsdorf marched in (said to have been engineered by the Spartacists); six men in workmen's clothes marched on to the platform, "theatrically," as *Vorwärts* notes in disgust, and demanded the General Strike in the name of the 7,000 whom they "represented." No resolution was passed, and the meeting proceeded to vote for the new Executive Committee, when, unfortunately, it was found that the hall was required to be cleared for a fancy dress ball. Müller suggested that the meeting should dissolve, and leave the result of the voting to be announced in the press. A great tumult arose; half the meeting left the hall with Müller, and half stayed behind. This latter half, the Communists, probably decided on the General Strike then and there. In any case, Sunday is a dangerous day in Berlin, and when the meeting met again on Monday, and was once more debating the General Strike, and once more inconclusively, news came that the General Strike had actually broken out that morning in the Berlin factories.

At this point the Prussian Government declared the State of Siege in Berlin, in virtue of which, Noske, as Minister for Defense, issued orders forbidding any open-air meetings, allowing indoor meetings only by license, permitting the issue of no new papers except by license, and setting up courts martial for treason, murder, riot, mutiny, incitement to mutiny, robbery, plunder, blackmail, arson, interference with the transport service. The attitude of *Vorwärts* (practically the government organ) was one of only qualified approval of these measures; in fact, it exerted itself, not without success, to take up a mediating position between the various groups and declared its intention of doing its best to "secure an honorable issue for this sufficiently confused movement."

The more radical group of Berlin Majority Socialists sent a deputation to Weimar, which, on Thursday, negotiated with the government some very important "concessions"; these were undoubtedly of great influence in ending the strike. The government offered to recognize the Soviet system in so far as the Workers' Councils were to be an integral part of, or incorporated in, the Constitution.

In spite of the government "concessions," the Independent Party was not satisfied, and advanced "Five Demands." Hermann Müller then put himself into telephonic communication with Scheidemann at Weimar, and received the following answers:

(1) In regard to any proposed punishment of strikers, Noske has promised that no measures shall be taken against them in state or municipal works, and the employers shall be told also to abstain from such; (2) as soon as the identity of those arrested has been satisfactorily established, those arrested during the strikes are to be released. . . . (3) In regard to the evacuation of the factories occupied by the military: all private factories, and all state factories which are purely industrial concerns, shall be evacuated at once. But the electric works, which are held by Volunteer Corps, can only be evacuated in relays, in such a manner that, as the soldiers are gradually withdrawn, the Workers' Guard shall take their place. . . . (4) The State of Siege was only declared after robbery had begun on a great scale. . . . The State of Siege will be raised as soon as public safety is somewhat restored in Berlin. The State of Siege was not directed against the strikers, but against robbers. . . . (5) The abolition of the courts martial depends on the abolition of the State of Siege.— From *Vorwärts*, March 9th.

The government reply seems to have been found satisfactory by the moderate elements; but the more extreme elements considered it a signal for sharpening the conflict and proposed to cut off water and gas from the city of Berlin. On this "insane proposal," the moderates took their courage in both hands, definitely repudiated the extremists, and at a meeting on March 8th declared the strike ended.

Thus the formal strike flickered out, as lifelessly as it had begun. But this want of persistence on the part of the moderates raised the extremists to that sense of desperation which governed their actions for the next few days of appalling fighting.

PROBLEMS OF THE PEACE CONFERENCE

THE OPEN THREAT OF RUPTURE

APRIL 7, 1919

SISLEY HUDDLESTON   RAY S. BAKER
EDWIN BORCHARD   GUILLAUME MARTIN

The surface harmony of the Peace Conference was always preserved. It would not be too much to say of the chief representatives
of the Powers, that each one of them retained   for each other one a
high respect and even a warm personal friendliness. Yet their differences of purpose rapidly developed to a point where the only question was as to which could and would hold out the longest to win his
way. The chief points of antagonism which thus divided the conference are here presented. Special emphasis is given, first, to the
principle of "mandatories," which meant a very real approach toward
universal freedom and equality, and second to the "League of Nations"
argument and the final crisis of April 7th when President Wilson summoned his ship, the *George Washington,* to meet him at Brest, and
was prepared to abandon the Conference, if the others would not bring
the Treaty into closer harmony with the "Fourteen Points" upon
which it was nominally based.

Of those trying days a general glimpse is here given from the
viewpoint of Sisley Huddleston, a British eye-witness. Then comes
the view of Wilson's supporters as ably presented by the official
leader of the American press-representatives on the spot, Ray S.
Baker. A French summary comes from the distinguished French political writer, Martin; and the scientific estimate of the value of the
"mandatory" system is by Prof. Borchard, professor of Law at Yale
University.

BY SISLEY HUDDLESTON

THE story of the two hundred odd days in Paris between the signing of the armistice and the signing of
the Peace Treaty contains more stirring episodes than years
of battle: event followed event with lightning rapidity, although the deliberations dragged, and the tense drama of
those months was, especially for those who lived close to
the heart of things and knew how frail was the peace
struggling to birth, who watched with apprehension every

129

dispute, every fresh outbreak of fighting, every current of popular opinion which threatened to make the task of the statesmen impossible, a drama which at times was too poignant. The future of mankind was at stake. There were two alternatives: reconciliation, the possibility of universal co-operation in a spirit of good will to repair the ravages of fifty months of war and to make war impossible, or—a blind, egoistic struggle, the fear of general bankruptcy and the definite crash of civilization. Many could see no middle course. The war for victor and vanquished had gone on too long and only heroic efforts could save us from utter economic ruin, from a moral *débâcle* and from the submerging of all humanity's hopes. It was the gravest task that ever faced any body of the peoples' leaders: it was not a mere territorial readjustment: it was the rebuilding of the world. Were they equal to their job? Had they only parochial minds or would they see things with a broad vision? Their work was interrupted by a series of incidents which time after time nearly broke up the Conference and threw everything into the melting-pot. Chaos threatened, with the black night of a mondial revolution for which many forces openly strove.

BY RAY S. BAKER

It is possible, now that it is all over, to look back along the troubled history of the Peace Conference and to measure, with a little clearer vision, what it was that happened there and what President Wilson did.

Each of the five crises in the Peace Conference centered upon some point in the President's leadership and arose directly out of the clash between President Wilson's principles and ideals with the interests of other nations or groups of nations.

In at least three of these crises the Peace Conference was much nearer breaking up than the world yet knows. Some of these crises, like the one that centered around the Shantung decision, are fairly well known to the public, while others, though equally important, like that which attended the struggle to decide the future colonial policy of the world,

attracted almost no attention either at the time or since—
this largely because the discussions were kept so secret. These
five crises briefly were as follows, in the order in which
they occurred:

First, the settlement of world colonial policy by the
adoption of the new mandatory system.

Second, the fight between those who wanted the League
of Nations Covenant made an integral part of the Treaty
and those who wanted it left for discussion after the Treaty
was adopted. It was really the struggle between those who
wanted an effective League and those who did not want
one.

Third, the crisis of April which led President Wilson to
order the *George Washington,* and to consider the possibility of the withdrawal of America from the Conference.

Fourth, the President's note to the Italian people regarding the situation at Fiume which caused the Italian delegates
to withdraw from the Conference.

Fifth, the Shantung settlement.

It was inevitable that President Wilson should be forced
at Paris to bear the brunt of the heavy fighting—fighting that
would have worn out a stronger, more robust man than he.
For he had a double problem, a double task. He had not only
to join the other delegates in making peace with Germany,
but he had the far more difficult and delicate task, which
grew more and more difficult as the Conference progressed,
of upholding the disinterested American position against the
insistent desires and necessities of the other allied nations.

Most people do not realize that most of the troubles at
Paris, and every one of the really serious crises, arose not
out of any differences of view regarding the terms to be imposed upon Germany, but out of deep-seated and often bitter
disagreements among the Allies themselves. Throughout
the six troubled months of the Conference the center and
focus of the struggle was the conflict between President Wilson demanding a settlement upon broad principles (which
every one had accepted!) and the other allied powers demanding various material reimbursements or advantages.

While the war was still in progress necessity united the

Allies: every one accepted Mr. Wilson's plan of settlement, and welcomed his strong leadership—for three reasons:

First, because his principles appealed to the great masses of the world as good in themselves, as the true, reasonable, and honest basis of settlement. This tended to disarm the opposition of the radicals in all European countries who were becoming more and more restless with the bloody continuation of the war.

Second, because a hearty acceptance of the American idea, and American leadership, helped to bring America with her vast resources more wholeheartedly into the war.

Third, because Wilson's diplomacy tended to divide and weaken German support of the war.

The moment the war ended in an unexpectedly complete victory, the high purpose and the unified spirit of the Allies began to fade away. They were not, after all, united nations. Each had its strong loyalties, its ambitions, its necessities, and these immediately began to reassert themselves. In the high moments of inspiration and enthusiasm of the war men had begun to believe in miracles: when it was over they found themselves back in the old world—and more than that, in a state of exhaustion and demoralization which some one has characterized as national shell-shock. It must never be forgotten that it was in this atmosphere of national shell-shock, exaggerated appearances, exaggerated fears, that the Treaty was made.

Even before the Peace Conference met, certain ominous things happened. At the same time that Wilson was making sanguine speeches in England regarding the league of nations, Clemenceau was telling the Chamber of Deputies in Paris that he still believed in the old-fashioned system of alliances as the only safe way of safety in the world and notable French leaders were advancing claims which would, if granted, defeat the very principles to which the Allies had agreed at the armistice. A little later the British elections returned a heavily conservative parliament endorsing a hard peace with Germany, and defeating some of Mr. Wilson's strongest supporters in the House of Commons. In Italy there began to be talk of the wide expansion of Italy in the

Adriatic and elsewhere. And finally, the November elections in America, which returned a Congress in opposition to the President, and the attacks made upon him by various Republican leaders in the Senate, tended to weaken his influence at Paris. To any one who had been in Europe during the last year of the war, before the Peace Conference began, as I had been, this change of attitude toward Wilson among the leaders (not among the people) was most evident.

No sooner had the Peace Conference got down to business, sitting within the double-doored, sound-proof room in the French Foreign Office, than the struggle began—and it centered at once upon an issue between President Wilson, demanding the acceptance of a broad principle of policy, and the Allies demanding that their interests be served. President Wilson had wished to have the hardest problems, those relating to European conditions, taken up first, because he believed that the danger to the world arose from the unsettled conditions there. But the irresistible temptation, as in all such conferences, was to put off hard questions, assign them to committees, and take up what seemed to be the easy problems first.

The easy problem here seemed to be the disposition of the German colonies. Every one was agreed from the beginning that they should not be returned to Germany. They appeared therefore to be the easy spoils of war : the jackpot of the great game. And one morning, without any introduction, without a word of warning, they prepared to carve them up and distribute them around.

That the plan for the division of the German colonies had all been worked out—and without any reference to the establishment of a new or a general principle—was clear enough when the prime ministers of several of the British colonies came into the Conference on January 24th, quite unexpectedly, and made prepared statements of their claims to the annexation of certain former German territory. Canada made no such demands. Although she had had great losses and made great sacrifices in the war—far greater in proportion than those of the United States—she made no selfish claim whatever for herself. It developed, also, at once, that Japan expected to annex certain colonies, and France certain others: and that possibly Italy and Belgium would have to be permitted more extensive territorial concessions.

It was January 27th before Mr. Wilson got an opportunity to present his idea of a new principle of world colonial policy. He was against annexation: he declared for the development of each colony, not for the advantage of the nation that controlled it, but for that of the people who lived there. He thought the emphasis should be placed upon the welfare of the people, not upon the ownership of the land. The world should act as a trustee for these weak and backward people until the day when the true wishes of the inhabitants could be ascertained. Colonies should be assigned to certain mandatories or trustees who should be under the supervision of the League of Nations. And he wanted the principle to apply not only to German colonies but to all those parts of Turkey which were not to be returned to the Turks.

This at once precipitated a red-hot controversy. Mr. Hughes of Australia, especially, attacked the whole mandatory principle, and was supported less vigorously by the other British colonial premiers. M. Simon, the French Colonial Minister, appeared and made a long statement in support of the idea of frank annexation and set forth the French colonial demands to the Cameroons and Togoland. In this it was clear that he had the support of Clemenceau who called attention to the various secret treaties or "conversations" under which some of the colonies had already been disposed of. Mr. Lloyd George said that he was in favor of the *principle* of the mandatory, but he was also in favor of having the British colonies get what they wanted. They were all in favor of dividing up the colonies first and adopting the principle afterward! It was clear enough, throughout the discussion, that no one of the three except Mr. Wilson, had any real faith in the League of Nations. M. Clemenceau treated both the mandatory system and the League of Nations with finely turned irony which mirrored his entire opposition more clearly than any direct attack could have done. Mr. Wilson was placed in the position of having to defend a new principle the working of which in minute detail no one could prophesy.

Finally Lloyd George held a separate meeting with the delegates of the British dominions, persuaded them to accept the mandatory principle and came in with a set of resolutions providing for its application. This caused further heated discussion, but finally, with certain changes, and after reservations by both France and Japan—for France was determined to have the privilege of raising troops in the colonies for her own defense—it was adopted by the Conference, and the essence of it was later incorporated as Article 22 in the League of Nations Covenant. This is the longest article, but one, and it establishes firmly the contention of the President. It places the control of colonies firmly upon a broad basis of principle. In short, the machinery for a new and liberal policy in world colonial administration is established; it will work or fail to work exactly in proportion to the good will and determination of the governments of the world to make it work—a generalization which is true also regarding the whole League of Nations Covenant.

BY PROF. EDWIN BORCHARD

The operation of the Covenant upon the evils arising out of the monopolistic control of backward areas is embodied in the principle of "mandatories" found in Article 22. The principle constitutes the "mandatory"—properly speaking, mandatary—a trustee for the League of Nations. Its application is limited to the "colonies" and "territories" which "have ceased to be under the sovereignty" of Germany and Turkey, "and which are inhabited by peoples not yet able to stand by themselves under the strenuous conditions of the modern world." The "well-being and development of such peoples form a sacred trust of civilization." Their "tutelage" is "entrusted" to "advanced nations, who, by reason of their resources, their experience or their geographical position, can best undertake this responsibility" as "mandatories on behalf of the league." It is expressly recognized that "the character of the mandate must differ according to the stage of the development of the people, the geographical situation of the territory, its economic conditions, and other similar circumstances"—a difference which is taken into account in outlining briefly the conditions which should apply to the areas formerly under Turkish rule, where the tutelage is to be provisional until "they are able to stand alone"; to areas such as Central Africa, where the beneficent principles of the Berlin Conference of 1885 are directed to be carried out, including "equal opportunities for the trade and commerce of other members of the league," that is, other than the mandatory; and to territories, such as Southwest Africa, which may be administered as "integral portions" of the mandatory state. The mandatory must render to the League an annual report of its trusteeship.

This form of trust administration appears to show a recognition by the Allies that the old rule of dividing outright in fee the territories of a defeated foe is not in conformity with their avowed principles, and in the particular cases before them would probably lead to differences among the victors. It also furnishes us with one of the best conceivable tests of the sincerity and efficacy of a league of nations. The colonial administration thus provided is not a joint administration, such as has been known in Samoa and other places, and has practically always been unsuccessful, but the management of given territory by a single power, under the direction and supervision of the League.

Interesting as the experiment seems, and useful as it may become as a solution of the complicated problem of exploiting monopolies by the great Powers in vassal states and protectorates, it will begin its precarious career under certain disadvantages, namely, the experience of history and the temptations confronting the mandatory state. We have in the past heard the powers speak of their functions as "trustees" of the backward races, and we know the extent to which the "trustee," in violation of all legal principles, has exploited its trust and appropriated all the profits. We know that Bosnia and Herzegovina were once administered by Austria as "mandatory," as was Egypt by Great Britain, and we know that such form of administration was merely the first step leading to ultimate annexation. We know that the

secret treaties assigned various portions of the territories
conquered in this war to different powers, and that in the
early days of the peace negotiations they vigorously asserted
their claims. Should these powers be made the mandatories
of the territories they were to receive under the secret treaties,
we may suspect the purity of the "sacred trust," and wish
particular assurance that trusteeship shall not merge into
ownership.

Again, inasmuch as no provision has been made for the
trustee's compensation, we must be on guard against its
yielding to the temptation of discriminating in commercial
matters in favor of its own nationals. Any such attempt
would fatally compromise the plan. More particularly, the
natural resources of the territory under mandatory administration should not be placed at the disposal of concessionaires
of the trustee state, or of that state itself. Such grants of
concessions, or governmental exploitation, would constitute
merely disguised economic annexations of the territories,
would defeat the altruistic purposes of the new scheme of administration, and would effect a complete reversion to the
evils of monopolistic control of backward areas which now
endanger the world's peaceful development. The evils of
such concessions would not be tempered by the grant of general freedom of commerce and trade, for the monopolistic
concessionaires would doubtless control and direct the bulk
of all the really important trade. In addition, the abuse of
native labor is a constant temptation and danger.

These are some of the more obvious pitfalls in the path
of the disinterested trustee, against which the League must
guard. The public will watch the new experiment with
some misgiving, and the passing of time will not lull its
watchfulness into a false sense of security. Should it prove
successful, it may afford in part a possible solution of the
still unsolved problem of the disposal and utilization of the
vast resources of the backward areas of the world, which, as
we have already seen, are the subject of attempted monopoly
and of intense competitive struggle for control which sooner
or later develops into armed conflict.

The solution of the problem is not easy. Yet until a

solution is found for the existing predatory exploitation, in the interests of particular nations or syndicates, of the resources of backward areas, we are not likely to make much progress toward disarmament or the dissipation of the danger of war. The often suggested solution of "internationalization" finds its difficulties in practical application. Yet the task can, I believe, be performed. Commercial statistics are sufficiently accurate to enable international industrial commissions appointed by the Powers to allocate the raw materials of the world to the manufacturing countries in proportion to their capacity to utilize them. Extortionate prices could be guarded against by some form of price-control. It will be recalled that the International Sugar Convention was inaugurated to prevent the grant of sugar bounties on the part of individual states, by cáusing an automatic tariff wall to be created against sugar produced under bounty. Commissions for the control of raw materials entering into general world consumption would not be impossible to create.

The indefiniteness of the suggestions here offered is an admission of the difficulty of the problem, but not of the hopelessness of a practicable solution. Possibly the era of international coöperation toward which the proposed Covenant endeavors to make a slight advance is still too far distant to present any hope of early realization of the international control of the resources of backward areas; but until that day, no agreements for the pacific settlement of international disputes will avert those economic crises which now lead to war.

BY GUILLAUME MARTIN

Mr. Wilson arrived in France in the month of December convinced that he would find adhesion to, and enthusiastic support for, his ideas. He offered to France an association for the establishment of justice in the world. That adhesion and that support failed him at least in official quarters. Why? Essentially because of the territory of the Saar, which should have been renounced at the beginning as an annexation. Mr. Wilson, in order not to rest isolated, turned to England, and there found the aid desired. France in her turn, menaced by isolation, approached Italy. There was thus created at the Conference that constellation in which the Anglo-Saxon Powers supported by Japan have the majority, with the two Latin Powers facing them.

Italy supported the claims of France. She has on her side historical and strategic rights to put forward, and she seeks auxiliaries. Thus, French policy has been led to defend, against the unanimous sentiment of the French people, the Italian pretensions and the application of the Treaty of London. In this way France is considered as an adversary both in Italy and in Serbia. She receives the imprecations of d'Annunzio. The Italians take to Fiume the French flag, and the Serbians believe themselves betrayed and abandoned.

Even the accord between Italy and France in the bosom of the Conference is not perfect and durable. The Italians lend all their forces to the reunion of Austria with Germany. This reunion is, in fact, inevitable if they obtain the line of the Brenner that French policy tends to concede to them. To obtain the Saar, therefore, France indirectly throws the Austrians into the arms of Germany. To take a number of kilometers from Germany, she gives Germany twenty times more. And it is clear that if Italy seeks to have a common frontier with Germany, it is not with the idea of fighting the Germans.

France presents then the spectacle of a man who lets fall the substance for the shadow. To have the Saar she has renounced the support of President Wilson and her intimacy with England. She pursues a policy of which the ultimate consequences will be to throw into the arms of Germany both Austria and Italy, and prepares for herself a position of isolation in Europe.

There are to-day two systems in opposition. One believes that it is necessary to seek in annexations, in buffer-States, in strategic frontiers, all the guarantees of peace. Twenty centuries of experience are not then sufficient? The other is the principle of justice, of moderation, of collaboration.

THE REPUBLIC CZECHO-SLOVAKIA

THE PEACE CONFERENCE FORMALLY RECOGNIZES THE MOST DEMOCRATIC OF REPUBLICS

JUNE 28, 1919

CZECHO-SLOVAK DECLARATION OF INDEPENDENCE
ALPHONSE DE GUILLERVILLE   PRESIDENT MASARYK
CHARLES PERGLER

Czecho-Slovakia is the name now formally given to the new republic occupying what were formerly the Austro-Hungarian territories of Bohemia, Moldavia and Slovakia. Its people are mainly of the ancient Bohemian or Czech race, a branch of the Slavs; and with the Czechs are associated another Slav race of close kinship, the Slovaks. The Czechs had made themselves famous during the War by their resistance to Teutonic dominance, and had formed Czech armies in many Ally lands, especially the celebrated Czech army which had marched across all Siberia to escape from the Russian Bolshevists.

It was, however, only the Czechs who had escaped from Bohemia who could thus openly defy their Austrian oppressors. These exiles formed a committee at Paris to rouse and unite the Czechs in all countries and ultimately rescue the homeland; and gradually this committee came to be recognized by all the Ally governments as the true government of Bohemia and Slovakia. Head of this remarkable committee, builder of a country from outside, was Professor Thomas Garrigue Masaryk, a champion of freedom already famed before the War. He became the accepted President of the Czecho-Slovakia which as yet existed only in exile. Chief of Masaryk's assistants were two men of a younger generation, Edward Benès the organizer, and Milan Stefanik, a Slovak scholar and soldier. Within Bohemia itself the bold leader of so much of legalized opposition as Austria allowed was Karel (which means Charles) Kramár or Kramarcz.

With the crumbling of Austrian power in 1918 came the opportunity for the Czechs to free themselves at home; but as the movement did not culminate in a general election and the formation of a government by an assembly thus fully and formally representative, there is no exact date which can be set as ending the period of Czecho-Slovak disorganization and reconstruction, as in Poland or Germany. Czecho-Slovakia only assumes its full and positive position as an independent self-governing nation with its recognition by the Peace Treaty of June 28th.

The chief steps toward self-government had been, first, the "Declaration of Independence" published by Masaryk's government in

Paris on October 18, 1918. Then followed the actual taking away of power from the Austrian officials in Prague, Bohemia's capital. This was accomplished on October 28, 1918, under Kramar; and on the next day Prague itself declared its independence. A "National Assembly" was then hastily named by the chief Czecho-Slovak organizations, not elected by the people; and this Assembly met at Prague on November 14th. It adopted a constitution, and confirmed Masaryk's presidency with Kramar as Prime Minister. The exile president reached Prague and was formally installed on December 20, 1918. Masaryk had always been a Democrat with marked Socialistic tendencies, and the government under his control promptly proceeded to make Czecho-Slovakia the most genuinely "radical" or popularistic state in eastern Europe and perhaps in the world.

DECLARATION OF INDEPENDENCE
OF THE CZECHO-SLOVAK NATION

Adopted and proclaimed by the "Provisional Government" of the Czecho-Slovak State at Paris, October 18, 1918

A T this grave moment, when the Hohenzollerns are offering peace in order to stop the victorious advance of the allied armies and to prevent the dismemberment of Austria-Hungary and Turkey, and when the Hapsburgs are promising the federalization of the Empire and autonomy to the dissatisfied nationalities committed to their rule we, the Czecho-Slovak National Council, recognized by the allied and American Governments as the Provisional Government of the Czecho-Slovak State and nation, in complete accord with the declaration of the Czech deputies made in Prague on January 6, 1918, and realizing that federalization and, still more, autonomy, means nothing under a Hapsburg dynasty, do hereby make and declare this our declaration of independence.

We do this because of our belief that no people should be forced to live under a sovereignty they do not recognize and because of our knowledge and firm conviction that our nation cannot freely develop in a Hapsburg mock federation, which is only a new form of denationalizing oppression under which we have suffered for the past 300 years. We consider freedom to be the first prerequisite for federalization, and believe that the free nations of central and eastern Europe may easily federate should they find it necessary.

We make this declaration on the basis of our historic and

natural right. We have been an independent State since the seventh century, and in 1526, as an independent State, consisting of Bohemia, Moravia, and Silesia, we joined with Austria and Hungary in a defensive union against the Turkish danger. We have never voluntarly surrendered our rights as an independent State in this confederation. The Hapsburgs broke their compact with our nation by illegally transgressing our rights and violating the constitution of our State, which they had pledged themselves to uphold, and we therefore refuse longer to remain a part of Austria-Hungary in any form.

We claim the right of Bohemia to be reunited with her Slovak brethren of Slovakia, once a part of our national State, later torn from our national body, and fifty years ago incorporated in the Hungarian State of the Magyars, who, by their unspeakable violence and ruthless oppression of their subject races, have lost all moral and human right to rule anybody but themselves.

The world knows the history of our struggle against the Hapsburg oppression, intensified and systematized by the Austro-Hungarian dualistic compromise of 1867. This dualism is only a shameless organization of brute force and exploitation of the majority by the minority; it is a political conspiracy of the Germans and Magyars against our own as well as the other Slav and the Latin nations of the monarchy. The world knows the justice of our claims, which the Hapsburgs themselves dared not deny. Francis Joseph in the most solemn manner repeatedly recognized the sovereign rights of our nation. The Germans and Magyars opposed this recognition, and Austria-Hungary, bowing before the Pan-Germans, became a colony of Germany and, as her vanguard to the East, provoked the last Balkan conflict, as well as the present world war, which was begun by the Hapsburgs alone without the consent of the representatives of the people.

We cannot and will not continue to live under the direct or indirect rule of the violators of Belgium, France, and Serbia, the would-be murderers of Russia and Rumania, the murderers of tens of thousands of civilians and soldiers of our blood, and the accomplices in numberless unspeakable crimes committed in this war against humanity by the two degenerate and irresponsible dynasties. We will not remain a part of a State which has no justification for existence and which, refusing to accept the fundamental principles of modern world-organization, remains only an artificial and immoral political structure, hindering every movement toward democratic and social progress. The Hapsburg dynasty, weighed down by a huge inheritance of error and crime, is a perpetual menace to the peace of the world, and we deem it our duty toward humanity and civilization to aid in bringing about its downfall and destruction.

We reject the sacrilegious assertion that the power of the Hapsburg and Hohenzollern dynasties is of divine origin; we refuse to recognize the divine right of kings. Our nation elected the Hapsburgs to the throne of Bohemia of its own free will and by the same right deposes them. We hereby declare the Hapsburg dynasty unworthy of leading our nation, and deny all of their claims to rule in the Czecho-Slovak Land, which we here and now declare shall henceforth be a free and independent people and nation.

We accept and shall adhere to the ideals of modern democracy, as they have been the ideals of our nation for centuries. We accept the American principles as laid down by President Wilson; the principles of liberated mankind—of the actual equality of nations—and of governments deriving all their just power from the consent of the governed. We, the nation of Comenius, cannot but accept these principles expressed in the American Declaration of Independence, the principles of Lincoln, and of the declaration of the rights of man and of the citizen. For these principles our nation shed its blood in the memorable Hussite Wars 500 years ago; for these same principles, beside her allies, our nation is shedding its blood to-day in Russia, Italy, and France.

We shall outline only the main principles of the Constitution of the Czecho-Slovak Nation; the final decision as to the constitution itself falls to the legally-chosen representatives of the liberated and united people.

The Czecho-Slovak State shall be a republic. In constant endeavor for progress it will guarantee complete freedom of conscience, religion and science, literature and art, speech, the press, and the right of assembly and petition. The Church shall be separated from the State. Our democracy shall rest on universal suffrage; women shall be placed on an equal footing with men, politically, socially, and culturally. The rights of the minority shall be safeguarded by proportional representation; national minorities shall enjoy equal rights. The government shall be parliamentary in form and shall recognize the principles of initiative and referendum. The standing army will be replaced by militia.

The Czecho-Slovak Nation will carry out far-reaching social and economic reforms; the large estates will be redeemed for home colonization; patents of nobility will be abolished. Our nation will assume its part of the Austro-Hungarian pre-war public debt; the debts of this war we leave to those who incurred them.

In its foreign policy the Czecho-Slovak Nation will accept its full share of responsibility in the reorganization of eastern Europe. It accepts fully the democratic and social principle of nationality and subscribes to the doctrine that all covenants and treaties shall be entered into openly and frankly without secret diplomacy.

Our constitution shall provide an efficient, rational, and just government, which will exclude all special privileges and prohibit class legislation.

Democracy has defeated theocratic autocracy. Militarism is overcome—democracy is victorious; on the basis of democracy mankind will be recognized. The forces of darkness have served the victory of light—the longed-for age of humanity is dawning.

We believe in democracy—we believe in liberty—and liberty evermore.

Given in Paris, on the eighteenth of October, 1918.

Professor Thomas G. Masaryk,
    Prime Minister and Minister of Finance.

General Dr. Milan R. Stefanik,
    Minister of National Defense.

Dr. Edward Benès,
    Minister of Foreign Affairs and of Interior.

BY ALPHONSE DE GUILLERVILLE

Narrative of a French observer in Prague

The revolution that triumphed in Prague on October 28 and 29, 1918, had been carefully prepared for many months before the final coup, awaiting only the signal from the recognized Czech leaders in Entente countries.

Bohemia had tried for three centuries, by all possible means, to regain its liberty, lost at the battle of the White Mountain in 1620. All Czech history is but the relation of the long struggle against the Germanic domination of Austria. In all the Bohemian towns the local associations and school societies were the headquarters of an ardent patriotic propaganda movement. These organizations, persecuted by the Austrian police and military authorities, became secret societies at the beginning of the war, the most famous of which assumed the name of the "Maffia," borrowed from Sicily. The conspirators, following the clever methods of the Carbonari of former times, did not know each other, save for two fellow-workers, with whom each member, respectively, carried on his work. Dr. Szarnal, the chief of the Maffia, who became the Mayor of Prague after the revolution, alone knew all of his fellow-workers.

It was this organization—to which belonged Dr. Benès; M. Stanck, the Minister of Labor in the new Government; Dr. Stefanik, who acted as Minister to Paris, and Dr. Borsky, who became Minister to Rome—which assured the Czech patriots at Prague and Vienna communication with the Czecho-Slovak committee at Paris. Czech women, employees, and even servants, undertook perilous missions, risking life and liberty in order to serve their cause. It should be known also that there were many Czechs in all the Ministries and in all the important administrative branches of the Austrian Government, who stopped at nothing when their cause against the oppressor was called into question.

The "Maffia" had placed a Czech manservant in the home of Count Stürgkh, the President of the Austrian Council, who was assassinated by Fritz Adler. This servant each night gathered up the papers which he found on his master's desk and took them home, where he made copies of them on a typewriter. Women placed these copies in umbrella handles and in that manner forwarded them to Switzerland or to Paris. They came back to Austria with the instructions of the Czecho-Slovak committees. The police arrested many suspected persons, among them President Masaryk's daughter and the wife of Dr. Benès, whom they imprisoned among thieves and prostitutes, but the secret was never discovered.

Thanks to this widespread organization, which was on the alert constantly, the Czechs were always informed of the most secret actions taken at the court and at the General Staff Headquarters. Even the decisions reached by Emperors William and Charles at their last meeting were learned. One of the conspirators, Dr. Rambousek, had discovered an invisible ink, and correspondence was exchanged by means of bulletin reviews, which the censorship permitted to pass, messages being written between the printed lines. In spite of all chemical reactions tried, the mysterious ink remained invisible to the police agents. Just eight days before the revolution the police forbade the sending of books and magazines outside of Austria. This did not prevent Dr. Benès from warning his friends at Prague "to prepare for the revolution."

On October 29th, when Prague was celebrating the triumph of the revolution, one of the members of the "Maffia" brought the last secret message of Dr. Benès to his colleagues: "Do not lose courage; the Czecho-Slovak Government is recognized by the Entente, with Thomas Masaryk as President."

BY PRESIDENT MASARYK

Address on entering Prague as President of the Republic, December 20, 1918

I am too moved to speak. This is the first time in four years that I have been so deeply touched. We know how much worked against us and how many difficulties we had to overcome, but we will find a friendly way out. Dr. Kramar said that you were impatiently waiting my coming. I also was impatiently awaiting the moment when I should come here to continue your work. How many sleepless nights I have passed during these four years! I knew you were oppressed and how hard was your task. You are all heroic and strong with a strength which showed that you were unitedly back of your leaders, though they were exiled. My heart speaks its thanks. I promise that my efforts will continue without wavering.

BY CHARLES PERGLER

Official explanation of the Czecho-Slovak Republic's policies by its official representative, the "Commissioner of the Czecho-Slovak Republic in the United States."

An indication of how thoroughly democratic the new Republic is, is found in the fact that one of the very first acts of the National Assembly was the abolition of all patents of nobility. Thus the new nation, through its duly authorized representatives, with one stroke gave earnest of its intention to do away with everything savoring of medievalism.

Of the economic and social problems one of the most important confronting the new state was that of the large landed estates. You will remember that hesitation to deal with this question was perhaps the fundamental reason why the Russian provisional government was wrecked, and why Bolshevism gained the upper hand. Czecho-Slovak statesmen do not propose to be caught unawares in this fashion. The estates in most cases are those held by alien nobility and the late imperial house. More often than not they came into the hands of these various clans during the carpet-bagging period of the Thirty Years' War, when Bohemia was plundered right and left by the Hapsburgs and their retainers. On April 16, 1919, the National Assembly adopted a law expropriating all large estates exceeding 150 hectares[1] of land under cultivation, or that can be cultivated, and 100 hectares of woodland. Under this law the state will take over 1,300,-000 hectares of cultivated land, and 3,000,000 hectares of woodland, which will furnish livelihood to 430,000 families. In the case of estates of the imperial family, estates illegally acquired, and estates of persons who during the war had been guilty of treason against the Czecho-Slovak nation, no com-

[1] A hectare is a measure of area containing ten thousand square meters, or 2.471 acres.

pensation will be paid. There will be compensation to all those who have not legally forfeited their right to it, or whose possession was not based upon robbery, theft or fraud.

Immediately following the abolition of all patents of nobility and the making private citizens of various princes, dukes and counts, the National Assembly passed a law establishing the eight-hour day. According to latest advices, the National Assembly is about to pass legislation aimed at doing away with unemployment and, in so far as this may not be possible, to alleviate the condition of the unemployed. No doubt ultimately this legislation will include some sort of a scheme of insurance against unemployment, against sickness and accident, and similar features of what is known in Europe as social legislation. The establishment of workingmen's chambers is being contemplated. This should not be confused with Soviet institutions. In Europe chambers of commerce and similar institutions have a legal status, and logically, if there can be chambers of commerce, there is no reason why there should not be workingmen's chambers, which will be the legally authorized representatives and spokesmen of the workingmen, even as the chambers of commerce speak for the manufacturer and the merchant. In the meantime, the government is undertaking emergency public works to reduce the number of unemployed and it has appropriated millions of crowns for these works, particularly in the city of Prague.

Radical as certain features of this legislation may appear to some Americans, considering European standards and the advanced standing of the labor movement in particular, as well as its tremendous influence, it is simply what the times call for, if violent upheavals are to be avoided. After all, we must remember that the laws of social development were not suspended on the day we were born, and that history is also a record of transition from one order to another. The problem for the statesman and the sound thinker is to seek an orderly way, one which can be pursued with the minimum of suffering to society as a whole, and to the individuals composing it. The art of real statesmanship may be said to consist in bringing about new social formations without violence and without bloodshed. This, so far, the Czecho-Slovak Republic has accomplished. It seems to have taken a leaf out of the book of Anglo-Saxon history, as exemplified both in Great Britain and the United States, the most marked feature of which is the fact that in most cases fundamental changes in government and society were accomplished peacefully.

Certainly the methods adopted by the Czecho-Slovaks are diametrically opposed to Bolshevism. The latter, if it has come to stand for anything, means revolutionary changes by violence, by civil war. It stands for the dictatorship of the proletariat, and for the Soviet system of government. There is not a trace of that in the measures I have enumerated. On the contrary, everything is being done in an orderly and legal way; by the parliamentary methods so well known to western democracies and to the United States.

Czecho-Slovak statesmen will be careful to prevent anything resembling militarism from striking roots in the Republic. The Czecho-Slovak army still standing in Siberia is very democratic, as is inevitable from its origin, having been organized voluntarily by the men themselves for the purpose of fighting for the independence of their native land, and against German, Magyar and Prussian militarism. President Masaryk himself is squarely opposed to militarism which means rule by an army clique, and the subordination of civic ideals to those of the military martinet. In a recent public speech in Prague, the President declared that the new nation must have a democratic army based upon free and voluntary discipline and convinced of its mission to defend the country against external enemies. This democratic army will be solely for purposes of defense. Naturally it will be governed by the exigencies of the international situation, and by the fact whether or not an international organization can be achieved which will do away entirely with the necessity of any armies except for purely police purposes.

Woman suffrage is already an accomplished fact in the Republic. Even now eight members of the National Assembly are women, among them Dr. Alice Masaryk, daughter of the president, well known in America. During the war, she was held by the Austrian authorities in jail for a period of nine months.

Under European constitutional practice the power of the president is usually meager indeed. It seems likely, however, that the Czecho-Slovak state will somewhat follow American examples. Thus, in accordance with a recent recommendation of the Constitutional Committee of the National Assembly, the president shall have the right to name and dismiss cabinet ministers, negotiate and ratify international agreements and treaties; shall be present and preside at the meetings of the Council of Ministers, having also the right to make recommendations to the National Assembly in matters of state. This does not mean that parliamentary control will be done away with, and that the president will have anything like autocratic powers. But it does mean that he is to possess a larger freedom of movement and more initiative than a European president usually has.

In mid-Europe no state can be created without certain national minorities, and this is a troublesome problem indeed. There is going to be in the Czecho-Slovak Republic a minority of Germans, not nearly so large as the Germans themselves claim, but still a minority. This fact entitles us to all the sympathy the world can give us, especially when we bear in mind that this is a German minority. This minority is entitled to fair treatment. The Czecho-Slovak delegation at the Peace Conference, in outlining our claims, declared that the new republic will guarantee to national minorities full freedom of development and cultivation of racial individuality.

Dr. Charles Kramar, the Prime Minister of the Czecho-Slovak Republic, in a speech delivered to the National Assembly in Prague on December 20, 1918, said that complete cultural, social and economic freedom will be granted to Bohemian Germans. Dr. Kramar said: "We do not want to be oppressors. We do not want to follow the former German policy in Austria, as we have seen what it leads to. The Germans in Bohemia, with their great economic strength, are shrewd enough calculators not to have any particular desire to be incorporated into Germany. For the Czecho-Slovak Republic the whole world is open. Germany, on the contrary, will be in the worse imaginable position. Even if there were no direct economic boycott, the indirect moral boycott will be far more terrible."

The Czech Social Democrats of Bohemia are certainly not jingoes, and their chief organ, the *Pravo Lidu,* on December 7, 1918, in writing on the question of the German minority, said: "The present German possession in Bohemia is not the result of natural development, but of terror and oppression. In the natural development and a free course, the German possessions in the north of Bohemia would assume quite another aspect. In spite of the terror and oppression and so-called assimilation, we can prove that German Bohemia does not exist, as this territory is everywhere mixed with the Czech population, which in many places forms, as a matter of fact, majorities. According to reliable estimates, there were in 1910 in the district of Most, in northern Bohemia, which the Germans claim, over 40,000 Czechs; in Litvinow, over 30,000; in Duchov, over 35,000; in Bilinia, about 30,000; in Teplice, over 20,000, etc. Since 1910 the development was in favor of the Czechs, so that it may be safely assumed that in many places the Czech minorities have now become majorities."

As regards the attitude of the Germans in Bohemia themselves, it is interesting to quote the German paper *Prager Tagblatt* of December 23, 1918: "Masaryk claims the integrity of Bohemia, but he wants to assure the German minorities not only equal rights, but also full rights of nationalities. This is a new idea. If a really democratic autonomy is introduced, we shall have no reason to complain."

In any event, because the Germans and Magyars oppressed the Czecho-Slovaks, it does not follow that the latter will oppress the former. It is a significant fact that during the whole of the nineteenth century not a single Czech statesman appeared who in any way advocated the oppression of other peoples. On the contrary, the Czechs always emphasized the fact that they would accord their German citizens complete civil rights which, of course, includes cultural rights.

It was the great Czech historian and statesman, Palacky, who said that we never had, nor ever shall have the intention of oppressing other people; that, true to our character, rejecting all desire for the revenge of past wrongs, we extend our right hand to all our neighbors who are prepared to recognize the equality of all nations without regard to their size or political power. And it was Havlicek, the Czech leader in 1848, who said that oppression never brings good results, and in time brings vengeance upon the heads of its own originators.

The new Czecho-Slovak Republic is the greatest experiment in really liberal and progressive government evei undertaken on the European Continent, and it is entitled to the sympathy and aid of the great American democracy.

THE PEACE OF VERSAILLES

GERMANY SIGNS THE TERMS DICTATED BY THE ALLIES

JUNE 28, 1919

HARRY HANSEN   VON BROCKDORFF-RANTZAU
GEORGES CLEMENCEAU   GABRIEL HANOTAUX
KARL KAUTSKY   PAUL ROHRBACH

The long and patient discussions by which the Allies sought to reach among themselves agreement as to just what peace terms they would impose upon Germany and upon one another, reached on May 6th a point where all were in accord, or at least so nearly in accord that they held a final session and agreed upon the terms to be presented to Germany. On the following day this treaty was presented to Count von Brockdorff-Rantzau, leader of the German delegation which had been summoned to receive it. Von Brockdorff refused to agree to the treaty. Instead he and his colleagues formally stated their objections to it in a lengthy protest summarized in the noted letter of their leader, which is given herewith.

To this protest M. Clemenceau responded in similar form, summarizing the position of the Allies in the letter here given, and presenting with it the full Ally reply. In effect the Allies refused to reconsider their treaty as prepared on May 6th. The German delegation thereon returned to Germany, placed the treaty in the hands of their government, and resigned from office. Only after much domestic tumult did the German government finally decide to accept the treaty; and two new representatives were then selected to go to France and sign the hated document.

Because of this delay, the actual signing, the final ceremony, did not take place until June 28th. The place selected for it was the great palace at Versailles, and the room the very "Hall of Mirrors" in which the victorious Germans had triumphed over France in 1871. The scene is here described by an American eye-witness, a special press representative, Harry Hansen. Then, after the formal protest and response of von Brockdorff and Clemenceau, we give the views of the peace from many other angles, less bitter than von Brockdorff's, less approving than Clemenceau's. The great French historian Hanotaux speaks gravely, seriously for his countrymen. A noted Holland editor gives an estimate supposedly neutral though obviously with a Teuton tinge. A noted Teuton socialist, Karl Kautsky, tells how the radical, "new" Teutons looked on it; and the well-known Prussian militarist, Dr. Rohrbach, sums up the peace in what he believes its influence upon the United States.

BY HARRY HANSEN

THE greatest attention had been given to the staging of the culminating event in the Hall of Mirrors. It is a long and narrow room, more like a corridor than a salon. The delegates ascended the marble staircase and passed through what at one time were the apartments of Marie Antoinette to the Salon de la Paix, the Hall of Peace, whence they entered the Hall of Mirrors. At this end of the hall were the chairs for the invited guests. Then came tables for secretaries of certain delegations. Beyond that stood the long horseshoe table that ran along the mirrored side of the hall. At the middle of the table, facing the high embrasured windows, was the place for M. Clemenceau, president of the conference. To his left, in the direction of the Hall of Peace, were reserved places for the delegates of Great Britain, the British dominions, and Japan. Here the angle in the table was reached, and then came the places reserved for Germany. There followed the seats of Uruguay, Peru, Panama, Nicaragua, Liberia, Honduras, Brazil, Haiti, Guatemala, Bolivia, and Equador. At the right hand of the President sat the commissioners from the United States. Then came France, Italy and Belgium. Beyond the turn of the table came the places of Greece, Poland, China, Cuba, Rumania, Hedjaz, Siam, Serbia, and Czecho-Slovakia. Behind this table were tables for secretaries, and behind them, extending toward the Hall of War, came seats for the representatives of the press of the world. Inside the horseshoe table were smaller tables for secretaries, and a small one before the chairman's place was reserved for the interpreter. In the middle stood the table on which lay the treaty of peace and three other documents to be signed simultaneously with it; the protocol, to be signed also by all the delegates; the Rhine province agreement, to be signed by the five great powers and Germany; and the Polish treaty, to be signed by the five great powers, Poland, and Germany.

On the day before the ceremony Herr von Haniel sent word to the Peace Conference that the German delegates had received no formal assurance that the document they were to sign in the Hall of Mirrors was identical with the treaty handed them on June 19th. M. Clemenceau immediately drafted a letter assuring them formally that the document was identical in all its parts, and this was carried to the Germans by M. Dutasta, general secretary of the conference.

Singularly, the places reserved for the delegation from China were not to be occupied. This was the one rift in the lute, for the Chinese commissioners, in protest against the clauses of the treaty agreeing to the transfer of the German leaseholds to Japan, decided not to sign the treaty. A month before the Chinese plenipotentiaries had made a formal request of the Peace Conference that the questions involved in the Shantung matter be not included in the treaty, but be postponed for future consideration. This request was denied. On the morning of June 28th M. Lou Tseng Tsiang, president of the Chinese delegation, asked that China be permitted to sign with the explanatory note, "Under the reservation made at the plenary session of May 6, 1919, and relative to the question of Shantung (Articles 156, 157, and 158)." He pointed out that the Swedish plenipotentiary signed the act of the Congress of Vienna with a reservation. The request was not acceded to by the conference, and when the time for signature came, the Chinese did not respond. The attitude of the Chinese delegation in this matter was consistent with its point of view that Japan should have been asked by the Peace Conference to vacate Shantung and turn all German property over to China.

There was to be only one official treaty of peace, printed on Japanese vellum, with a large margin and held together by red tape. This copy was to be placed in the archives of the Ministry of Foreign Affairs of France, and a copy given to all the governments concerned in its signing. In order to expedite the signing, which at the best speed possible would take nearly an hour, the seals of the commissioners, which were considered necessary, had been placed on the document before the signing. These were the personal seals of the signatories, for these men signed in person and not as officials of their governments. For this reason it was not considered proper for President Wilson to use the seal that had been selected for him, one bearing the American eagle and the words, "The President of the United States of America." President Wilson thereupon substituted a seal from a ring given him at the time of his marriage by the State of California, which bore his name in stenographic characters. Some of the commissioners did not possess personal seals, but obtained them before they were needed.

When the time came for opening the historic session, the long hall was crowded with delegates, visitors, and newspaper representatives. The commissioners had put in almost an hour passing from table to table to seek autographs of men as notable as themselves. The guests bobbed up and down in their chairs, trying to observe the great men of the conference. A score of *Gardes Municipaux* circulated among the crowd for a very good reason: they were instructed to keep a watch on the pens and ink-wells in the hall, and to prevent these articles being pilfered by souvenir-hunters.

At about 2.30 o'clock M. Clemenceau entered the room and looked about him to see that all arrangements were in perfect order. He observed a group of wounded, with their medals of valor on their breasts, in the embrasure of a window, and, walking up to them, engaged them in conversation. At 2.45 o'clock he moved up to the middle table and took the seat of the presiding officer. It was a singular fact that he sat almost immediately under the ceiling decoration that bears the legend *"Le roi gouverne par lui-même,"* in other words, almost on the exact spot where William I. of Prussia stood when he was proclaimed German Emperor in 1871. President Wilson entered almost immediately after M. Clemenceau and was saluted with discreet applause. The German delegation entered by way of the Hall of Peace and slipped almost unnoticed into its seats at this end of the hall. It was led by Herr Müller, a tall man with a scrubby little mustache, wearing black, with a short black tie over his white shirt front. The Germans bowed and seated themselves.

At 3.15 o'clock M. Clemenceau rose and announced

briefly that the session was opened—*"La séance est ouverte."*
He then spoke briefly in French as follows:

"An agreement has been reached upon the conditions of
the treaty of peace between the allied and associated powers
and the German empire.

"The text has been verified; the president of the conference has certified in writing that the text about to be signed
conforms to the text of the 200 copies which have been
sent to Messieurs the German delegates.

"The signatures about to be given constitute an irrevocable
engagement to carry out loyally and faithfully in their entirety all the conditions that have been decided upon.

"I therefore have the honor of asking Messieurs the German plenipotentiaries to approach to affix their signatures to
the treaty before me."

M. Clemenceau ceased and sat down, and Herr Müller
rose as if to proceed to the table. He was interrupted, however, by Lieutenant Mantoux, official interpreter of the conference, who began to translate M. Clemenceau's words into
German. In his first sentence, when Lieutenant Mantoux
reached the words "the German empire," or, as M. Clemenceau had said in French: *"l'empire allemand,"* he translated
it "the German republic." M. Clemenceau promptly whis-
pered, "Say German *Reich,"* this being the term consistently
used by the Germans.

M. Dutasta then led the way for five Germans—two
plenipotentiaries and three secretaries—and they passed to
the table, where two of them signed their names. Müller
came first, and then Bell, virtually unknown men, performing
the final act of abasement and submission for the German
people—an act to which they had been condemned by the
arrogance and pride of Prussian Junkers, German militarists,
imperialists, and industrial barons, not one of whom was
present when this great scene was enacted.

The delegation from the United States was the first to
be called up after the Germans. President Wilson rose, and
as he began his walk to the historic table, followed in order
by Secretary Lansing, Colonel House, General Bliss, and
Mr. White, other delegates stretched out their hands to con-

gratulate him. He came forward with a broad smile, and signed his name at the spot indicated by M. William Martin, director of the protocol. Mr. Lloyd George followed the American delegation, together with Mr. Balfour, Lord Milner, Mr. Bonar Law, and Mr. Barnes; and when these five men had signed, the delegates from the British dominions followed, a notable array of men representing the greatest power the world has ever seen. Then came the delegation of the French Republic, in order, Messieurs Clemenceau, Pichon, Klotz, Tardieu, and Cambon, the president of the council signing his name without seating himself. Then came the delegations of Italy, Japan, and Belgium. At 3.50 o'clock all signatures had been completed, and the president of the conference announced:

"Messieurs, all the signatures have been given. The signature of the conditions of peace between the Allied and Associated powers and the German Republic is an accomplished fact. The session is adjourned."

The official protocol verifies the fact that M. Clemenceau used the word "republic" in his final statement.

Immediately afterward the great guns began to boom from the battery near the *orangerie*. The delegates rose and congratulated one another. The notables streamed out of the palace to join the crowd, which had begun shouting in wild enthusiasm with the first sound of the guns. The great fountains of the park were turned on, and the water marvels of Lenôtre began to play in the mellow sunshine throughout one of the most impressive playgrounds of the world.

The Germans were the first to leave the Hall of Mirrors, passing out alone, and immediately taking their automobiles for the hotel. A short time later M. Clemenceau invited President Wilson and Mr. Lloyd George to view the fountains with him. The moment that the three men appeared before the crowd a great wave of wildly cheering humanity rushed toward them. They locked arms, and preceded by a protecting guard of soldiers and attendants attempted to gain the terrace above the fountain of Latona, in order to look over the broad expanse of the *tapis vert* to the vista of canals and woods beyond. Even here the crowd pushed forward; men slapped them on the back in their exuberance, strangers shouted hoarse greetings into their ears, and it was a most fortunate and remarkable fact that they returned to the palace in safety. They then went to the salon of the old senate, where they met Baron Sonnino and later Baron Makino, and indulged in the beverage of the conference—tea.

After signing the treaty of peace the German plenipotentiaries gave the following statement to the United Press:

"We have signed the treaty without any mental reservation. What we have signed we will carry out. The German people will compel those in power to hold to and conform to the clauses. But we believe that the Entente in its own interest will consider it necessary to modify some articles when it becomes aware that the execution of these articles is impossible.

"We believe that the Entente will not insist upon the delivery of the Kaiser and upon that of the high officers.

"The central government has not aided any attack against Poland. Germany will make every effort to prove that she is worthy of entering the League of Nations."

For the rest of that day and night Versailles and Paris, throwing aside *"le calme et la dignité,"* gave themselves up to a delirium of joy, a revel that came as the logical reaction to five years of pent-up grief and suffering.

BY COUNT VON BROCKDORFF-RANTZAU

Letter to M. Clemenceau as President of Peace Conference, delivered as introducing and summarizing the German Delegation's objections to the terms offered them and making counter-proposals.

Mr. President: I have the honor to transmit to you herewith the observations of the German delegation on the draft treaty of peace. We came to Versailles in the expectation of receiving a peace proposal based on the agreed principles. We were firmly resolved to do everything in our power with a view of fulfilling the grave obligations which we had undertaken. We hoped for the peace of justice which had been promised to us. We were aghast when we read in documents the demands made upon us, the victorious violence of our enemies. The more deeply we penetrate into the spirit of this treaty, the more convinced we become of the impossibility of carrying it out. The exactions of this treaty are more than the German people can bear.

With a view to the reëstablishment of the Polish State we must renounce indisputably German territory—nearly the whole of the Province of West Prussia, which is preponderantly German; of Pomerania; Danzig, which is German to the core; we must let that ancient Hanse town be transformed into a free State under Polish suzerainty. We must agree that East Prussia shall be amputated from the body of the State, condemned to a lingering death, and robbed of its northern portion, including Memel, which is purely German. We must renounce Upper Silesia for the benefit of Poland and Czecho-Slovakia, although it has been in close political connection with Germany for more than 750 years, is instinct with German life, and forms the very foundation of industrial life throughout East Germany.

Preponderantly German circles (*Kreise*) must be ceded to Belgium, without sufficient guarantees that the plebiscite, which is only to take place afterward, will be independent. The purely German district of the Saar must be detached from our empire, and the way must be paved for its subsequent annexation to France, although we owe her debts in coal only, not in men.

For fifteen years Rhenish territory must be occupied, and after those fifteen years the Allies have power to refuse the restoration of the country; in the interval the Allies can take every measure to sever the economic and moral links with the mother country, and finally to misrepresent the wishes of the indigenous population.

Although the exaction of the cost of the war has been expressly renounced, yet Germany, thus cut in pieces and weakened, must declare herself ready in principle to bear all the war expenses of her enemies, which would exceed many times over the total amount of German State and private assets.

Meanwhile her enemies demand, in excess of the agreed conditions, reparation for damage suffered by their civil population, and in this connection Germany must also go bail for her allies. The sum to be paid is to be fixed by our enemies unilaterally, and to admit of subsequent modification and increase. No limit is fixed, save the capacity of the German people for payment, determined not by their standard of life, but solely by their capacity to meet the demands of their enemies by their labor. The German people would thus be condemned to perpetual slave labor.

In spite of the exorbitant demands, the reconstruction of our economic life is at the same time rendered impossible. We must surrender our merchant fleet. We are to renounce all foreign securities. We are to hand over to our enemies our property in all German enterprises abroad, even in the countries of our allies. Even after the conclusion of peace the enemy States are to have the right of confiscating all German property. No German trader in their countries will be protected from these war measures. We must completely renounce our colonies, and not even German missionaries shall have the right to follow their calling therein. We must thus renounce the realization of all our aims in the spheres of politics, economics, and ideas.

Even in internal affairs we are to give up the right to self-determination. The international Reparation Commission receives dictatorial powers over the whole life of our people in economic and cultural matters. Its authority extends far beyond that which the empire, the German Federal Council, and the Reichstag combined ever possessed within the territory of the empire. This commission has unlimited control over the economic life of the State, of communities, and of individuals. Further, the entire educational and sanitary system depends on it. It can keep the whole German people in mental thraldom. In order to increase the payments due, by the thrall, the commission can hamper measures for the social protection of the German worker.

In other spheres also Germany's sovereignty is abolished. Her chief waterways are subjected to international administration; she must construct in her territory such canals and such railways as her enemies wish; she must agree to treaties the contents of which are unknown to her, to be concluded

by her enemies with the new States on the east, even when
they concern her own functions. The German people, if
excluded from the League of Nations, to which is intrusted
all work of common interest to the world.

Thus must a whole people sign the decree for its own
proscription, nay, its own death sentence.

Germany knows that she must make sacrifices in order
to attain peace. Germany knows that she has, by agreement,
undertaken to make these sacrifices, and will go in this matter to the utmost limits of her capacity.

Counter-proposals

1. Germany offers to proceed with her own disarmament in advance of all other peoples, in order to show that
she will help to usher in the new era of the peace of justice.
She gives up universal compulsory service and reduces her
army to 100,000 men, except as regards temporary measures. She even renounces the warships which her enemies
are still willing to leave in her hands. She stipulates, however, that she shall be admitted forthwith as a State with
equal rights into the League of Nations. She stipulates that
a genuine League of Nations shall come into being, embracing all peoples of good-will, even her enemies of to-day.
The League must be inspired by a feeling of responsibility
toward mankind and have at its disposal a power to enforce
its will sufficiently strong and trusty to protect the frontiers
of its members.

2. In territorial questions Germany takes up her position unreservedly on the ground of the Wilson program.
She renounces her sovereign right in Alsace-Lorraine, but
wishes a free plebiscite to take place there. She gives up
the greater part of the province of Posen, the district in-
contestably Polish in population, together with the capital.
She is prepared to grant to Poland, under international guarantees, free and secure access to the sea by ceding free ports
at Danzig, Königsberg, and Memel, by an agreement regu-
lating the navigation of the Vistula and by special railway
conventions. Germany is prepared to insure the supply of
coal for the economic needs of France, especially from the

Saar region, until such time as the French mines are once more in working order. The preponderantly Danish districts of Schleswig will be given up to Denmark on the basis of a plebiscite. Germany demands that the right of self-determination shall also be respected where the interests of the Germans in Austria and Bohemia are concerned.

She is ready to subject all her colonies to administration by the community of the League of Nations, if she is recognized as its mandatory.

3. Germany is prepared to make payments incumbent on her in accordance with the agreed program of peace up to a maximum sum of 100,000,000,000 gold marks, 20,000,-000,000 by May 1, 1926, and the balance (80,000,000,000) in annual payments, without interest. These payments shall in principle be equal to a fixed percentage of the German Imperial and State revenues. The annual payment shall approximate to the former peace budget. For the first ten years the annual payments shall not exceed 1,000,000,000 gold marks a year. The German taxpayer shall not be less heavily burdened than the taxpayer of the most heavily burdened State among those represented on the Reparation Commission.

Germany presumes in this connection that she will not have to make any territorial sacrifices beyond those mentioned above and that she will recover her freedom of economic movement at home and abroad.

4. Germany is prepared to devote her entire economic strength to the service of the reconstruction. She wishes to coöperate effectively in the reconstruction of the devastated regions of Belgium and Northern France. To make good the loss in production of the destroyed mines of Northern France, up to 20,000,000 tons of coal will be delivered annually for the first five years, and up to 80,000,000 tons for the next five years. Germany will facilitate further deliveries of coal to France, Belgium, Italy, and Luxemburg.

Germany is, moreover, prepared to make considerable deliveries of benzol, coal tar, and sulphate of ammonia, as well as dyestuffs and medicines.

5. Finally, Germany offers to put her entire merchant

tonnage into a pool of the world's shipping, to place at the disposal of her enemies a part of her freight space as part payment of reparation and to build for them for a series of years in German yards an amount of tonnage exceeding their demands.

6.   In order to replace the river boats destroyed in Belgium and Northern France, Germany offers river craft from her own resources.

7.   Germany thinks that she sees an appropriate method for the prompt fulfillment of her obligation to make reparations conceding participation in coal mines to insure deliveries of coal.

8.   Germany, in accordance with the desires of the workers of the whole world, wishes to insure to them free and equal rights.   She wishes to insure to them in the Treaty of Peace the right to take their own decisive part in the settlement of social policy and social protection.

9.   The German delegation again makes its demand for a neutral inquiry into the responsibility for the war and culpable acts in conduct.   An impartial commission should have the right to investigate on its own responsibility the archives of all the belligerent countries and all the persons who took an important part in the war.

Nothing short of confidence that the question of guilt will be examined dispassionately can leave the peoples lately at war with each other in the proper frame of mind for the formation of the League of Nations.

These are only the most important among the proposals which we have to make.   As regards other great sacrifices, and also as regards the details, the delegation refers to the accompanying memorandum and the annex thereto.

The time allowed us for the preparation of this memorandum was so short that it was impossible to treat all the questions exhaustively.   A fruitful and illuminating negotiation could only take place by means of oral discussion.   This treaty of peace is to be the greatest achievement of its kind in all history.   There is no precedent for the conduct of such comprehensive negotiations by an exchange of written notes only.   The feeling of the peoples who have made such immense sacrifices makes them demand that their fate should be decided by an open, unreserved exchange of ideas on the principle: "Quite open convenants of peace openly arrived at, after which there shall be no private international understandings of any kind, but diplomacy shall proceed always frankly in the public view."

Germany is to put her signature to the treaty laid before her and to carry it out. Even in her need, justice for her is too sacred a thing to allow her to stoop to achieve conditions which she cannot undertake to carry out. Treaties of peace signed by the great powers have, it is true, in the history of the last decades, again and again proclaimed the right of the stronger. But each of these treaties of peace has been a factor in originating and prolonging the world war. Whenever in this war the victor has spoken to the vanquished, at Brest-Litovsk and Bucharest, his words were but the seeds of future discord. The lofty aims which our adversaries first set before themselves in their conduct of the war, the new era of an assured peace of justice, demand a treaty instinct with a different spirit. Only the coöperation of all nations, a coöperation of hands and spirits, can build up a durable peace. We are under no delusions regarding the strength of the hatred and bitterness which this war has engendered, and yet the forces which are at work for a union of mankind are stronger now than ever they were before. The historic task of the Peace Conference of Versailles is to bring about this union.

Accept, Mr. President, the expression of my distinguished consideration.

BROCKDORFF-RANTZAU.

BY GEORGES CLEMENCEAU

Letter to the President of the German Delegation covering the Reply of the Allied and Associated Powers

Sir:

The Allied and Associated Powers have given the most earnest consideration to the observations of the German Delegation on the conditions of peace. The reply protests against the peace, both on the ground that it conflicts with the terms upon which the armistice of November 11, 1918,

was signed, and that it is a peace of violence and not of justice.
The protest of the German Delegation shows that they utterly
fail to understand the position in which Germany stands
to-day. They seem to think that Germany has only to "make
sacrifices in order to attain peace," as if this were but the
end of some mere struggle for territory and power.

I

The Allied and Associated Powers therefore feel it necessary to begin their reply by a clear statement of the judgment passed upon the war by practically the whole of civilized mankind.

In the view of the Allied and Associated Powers the
war which began on August 1, 1914, was the greatest crime
against humanity and the freedom of peoples that any nation,
calling itself civilized, has ever consciously committed. For
many years the rulers of Germany, true to the Prussian tradition, strove for a position of dominance in Europe. They
were not satisfied with that growing prosperity and influence
to which Germany was entitled, and which all other nations
were willing to accord her, in the society of free and equal
peoples. They required that they should be able to dictate
and tyrannize to a subservient Europe, as they dictated and
tyrannized over a subservient Germany.

In order to attain their ends they used every channel in
their power through which to educate their own subjects in
the doctrine that might was right in international affairs.
They never ceased to expand German armaments by land and
sea, and to propagate the falsehood that this was necessary
because Germany's neighbors were jealous of her prosperity
and power. They sought to sow hostility and suspicion instead of friendship between nations. They developed a system of espionage and intrigue which enabled them to stir
up internal rebellion and unrest and even to make secret
offensive preparations within the territory of their neighbors
whereby they might, when the moment came, strike them
down with greater certainty and ease. They kept Europe
in a ferment by threats of violence, and when they found
that their neighbors were resolved to resist their arrogant

will they determined to assist their predominance in Europe by force.

As soon as their preparations were complete, they encouraged a subservient ally to declare war against Serbia at forty-eight hours' notice, knowing full well that a conflict involving the control of the Balkans could not be localized and almost certainly meant a general war. In order to make doubly sure, they refused every attempt at conciliation and conference until it was too late, and the world war was inevitable for which they had plotted, and for which alone among the nations they were fully equipped and prepared.

Germany's responsibility, however, is not confined to having planned and started the war. She is no less responsible for the savage and inhuman manner in which it was conducted.

Though Germany was herself a guarantor of Belgium, the ruler of Germany violated, after a solemn promise to respect it, the neutrality of this unoffending people. Not content with this, they deliberately carried out a series of promiscuous shootings and burnings with the sole object of terrifying the inhabitants into submission by the very frightfulness of their action. They were the first to use poisonous gas, notwithstanding the appalling suffering it entailed. They began the bombing and long distance shelling of towns for no military object, but solely for the purpose of reducing the morale of their opponents by striking at their women and children. They commenced the submarine campaign with its piratical challenge to international law, and its destruction of great numbers of innocent passengers and sailors, in mid-ocean, far from succor, at the mercy of the winds and the waves, and the yet more ruthless submarine crews. They drove thousands of men and women and children with brutal savagery into slavery in foreign lands. They allowed barbarities to be practiced against their prisoners of war from which the most uncivilized peoples would have recoiled.

The conduct of Germany is almost unexampled in human history. The terrible responsibility which lies at her doors can be seen in the fact that not less than seven million dead lie buried in Europe, while more than twenty million others carry upon them the evidence of wounds and sufferings, because Germany saw fit to gratify her lust for tyranny by resort to war.

The Allied and Associated Powers believe that they will be false to those who have given their all to save the freedom of the world if they consent to treat this war on any other basis than as a crime against humanity and right.

This attitude of the Allied and Associated Powers was made perfectly clear to Germany during the war by their principal statesmen. It was defined by President Wilson in his speech of April 6, 1918, and explicitly and categorically accepted by the German people as a principle governing the peace:

"Let everything that we say, my fellow countrymen, everything that we henceforth plan and accomplish, ring true to this response till the majesty and might of our concerted power shall fill the thought and utterly defeat the force of those who flout and misprize what we honor and hold dear. Germany has once more said that force, and force alone, shall decide whether justice and peace shall reign in the affairs of men, whether Right as America conceives it or Dominion as she conceives it shall determine the destinies of mankind. There is, therefore, but one response possible from us: Force, Force to the utmost, Force without stint or limit, righteous and triumphant Force which shall make Right the law of the world, and cast every selfish dominion down in the dust."

It was set forth clearly in a speech of the Prime Minister of Great Britain, of December 14, 1917:

"There is no security in any land without certainty of punishment. There is no protection for life, property, or money in a state where the criminal is more powerful than the law. The law of nations is no exception, and until it has been vindicated, the peace of the world will always be at the mercy of any nation whose professors have assiduously taught it to believe that no crime is wrong so long as it leads to the aggrandizement and enrichment of the country to which they owe allegiance. There have been

many times in the history of the world criminal states. We
are dealing with one of them now. And there will always
be criminal states until the reward of international crime
becomes too precarious to make it profitable, and the punishment of international crime becomes too sure to make it
attractive."

It was made clear also in an address of M. Clemenceau of
September, 1918:

"What do they (the French soldiers) want? What do
we ourselves want? To fight, to fight victoriously and unceasingly, until the hour when the enemy shall understand
that no compromise is possible between such crime and
'justice.' . . . We only seek peace, and we wish to make it
just and permanent in order that future generations may be
saved from the abominations of the past."

Similarly, Signor Orlando, speaking on October 3, 1918,
declared:

"We shall obtain peace when our enemies recognize that
humanity has the right and duty to safeguard itself against
a continuation of such causes as have brought about this terrible slaughter; and that the blood of millions of men calls
not for vengeance but for the realization of those high ideals
for which it has been so generously shed. Nobody thinks
of employing—even by way of legitimate retaliation—methods of brutal violence or of overbearing domination or of
suffocation of the freedom of any people—methods and
policies which made the whole world rise against the Central
Powers. But nobody will contend that the moral order can
be restored simply because he who fails in his iniquitous
endeavor declares that he has renounced his aim. Questions
intimately affecting the peaceful life of nations, once raised,
must obtain the solution which justice requires."

Justice, therefore, is the only possible basis for the settlement of the accounts of this terrible war. Justice is what
the German Delegation asks for and say that Germany had
been promised. Justice is what Germany shall have. But
it must be justice for all. There must be justice for the dead
and wounded and for those who have been orphaned and
bereaved that Europe might be freed from Prussian despot-

ism. There must be justice for the peoples who now stagger under war debts which exceed £30,000,000,000 that liberty might be saved. There must be justice for those millions whose homes and lands, ships and property German savagery has spoliated and destroyed.

That is why the Allied and Associated Powers have insisted as a cardinal feature of the treaty that Germany must undertake to make reparation to the very uttermost of her power; for reparation for wrongs inflicted is of the essence of justice. That is why they insist that those individuals who are most clearly responsible for German aggression and for those acts of barbarism and inhumanity which have disgraced the German conduct of the war, must be handed over to a justice which has not been meted out to them at home. That, too, is why Germany must submit for a few years to certain special disabilities and arrangements. Germany has ruined the industries, the mines, and the machinery of neighboring countries, not during battle, but with the deliberate and calculated purpose of enabling her industries to seize their markets before their industries could recover from the devastation thus wantonly inflicted upon them. Germany has despoiled her neighbors of everything she could make use of or carry away. Germany has destroyed the shipping of all nations on the high seas, where there was no chance of rescue for their passengers and crews. It is only justice that restitution should be made and that these wronged peoples should be safeguarded for a time from the competition of a nation whose industries are intact and have even been fortified by machinery stolen from occupied territories. If these things are hardships for Germany, they are hardships which Germany has brought upon herself. Somebody must suffer for the consequences of the war. Is it to be Germany, or only the peoples she has wronged?

Not to do justice to all concerned would only leave the world open to fresh calamities. If the German people themselves, or any other nation, are to be deterred from following the footsteps of Prussia, if mankind is to be lifted out of the belief that war for selfish ends is legitimate to any state, if the old era is to be left behind and nations as well as indi-

viduals are to be brought beneath the reign of law, even if
there is to be early reconciliation and appeasement, it will
be because those responsible for concluding the war have had
the courage to see that justice is not deflected for the sake
of convenient peace.

It is said that the German Revolution ought to make a difference and that the German people are not responsible for
the policy of the rulers whom they have thrown from power.

The Allied and Associated Powers recognize and welcome the change. It represents a great hope for peace, and
for a new European order in the future. But it cannot affect
the settlement of the war itself. The German Revolution
was stayed until the German armies had been defeated in the
field, and all hope of profiting by the war of conquest had
vanished. Throughout the war, as before the war, the German people and their representatives supported the war, voted
the credits, subscribed to the war loans, obeyed every order,
however savage, of their government. They shared the responsibility for the policy of their government, for at any
moment, had they willed it, they could have reversed it. Had
that policy succeeded they would have acclaimed it with the
same enthusiasm with which they welcomed the outbreak of
the war. They cannot now pretend, having changed their
rulers after the war was lost, that it is justice that they should
escape the consequences of their deeds.

II

The Allied and Associated Powers therefore believe that
the peace they have proposed is fundamentally a peace of justice. They are no less certain that it is a peace of right fulfilling the terms agreed upon at the time of the armistice. There
can be no doubt as to the intentions of the Allied and Associated Powers to base the settlement of Europe on the principle
of freeing oppressed peoples, and re-drawing national boundaries as far as possible in accordance with the will of the peoples concerned, while giving to each facilities for living an
independent national and economic life. These intentions were
made clear, not only in President Wilson's address to Congress of January 8, 1918, but in "the principles of settlement

enunciated in his subsequent addresses" which were the agreed basis of the peace. A memorandum on this point is attached to this letter.

Accordingly the Allied and Associated Powers have provided for the reconstitution of Poland as an independent state with "free and secure access to the sea." All "territories inhabited by indubitably Polish populations" have been accorded to Poland. All territory inhabited by German majorities, save for a few isolated towns and for colonies established on land recently forcibly expropriated and situated in the midst of indubitably Polish territory, has been left to Germany. Wherever the will of the people is in doubt a plebiscite has been provided for. The town of Danzig is to be constituted a free city, so that the inhabitants will be autonomous and not come under Polish rule and will form no part of the Polish state. Poland will be given certain economic rights in Danzig and the city itself has been severed from Germany because in no other way was it possible to provide for that "free and secure access to the sea" which Germany has promised to concede.

The German counter-proposals entirely conflict with the agreed basis of peace. They provide that great majorities of indisputably Polish population shall be kept under German rule.

They deny secure access to the sea to a nation of over twenty million people, whose nationals are in the majority all the way to the coast, in order to maintain territorial connection between East and West Prussia, whose trade has always been mainly sea-borne. They cannot, therefore, be accepted by the Allied and Associated Powers. At the same time, in certain cases the German note has established a case for rectification, which will be made; and in view of the contention that Upper Silesia, though inhabited by a two to one majority of Poles (1,250,000 to 650,000, 1910 German census), wishes to remain a part of Germany, they are willing that the question of whether Upper Silesia should form part of Germany or of Poland should be determined by the vote of the inhabitants themselves.

In regard to the Saar basin, the régime proposed by the Allied and Associated Powers is to continue for fifteen years. This arrangement they considered necessary both to the general scheme for reparation, and in order that France may have immediate and certain compensation for the wanton destruction of her northern coal mines. The district has been transferred not to French sovereignty, but to the control of the League of Nations. This method has the double advantage that it involves no annexation, while it gives possession of the coal field to France and maintains the economic unity of the district, so important to the interests of the inhabitants. At the end of fifteen years the mixed population, who in the meanwhile will have had control of its own local affairs under the governing supervision of the League of Nations, will have complete freedom to decide whether they wish union with Germany, union with France, or the continuance of the régime established by the treaty.

As to the territories which it is proposed to transfer from Germany to Denmark and Belgium, some of these were forcibly seized by Prussia, and in every case the transfer will only take place as the result of a decision of the inhabitants themselves, taken under conditions which will insure complete freedom to vote.

Finally, the Allied and Associated Powers are satisfied that the native inhabitants of the German colonies are strongly opposed to being again brought under Germany's sway, and the record of German rule, the traditions of the German Government and the use to which these colonies were put as bases from which to prey upon the commerce of the world, make it impossible for the Allied and Associated Powers to return them to Germany, or to entrust to her the responsibility for the training and education of their inhabitants.

For these reasons, the Allied and Associated Powers are satisfied that their territorial proposals are in accord both with the agreed basis of peace and are necessary to the future peace of Europe. They are therefore not prepared to modify them except as indicated.

III

Arising out of the territorial settlement are the proposals in regard to international control of rivers. It is clearly in accord with the agreed basis of the peace and the established public law of Europe that inland states should have secure access to the sea along navigable rivers flowing through their territory. The Allied and Associated Powers believe that the arrangements which they propose are vital to the free life of the new inland states that are being established and that they are no derogation from the rights of the other riparian states. If viewed according to the discredited doctrine that every state is engaged in a desperate struggle for ascendancy over its neighbors, no doubt such arrangement may be an impediment to the artificial strangling of a rival. But if it be the ideal that nations are to coöperate in the ways of commerce and peace, it is natural and right. The provisions for the presence of representatives of non-riparian states on these river commissions is security that the general interest will be considered. In the application of these principles, some modifications have however been made in the original proposals.

IV

The German Delegation appear to have seriously misinterpreted the economic and financial conditions. There is no intention on the part of the Allied and Associated Powers to strangle Germany or to prevent her from taking her proper place in international trade and commerce. Provided that she abides by the treaty of peace and provided also that she abandons those aggressive and exclusive traditions which have been apparent no less in her business than in her political methods, the Allied and Associated Powers intend that Germany shall have fair treatment in the purchase of raw materials and the sale of goods, subject to those temporary provisions already mentioned in the interests of the nations ravaged and weakened by German action. It is their desire that the passions engendered by the war should die as soon as possible, and that all nations should share in the prosperity which comes from the honest supply of their mutual needs. They wish that Germany shall enjoy this prosperity like the rest, though much of the fruit of it must necessarily go, for many years to come, in making reparation to her neighbors for the damage she has done. In order to make their intention clear, a number of modifications have been made in the financial and economic clauses of the treaty. But the principles upon which the treaty is drawn must stand.

V

The German Delegation have greatly misinterpreted the reparation proposals of the treaty.

These proposals confine the amount payable by Germany to what is clearly justifiable under the terms of armistice in respect of damage caused to the civilian population of the Allies by German aggression. They do not provide for that interference in the internal life of Germany by the Reparation Commission which is alleged.

They are designed to make the payment of that reparation which Germany must pay as easy and convenient to both parties as possible and they will be interpreted in that sense. The Allied and Associated Powers therefore are not prepared to modify them.

But they recognize with the German Delegation the advantage of arriving as soon as possible at the fixed and definite sum which shall be payable by Germany and accepted by the Allies. It is not possible to fix this sum to-day, for the extent of damage and the cost of repair have not yet been ascertained. They are therefore willing to accord to Germany all necessary and reasonable facilities to enable her to survey the devastated and damaged regions, and to make proposals thereafter within four months of the signing of the treaty for a settlement of the claims under each of the categories of damage for which she is liable. If, within the following two months, an agreement can be reached, the exact liability of Germany will have been ascertained. If agreement has not been reached by then, the arrangement as provided in the treaty will be executed.

VI

The Allied and Associated Powers have given careful consideration to the request of the German Delegation that Germany should at once be admitted to the League of Nations. They find themselves unable to accede to this request.

The German Revolution was postponed to the last moments of the war and there is as yet no guarantee that it represents a permanent change.

In the present temper of international feeling, it is impossible to expect the free nations of the world to sit down immediately in equal association with those by whom they have been so grievously wronged. To attempt this too soon would delay and not hasten that process of appeasement which all desire.

But the Allied and Associated Powers believe that if the German people prove by their acts that they intend to fulfill the conditions of the peace, and that they have abandoned those aggressive and estranging policies which caused the war, and now have become a people with whom it is possible to live in neighborly good fellowship, the memories of the past years will speedily fade, and it will be possible at an early date to complete the League of Nations by the admission of Germany thereto. It is their earnest hope that this may be the case. They believe that the prospects of the world depend upon the close and friendly coöperation of all nations in adjusting international questions and promoting the welfare and progress of mankind. But the early entry of Germany into the League must depend principally upon the action of the German people themselves.

VII

In the course of its discussion of their economic terms, and elsewhere, the German Delegation have repeated their denunciation of the blockade instituted by the Allied and Associated Powers.

Blockade is and always has been a legal and recognized method of war, and its operation has from time to time been adapted to changes in international communications.

If the Allied and Associated Powers have imposed upon Germany a blockade of exceptional severity, which throughout they have consistently sought to conform to the principles of international law, it is because of the criminal character of the war initiated by Germany and of the barbarous methods adopted by her in prosecuting it.

The Allied and Associated Powers have not attempted to make a specific answer to all the assertions made in the German note. The fact that some observations have been passed over in silence does not indicate, however, that they are either admitted or open to discussion.

VIII

In conclusion the Allied and Associated Powers must make it clear that this letter and the memorandum attached constitute their last word.

They have examined the German observations and counter-proposals with earnest attention and care. They have, in consequence, made important practical concessions, but in its principles, they stand by the treaty.

They believe that it is not only a just settlement of the great war, but that it provides the basis upon which the peoples of Europe can live together in friendship and equality. At the same time it creates the machinery for the peaceful adjustment of all international problems by discussion and consent, whereby the settlement of 1919 itself can be modified from time to time to suit new facts and new conditions as they arise.

It is frankly not based upon a general condonation of the events of 1914-1918. It would not be a peace of justice if it were. But it represents a sincere and deliberate attempt to establish "that reign of law, based upon the consent of the governed, and sustained by the organized opinion of mankind" which was the agreed basis of the peace.

As such the treaty in its present form must be accepted or rejected.

The Allied and Associated Powers therefore require a declaration from the German Delegation within five days from the date of this communication that they are prepared to sign the treaty as it stands to-day.

If they declare within this period that they are prepared to sign the treaty as it stands, arrangements will be made for the immediate signature of the peace at Versailles.

In default of such a declaration, this communication constitutes the notification provided for in Article II. of the Convention of February 16, 1919, prolonging the armistice which was signed on November 11, 1918, and has already been prolonged by the agreement of December 13, 1918, and January 16, 1919. The said armistice will then terminate, and the Allied and Associated Powers will take such steps as they think needful to enforce their terms.

French text signed: CLEMENCEAU.

BY GABRIEL HANOTAUX

Peace at last! Peace so tragically disturbed, and so tragically restored, peace which covers all things, whose very features are hidden by the splendor of its appearance,—Peace!

We are not in a mood to discuss peace; it is for us to accept it. It is here at last at the end of five years. Only a year ago, Paris was living in the alternate agonies of high explosives and black *communiqués*. The enemy was at the gates. And now,—he is at Versailles. M. de Brockdorff-Rantzau allows his tranquil cigarette to go out and listens. He receives the heavy volume, a weight to which he had not looked forward. And, accepting, he could find nothing better to babble than the vain protestations of a crushed militarism. It might have been more worth while for him, in the manner of our Premier, to have cut through this loquacity with one trenchant word.

To allow it to be said that France, Belgium, and the other Powers which have struck down conquering Germany are guilty of crimes similar to those of the Central Empires, is to permit the growth, in a solemn hour, of a false and dangerous legend. The future will read that. Now and as ever, historical fiction is being written.

Let us first consider that word in which the thought of

the leader of the German delegation is resumed—"The peace
which you are imposing on us," he has said, "is a peace of
hatred." And he adds that an Allied imperialism is merely
dictating its conditions to a German imperialism.

Let us now limit our discussion to France. M. de Brockdorff-Rantzau's allegation is cruel and unjust.

France, attacked, defended herself; she never was guilty
of the least imperialism or of the spirit of conquest, either
at the moment in which she went to war, or that in which she
closed it with victory; she has claimed and obtained nothing
more than her due.

The proof of this is inscribed on every page of the
enormous volume. All in all, what has the Treaty given to
France? Simply Alsace-Lorraine, and the coal which was
stolen from her!

In spite of the dangerous "lists" which fill the columns
of the newspapers, the "reparation" amounts to just that.
The fair-minded will admit that we have not reckoned in
either the horses, cattle, or equipages pillaged from us; or
Morocco and the Congo, pick-pocketed from our too feeble
diplomacy. As for the dead, the wounds, the atrocious miseries of war in our invaded regions, the immense debt under
which we are staggering—all these have been summarily
passed over. Does this indicate a peace of hatred? Of what,
then, should a peace of abnegation, moderation, and patience be made?

The situation is clear. Our enemy lies at our feet. The
ogre who sharpened his knife on our doorstone lies full
length upon the ground. He will need years in which to
retemper his bloody soul in the gall of his rancor. Who can
say but this soul may really be transformed? May we not
some day discover a Germany with whom Europe can live?
Is this a hope, an illusion, a lure? We have faith in this
trial. Therein lies the true sense of the Treaty.

The fourteen articles of President Wilson, to which our
conquered enemies proclaim their allegiance with high fervor,
promise us a new world in which humanitarian faith shall
reign. We adhere to it. Is it wise that on the day which
beholds the raising of this improvised shelter a lasting *"ha-*

tred" should be sealed in its foundations? This Brockdorff-Rantzau is scarcely a wise diplomat; he would have done well to swallow his venom before entering the Trianon Palace.

Under the authority of President Wilson, the Powers, —and France in particular,—far from dictating a peace of conquest, resign themselves to an arbiter's peace. How shall France rescue herself from the disaster in which she is half entombed? That is what the future and France's faith in herself must show us. In any case, it is neither by the new resources which may come to her from the ransom of the enemy nor by the colonies which she will gain; nor by the labor of those soldiers who, having destroyed all, will now return, having rebuilt nothing, nor by the recovery of that French capital which the nation's laborious frugality poured forth upon the world.

France will set to work anew, once again she will begin to save, she will be, nevertheless, perhaps for centuries the prisoner of this terrible catastrophe. It is not for them to approach us saying that the restoration of Alsace-Lorraine, the return of children to a mother's house, is a work of hatred, a work of imperialism. Such is not the character of this peace.

France is as noble and disinterested in victory as she was unconquerable in the struggle. Her character remains faithful to itself, since nothing has been awarded her beyond the bounds of her legal right, and she has asked nothing, insisted on nothing. She even added no conditions to that famous Pact of London, which all begged her to hold fast to for the sake of the world. She accepts peace as she accepted war. She accepts it with joy, with enthusiasm, with confidence: it is *Peace!*

May this breath of generosity spread throughout the world; may all others do as we have done. The great patriot who will sign the Treaty in the name of France is not a business man. Soon an octogenarian, he sees the life of men and even the life of peoples with the solemn detachment of a chief through whom destiny is accomplished.

In a certain sense, destiny acts within him and beyond

him. Gathering together into his mind and conscience all the various facets of the European problem, he has thought it wise to hold us where we are. And there we shall stay, ready to receive from his hands what they shall bring us.

France rejoices. England rejoices, and stands by, discreet; America, who finds herself already too deeply entangled in universal conflicts and is seeking a way to withdraw, voices her full and vigorous assent. There are but a few timid objections from our comrade in the struggle, Belgium, from our friend and sister, Italy, from Russia, and from those eastern lands impatiently waiting for a solution.

One great person alone is absent from Versailles, and will probably be surprised that she has not been called to a place—Europe. For, by a singular contrast which will become more marked with the advance of time, the Treaty submitted deals with everything except the fate of the continent which has undergone war and the Prussian's ambition.

Europe remains even as Bismarck made it; this, to my way of thinking, is the grave lacuna in the world task now submitted to us. One seeks the constitution of a future Europe among those numberless articles and clauses, and seeks in vain. One precaution, one alone, has been taken; German-Austria has been forbidden to join Germany. There lay the good road, it has been opened, but not followed.

Again, there will have to be a real decision made in the matter of whether peoples are or are not free to dispose of themselves. If the thesis of pan-Germanism is to be accepted; upon what integral principle is the exclusion of Austria to be based? And if the thesis is not to be accepted, why incline before it when the matter in hand concerns one of those violent annexations, torn, a hundred years ago, by the force of Prussia, from the body of European liberties?

One of our friends well situated for knowing all that is taking place in the Palatinate and the Rhine country wrote to me yesterday, "I am living here and I am reading all the time. I talk with people belonging to all ranks and I have been able to gather and examine many documents. Here we are literally walking on the souvenirs of France. The mental attitude of the inhabitants of the Palatinate has, for four years, been turning in a very marked fashion toward France. An immense future is opening here in front of us. What deception the entirely negative decisions of the Conference are bringing to us! . . ." People who see things from close at hand see them thus. Why should we have closed and padlocked the gates of the future to such deliverances?

Since the veto has been pronounced in relation to Austria, why should we not have disentangled that new combination of Bavaria, Saxony, Würtemburg, and Baden, a country of recent allegiance which only half a century ago represented that admirable hope which enchanted our fathers; the hope of a non-Prussian Germany, the true Germany? Why did they suppose these states to hold either this or that sentiment? Why did they not consult them?

Under our eyes, under the eyes of our soldiers who are maintaining guard along the Rhine, Prussian militarism has just entered Munich in triumph, and is crushing out under its hobnailed boots the attempt at separation lately manifested there. Bavaria is being treated as was Belgium, and we are looking on.

Therefore, there is no longer a Europe, there are peoples new-born, rich in a future, singing their first songs and ignorant of the "difficulty of being," Poland, Czecho-Slovakia, greater Serbia,—but Russia has disappeared. No one can tell what she is or what she will be. Upon this devastated continent there remains to-day, to oppose that inexpiable "hatred" of which the rhetorician of Versailles has spoken, only France.

France, it is true, can count upon her strong friends from beyond the channel and beyond the sea; they will fly to her aid. At the least peril, the Society of Nations will warn them. They will hasten hither, obedient to their oath, to their fidelity of heart, and to their Treaty pledges. The sea belongs to them. They need fear no longer the assault either of the battleships or the submarines of Wilhelm II. They will be at hand and at once. Let us count upon them, but, also, let us count upon ourselves.

The peace is good in itself; our enemy has been laid

low, we breathe freely. To every day its task. To-day, let us sign this peace. To-morrow, by our courage, our perseverance, and our proved abnegation, we shall improve it, we shall develop it. Europe, if she only finds here foundations, has the whole future in which to build. Only let us take care that the rôles of the play are not reversed; the sowers of hatred are not the conquerors, they are the conquered.

BY THE ALGEMEEN HANDELSBLAD
An editorial in a prominent Holland paper

The peace conditions imposed upon Germany are so hard, so humiliating, that even those who have the smallest expectation of a "peace of justice" are bound to be deeply disappointed. Has Germany actually deserved such a "peace"? Everybody knows how we condemned the crimes committed against humanity by Germany. Everybody knows what we thought of the invasion of Belgium, the submarine war, the Zeppelin raids. Our opinion on the lust of power and conquest of Germany is well known. But a condemnation of war-time actions must not amount to a lasting condemnation of a people. In spite of all they have done, the German people is a great and noble nation. The question is not whether the Germans have been led by an intellectual group to their destruction, or whether they are accomplices in the misdeeds of their leaders—the question is, whether it is to the interest of mankind, whether there is any sense in punishing a people in such a way as the Entente governments wish to chastise Germany. The Entente evidently desires the complete annihilation of Germany. Not only will the whole commercial fleet be confiscated, but the shipbuilding yards will be obliged to work for the foreigner for some time to come. Whole tracts of Germany will be entirely deprived of their liberty; they will be under a committee of foreign domination, without adequate representation. The financial burden is so heavy that it is no exaggeration to say that Germany is reduced to economic bondage. The Germans will have to work hard and incessantly for foreign masters, without any chance of personal gain, or any prospect of regaining liberty or economic independence. This "peace" offered to Germany may differ in form from the one imposed upon conquered nations by the old Romans, but certainly not in essence. This peace is a mockery of President Wilson's principles. Trusting to these, Germany accepted peace. That confidence has been betrayed in such a manner that we regard the present happenings as a deep humiliation, not only to all governments and nations concerned in this peace offer, but to all humanity. These conditions will never give peace. All Germans must feel that they wish to shake off the heavy yoke imposed by the cajoling Entente, and we fear very much that that opportunity will soon present itself. For has not the Entente recognized in the proposed so-called "League of Nations" the evident right to conquer and possess countries for economic and imperialistic purposes? Fettered and enslaved, Germany will always remain a menace to Europe.

The voice and opinion of neutrals have carried very little weight in this war. But, however small their influence and however dangerous the rancorous caprice of the Entente powers may be to neutrals, it is our conviction and our duty to protest as forcibly as possible against these peace conditions. We understand the bitter feelings of the Entente countries. But that does not make these peace conditions less wrong, less dangerous to world civilization, or any less an outrage against Germany and against mankind.

BY KARL KAUTSKY

Universal disarmament has ceased to be a dream of the pacifists, and has become an economic necessity. International disarmament, however, is impossible without international institutions for controlling or deciding controversies between peoples and governments, which otherwise would resort to weapons to solve their differences. We do, indeed, anticipate that the coming peace will settle important disputes between the leading nations for a considerable time to come. But there will be innumerable questions of controversy between the small governments just being erected in eastern Europe after peace has been made. It is vain to hope that the peace treaty will succeed in establishing things upon a final basis in that region that will be satisfactory to all the parties affected. Mistakes in drawing boundaries are possible. Changes of attitude may occur as soon as the existing excitement and hostility have disappeared. These conditions will create a continued effort for revising the peace treaty, and result either in perpetual war or perpetual danger of war, such as we had in the Balkans for some time before the present world catastrophe. The only way to avoid this will be to create some institution authorized to pass judicially upon such controversies, and supported by the community of nations, so that no individual government will even consider an attempt to resist, by force of arms, its superior authority.

But if we have universal disarmament and international arbitration, then national frontiers will lose their strategic importance. Consequently, those governments born out of the present war, whose frontiers are not favorable from a strategic point of view, are the most interested in having universal disarmament and international arbitration.

The world-war has also dealt a vital blow to the previous tariff system. It has produced an extraordinary shortage of food and raw material, and an abnormal increase in prices of every manufacturing country. At the same time it has accentuated in a high degree the conflict of interest between the farming population and the city working classes, which already was manifesting itself before the war. Finally, it has—at least in Eastern Europe—started a contest to overthrow the still feudalistic tenures of the great landholders.

The latter conflict is as real and present in Bohemia as in Poland and Hungary. To be sure, the Bohemian nobleman is of a different sort from the Hungarian. He has not fought for centuries for masters and existence, but has withdrawn from political activity since the battle of White Mountain, and contented himself with a quiet and retired life of ease and luxury. He is the peer of the Hungarian nobility in avarice and extortion, but not in talent and energy. His power will be broken more easily than that of his Hungarian fellow.

The characteristic features of the period following the war will everywhere be the overthrow of Junker authority, the steady growth of opposition on the part of the city population to agrarian demands, and an unendurable increase of prices. It is hardly likely, under these conditions, that we shall see protective duties on agricultural products restored.

But when the tariff on agricultural products disappears, the justification for a tariff on manufactures disappears. For a long period, the latter has not been a measure to stimulate manufacturing, but to insure manufacturers a monopoly market. Other methods of encouraging manufacturers in industrially backward countries may be employed with equal confidence, and at the same time be free from the objection of increasing the prices of products. Indeed they may even lower the price of products. This latter consideration will be a determining one during the era of poverty and want that is to follow the present war.

To the extent that tariffs lose their old importance and that freedom of trade becomes possible, individual States will cease to attach importance to particular economic territories, and the principles of national self-determination will be correspondingly unaffected by considerations of international commerce.

We must oppose firmly the plan of substituting tariff unions for general free trade. The latter was merely a way of grouping nations together in order to build up trade barriers between the groups. Every such group is instinctively hostile to every other, and the system bears within it the germ of economic warfare. That germ is incompatible with the ideals of universal disarmament and permanent peace.

A Balkan federation, or a Danube federation, or a Middle Europe or Russian federation, or whatever other such scheme may be devised, will indicate no progress, but rather an obstacle, so far as these leagues are tariff unions, likely to prevent a general federation of the world. If economic necessities force nations to unite for purposes of general disarmament and international arbitration, economic necessity will rapidly extend this community of action to other fields of

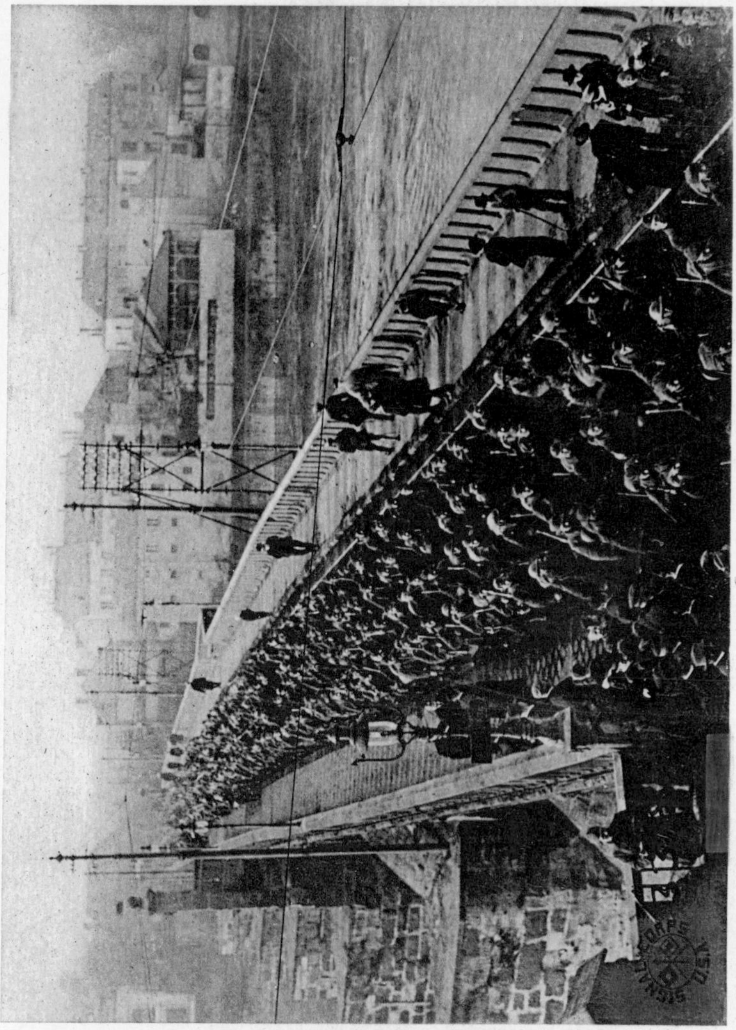
SIGNAL CORPS U.S.A.

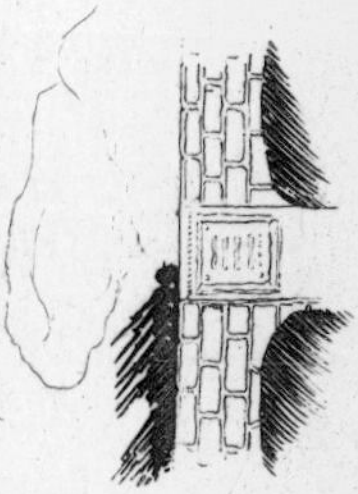

political and business life. We are dealing with forces whose initial manifestations are only a beginning of wider effects. But the possibility of internationalizing colonies, and open seas and canals, has been suggested. The demand that many waterways be internationalized and the freedom of the sea assured arises from a recognition that unrestricted participation in international trade, unrestricted use of international channels of communication, are questions of life and death for every modern nation. This is why it is so important now for a government to control its own access to the sea.

To be sure, in this age of railways the sea is far from being the only international route of traffic. Railways have already become more important for many nations. It may be as detrimental to the interests of a country to be dependent on the railway policies of a neighbor as to be cut off from the sea.

It was a great and significant ideal of modern German statesmen to control a railway connection extending from Hamburg to Bagdad. The only bad thing about it was that trade routes are also military routes, and that the route we planned would serve our purpose of world mastery as much as it would our desire for world commerce. But that is no reason for dropping the idea entirely; for we can deprive it of all its associations of military objects and plans of domination.

The Balkan war and the world-war, which have separated Turkey, Austria, and Russia into a series of smaller States, have not improved the conditions for standardizing international railway traffic, but have impaired them. When we started to build the Bagdad railway, communication between Hamburg and Bagdad would have been subject to the control of but three governments, Germany, Austria, and Turkey. From now on, goods passing between Germany and Bagdad will have to pass through Czech, German-Austrian, Hungarian, Serb, Bulgarian, and Turkish jurisdictions in order to arrive at an Arabian destination.

Unless this is to remain a serious step backward, it is urgently important that this particular line, and every railway line of international importance, shall have an international administration, although it need not be international property. Every country engaged in international trade has equal interest in such a plan, particularly those nations which are cut off from the sea. On the other hand, such an arrangement, combined with universal free trade, would deprive governments of every principal motive for seeking access to the sea, and countries like Hungary, Poland, and Bohemia would feel assured of their economic future without such access.

Other new countries, whose national enthusiasm is not at high flood, and that most zealously proclaim and define their national autonomy, have a principal interest in seeing that the international institutions that will inevitably be created by the peace treaty, are given the greatest possible power and the widest possible jurisdiction.

Those countries are also mainly interested in having the international Socialist proletariat exercise the most powerful possible influence in the course of world events.

We must not undervalue the international institutions which are to be called to life,—as do many radical Socialists,—because these institutions will be established in the first place by bourgeois governments. Such Socialists forget the dominant rôle in historical evolution that economic demands play hand in hand with the plans of governments. This dominant influence is what, in our opinion, will force the creation of international institutions that will not be the product of political desires. Such institutions are among the conditions precedent to the final victory of the working class, predicted by Engels as an absolutely certain result of the world-war, which he foresaw.

Consequently, we do not underestimate the value of these institutions. But there is no doubt but what some bourgeois governments will take this unaccustomed course with hesitation, while others will continue to strive for directed ways of attaining their selfish objects. One of the first and most important duties of the international proletariat, which is just reviving, will consist in stimulating the laggard governments and preventing these new institutions from being employed for political purposes.

The more successful we are in thus making permanently secure the self-determination of all nations, and in preventing national wars, which engage the attention and disperse the energy of the proletariat, the more readily we shall be able to unite our forces for the great final struggle against the capitalist system of production, which the conclusion of peace makes the next item upon the program of every nation.

BY DR. PAUL ROHRBACH

Two schools of thought have come into conflict in the American Senate and in public discussion in the United States. The nominal issue is whether that country shall ratify or reject the Treaty of Versailles. Party politics, presidential ambitions, and material interests inevitably play a part in this discussion. Both schools of thought are hostile to Germany. The American people were induced to go to war by being convinced of the necessity of a crusade against German imperialism. That sentiment still persists. Furthermore, English and French propagandists have not relaxed for a moment the efforts they made during the war to propagate distrust and hatred of Germany by biased reports. We have but one recourse against this—persistent labor to make the world understand how much of the responsibility for the war, how much of the inhumanity during the war, and how much of the selfishness that inspired that conflict, also stand to the account of the rulers of the Entente. Thanks to the skill of the political leaders of our opponents, the Americans comprehend these things less than any other nation. German propaganda may well be devoted now to reëstablishing a fair balance of judgment among the American people. This is neglected because our government fails to comprehend the part psychology plays in foreign policy. We might say that it understands less than the old government did—if that would not be incredible. The better informed among us will have to resign ourselves to this fatal misunderstanding. It is impossible as yet to foresee a time when the opinion of the world will refuse to be biased longer in our disfavor.

One of the principal opponents of ratification, Senator

Knox, has criticized the irrational and unjust provisions of the treaty. At the same time he felt it necessary, in view of public sentiment and probably of his own feelings, to assure his hearers that he had no sympathy for the Germans, and that he assumed as a matter of course that their misdeeds must be punished. He did not refer to the inhumanity of killing 800,000 non-combatants in Germany by a famine blockade, and of crushing the spirit and ambition of the survivors by forcing upon them years of undernourishment, and of the moral degeneration which that produces. We are, therefore, called upon to emphasize this distinctly. He and his associates, however, have something else to say, something very important for America and indirectly for the rest of the world and for ourselves. These gentlemen are not willing to have their country become more deeply involved in the affairs of Europe and Asia. The only exception they consider are those parts of Eastern Asia which face the Pacific.

If America ratifies the Treaty, thereby engaging to assist in its enforcement, every one of the innumerable difficulties that will inevitably arise in so doing will force America to interest itself in the affairs of Germany, Austria, France, Italy, Russia, the Balkans, and the Orient. Their country will have to form an opinion and to take sides and to make decisions in connection with each one of these countries. The result will be inevitable domestic dissension and internal conflict. The government of a people as powerful as that of the United States, with the self-confidence, the national sensitiveness, and the love of sensation, which the Americans possess, will be unable to confine themselves, if they are members of a league of nations, to merely academic and theoretical declarations concerning the innumerable complications which will flow from the Versailles Treaty. If America speaks, it will be with authority and self-assertion, and it will have to take its stand in accordance with its sympathies and interests.

The party opposed to ratification maintains that the interests of the United States are in the Western Hemisphere, and that if they extend beyond that limit, it is only in the region of the Pacific. America had a moral mission in Europe which it could not escape. It was America's duty to assist the western democracies to overthrow Germany, because they alone were too weak to throttle the monster. Now that the object is attained, America should withdraw. Beneath this sentiment lies also the thought that every European nation and government retains certain traces of backwardness, the outcome of irrational and misguided historical tendencies, and that the ideals of America can be realized only in the New World.

The question arises whether the Americans will be able to avoid actively participating in the political supervision of the reorganized world, no matter how sincerely they desire to do so. There are two conditions which make their withdrawal difficult: the first is that the war has made them too powerful to pursue such a policy; the second is that American interests in Eastern Asia, which are of supreme importance, inevitably are inter-related with broader international questions. In addition we have the influence of America's commercial interests, which the war has greatly widened. Of these three considerations the most important is the first. Even if we assume that the anti-European party wins, for the time being, that will not prevent the constant references of European controversies to America's judgment, and the repeated efforts of the contestants to win America's support. The Americans have sacrificed money and blood for Europe. The President has voiced an ideal of extraordinary importance for the orderly development of a world in which Europe still remains the most highly civilized, and relatively the most densely populated portion. He promulgated that ideal in the name of America's people, and the nation has gained from his pronouncements definite opinions of the condition of the old governments east of the Atlantic. Besides the conviction that they have the power to make their ideals prevail, the Americans realize at heart that it is impossible to withdraw again into their old political seclusion by a mere effort of will, and that they will not be able to maintain that seclusion in the future for both psychological and practical reasons. This would be impossible. A nation that actually has supreme power, and is conscious that it is a preponderant force in the world, cannot artificially isolate itself in its own hemisphere.

A majority of the Americans now begin to feel keenly that they have been placed in an awkward position because their President has not measured up, either morally or intellectually, to the demands made upon him. Wilson promulgated a lofty ideal. He did it with a great expenditure of pathos and in the pose of a world-judge, as though it depended upon him personally to direct the nations into the path they should pursue. We are justified in saying that hardly ever in modern times has the head of a government stood so high in the world's esteem and temporarily possessed such vast influence as Wilson.

The whole world looked up to him and felt that its fate hung from his decisions. But this man, elevated to such a height, revealed himself as a surprisingly small soul in the hour of decision. The conception of a League of Nations must have resided in his head as a cloudy dream, never theoretically or practically workable. If Wilson had been capable of conceiving the league as a political actuality, he would have seen beforehand that such an institution, in the form he proposed it, would encounter insuperable opposition from his own allies. Only a dreamer—a political simpleton—could imagine for a moment that the rulers of the Entente would consent to anything but a predatory peace. No league of nations was compatible with this. If Wilson was really determined to have a league, he should have insisted in the very beginning upon sufficient guarantees from England, Italy, and France. As soon as Clemenceau and Lloyd George had succeeded in completely disarming Germany by the conditions of the armistice, Wilson's League of Nations was dead and buried. The world saw its author dandling a mere inflated rubber image of the League, in place of the real thing. He no longer imposed his ideals on any one, least of all upon his allies. Thereupon, he preferred to accept the mere mockery of his plan, instead of frankly acknowledging his defeat and withdrawing with dignity from the unsuccessful contest.

A feeling is spreading among the Americans, in spite of the fact that they are more easily misled concerning European and international affairs than most other nations, that the true story of what occurred at Versailles has not been told them. They have a suspicion that the President did not win much glory for their country there. But Wilson is a shrewd enough political tactician to perceive that the Americans will find it difficult not to enter the League under one condition or another. If ratification is actually to be rejected, Wilson's opponents must find a skillful political formula in order to escape the charge that the defeat of the President has dishonored the American nation as a whole.

Whether such a formula is discovered or not, America's participation in world policies cannot be recalled. Naturally the English would find it unpleasant for the United States to accept a mandate for Constantinople, or Asia Minor, or even Armenia; for the English want to be unhindered there. They skillfully arranged that the Indian and Mohammedan princes should rally to the support of the Sultan as soon as his capital of Constantinople was seriously threatened with American control. England wants to remain sole master in that quarter of the world, where it is now so skillfully establishing itself. It is seeking to elbow the French out of Syria by supporting a native president under the pretext of "Syrian self-determination."

China and Japan are much more important for America than these regions in Western Asia. It is a vital necessity for the United States to keep the Japanese from carrying out the economic and military organizations of China. On the other hand, it is a vital necessity for Japan to do just this thing. The Japanese are determined to be absolute masters of the Japan Sea. They intend to rule its continental as well as its island shores. They propose to occupy a position upon the mainland that will make it impossible for China to escape from their grasp. Their domination over Manchuria and Eastern Mongolia, the important highways to China from the north, is the first step in this program. Japan has already accomplished this. But a wide stretch of coast lies between these regions and the iron deposits at the head of the lower reaches of the Yangtze-kiang, opposite Hankow. These deposits are essential to the Japanese, because their country does not now possess large enough iron resources to become a great power. Unless it has assured control of Chinese ore, Japan's policy is a failure, because in case of war it would be unable to maintain its army and navy.

England and America are united in a wish to keep Japan within limits and to prevent its annexing China's iron. If Japan succeeds, its remoteness from England and America will make it a dangerous military opponent, because it will be difficult to attack. Without iron it will be a negligible factor. Japan must hold Shantung, if it is to control the Yangtze mines; therefore, the promise made to China, that its territorial integrity would be respected as compensation for its declaration of war against Germany, was very agreeable both to the English and the Americans. But Wilson let himself be intimidated by the Japanese at Paris, just as he was intimidated by the English and French military party, and so he yielded Shantung to Japan. Shantung goes to Japan in violation of the solemn promise to China. But since the Chinese are more fortunate than Germany and the fourteen points, in having the hostility of powerful circles in both America and England toward Japan on their side, their prospects are better than our own.

This incident is merely one illustration of how difficult it will be for Americans to avoid intervening in things outside of America. There is the further consideration, that if a controversy should ever arise between America and England, Japan would be most assiduously courted by both parties. The effect of such an estrangement upon India, and even upon Europe, is obvious. This possibility in turn would arouse bitter domestic conflicts in America itself.

APPENDICES

STATISTICS OF THE GREAT WAR

Including Pronouncing Vocabulary, Chronologies, Bibliography, etc.

PRONOUNCING VOCABULARY

The sound of vowels as here marked is: āle, fâre, härm, tȧsk, ăm, sofȧ, ēve, ĕnd, īce, ĭll, ōld, ȯbey, ôrb, ŏdd, cŏmbine, ūse, ûrn, ŭp, fōod, fŏot, out, oil, menü (this ü is between ōo and ē, nearer ē).

The sound of consonants when marked, is: g=hard g, as in get; ᴋ=guttural *ch* as in loch or German *ich*; N=nasal *ng*, as in French *bon*; *n*=ng, as in bank.

Accents are marked. Their general rule is: in French all syllables are equal with a faint extra accent on the final syllable; in Italian and Polish a slight accent marks the next to the last syllable; in English and German the antepenult or third from the closing end usually gets a strong accent, but this is by no means regular; in Russian and most Slavic tongues the accent is very strong and irregular.

Aachen, ä′ᴋĕn
Aalst (*or* Alost), älst
Aboukir, ä-bōo-kēr′
Aegean, ē-jē′ăn
Agincourt, ȧ′zhäN′kōor′; *Eng.* ăj′ĭn-kōrt
Aidin, ī-dēn′
Aisne (river), ân
Aix-la-Chapelle, āks′lä′shȧ′pĕl′
Albert, ȧl′bâr′
Alexief, ȧl-ĕks′ĭ-ĕf
Allenby, ăl′ĕn-bē
Allenstein, äl′ĕn-shtīn′
Alost (*or* Aalst), ä′lŏst
Alsace, äl-säs′
Altkirch, ält′kĭrᴋ′
Amiens, ȧ′myäN′
Ancre (river), äN′kr′
Andrassy, ŏn′drä-shĕ
Antwerp, ănt′wĕrp
Ardahan, är′dȧ-hän′
Ardennes, är-dĕn′
Argonne, ȧr′gŏn′
Arlon, är′lŏN′
Armentières, ȧr′mäN′tyâr′
Arnim, är′nĭm
Arras, ȧ′räs′
Arsiero, är-sē-ā′rō
Artois, ȧr′twä′
Arz, ärdz
Asiago, ä-sē′ä-gō
Asquith, ăs′kwĭth
Attigny, ȧ′tē′nyē′
Aube (river), ōb
Aubenton, ō′bäN′tôN′
Aubigny, ō′bē′nyē′
Audenarde (*or* Oudenarde), ou′dē-när′de
Augustowo, ou′gōos-tō′vō

Avesnes, ȧ′väN′
Avricourt, ȧ′vrē′kōor′

Bagdad, bäg′däd
Bainsizza, bīn′sē-zä
Baku, bȧ-kōo′
Bâle (*or* Basel), bäl
Balfour, băl′fẽr
Bapaume, bȧ′pōm′
Bar-le-Duc, bâr′lē-dük′
Basel (*or* Bâle), bä′zĕl
Bassée, La, lä′bȧ′sä′
Bastogne, bäs′tôN′y′
Batum, bȧ-tōom′
Bavay, bȧ′vĕ′
Beatty, bē′tĭ
Beaumont, bō′môN′
Beauvais, bō′vĕ′
Belfort, bĕl′fôr′
Belgrade, bĕl′grād′
Belleau, bä-lō′
Berchtold, bĕrᴋ′tōld
Berlaimont, bĕr′lĕ′môN′
Bernstorff, bĕrns′tôrf
Bertincourt, bĕr′täN′kōor′
Besançon, bē′zäN′sôN′
Bethmann-Hollweg, bĕth′mĕn-hŏl′-wĕg
Béthune, bā′tün′
Beuthen, boi′tĕn
Bialystok, byä′lĭ-stŏk
Blamont, blä′môN′
Bohain, bō′äN′
Bordeaux, bŏr-dō′
Bosphorus (*or* Bosporus) bŏs′pô-rŭs′
Botoshani, bō-tō-shȧn′y′
Bouchain, bōo′shän′
Bouillon, bōo′yôN′
Boulougne, bōo′lŏN′y′; *Eng.* bōo-lōn′

Bourlon, bōōr-lŏN'
Bouvines, bōō'vēn'
Boves, bŏv
Brabant-le-roi, brȧ'bäN'-lē-rwä'
Braila, brȧ-ē'lȧ
Braine-le-Comte, brȧn'lē-kŏNt'
Braunsberg, brounz'bĕrк
Bray-sur-Seine, brĕ'-sür'sȧn'
Brenta, brĕn'tä
Brest-Litovsk, brĕst'-lyē-tŏfsk'
Briand, brē-äN'
Briey, brē'ĕ'
Bruges, brüzh
Brusa (or Brussa), brōō'sä
Brusiloff, brōō-sē-lŏf'
Buczacz, bōō'chȧch
Bug (river), bŏŏg
Bukharest (or Bucharest), bōō'kȧ-rĕst'
Bukowina (Bukovina), bōō'kŏ-vē'nä
Bülow, bü'lō
Byng, bĭng

Cadorna, cä-dōr'nä
Calais, kȧ'lĕ'; Eng. kăl'ā
Cambrai (or Canbray), käN'brĕ'
Cantigny, cäN-tēn-yĕ'
Capelle, cä-pĕl'
Caporetto, cä-pō-rĕt'ō
Carignan, ka'rēn'yäN'
Carpathians, cär-pä'thĭ-ăns
Carso, cär'sō'
Cary, cä-rē'
Castelnau, cäs'tĕl-nō'
Cateau, Le, lē kȧ'tō'
Cernavoda (or Tchernavoda), chĕr'nȧ-vô'dä
Cetinje (or Cettinje), tsĕt'ēn-yä
Châlons-sur-Marne, shä'lôN'-sür'-märn'
Chalon-sur-Saône, shȧ'lôN'-sür'sōn'
Champagne, shăm-pän'
Champigny, shäN'pĕ'nye'
Charleroi (or Charleroy), shȧr'lē-rwä'
Charleville, shȧrl'vēl'
Châteauroux, shä'tō'rōō'
Château-Thierry, shä'tō'-tyĕ'rē'
Châtel, shä'tĕl'
Chatillon-sur-Marne, shä'tē'yôN'sür-märn'
Chaudefontaine, shōd'fôN'tän'
Chaulnes, shō'n'
Chaumont, shō'môN'
Chauny, shō'nĕ'
Chemin des Dames, shä-măN'-dä-däm
Chimay, shē'mĕ'
Chiny, shē'nē'
Ciney, sē'nĕ'
Clary, klä'rē'
Clemenceau, clä'mäN-sō'

Combles, kōN'bl'
Comines, kŏ'mēn'
Commercy, kŏ'mĕr'sĕ'
Compiègne, kôN'pyĕn'y'
Condé, kôN'dä'
Conflans, kôN'fläN'
Constanta (or Kustendje), kŏn-stän'-tsä
Coronel, cō-rō-nĕl'
Coucy-le-Château, kōō'se'-lē-shä'tō'
Coulommiers, kōō'lŏ'myäōō'
Courland, cōōr-länd
Courtrai, kōōr'trĕ'
Cracow (or Krakow), krä'kō
Crajova (or Craiova), krȧ-yō'vȧ
Craonne, krä'ôn'
Crécy, krä'sē'; Eng. krĕs'ĭ
Crécy-sur-Serre, krä-sē'-sür'-sȧr'
Cressy, krĕs'ĭ
Crimea, krī-mē'ȧ; krī-mē'ȧ
Croiselles, krwä'sĕl'
Czechoslovakia, chĕck'ō-slō-väk'ĭä
Czechs, chĕcks
Czenstochowa, chĕN'stŏ-kŏ'vȧ
Czernowitz, chĕr'nŏ-vĭts

Dammartin, däN'mȧr'tăN'
Damvillers, däN'vē'yä'
D'Annunzio, dăn-nun'tzĭ-ō
Danzig (or Dantzic), dän'tsĭk
Dardanelles, där'dȧ-nĕlz'
Dégoutte, dä-güt
Delatyn (pass), dĕ-lä'tĭn
Denain, dē-năN'
Dendermonde (or Termonde), dĕn'-dĕr-mŏn'dē'
Deutschland, doitsch'länd
Diarbekr (or Diarbekir), dê-är'bĕk'r
Diaz, dē'äth
Diedenhofen (or Thionville), dē'dĕn-hŏ'fĕn
Dijon, dē'zhôN'
Dimitrieff, dē-mē'-trē-ĕf
Dinant, dē'näN'
Dixmude, dēks'müd'; dē'müd'
Dneiper (river), nē'pĕr
Dneister (river), nēs'tēr
Dobrudja, dō-brō'jä
Dompaire, dôN'pär'
Dormans, dôr'mäN'
Douai (or Douay), dōō'ā'
Douaumont, dŏō-ō-môN'
Doullens, dōō'läN'
Drohobycz, drŏ-hŏ'bĭch
Dubno, dŏŏb'nŏ
Dukla, dŏŏk'lä
Duma, dŏŏ'mä
Dumba, dŏŏm'bă
Dunajec, dü'nä-jĕc

Durazzo, dōōrät′sō
Dwina, dwē′nä

Ebert, ā′bĕrt
Emden, ĕm′dĕn
Emmich, ĕm′ĭк
Épernay, ā′pĕr′nĕ′
Épinal, ā′pē′nál′
Epirus, ē-pī′rŭs
Eregli, ēr′ē-glē′
Erivam, ĕr′ē-vän′
Erzberger, ĕrtz′bĕrg-ĕr
Erzerum, ĕrz-rōōm′
Erzingan, ĕr′zĭn-gän′
Esperey, ā-spä-rä′
Étain, ā′täN′
Euphrates (river), ū-frä′tēz
Eydtkuhnen, īt-kōō′nĕn

Falkenhayn, fälk′ĕn-hän
Fère, La, lä′ fâr′
Fère-Champenoise, fâr′-shäN′pē-nwáz′
Fère-en-Tardenois, fâr′-äN′-tàrd′nwä′
Ferté-Gaucher, La, lä′ fĕr′tä′-gō′shä′
Ferté-sous-Jouarre, La, lä′ fĕr′tä′sōō′-
    zhōō′är′
Fiume, fyōō′mä
Foch, fôsh
Fourmies, fōōr′mē′
Fresnes-en-Woëvre, frĕn′-äN′-vŏ′ĕv′r′

Galatz, gä′läts
Galicia, gà-lĭsh′ĭ-à
Gallieni, gä-lē-nē′
Gallipoli, gäl-lē′pŏ-lē
Genappe, zhē-náp′
Ghent, gĕnt
Giolitti, jō-lē′tē
Gironville, zhē′rŏN′vēl′
Givenchy, zhē′vän′shē′
Givet, zhē′vĕ′
Gleiwitz, glī′vĭts
Gnesen, g′nä′zĕn
Goeben, gĕ′bĕn
Gorizia (or Görz), gŏ′rĭd′zē-ä
Gorlice, gör′lĭs
Görz (or Gorizia), gûrts
Gouraud, gōō-rō′
Gourko, gōōr′kō
Grand pré, grôN-prä′
Gravelotte, gräv′lôt′
Guiscard, gēz′kär′
Guise, güēz′
Gumbinnen, gŏŏm-bĭn′ĕn

Hague, häg
Haig, häg
Hal, häl
Halicz, hä′lĭch

Hausen, how′zĕn
Hautmont, ō′mŏN′
Helgoland (or Heliogoland), hĕl′gŏ-
    länt
Hertling, hĕrt′lĭng
Herzegovina, hĕr′tsĕ-gŏ-vē′nä
Hindenburg, hĭn′dĕn-bĕrg
Hirson, ēr′sŏN′
Horodenka, hō′rŏ-dĕn′kä
Hutier, ü′tē-ä
Huy, hoi

Isonzo, ēs-ŏn′zō
Ivangorod, ē-vän′gō-rŏt

Jamboli (or Yamboli), yàm′bŏ-lē
Jaroslaw (or Jaroslau), yà-rôs′làf
Jassy (or Yassy), yäs′ē
Jellicoe, jĕl′ĭ-cō
Joffre, zhŏf
Jonescu, zhō-näs′kē
Jonnart, zhŏN-är′
Jugoslavia, yü-gō-släv′ĭ-ä
Juniville, zhü′nē′vēl′

Kaisarieh (or Kaisariyeh), kī′sà-rē′yĕ
Kalisz, kä′lyкsh
Keltsy (or Kielce), kyĕl′tsĭ
Kerensky, kä-rĕn′skĭ
Kholm, кŏlm
Khotin, кŏ′tyкn
Kiau-chau, kē-ow-chow
Kief (or Kiev), kē′yĕf
Kielce (or Keltsy), kyĕl′tsĕ
Kishinef (or Kishinev), kк-shкnyĕf′
Kitchener, kĭch′ĕn-ĕr
Kluck, klük
Kolomea, kŏ′lō-mä′ä
Königsberg, kü′nĭкs-bĕrk
Korniloff, kŏr′nē-lŏf
Kovel, kŏ′vĕl-y′
Kragojevatz (or Kraguyevatz), krà-
    gōō′-yĕ-vàts
Krakow (or Cracow), krä′kō
Kremenchug (or Krementchug),
    krĕm′ĕn-chŏŏk′
Kremnitz, krĕm′nĭts
Kuhlmann, kül′mŏn
Kur or Kura (river), kōōr; kōō′rà
Kurisches Haff, kōō′rĭsh-ĕs häf
Kustendje (or Constanta), küs-tĕn′jĕ
Kut-el-Amara, kōōt′ĕl-ä-mä-rä

La Bassée, lä′bá′sä′
La Fère, la′fâr′
La Fère-Champenoise, lä fâr′-shäN′-
    pē-nwáz′
Lagny, làn′yē′
Landrecies, läN′drä′sē′

Langres, län'gr'
Languion, län'gē'ôn'
Laon, län
Le Cateau, lē' kå'tō'
Lemberg (or Lwów), lĕm'bĕrк
Leman, lå-män'
Lenine, lĕn'ĭn
Lens, läns
Le Quesnoy, lē kā'nwȧ'
Liancourt, lē'än'kōōr'
Libau, lē'bou
Lichnowski, lĭк-now'skĭ
Liége, lē'ĕzh'
Lierre, lē'âr'
Ligny, lēn'yē'
Ligny-en-Barrois, lēn'yē'-än'-bȧ'rwä'
Lille (or Lisle), lēl
Lodz (or Lódz), lôdz; lŏŏj
Lomza, lôm'zhȧ
Longwy, lôn'vē'
Loos, lō'ôs'
Lorraine (or Lothringen), lô-rän'
Lothringen (or Lorraine), lôt'rĭng-ĕn
Lötzen, lût'sĕn
Louvain, lōō'vän'
Lublin (or Lyublin), lyŏŏ'blyкn
Ludendorff, lōōd'ĕn-dôrf
Lunéville, lü'nä'vël'
Lutzk (or Lutsk), lŏŏtsk
Luxemburg, lŭks'ĕm-bŭrg
Lwów (or Lemberg), lvŏŏf
Lys (river), lēs

Mackensen, mäk'ĕn-sĕn
Mährisch-Ostrau, mä'rĭsh-ôs'trou
Mainz (or Mayence), mīnts
Maisons-Alfort, mä'zôn'-zȧl'fôr'
Mangin, män-zĕn'
Manoury, mä-nōō-rē'
Marcoing, mȧr'kwăn'
Marienburg, mä-rē'ĕn-bŏŏrk
Masourian Lakes, mä-sōō'rē-ăn
Maubeuge, mō'bûzh'
Mayence (or Mainz), mȧ'yäns'
Meaux, mō
Melun, mē'lūn'
Mesopotamia, mĕs'ō-pō-tä'mĭ-ă
Messancy, mē-sän'sē'
Messines, mä-sĕn'
Meuse (river), mûz; Eng. mūz
Mézières, mä'zyâr'
Michaelis, mē-kä-ā'lĭs
Millerand, mē-yä-răn'
Mitrovicza (or Mitrovitz), mē'trŏ-
vкt'-sä
Moldava (river), môl-dä'vȧ
Moltke, mōlt'kĕ
Monastir, mŏn'ȧs-tēr'
Mons, môns

Montdidier, môn'dë'dyā'
Montfaucon, môn'fō-kôn
Monthureux, môn'tü'rû'
Montmédy, môn'må'dē'
Montmirail, môn'mē'rȧ'y'
Moreuil, mō'rû'y'
Morhange, mōr-hänj'
Mouvaux, mōō'vō'
Moyenmoutier, mwȧ'yän'mōō'tyä'
Mülhausen, mül'hou'zĕn
Mush, mōōsh

Nakhitchevan, nȧ'кк-chĕ-vän'
Namur, nȧ'mür'
Nancy, nän'sē'; Eng. năn'sĭ
Narew or Narev (river), nä'rĕf
Nesle, näl
Neufchâteau, nû'shȧ'tō'
Neuilly-sur-Marne, nû'yē'-sür'-mȧrn'
Neutitschein, noi'tĭt'shĭn
Neuve Chapelle, nûv'shȧ'pĕl'
Niemen, nē'mĕn
Nieuport, nē'ŏŏ-pôrt
Nikolaief (or Nikolayev), nyē'kŏ-lä'-
yĕf
Nîmes (or Nismes), nēm
Nivelle, nē-väl'
Novogeorgievsk, nŏ'vŏ-gé-ôr'gk-yĕĭsk
Noyons, nŏ-yōn'

Oise, wȧz
Olmütz, ôl'müts
Orchies, ôr'shē'
Orlando, ôr-län'dō
Ostend, ŏst-ĕnd'
Ostrog, ŏs-trôk'
Ostrow, ŏs'trôf
Oudenarde (or Audenarde), ou'dē-
när'dē
Ourcq (river), ōōrk
Orthe (river), ōōrt

Painlevé, pän-lä-vä'
Passchendaele, pä'shĕn-dāl
Peremysl (or Przemyśl), pĕ-rĕ'mĭshl-
y'; pshē'mĭshl-y'
Péronne, pā'rŏn'
Pershing, pĕrsh'ĭng
Petain, pa-tän'
Petrokov (or Piotrków), pyĕ'trŏ-kôf'
Philippeville, fē'lēp'vĕl'
Piave, pē-ä'vē
Picardy, pĭk'är-dē
Pierrefitte, pyâr'fēt'
Pierrefonds, pyâr'fôn'
Pinsk, pĭnsk
Piotrków (or Petrokov), pyôtr'kŏŏf
Podgorze, pŏd-gōō'zhĕ
Poincaré, pwŏn-cä-rä'

Poitiers, pwä'tyā'
Poix, pwä
Pont-à-Mousson, pôn'-tä'mōō'zôn'
Pont Ste. Maxence, pôn' sänt'-mȧ'-zäns'
Pripet, prē'pĕt
Prisrend, prē'zrĕnt
Proskurof (or Proskurov), prŏ'skōō-rŏf'
Pruth (river), prōōt
Przasnysz, pshäs'nĭsh
Przemysl (or Peremyśl), pshĕ'mĭshl-y'
Pultusk, pōōl'tōōsk
Putnick, pōōt'nĭk

Quatre-Bras, kȧ'tr'-brä'
Quesnoy, Le, lē kä'nwȧ'

Radom, rä'dŏm
Radzivilov, räd'zk'vk-lŏf'
Ramillies, rȧ'mē'yē'
Raon-l'Etape, rän'lä'tȧp'
Rastenburg, räs'tĕn-bōōrk'
Raucourt, rŏ'kōōr'
Rava (or Rawa), rä'vä
Rawaruska, rä'vä-rōōs'kȧ
Rennenkampf, rĕn'ĕn-kämf
Rethel, rē-tĕl'
Rheims (or Reims), rēmz; Fr. räns
Ribecourt, rēb'kōōr'
Ribemont, rēb'môn'
Riga, rē'gȧ
Rochefort, rŏsh'fôr'
Rocroi, rŏ'krwä'
Roisel, rwä'zĕl'
Roubaix, rōō'bä'
Roulers, rōō'lä'
Roye, rwä
Rozoy-sur-Serre, rŏ'zwä'-sür'-sâr'
Rupprecht, rü'prĕkt
Russky, rōō'skē
Rzeszow, zhĕ'shōōf

Saar (river), zär
Saarbrücken, zär'brük'ĕn
Saint-Amand, săn'tȧ'män'
Saint-Denis, săn'dē-nē'
Saint-Dié, săn'dyä'
Saint Hubert, săn'tü'bâr'
Saint-Mihiel, săn'mē'yĕl'
Saint-Omer, săn'tŏ'mâr'
Saint-Quentin, săn'kän'tän'
Saint-Trond, săn'-trôn'
Saloniki (or Salonica), sä'lŏ-nē'kē
Sambre (river), sän'br'
Samsonoff, säm'sŏn-ŏf
San (river), sän
Sarajevo (or Sarayevo), sä'rȧ-yŏ-vŏ
Sarrail, sär-rīl'

Sarre (or Saar), sär
Scapa Flow (or Skalpa), skä'pă
Scheer, shär
Scheldt, skĕlt
Scutari(or Skutari), skōō'tä-rē
Sedan, sē-dän'
Senlis, sän'lēs'
Seres, sĕr'ĕs
Sereth (river), sȧ-rĕt'
Sézanne, sä'zȧn'
Siedlce (or Syedlets), shĕl'tsĕ
Signy l'abbaye, sēn'yē' läbä'
Sinn Fein, shĭn-fän
Sinob (or Sinope), sê-nŏb'
Sinope (or Sinob), sĭ-nŏ'pk
Sissonne, sē'sŏn'
Sivas, sē'väs'
Skoda, skŏ'dă
Skoplje (or Usküp), skŏp'lyĕ
Sofia, sŏ-fē'ä
Soissons, swä'sôn'
Sokolof, sŏ'kŏ-lŏf
Solesmes, sŏ'läm'
Somme (river, department), sŏm
Sonnino, sŏn-nē'no
Stettin, shtĕ-tēn'
Stralsund, shträl'zōōnt
Stryj, strĕ'yĕ
Stuermer, stēr'mēr
Suippes, swēp
Suwalki, sōō-väl'kĕ

Tabriz, tȧ-brēz'
Tagliamento, täl-yä-mĕn'tō
Tarnopol, tär-nŏ'pŏl-ĕ
Tarnow, tär'nōōf
Termonde (or Dermonde), tĕr'-mônd'
Thiaucourt, tyŏ'kōōr'
Thielt, tēlt
Thionville (or Diedenhofen), tyôn'vēl'
Thuin, tü'ăn'
Tirlemont, tēr'l'môn'
Tirpitz, tĭr'pĭts
Tomasof, tō-mä'sŏŏf
Tongres, tôn'gr'
Toul, tōōl
Tourcoing, tōōr'kwăn'
Tournay (or Tournai), tōōr'nä'
Trélon, trä'lôn'
Trentino, trĕn-tē'nō
Triest (or Triest), trē-ĕst'
Trotsky, trŏt'skĭ

Ukraine, ōō-crän
Urmia, ōōr'mē'ä
Uskup (Skoplje), üs-küp'

Valenciennes, vȧ'län'syĕn'
Valjevo, väl'y-vŏ

Vardar, vär-där′
Varennes-en-Argonne,   vȧ′rĕn′-zäN′-
    är′gŏn′
Veles, väl
Venizelos, vĕn-ĭ-zä′lōs
Verdun, vĕr′dŭn′
Versailles, vĕr′sä′y′; *Eng.* vẽr-sälz′
Vervins, vĕr′văN′
Villers-Bretonneux, vẽ′lâr′-brē-tŏ′nû′
Villers-Cotterets, vẽ′lâr′-kŏ′tē-rĕ′
Villers-la-Ville, vẽ′lâr′-lȧ′-vēl′
Vimy, vē-mē
Visé, vē′zä′
Vistula, vĭs′tü-lȧ
Vitry-en-Artois, vē′trē′-äN′-är′twä′
Vitry-le-François, vē′trē′-le-fräN′swä′
Volga, vŏl′gä
Volhynia, vŏl-ĭn′ĭ-ȧ
Vosges, vōzh

Vouziers, vōō′-zyä′

Wassigny, vȧ′sē′nye′
Wavre, vȧv′r′
Woëvre, vŏ′ĕv′r′
Wurtemberg, vür′tĕm-bŭrg
Wytschaete, wĭt′shät

Yassy (*or* Jassy), yäs′ĭk
Ypres, ē′pr′
Yser (river), ē′sĕ′
Yvoire, ē′vwâr′

Zabern, tsä′bērn
Zamosc, zä′mŏshch
Zeebrugge, tsä-brōōg′ē
Zimmermann, tsĭm′ĕr-măn
Zittau, tsĭt′ou
Zloczow, zlŏ′chŏŏf

CHRONOLOGY OF THE WAR

1914

June 28—Archduke Francis Ferdinand of Austria-Hungary assassinated.

July 23—Austrian ultimatum to Serbia.

July 28—Austria declares war on Serbia.

July 29—Russia calls reserves to colors.

July 29—Bombardment of Belgrade.

July 29—Britain gathers her navy in the North Sea.

July 31—Germany sends ultimatum to Russia and declares martial law. Stock markets of the world close.

Aug. 1—Germany declares war on Russia.

Aug. 1—France orders mobilization.

Aug. 2—Germans enter Luxemburg.

Aug. 2—German ultimatum to Belgium.

Aug. 3—Germany declares war on France.

Aug. 4—Austria begins invasion of Serbia.

Aug. 4—Germany invades Belguim.

Aug. 4—Great Britain declares war on Germany.

Aug. 5—Germans attack Liege.

Aug. 6—Austria declares war on Russia.

Aug. 7—Russians invade East Prussia. French invade Alsace.

Aug. 8—Montenegro declares war on Austria.

Aug. 9—French take Mulhausen in Alsace.

Aug. 9—Germans take Liege.

Aug. 9—Serbia declares war on Germany.

Aug. 10—France declares war on Austria.

Aug. 11—Germans enter F r a n c e through Luxemburg.

Aug. 11—French driven from Mulhausen.

Aug. 12—Great Britain declares war on Austria-Hungary.

Aug. 15—Japan's ultimatum sent to Germany.

Aug. 15—Last of Liege forts captured by Germans.

Aug. 17—B e l g i a n government removed from Brussels to Antwerp.

Aug. 16-23—Serbians drive Austrian invaders out of Serbia in battle of the Jadar.

Aug. 19—Belgians defeated before Louvain.

Aug. 20—French invasion of Germany defeated in battle of Morhange.

Aug. 20—Germans enter Brussels.

Aug. 20-21—Russians defeat Germans at Gumbinnen.

Aug. 22—Germans take Namur.

Aug. 22—French and Germans meet in Belgium in battle of Charleroi.

Aug. 23—British and French defeated at Mons.

Aug. 23—Japan declares war on Germany.

Aug. 23-Sept. 6—Retreat of British-French, Mons to the Marne.

Aug. 23-26—Austrians defeat Russians at battle of Krasnik.

Aug. 25—Austria declares war on Japan.

Aug. 26—The sacking of Louvain.

Aug. 26—Germans surrender Togoland.

Aug. 26—First bomb dropped from Zeppelin on Antwerp.

Aug. 27—Surrender of Longwy.

Aug. 28—Naval battle of Helgoland.

Aug. 28—Austria declares war on Belgium.

Aug. 29-31—Germans defeat Russians in battle of Tannenberg.

Sept. 1-7—First battle of Nancy checks the German attack on France from the east.

Sept. 2—Japanese land on Shantung peninsula.

Sept. 2—Russians take Lemberg.

Sept. 3—French government removes from Paris to Bordeaux.

Sept. 4-8—Russians defeat Austrians, Rawaruska, and Tomaszov.

Sept. 5-10—Battle of the Marne.

Sept. 9—Surrender of Maubeuge.

Sept. 7-13—Germans defeat Russians in East Prussia.

Sept. 12-15—Battle of the Aisne.

Sept. 13—French retake Rheims.

Sept. 16—Germans bombard Rheims cathedral.

Sept. 22—British cruisers "Aboukir," "Cressy" and "Hogue" sunk by submarine.

Sept. 26—Germans take St. Mihiel.

Sept. 25—Bombardment of Antwerp begun.

Sept. 29—First German advance into Poland begun; battle of Tarnow.

Oct. 3-14—The first Canadian army crosses the Atlantic to aid Britain.

Oct. 5—British troops join Belgians in Antwerp.

Oct. 9—Germans capture Antwerp.

Oct. 10-12—Battle of Lille.

Oct. 12—Germans capture Ghent.

Oct. 14—Dutch revolt begun against British in South Africa.

Oct. 15—Germans take Ostend.

Oct. 15-23—Germans driven back from Poland in battle of Warsaw.

Oct. 17-Nov. 11—Battle of Ypres and the Yser.

Oct. 18—Battle of destroyers off Dutch coast.

Oct. 26—Italians occupy Avlona, Albania.

Oct. 29—Turkey begins hostilities against Russia.

Oct. 29—Belgians block Germans by opening the Yser dykes.

Nov. 1—Sea battle off Coronel, Chili.

Nov. 4—British attack on Tanga, German East Africa, defeated.

Nov. 5—Great Britain declares war on Turkey.

Nov. 5—Second Austrian invasion of Serbia begun.

Nov. 7—Japanese take Tsing-tau.

Nov. 9—German cruiser "Emden" destroyed.

Nov. 12—Second German invasion of Poland begun.

Nov. 16—German success on Plock-Warthe line, Poland.

Nov. 19-28—Battle of Lodz.

Nov. 23—Portugal joins the Allies.

Dec. 1—South African revolt breaks down.

Dec. 2—Austrians take Belgrade.

Dec. 6—Germans take Lodz.

Dec. 6-14—Serbians defeat Austrians; retake Belgrade.

Dec. 8—Naval battle off Falkland Islands.

Dec. 9—British advance in Mesopotamia.

Dec. 16—German raid on Scarborough, England.

Dec. 17—British proclaim protectorate over Egypt.

Dec. 18—Germans take Lowicz.

Dec. 25—British sea and air raid on Cuxhaven.

Dec. 28—Germans repulsed from Warsaw.

1915

Jan. 3-4—Turkish defeat in the Caucasus.

Jan. 3—French take Steinbach.

Jan. 14—French defeated at Soissons.

Jan. 17—Russians take Kirlibaba pass.

Jan. 24—Naval battle off Dogger Bank.

Feb. 2-4—Turks attempt invasion of Egypt at Suez. British rout Turks.

Feb. 4—Germans proclaim submarine blockade of British Isles to begin February 18th.

Feb. 10—The United States' President warns Germany against injuring neutrals by submarine attacks.

Feb. 11-12—Russians driven from East Prussia.

Feb. 16—French take Perthes.

Feb. 18—Austrians take Czernowitz.

Feb. 19—Naval attack on Dardanelles forts.

Feb. 23—South Africans invade German West Africa.

Feb. 25—Second naval attack on Dardanelles.

Feb. 28–Mar. 1—Russian offensive in Northern Poland.

Mar. 1—Britain proclaims blockade of all German coast.

Mar. 10–12—Battle of Neuve Chapelle.

Mar. 18—Third naval attack on Dardanelles forts; three battleships sunk.

Mar. 20—Russians take Memel.

Mar. 22—Surrender of Przemysl and Austrian army.

Mar. 28—Passenger steamer "Falaba" sunk by submarine; 111 lost.

Apr. 4—Germany protests at sale of munitions by United States merchants.

Apr. 4—Russians through the Beskid range, Hungary.

Apr. 4–9—Battle of Les Eparges.

Apr. 22–24—Second battle of Ypres (St. Julien); first use of gas.

Apr. 23—British victory at Shaiba, Mesopotamia.

Apr. 25—British and French land on Gallipoli.

Apr. 30—Germans advance into Kovno and Courland.

May 1—German great artillery attack crushes Russians at battle of Dunajec.

May 2—Germans take Shavli.

May 7—"Lusitania" sunk.

May 11—French take Carency and Notre Dame de Lorette.

May 13—President Wilson protests "Lusitania" sinking.

May 14–17—Retreating Russians driven back across the San.

May 16—Four Zeppelins destroyed in air raid on England.

May 16—Battle of Festubert.

May 19—Britain establishes a coalition ministry.

May 23—Italy declares war on Austria.

June 2—Germans retake Przemysl.

June 5—South Africans complete the conquest of German West Africa.

June 20—German victory at Rawaruska.

June 22—Austrians retake Lemberg.

June 28—United States protests sinking of the "Frye."

July 2–6—Germans cross the Niemen into Russia and win battle of Krasnik.

July 14—German offensive in North Poland.

July 22—Advancing Germans cross the Vistula in Poland; Warsaw doomed.

Aug. 4—Russians evacuate Warsaw.

Aug. 6–10—Chief British effort to storm the Turkish lines at Gallipoli fails. The Anzacs repulsed at Sari-bair.

Aug. 15—American reply to Austria-Hungary protests on arms traffic.

Aug. 18—Germans take Kovno.

Aug. 19—"Arabic" torpedoed.

Aug. 19—Germans take Novogeorgievsk.

Aug. 21—Italy declares war on Turkey

Aug. 26—Germans take Bialystok and Brest-Litovsk.

Sept. 1—Austrians take Lutsk.

Sept. 2—Germans take Grodno.

Sept. 6—End of the great Russian retreat. The Czar takes command of his armies.

Sept. 9—United States demands recall of Austrian Ambassador Dumba.

Sept. 9—Russian success on Sereth River.

Sept. 9—Austrians take Dubno.

Sept. 18—Germans take Vilna.

Sept. 22—Bulgaria orders mobilization.

Sept. 24–Oct. 2—Greece mobilizes; Allies land troops at Salonika; Greece protests.

Sept. 25—Battle of Loos.

Sept. 25—Battle of Champagne.

Oct. 3—Russian ultimatum to Bulgaria.

Oct. 5—German reply in "Arabic" case concedes American points; no merchant ships to be sunk without warning and protection of life.

Oct. 6—German-Austrian offensive against Serbia; Danube crossed.

Oct. 8—Belgrade taken.

Oct. 12—Bulgarians invade Serbia.

Oct. 13—Execution of Edith Cavell.

Oct. 14—Bulgaria declares war on Serbia.

Oct. 15—Britain declares war on Bulgaria.

Oct. 22—Greece refuses offer of Great Britain to cede Cyprus.

Oct. 24—Bulgarians take Uskub.
Oct. 28—Viviani resigns as premier of France.
Oct. 29—Italian attack on the Isonzo.
Nov. 5—Germans repulsed by Russians at Riga.
Nov. 5—Bulgarians take Nish.
Nov. 9—Italian liner "Ancona" torpedoed.
Nov. 22-24—Battle of Ctesiphon, Mesopotamia; end of the British advance toward Bagdad.
Nov. 25—Dec.—Serbian exodus into Albania.
Nov. 30—Second Italian attack on the Isonzo.
Dec. 3—United States demands recall of Boy-Ed and Von Papen.
Dec. 3-12—Anglo-French troops defeated on Vardar.
Dec. 5—Bulgarians take Monastir.
Dec. 6—British retreat to Kut-el-Amara.
Dec. 15—Sir Douglas Haig succeeds Sir John French in command of British.
Dec. 20—British withdraw from Gallipoli.
Dec. 21-22—French take Hartmans-Weilerkopf.
Dec. 27—British defeat Arab revolt in West Egypt.

1916

Jan. 13—Austrians take Cettinje, Montenegro.
Jan. 16—Russians begin drive in Caucasus.
Jan. 19—King Nicholas of Montenegro flees.
Feb. 16—Russians take Erzerum.
Feb. 18—Allied conquest of Cameroons.
Feb. 20—German offensive at Verdun begun.
Feb. 26—Germans take Fort Douaumont.
Mar. 10—Germany declares war on Portugal.
Mar. 15—Von Tirpitz retires as head of German navy.
Mar. 19—Ispahan in Persia occupied by advancing Russians.
Mar. 24—Channel steamer "Sussex" torpedoed; the United States again protests.

Mar. 26—British naval air raid on Jutland.
Mar. 31—Russian hospital ship "Portugal" sunk.
Apr. 18—United States sends ultimatum to Germany on "Sussex" case; Germany yields.
Apr. 18—Russians take Trebizond.
Apr. 21—Arrest of Sir Roger Casement.
Apr. 24—Irish rebellion.
Apr. 28—General Townshend surrenders British force at Kut-el-Amara.
May 1—Dublin rebels surrender.
May 5—Germany promises to stop sinkings without warning.
May 15—Austrian drive in Trentino begun.
May 23—British Commons adopt conscription.
May 27—Austrians take Asiago.
May 31—Naval battle off Jutland.
June 1-7—German drive on Douaumont-Vaux.
June 2-16—Third battle of Ypres.
June 4-Aug. 15—Russia rallies and makes her third great advance into Austrian lands; Brusiloff captures Bukowina and threatens Hungary.
June 6—Lord Kitchener drowned by sinking of cruiser "Hampshire."
June 6—Russians take Lutsk.
June 7—Germans take Fort Vaux.
June 10—Russians take Dubno.
June 13—Shereef of Mecca revolts from Turkey.
June 17—Russians take Czernowitz.
June 25—Russians complete conquest of Bukowina.
July 1—First battle of the Somme begun.
July 9—German merchant submarine "Deutschland" crosses the Atlantic.
July 11—British take Contalmaison.
July 26—Russians take Erzingam.
Aug. 1-10—Russian advance into Austria checked at Stochod River.
Aug. 4—Roger Casement executed.
Aug. 4—French retake Fleury and Thiaumont.
Aug. 9—Italians take Gorizia.
Aug. 11—Italians take Corso plateau.

Aug. 18—Bulgarians invade Northern Greece.

Aug. 27—Italy declares war on Germany.

Aug. 27—Bulgarians enter Greek Macedonia.

Aug. 28—Rumania declares war on Austria.

Aug. 29—Hindenburg becomes German chief of staff.

Aug. 30—Rumanians take Kronstadt.

Sept. 2—Rumanians take Hermanstadt.

Sept. 2-8—Bulgarians defeat Rumanians in Dobrudja.

Sept. 6—Russian victory near Halicz.

Sept. 15—First use of British tanks.

Sept. 19—Allies blockade the coast of Greece

Sept. 19-23—Rumanians defeated at Vulcan Pass.

Sept. 26—British take Combles and Thiepval.

Oct. 7—German submarine "U-53" crosses Atlantic to United States coast.

Oct. 8—"U-53" sinks six ships off Massachusetts coast.

Oct. 11-13—Italian advance on the Carso.

Oct. 17—Allies take over Greek fleet and land forces.

Oct. 23—Rumanians lose Constanza.

Oct. 24—French retake Fort Douaumont.

Nov. 15-17—Rumanians defeated in battle of Tirgu-Juil.

Nov. 19—Serbians take Monastir.

Nov. 21—Emperor Francis Joseph dies; Carl succeeds.

Nov. 25—French retake Fort Vaux.

Nov. 29—Sir David Beatty succeeds Sir John Jellicoe in command of British fleet.

Dec. 2—Entente troops move on Athens.

Dec. 3—Rumanians beaten in battle of Argechu.

Dec. 5—Asquith resigns as premier of Britain.

Dec. 6—Teutonic allies take Bucharest.

Dec. 10—Lloyd George forms ministry.

Dec. 11—Nivelle succeeds Joffre in command of French.

Dec. 15—Brilliant French victory north of Verdun.

Dec. 21—Peace proposals made by United States.

1917

Jan. 9—Allies state their terms of peace "restitution and reparation."

Jan. 11—British take Rafa, Sinai Peninsula.

Jan. 31—Germany announces resumption of submarine ruthlessness after Feb. 1st.

Feb. 3—United States announces severance of diplomatic relations with Germany.

Feb. 3-5—British advance on the Ancre.

Feb. 24—German withdrawal on Somme detected; the Hindenburg retreat.

Feb. 24—British take Sanna-y-Yat.

Feb. 25—"Laconia" sunk.

Feb. 25—British advancing in Mesopotamia retake Kut.

Feb. 28—Zimmermann's Mexican plot exposed.

Mar. 9—President Wilson orders arming of merchant ships.

Mar. 9-11—Revolutionary riots in Petrograd.

Mar. 11—British take Bagdad.

Mar. 15—Czar Nicholas abdicates; republic organized, Lvoff premier.

Mar. 17—Briand cabinet resigns.

Mar. 31—British before Hindenburg line.

Apr. 4—Germans defeat Russians on the Stokhod.

Apr. 6—United States declares war on Germany.

Apr. 7—Cuba declares war on Germany.

Apr. 9—British begin battle of Arras; Canadians take Vimy Ridge.

Apr. 10—Brazil severs diplomatic relations with Germany.

Apr. 14-17—U. S. Congress passes $7,000,000,000 war bond bill.

Apr. 16—Nivelle's offensive begun.

Apr. 21-25—British and French commissioners reach U. S. for consultation on war plans.

Apr. 22—Hospital ships "Lanfranc" and "Donegal" torpedoed.

Apr. 28—U. S. Congress passes conscription bill.

May 4—First squadron U. S. navy reaches England.

May 5—French take Chemin des Dames.

May 6—First meeting of the Allied War Council in Paris.

May 7—Greek Venizelist troops first go into action beside Allies.

May 12-31—Italian offensive on the Isonzo.

June 7—British take Messines ridge.

June 12—King Constantine of Greece abdicates.

June 26-27—First United States contingent lands in France.

July 1—Russians begin offensive in Galicia.

July 2—Greece declares war.

July 8-10—Russians win battle of Dolina.

July 11—British reverse on Yser.

July 17—Bethmann-Hollweg resigns as German Chancellor.

July 19—German counter-offensive breaks Russian front in Galicia.

July 22—Kerensky succeeds Lvoff as premier of Russia.

July 22—Russian soldiers in Galicia refuse obedience and start flight.

July 23—Germans take Tarnopol.

July 23—Council of workmen and soldiers makes Kerensky dictator.

July 25—Rumanians take offensive.

July 31—Allies begin fourth battle of Ypres.

Aug. 2—Brusiloff and Dimitrieff resign. Russian forces broken.

Aug. 7—Liberia declares war on Germany.

Aug. 14—Pope makes peace proposal.

Aug. 14—China declares war on Germany and Austria-Hungary.

Aug. 18-24—Italian offensive on Isonzo; take Bainsizza plateau, Monte Santo and Monte San Gabriele.

Aug. 20—French take Dead Man's Hill.

Aug. 25-27—Moscow conference.

Sept. 3—Germans take Riga.

Sept. 8—Luxburg sink-without-trace dispatch disclosed.

Sept. 8—Korniloff rebels against Kerensky.

Sept. 15—Korniloff surrenders to Alexieff.

Sept. 22—Germans take Jacobstadt.

Oct. 13—Germans land on Oesel Island, Baltic Sea.

Oct. 18—Battle of German and Russian fleets in Moon Sound.

Oct. 20—Five Zeppelins destroyed in raid on London.

Oct. 21-23—Battle of Caporetto; Italian front broken.

Oct. 25—French drive Germans across the Ailette.

Oct. 26—Brazil declares war on Germany.

Oct. 28—Gorizia retaken by Austrians; Bainsizza and Carso lost.

Oct. 30—Austrians take Udine.

Oct. 31—British take Beersheba, Palestine.

Nov. 3—First American trench fight on Rhine-Marne canal.

Nov. 6—British take Passchendaele.

Nov. 7—Kerensky overthrown by Bolsheviki.

Nov. 8—Italians defeated on the Tagliamento.

Nov. 9—General Diaz succeeds Cadorna in command of Italians.

Nov. 10—British take Askalon.

Nov. 16-17—Kerensky forces defeated by Bolsheviki.

Nov. 18-19—Battle of the Piave; Italians hold.

Nov. 18—British take Jaffa.

Nov. 19—Death of General Cyril Maude.

Nov. 20—Battle of Monte Tomba.

Nov. 20—British attack at Cambrai.

Nov. 30-Dec. 7—German counter-attack at Cambrai.

Dec. 4—Last German colony, East Africa, conquered.

Dec. 7—United States declares war on Austria-Hungary.

Dec. 7—Rumania agrees to armistice.

Dec. 8—Trotsky announces suspension of hostilities.

Dec. 10—British take Jerusalem.

Dec. 14—Germans and Bolsheviki sign armistice.

Dec. 19-21—Battle of Monte Asolone.

Dec. 28—Provisional peace agreement between Bolsheviki and Germans.

1918

Jan. 8—President Wilson's speech stating fourteen peace articles.

Jan. 20—Bolsheviki dissolve Constituent Assembly.

Jan. 24-28—Italian success on Aisago plateau.

Feb. 6—"Tuscania" torpedoed; 212 U. S. soldiers lost.

Feb. 9—Ukraine government signs separate peace.

Feb. 11—Bolsheviki declare end of war.

Feb. 17—Germans announce end of armistice with Bolsheviki.

Feb. 18—Germans advance across the Dvina.

Feb. 19—Germans take Dvinsk and Lutsk.

Feb. 20—Germans enter Esthonia.

Feb. 22—British take Jericho.

Feb. 23—New German terms to Bolsheviki.

Feb. 25—Germans take Reval and Pskov.

Mar. 1—Austrian armies enter Ukraine.

Mar. 3—Bolsheviki agree to German terms.

Mar. 7—Peace treaty with Rumania.

Mar. 10—Germans land in Finland.

Mar. 13—Austrians take Odessa.

Mar. 21—German drive on Cambrai-Saint Quentin front begins.

Mar. 23—British front breaks and Germany's great drive threatens to overthrow the Allies.

Mar. 23—Germans first shell Paris with 76-mile gun.

Mar. 28—Germans reach Montdidier.

Mar. 28—Germans repulsed before Arras.

Mar. 29—Foch appointed Allied generalissimo.

Apr. 5—Japanese land at Vladivostok.

Apr. 9—Second great German thrust begun in France; British attacked on Lys.

Apr. 11—Germans take Armentières.

Apr. 12—Haig's back-to-wall order.

Apr. 14—British and French land on Kola Peninsula.

Apr. 16—Germans take Bailleul and Wytschaete; British retire from Passchendaele.

Apr. 17—French reinforce British on the Lys.

Apr. 20—U. S. troops repulse German raid at Seicheprey.

Apr. 23—British naval raid on Zeebrugge and Ostend.

Apr. 25-26—Germans take Mont Kemmel.

Apr. 29—General German attack on Lys sector repulsed.

May 10—Second British naval raid on Ostend.

May 16—Italian naval raid on Pola sinks battleship.

May 27—Third great German attack captures Chemin des Dames and hurls French back toward Paris.

May 28—Germans advance to the Vesle.

May 28—First U. S. offensive; take Cantigny.

May 29—Germans take Soissons.

May 30—Germans cross the Ourcq.

May 31—Germans reach the Marne.

June 2—Germans take Château-Thierry.

June 2—U. S. troops reach front at Château-Thierry.

June 3—Submarine off American coast sinks "Carolina" and other ships.

June 6-11—U. S. marines take Belleau Wood.

June 9—Fourth great German drive meets but small success against French.

June 15-23—Austrian drive on Piave.

June 25—Austrians driven across Piave.

June 30—Italians take Monte de Valbella and Monte del Rosso.

July 4—Czecho-Slovaks take Vladivostok.

July 6—Italians clear Piave delta.

July 7—German ambassador at Moscow assassinated.

July 7-12—Italians advance in Albania.

July 15—Germans begin Marne-Champagne drive.

July 18—Allied counter-attack on Aisne and Marne.

July 20—Germans recross the Marne.

July 27—Germans retire to the Ourcq.

July 28—Allies take Fère-en-Tardenois.

Aug. 2—French take Soissons.

Aug. 3—Germans retire across the Vesle.

Aug. 5—Allies land at Archangel.

Aug. 6—Foch made marshal.

Aug. 8—Allied drive on Amiens front begun.

Aug. 10—Montdidier retaken.

Aug. 14—French take Ribecourt.

Aug. 14—U. S. troops land at Vladivostok.

Aug. 14—British reach Baku.

Aug. 19—French begin drive south of the Oise.

Aug. 21—French take Lassigny.

Aug. 21—British attack Albert to Arras.

Aug. 21—Germans driven across Oise.

Aug. 22—Bolsheviki declare war exists with United States.

Aug. 24—Austrians retake Berat.

Aug. 27—French take Roye and Nesle.

Aug. 28—U. S. troops attack Juvigny.

Aug. 29—British recross the Somme.

Aug. 31–Sept. 2—Japanese defeat Bolsheviki on Ussuri River.

Sept. 2—British break Drocourt-Queant line.

Sept. 5—French recover Aisne-Ailette line.

Sept. 6—Germans retreat to Hindenburg line.

Sept. 12—U. S. army takes St. Mihiel salient.

Sept. 14—Drive on Macedonian front begun.

Sept. 16—French take Vailly.

Sept. 18—British attack Cambrai-St. Quentin front.

Sept. 20—Turks defeated north of Jerusalem.

Sept. 22—British take Nazareth.

Sept. 22—Salonika army of Allies advances against Bulgaria.

Sept. 23—Serbians reach the Vardar.

Sept. 26—U. S. campaign on the Meuse begun.

Sept. 26—French drive in Champagne.

Sept. 27—Bulgarians ask armistice.

Sept. 27—British attack on Hindenburg line.

Sept. 29—27th U. S. division goes through Hindenburg line near Le Catelet.

Sept. 29—Belgians begin drive; take Houthoulst forest.

Sept. 30—Bulgaria surrenders.

Sept. 30—Messines ridge retaken.

Sept. 30—Turks surrender west of Jordan.

Oct. 1—British take Damascus.

Oct. 2—French retake St. Quentin.

Oct. 4—Naval attack on Durazzo.

Oct. 6-19—U. S. advance on the Meuse.

Oct. 5—King Ferdinand of Bulgaria abdicates.

Oct. 6—Germany asks peace on Wilson's terms.

Oct. 7—Germans retreat north of Rheims.

Oct. 8—Cambrai-St. Quentin front smashed.

Oct. 12—French take Craonne and Vouziers.

Oct. 13—Serbians take Nish.

Oct. 15—U. S. troops take Grand Pré.

Oct. 17—Ostend, Courtrai and Lille retaken.

Oct. 18—Bruges, Zeebrugge and Thielt taken.

Oct. 18—Turcoing, Roubaix and Douai taken.

Oct. 22—British reach the Scheldt.

Oct. 25—Italians begin offensive on the Piave.

Oct. 27—German note; await Allies' terms.

Oct. 27—Ludendorff resigns.

Oct. 27—Italians cross the Piave.

Oct. 27—British take Aleppo.

Oct. 28—Austria sends note to Wilson accepting terms and asking armistice.

Oct. 30—Italians take Vittorio.

Oct. 30—British defeat Turks on the Tigris.

Oct. 31—Turkey surrenders.

Oct. 31—Austria sends commissioners to Diaz.

Nov. 1—U. S. army again attacks on the Meuse.

Nov. 3—Italians occupy Trent, Rovereto and Trieste.

Nov. 3—Austria surrenders.

Nov. 3—British take Valenciennes.

Nov. 3—Serbians take Belgrade.

Nov. 3—Count Tisza assassinated.

Nov. 3—German sailors successfully defy their officers.

Nov. 4—Allied war council agrees on armistice terms.

Nov. 4—Italians take Scutari.
Nov. 7—U. S. army reaches Sedan.
Nov. 9—Kaiser abdicates.
Nov. 11—British take Mons.
Nov. 11, 11 A.M.—ARMISTICE.

Nov. 12—Republic proclaimed in Berlin.
Nov. 19—French enter Metz.
Nov. 21—German fleet surrenders.
Dec. 1—Ally armies enter Germany.

BIBLIOGRAPHY OF THE GREAT WAR

I. The Causes of the War

NICOLAI, G. F., *The Biology of War*. A profound analysis of the nature and history of war, with special reference to the Great War.

ZIMMERN, A. E., *Nationality and Government*. A thorough and convincing study of the contrasting ideals set forth by Prussianism, by Bolshevism and by Democracy.

SCHAPIRO, J. SALWYN, *Modern and Contemporary European History*. Reviews history from 1815 up to the Great War; carefully and clearly and thoroughly, with the War always in view.

DAVIS, W. S., *The Roots of the War*. Reviews European history after 1870, and summarizes simply but thoroughly the antagonisms which led to the Great War.

ROSE, J. H., *Origin of the War*. Gives the British viewpoint, as seen by a noted and highly honored historian.

CHERADAME, A., *The Pan-German Plot Unmasked*. A widely read and striking work by a French writer who had foreseen the War.

ARCHER, WILLIAM, *Gems of German Thought*. A popular English work made up of quotations from ambitious Germans before and during the early stages of the War.

Out of their Own Mouths. (Published by Appleton). An anonymous collection similar to the preceding.

BERNHARDI, F. VON, *Germany and the Next War*. This work, published shortly before the War, is the clearest authoritative German book upholding German plans of conquest.

BULOW, PRINCE VON, *Imperial Germany*. Revised during the early stages of the War and so republished, this may be accepted as the popular, patriotic German view of the sources of the contest.

NAUMANN, F., *Central Europe*. A really brilliant study of Germany's possibilities and powers for developing a great Middle Europe empire. The author, who died shortly after the War, was one of Germany's ablest thinkers.

NIPPOLD, O., *German Chauvanism*. A noted German scholar portrays the aggressive spirit of his people just before the war, and cautions them against it.

WILLMORE, J. S., *The Great Crime and its Moral*. A patriotic British work published during the War, tracing the origins of the Prussian system, and picturing the resulting horrors.

HAUSER, HENRI, *Germany's Commercial Grip*. A brief but powerful French picture of Germany's control of world finance just before the War.

PHILLIPSON, COLEMAN, *Alsace Lorraine*. A British work much noted by Germans because it does not wholly condemn their claims to or treatment of Alsace-Lorraine. A full and scholarly work fair to both sides.

JASTROW, M., *The War and the Bagdad Railway*. An American scholar's study of conditions in the Near East, leading up to the War.

BRAILSFORD, H. N., *The War of Steel and Gold*. A sincere and thoughtful "Pacifist" book, tracing the War back to capitalistic imperialism.

BARKER, J. E., *The Foundations of Germany*. A careful and thoughtful review of the construction of German government and its tendencies, by a noted British economist, Professor of History at Oxford. Written during the War.

HALDANE, LORD, *Before the War*. One of the earliest and most valuable books of "memoirs" dealing with conditions before the War. Lord Haldane was the "liaison" official, the Britisher who sought to keep his country on kindly terms with Germany. He conducted frequent negotiations in the old diplomatic style.

POINCARE, RAYMOND, *The Origins of the War*. Poincaré, having been President of France at the opening of the War, was accused by some of his own country men of having helped to bring on the disaster. In answer he wrote this work, which is thus a personal defense. It is full, and frank of tone, and gave much new light upon diplomatic intrigue. It depicts the position of Russia as well as that of France.

TARDIEU, A., *France and the Alliances*. A powerful semi-official presentation of the French viewpoint as to the actual outbreak of the War.

Collected Diplomatic Documents Relating to the Outbreak of the European War (published by Doran). A useful collection of the various statements issued by European governments as their justification in entering the War.

CHITWOOD, O. P., *The Immediate Causes of the War*. A clear and convincing American picture of the German "Will to War."

AHCHER, W., The Thirteen Days. An exhaustive British narrative of the exciting days immediately preceding the outbreak of fighting in the War.

BECK, J. A., *The Evidence in the Case*. A vigorous American indictment of Germany, approaching the charges from a lawyer's viewpoint of probability and proof.

FERRERO, G., *Who Wanted the European War*. This famous Italian historian here dramatically voices the Italian view, and presents the special evidence possessed by Italy as a member of the former Alliance of Central Europe.

MURRAY, G., *The Foreign Policy of Sir Edward Grey*. A careful British review and exposition of Britain's efforts for freindly relations under Grey as Foreign Minister, leading up to his handling of the situation with Germany.

LOREBURN, EARL, *How the War Came*. This work gives a reverse British view from the preceding. It pictures Grey as a bungler fussing over trifles while missing essentials which might have prevented the War.

GRELLING, R., *I Accuse* and *The Crime*. Two powerful books by a German scholar accusing his Government of having planned the War and his people of having welcomed it. For the first book, issued early in the War, he was compelled to flee from Germany. The second book is an enlargement and continuation of the first.

SCHIEMANN, PROF., *Germany's and Kaiser William II's Alleged Re-*

sponsibility for the Outbreak of the World's War. This is the semi-official German defense. It admits little and repudiates much that has become established history.

KAUTSKY, KARL, *Guilt of William Hohenzollern.* For six weeks only the Independent Socialists took part in governing Germany just after the Armistice. They set "Comrade Kautsky" to publishing the secret archives, and even in the brief time before his work was stopped he gathered the evidences of the militarists' guilt which the book reveals.

JAGOW, GOTTLIEB VON, *Causes and Outbreak of the World War.* The author was "Secretary of State for Foreign Affairs" in Germany in 1914. As such he was the buffer between the German leaders and foreign statesmen who sought peace. His work is important, but conceived in the old diplomatic style of "loyalty to the government."

LUDENDORFF, GENERAL ERICH VON, *Secret Documents of the German High Staff.* This work published in 1921 has less interest than the author's other War books, but it shows the years of preparation pointed toward a war in 1914.

Comparative Historical Tablets. Published anonymously, this little work owes its interest wholly to the fact that it has been generally accepted as the work of the Kaiser himself. It groups historic incidents of the past to show other nations as the constant aggressors, Germany as the consistent friend of peace.

EMPEROR WILLIAM II, *Memoirs.* Like the preceding book, this work owes its interest solely to its authorship. It says surprisingly little and nothing surprising. Historical fact has become strangely perverted in the author's mind.

FREDERICK WILLIAM HOHENZOLLERN, *Memoirs of the Crown Prince of Germany.* This work is much more one of memoirs than of military history. It gives briefly the writer's opinion of his various campaigns, but is much more a glorification and defense of the royal house.

ANDRASSY, COUNT JULIUS, *Diplomacy and the World War.* Count Andrasay was a leading Austrian statesman, but not a member of the cabinet which declared War. He was not of the innermost circle. What he knows of Austria's approach to the War is told vividly and convincingly.

WOODS, H. C., *The Cradle of the War.* An authoritative work on the Balkans and Turkey by one who has dwelt and traveled there. An examination of the Middle Europe plans of Germany.

SETON-WATSON, R. W., *The Rise of Nationality in the Balkans.* A study by a British authority, published after the War, and reviewing former affairs in the new light of today.

MASARYK, T. G., *The Slavs amongst Nations.* An authoritative work written in 1915 by the leader who was to be the first president of Czecho-Slovakia.

GAUSS, CHR. *Why We Went to War.* An American work clearly reviewing the steps by which the United States was driven into antagonism to Germany, including a study of German propaganda in America.

Scott, J. B., *Diplomatic Correspondence between the United States and Germany.* A collection of all the important documents, with careful explanations and discussions.

Bernstorff, Count Julius von, *My Three Years in America.* A work of special pleading to show that the author did everything for peace and avoided intrigue.

II. Military and Naval History

Buchan, J., *Nelson's History of the War.* A very full British history of the War written year by year or almost month by month as the War continued. It is the work of an established scholar and the best of its kind.

The Times History of the War (London). A similar British work in many volumes, anonymous but semi-official, and accepted by the British as the standard history.

Hanotaux, G., *History of the War.* A similar French work by a really great historian.

Simonds, F., *History of the Great War.* The best of the similar American works, written as the War progressed.

New York Times Current History. A binding into volumes of the monthly magazine, with all its articles, some valuable, some mistaken, and most of them now out of date and filling much space with little value. This was a masterly work as a magazine.

Hayes, Carlton, *Brief History of the Great War.* A standard American work, concise and reliable.

Frothingham, Captain Thomas. *A Guide to the Military History of the Great War.* A painstaking work giving facts, figures and data with satisfactory accuracy.

McPherson, Wm. L., *Strategy of the Great War* and *Short History of the Great War.* Two brief American reviews, clear and accurate. The "Strategy" is a work of knowledge and insight and very helpful for an understanding of general principles.

Doyle, A. Conan, *History of the Great War.* This deals wholly with the British efforts in the War, giving these with great detail, and written year by year during the War, a volume for each year.

Wallace, W. K., *Greater Italy.* The best work available in English to present the War from the Italian viewpoint.

Arnoux, Anthony, *The European War.* A resolutely pro-German work in several volumes, issued in America up to 1917, and most interesting in its divergence from other American war books.

Malherbe, Henri, *The Flame that is France.* A picture of the French effort and suffering in the War. This work won the literary Goncourt Prize in Paris in 1917.

Bernhardi, General F. von, *Germany's Heroic Struggle.* The author's books praising militarism before the War (see page 213) make his courage admirable in that he writes after as before with all faith in Germany. A vehement and most interesting old wardog condemning every civilian authority including the Kaiser.

Malkowsky, E., *Der Weltkrieg.* A popular German history widely read in Germany during the War and now available in other lands.

BREITNER, ERHART, *Kriegsbilder.* A work similar to the above, but more emphatically Prussian.

RITTER, CAPTAIN H., *A Criticism of the World War.* This has not yet been translated into English. All readers of German will find it what German critics have called it "the best study of the War campaigns." Each German blunder and each blunder of the Allies is pointed out sharply and convincingly. The author is wholly impartial.

FALKENHAYN, GENERAL E. VON, *General Headquarters, 1914-1916.* The author was in strategic command of all the German armies from the defeat at the Marne until Ludendorff superseded him. His work, though one-sided, is extremely instructive. It pictures Germany as never recovering from the Marne defeat, struggling always against overwhelming numbers.

LUDENDORFF, GENERAL E. VON, *My War Memories.* This important work, promptly translated into all leading tongues, is a narrow review and defense of this great general's own acts throughout the War. It is as instructive as it is unreliable. The author frankly admits using deception in all his statements issued during the War, and gives evidence that he has not abandoned this policy in peace.

LUDENDORFF, E. VON, *The General Staff and its Problems.* This, the General's second book, is more technical than the first and much more reliable. His third work, "War and Politics," has not yet been made available to English readers, except in the extracts given in the present volumes.

DELBRUCK, PROF. HANS, *Ludendorff's Self-portrait.* A noted German historian here picks to pieces Ludendorff's series of books, branding them as false and pretentious and arrogant. Delbruck should be read side by side with Ludendorff.

TIRPITZ, ADMIRAL A. VON, *Memoirs.* Less involved than Ludendorff in the final disaster of the War, von Tirpitz is able to speak more securely. His criticisms of the other German leaders are frank. The only man who is always right in his book is himself.

HINDENBURG, MARSHAL P. VON, *Out of My Life.* While professing to be an autobiography, this deals almost wholly with the Marshal's campaigns in the war. It is simple, straightforward and extremely valuable, though all too brief.

JOFFRE, MARSHAL J., *Preparation of the War and Conduct of Operations in 1914-1915.* The title explains the contents. This is an authoritative work but not illuminative. It is restrained and technical.

FRENCH, GENERAL J., *"1914": Memoirs.* The British Marshal's own story with an introduction by Marshal Foch.

BELLOC, H., *Elements of the Great War.* An American study of the early battles, written in masterly fashion, but at too early a period for the writer to have much real information.

WYRALL, E., *Europe in Arms.* A vivid narrative of the early battles from a British viewpoint.

PERRIS, G. H. *The Campaign of 1914 in France and Belgium.* The clearest, early picture of its period.

SAROLEA, C., *How Belgium Saved Europe.* Deals equally with the sufferings and with the achievements of Belgium in 1914.

DE GERLACHE DE GOMMERY, *Belgium in War Time.* A Belgian book, published in Europe as "The Country that will not Die," and translated into all leading languages. A remarkably vivid pitcure of Belgium's effort.

ESSEN, LEON VAN DER, *Invasion and War in Belgium.* The Belgian professor of History at Louvain University gives the completed picture of his country's effort in the first year of warfare, scholarly, moderate, complete.

SOUZA, COUNT CHARLES DE, *Germany in Defeat.* (4 vols.) A powerful tactical study of the various campaigns by a critic who insisted that Germany was defeated at the Marne and was always thereafter struggling helplessly against fate.

KUHL, GENERAL H. VON, *The Marne Campaign.* As one of the lesser leaders in the first German rush, von Kuhl knows his theme. He is patient, methodical and full of detail. While refusing to admit a full German failure, he talks instructive truth about the campaign.

VON KLUCK, A., *The March on Paris and the Battle of the Marne, 1914.* This work by the leader of the German army which advanced nearest to Paris in the first rush, is like the books of the other German leaders, an attempt to explain how well the author did everything, and how failure was not really failure after all.

RECOULY, CAPTAIN F., *General Joffre.* French pen picture by a staff officer serving with and greatly admiring the French Marshal.

RECOULY, F., *Foch, the Winner of the War.* In this later work, this vivid, French historian, readjusts his earlier enthusiasm for Joffre, and finds in Foch the supreme general of France. A well-drawn picture.

HAMILTON, GENERAL IAN, *Gallipoli Diary.* Since Hamilton commanded at Britain's Gallipoli disaster, his story of it becomes of real importance. He makes little effort to theorize or generalize; but simply and in a manly way he states that confronted by these conditions he took these steps.

MINTO, P., *The Most Glorious Page in the History of Italy.* An enthusiastic account of the great Italian victory on the Piave.

POWELL, E. A., *Italy at War.* A good though only very general picture of the Italian struggle, from a single observer's viewpoint.

TREVELYAN, G. M., *Scenes from Italy's War.* A masterly review by a sympathetic British Red Cross chief, who served in Italy throughout the War.

GOURKO, GENERAL BASIL, *Russia 1914-1917.* A military history by a leading Russian general. The author is not always thoroughly informed; but the work is as interesting as it is important.

WASHBURN, S., *Field Notes from the Russian Front.* The British official observer has here written his personal experiences in several volumes, professionally hopeful and admiring, yet full of informative fact.

ACKERMAN, C. W., *Trailing the Bolsheviki.* Narrative of an American journalist in Siberia during the revolution there, concise, clear, vivid.

GORDON-SMITH, G., *Serbia, Her Part in the Great War*. An authoritative survey of Serbia's efforts and her suffering.

PRICE, G. WARD, *Story of the Salonica Army*. A British observer tells in full the delays, difficulties and final success of the Ally troops in the southern Balkans.

HOPKINS, J., *Canada at War*. A full, vigorous, patriotic résumé of Canada's efforts and accomplishments.

NESMITH, G., *Canada's Sons and Great Britain in the World War*. A similar work to the above but more strictly military.

MACPHERSON, J. S. P., *Canada in the Great World War*. A full six volume work, going into detail of efforts at home and in Europe.

STEELE, H. E. R., *Canadians in France*. A fair-minded and patriotic picture of the splendid work accomplished by the Canadian forces.

SHELDON-WILLIAMS, R. F., *The Canadian Front in France and Flanders*. The most complete and carefully prepared work yet issued to tell of Canada's part on the actual fields of battle.

MASSEY, W. T., *Desert Campaigns*. Narrative of the official press representative with the British armies in the Near East.

CANDLER, E., *The Long Road to Bagdad*. A similar account of the Mesopotamian campaigns of the British.

PORTER, R. N., *Japan*. An excellent brief history carried down to 1918.

BASSETT, J. S., *Our War with Germany*. A brief, clear picture of the United States' part in the War.

PALMER, MAJOR F., *America in France*. Eye-witness story by a noted American writer who had many special facilities for seeing and judging.

McMASTER, J. B., *The United States in the World War*. A standard work by a standard historian. The first volume deals with the opening phases of the War. The second with the active forces during the War.

PAGE, A. W., *Our 110 Day's Fighting*. A full record of the actual fighting done by each United States Army Division.

THOMAS, SHIPLEY, *History of the A. E. F.* A careful and vigorous account of the great expedition, covering all the details of landing, drilling the troops, auxiliary services, etc.

DE CHAMBRUN, COLONEL J. A., *The American Army in the European Conflict*. An authoritative review by the French officer in charge of the work of "harmonizing" the French and American armies. Deals with all the American activities in France, fully, carefully and with much laudation.

WRIGHT, PETER, E., *At the Supreme War Council*. The author was present at the council during the latter part of the War. He acted as interpreter and secretary. He admired Foch as opposed to Haig and Pétain; and he quotes freely from the minutes of the council to uphold his views.

MAURICE, GENERAL SIR F., *The Last Four Months*. An authoritative work by Britain's great military expert. No clearer or more convincing book has explained the final drive of the Allies.

GIBBS, P., *Now it can be Told*. An "after the war" book of reminiscences by Britain's most noted press representative on the French front, criticizing many details especially of British leadership, on which he had been silent in earlier writings.

GIBBS, P., *The Way to Victory*. A two-volume account of the author's experiences on the British front, told with much patriotic enthusiasm.

JELLICOE, LORD, *The Grand Fleet, 1914-1916*. The main British work on the naval war, by the chief Admiral, well written, but chiefly made up of official reports. A second volume carries the record on to 1920.

HURD, A. S., *Heroic Record of the British Navy*. Britain's chief naval writer reviews and sums up the naval battles and labors of the War, from the British viewpoint.

TERRY, C. S., *Zeebrugge and Ostend Dispatches*. The author does little more than edit the various dispatches and reports about the celebrated Zeebrugge Raid which blocked the submarine base. Even in this shape the heroic tale thrills the blood.

SIMS, WILLIAM LOWDEN, *The Victory at Sea*. Rear Admiral Sims, the chief United States naval leader in the War, here gives his view of the difficulties which the United States navy had to face, and of the splendid success with which it overcame these difficulties. The book has caused much discussion because of its striking picture of the unpreparedness of the navy at the beginning of the War.

GILL, C., *Naval Power in the War*. An American study, careful and clear, of each naval contest in the earlier years of the War.

ISAACS, LIEUT. E. V., *Prisoner of the U-90*. Personal narrative of a United States naval officer, with an introduction by the Secretary of the Navy, Josephus Daniels. A vivid picture of U-boat life, prison life in Germany, and escape.

TURNER, C. C., *The Struggle in the Air*. A complete, brief record of aerial flights and fighters and the development of aviation during the War.

NEUMANN, G. P., *German Air Forces in the Great War*. This is merely a compilation of translations of German statements and reports. Even so, it gives the fullest available knowledge of the Germans' really remarkable aerial efforts.

BORDEAUX, H., *Guynemer, Knight of the Air*. A romantic, enthusiastic sketch of the achievements and death of the most famed of French aviators.

GIBBS, A. H., *Gun Fodder*. Personal narrative of a British soldier during four years of the War as enlisted man and artillery officer.

TASLAUANU, O., *With the Austrian Army*. A frank, chatty volume, wholly free from pose or pretense, showing Austria's levies upon her subject races.

Narrative of a German Destrter. An anonymous and unestablished story, but of extreme human interest and convincing. The author declares himself a German Socialist forced into the War but at first believing it righteous.

BLANCHON, G., *The New Warfare*. The War and its new methods and inventions, a study from the technical and scientific standpoint.

III. POLITICAL AND ECONOMICAL HISTORY

SCOTT, JAMES B., *The Hague Peace Conferences*. The best authority on the efforts to establish International Law through the Hague Conferences of 1899 and 1907, thus portraying the status of International Law at the opening of the War.

CLARK HAMILTON AND MOULTON, *Readings in the Economics of War*. A valuable compendium, covering a wide field, and most important for any general study of conditions.

OGG, F. A., *National Governments and the World War*. A comprehensive review of the growth of the main governments concerned in the War, and of the effects of the War upon each.

SEYMOUR, C., *Diplomatic Background of the War*. A standard work for all details of the actual breaking off of diplomatic relations in 1914.

STODDARD, L., *Stakes of the War*. This gives the facts of race, trade and territory involved in the War, with special reference to Middle Europe, the Balkans, the Russian border lands, and the Rhine frontier. It has received wide American indorsement.

ALBERTI, M., *Italy's Great War and her National Aspirations*. The military as well as the economic aspects of the War are here covered in a vigorous, patriotic manner.

GIBBONS, H. A., *The New Map of Asia*. An authoritative summary by an American who had examined all the regions and studied their problems. Covers the War, the years immediately preceding it, and the new problems arising from the War.

GRUMBACH, S., *Germany's Annexationist Aims*. A work mainly of quotations from German publications, to show German plans and dreams of glory.

ZANGWILL, I., *The War for the World*. A powerful picture of the causes and of the opening efforts and effects of the War.

BETHMANN-HOLLWEG, T. VON, *Reflections on the Great War*. An instructive though unconvincing book from the German viewpoint of before the War, stating what the German Imperial Chancellor hopes the world will ultimately believe.

CZERNIN, COUNT O., *In the World War*. We have here the memoirs of the Austrian Imperial Chancellor, very similar in character to the preceding.

ERZBERGER, MATHIAS, *Experiences in the World War*. The writer, since assassinated, was the leader of the German Catholic party during the War, and a government leader afterward. He probably knew much more than he writes, as the book is chiefly an explanation of his course.

HELFFERICH, KARL, *The World War*. A ponderous three-volume work by Germany's government financier, plausible but unconvincing.

WINDISCHGRAETZ, PRINCE LUDWIG, *Memoirs*. The author, a Hungarian aristocrat of the old school, was confidential adviser to the young Emperor Charles. He had also known Emperor Franz Josef intimately. His book is an exceptionally vivid picture of the last days of the crumbling Austro-Hungarian Empire.

MARGUTTI, VON *Recollections of the Old Kaiser*. Margutti was private secretary to Franz Josef and writes intimately of many trifles. He declares that the Germans coerced and misled Austria into the War, and that his master sent the ultimatum "in order to please Germany."

JONESCU, T., *Some Personal Impressions.* Rumania's leading states- man before the War and during the armistice, adds his interesting reminiscences to the list of those presented by the chief statesmen of the War.

WILSON, W., *The Triumph of Ideals.* This is little more than a col- lection from President Wilson's speeches, but the best summary of his views, preceding his promised history of the War.

TUMULTY, J. P., *Woodrow Wilson as I know Him.* Tumulty, the President's personal secretary, has here given us a most sym- pathetic and appreciative sketch of the efforts and difficulties of his chief.

LLOYD GEORGE, *Memoirs.* These cover not only the War but also his earlier career. They give an easy explanation of the author's ideas, and are full of their author's charm and patriotic enthusiasm.

MERCIER, CARDINAL DESIREE, *Cardinal Mercier's Own Story.* The author depicts himself most impressively. It is a tragic picture of what Belgium suffered and of how he struggled for his people. You live the awful years over again with him.

MAETERLINCK, M., *The Wrack of the Storm.* A passionate vision of the Belgian outlook and the Belgian suffering.

WAXWEILER, E., *Belgium Neutral and Loyal.* A full and semi- authoritative picture of Belgium's stand and of her efforts.

TOYNBEE, J. A., *The German Terror in Belgium. The German Terror in France. The Destruction of Poland.* Three carefully compiled, semi-official books depicting the miseries inflicted by the Germans.

WHITLOCK, BRAND, *Belgium, A Personal Narrative.* This personal narrative of the chief representative of the United States in Bel- gium during the period of its invasion thrills with the writer's horror and disgust against the German military leaders. The work forms an unanswerable accusation against Germany.

JORGENSEN, J., *False Witness.* A remarkable book by a Danish neu- tral, analyzing the German charges against Belgium. This work did much to convince the neutral world of German falsity.

ELLIOT, A. D., *Traditions of British Statesmanship.* A brief re- view of Britain's problems before the War, leading to a full ex- position of her internal problems and struggles during its progress.

DESTREE, JULES, *Britain in Arms.* Considers Britain's efforts from the French standpoint, and traces the increasing growth of Democ- racy in Britain during the War.

BARKER, E., *Ireland in the Last Fifty Years.* A friendly review by a well-known scholar, issued in London in 1917.

WELLS, W. B., *History of the Irish Rebellion of 1916.* A fair and thoughtful account by a scholar, an eye-witness of many of the scenes.

JOY, M., *Irish Rebellion of 1916 and its Martyrs.* This is the semi- official account from the side of the Irish sympathisers.

RADZIWILL, PRINCESS CATHERINE, *Russia's Decline and Fall.* A lady of the highest court circles, American by birth but Russian by marriage and long residence, describes all she saw and knew up to 1917.

KERENSKY, A. F., *The Prelude to Bolshevism.* The Russian leader's own view of Russia's downfall.

LEVINE, I. D., *The Russian Revolution.* An early and brief but very clear picture of the First Revolution of 1917, that against the Czar.

DILLON, E. J., *The Eclipse of Russia.* Though this was one of the earliest works written on the Russian downfall, yet the author's knowledge of his theme was so broad that the book remains one of our best sources, and has gone through repeated editions.

SAYLER, O. M., *Russia White or Red.* Personal narrative of a British witness, who saw the efforts of both the Czarists and the Bolshevists.

TROTSKY, L., *History of the Russian Revolution to Brest-Litovsk.* The Bolshevist leader here gives his own view of what he had accomplished for Russia up to the time of his "peace-struggle" against Germany. History has since contradicted most of his conclusions.

NOSEK, V., *Independent Bohemia.* An account of the Czecho-Slovak struggle for liberty, carried through 1918, authoritative and including most of the documents.

BAILEY, V. F., *The Slavs of the War Zone.* Mainly a picture of conditions among the South Slavs under Austrian rule, but with some vivid war scenes.

BENES, E., *Bohemia's Case for Independence.* An authoritative statement written during the War.

GORDON, MRS. W., *Roumania* [Sic.]. Narrative of Rumanian purposes, scenes and sufferings by an eye-witness in the Rumanian capital.

SAVIC, V. R., *South-Eastern Europe.* A Serbian writing during the War pictures the downfall of his country and its hopes and plans for a new life.

HIBBON, PAXTON, *Constantine I and the Greek People.* Hibbon, a well-known and highly reputed American traveler and author, here takes the standpoint that Constantine was never pro-German but only pro-Greek, and that he was a true patriot who saved his country from much of the misery of the War.

GIBBONS, H. A., *Venizelos.* Dr. Gibbons was in close touch with the great Greek statesman in Paris during the Peace Conference. Hence he writes with fullest knowledge and with sympathy, showing Venizelos as a great man directing a great movement.

LATZKO, ANDREAS, *Men in War.* An Austrian work, probably the most powerful "pacifist" argument produced by the War, an awful picture of the sufferings, mental rather than physical, of the soldiers at the front and at home.

DAVISON, H. P., *The American Red Cross in the Great War.* A straight-forward, unpretentious work which manages nevertheless to give a most impressive outline of the widespread effort and enthusiasm of non-combatant America.

JONES & HOLLISTER, *The German Secret Service in America.* A complete and semi-official review of the "War within the War" conducted by the Germans.

GOMPERS, SAMUEL, *American Labor and the War.* The collected war speeches of this noted labor leader, expressing the views and efforts of his followers.

GERARD, J. W., *My Four Years in Germany.* Personal narrative of the United States Ambassador in Germany before and during the early years of the War.

MORGENTHAU, HENRY, *Ambassador Morgenthau's Story.* A welltold and most impressive narrative of events in Constantinople during the early years of the War. The author saw to the heart of the great contest, and makes others see with him.

SCHINZ, A., *French Literature of the Great War.* A very useful summary of French writings and French views throughout the War.

IV. RECONSTRUCTION

VANDERLIP, F., *What Happened to Europe.* A keen analysis by a keen American financier who investigated in Europe. He notes the nature of the losses and the needs in each European land.

GARVIN, J. L., *Economic Foundations of Peace.* A broad and valuable study of the past and future economic relations of the nations and the conditions of the peoples.

CHERADAME, A., *The Essentials of an Enduring Victory.* A valuable French study written while the War was still in progress, and prophetic of what would follow. A study of how Germany could and should be restrained hereafter.

FERRERO, G., *Problems of Peace.* A famous Italian scholar's review of the past from 1815 down, in order to apply its lesson to the era of reconstruction.

NITTI, FRANCISCO, *The Wreck of Europe.* Nitti was Italy's premier in 1919, 1920. He writes therefore with knowledge as with bitterness. He condemns French militarism since the War, especially her use of colored troops in Germany. He sees Europe staggering from bad to worse.

HOBBS, W. H., *The World War and Its Consequences.* A powerful American work, written during the War, endorsed in an introduction by Theodore Roosevelt.

MARCOSSON, I. F., *The War After the War.* Problems of reconstruction are here shrewdly looked forward to by an American, just as his nation entered on the War.

KEYNES, J. M., *Economic Consequences of the Peace.* A powerful work in opposition to the peace terms as creating a "peace of revenge" rather than one of justice and wisdom in dealing with Central Europe.

KEYNES, J. M., *A Revision of the Treaty.* In this, a continuation of his preceding book, Mr. Keynes pleads for readjustments. This is a thoroughly scholarly and scientific amplification of the earlier work; but the author is still a theorist not a statesman.

LANE, R. (Norman Angell), *The British Revolution and the American Democracy.* An interpretation of the British labor movement and a prophecy for America.

FRIEDMAN, E. M., *Labor and Reconstruction in Europe.* A very valuable and instructive study of labor legislation of the past and present, combined with the author's judgment as to what future legislation should attempt.

HENDERSON, A., *The Aims of Labor.* A labor leader's clear, plain statement of the chief problems of the future.

WOOD, C. W., *The Great Change.* A study of the "new America" produced by the War, and the new problems confronting it.

COMMONS, J. R., *History of Labor in the United States.* A comprehensive and scholarly two-volume work giving a clear and fair review of the development of the labor movement.

VANDERWELDE, EMIL, *Socialism versus the State.* Belgium's most noted Socialist statesman sums up the desires and plans of European Socialism as learned by the War's experience.

SPARGO, JOHN, *Bolshevism.* A Socialist's careful study of the origin and results of the Russian movement. The author rejects Bolshevism wholly, while strongly supporting Socialism.

LENIN, NICHOLAI, *The Soviets at Work.* The master revolutionist's passionate devotion to his work makes his explanations interesting. In this book he discusses "the international position of the Russian Soviet Republic and the fundamental problems of the Socialist revolution."

COOLEY, C. H., *Social Process.* An effort to establish the laws of society's development, so as to apply them to present problems.

THAYER, W. R., *Democracy, Discipline, Peace.* An effort to establish the fundamental principles of self-government by the peoples, as viewed in the light of the War.

DOMBROWSKI, E., *German Leaders of Yesterday and Today.* This is the work of a Berlin journalist. It is clever and frankly satiric. Indeed the author's estimate of all the German leaders is such as could only have been published in the new Germany of today. The book contains much new material.

SCHEIDERMANN, PHILIP, *The Collapse.* The author was one of the two chief leaders of Germany in the first days of the German Republic and he had been long a Socialist and member of the Reichstag. He tells of his own efforts in founding the Republic, unconsciously picturing himself as a "feeble little bourgeois fussing over trifles while the world sweeps by."

YOUNG, G., *The New Germany.* This is a good journalistic account of the revolution of 1918 and the reconstruction that followed. No work really authoritative on this subject has yet been issued; but from Mr. Young we at least get a clear outline of fact.

TEAD, O., *The People's Part in Peace.* Discusses what the mass of the peoples in all lands want, and what would be wise and good for them.

MILLARD, T. F., *Democracy and the Eastern Question.* A careful and thorough study of the rights and also of the practical possibilities of the peoples of the East as regards self-government.

JASTROW, M., *The Eastern Question.* Reviews the situation after the War, and the needs and prospects in the Balkans, Arabia, Palestine, and Armenia.

BUTLER, RALPH, *The New Eastern Europe.* An authoritative study of the problems of reconstruction along the Russian and Balkan frontiers.

GORDON-SMITH, G., *From Serbia to Jugo-Slavia.* A narrative of the union of the South Slavs under Serbian leadership, clear and impressive.

MASARYK, T. G., *Small Nations in the European Crisis.* A patriotic and philosophic work by the scholar president of Czecho-Slovakia.

HUDDLESTON, S., *Peace Making at Paris.* A bright and keen British account of the Peace Conference.

TEMPERLEY, H. W. V., *History of the Peace Conference at Paris.* A five-volume work, the most complete and comprehensive history of the Conference. Its standpoint is distinctly British; but its facts are indisputable.

BAKER, R. S., *What Wilson did at Paris.* An authoritative American narrative from the standpoint of President Wilson's adherents.

HANSEN, H., *Adventures of the Fourteen Points.* Narrative by an American eye-witness, from a less approving stand than the preceding.

HOUSE, EDWARD M., *What Really Happened at Paris.* Colonel House here writes in conjunction with Professor Charles Seymour of Yale. Thus an actual knowledge of facts is here united with the broadest scholarship. The book is the outcome of a series of lectures delivered by delegates to the Peace Conference. The lectures and discussions that followed upon them are here condensed into one comprehensive work.

LANSING, ROBERT, *The Big Four and others of the Peace Conference.* The United States Secretary of State and delegate to the Conference here gives his personal impressions of the Treaty and the way it was made. He differed from President Wilson on several points and devotes himself chiefly to these points of disagreement.

TARDIEU, ANDRE, *The Truth about the Treaty.* This may be regarded as a semi-official statement of France's views. M. Tardieu was M. Clemenceau's confidential adviser throughout the treaty discussions.

DILLON, E. J., *The Inside Story of the Peace Conference.* The most powerful review of the Conference from an antagonistic standpoint. Dr. Dillon is a noted British economist who disapproved almost everything the Conference did.

LATANE, J. H., *From Isolation to Leadership.* A shrewd review of the development of international policy in Britain and the United States.

BASS, JOHN F., AND MOULTON, H. G., *America and the Balance Sheet of Europe.* A brief work in almost primer style that everyone should read. It is elementary but complete in its establishing of the first principles of economics.

V. THE LEAGUE OF NATIONS

SAYRE, F. B., *Experiments in International Administration.* A thoughtful, analytic study of previous efforts and of the causes that threaten failure to the present League.

sinking, III, 189; Germany accuses Britain of, III, 220; Germany convicted of inventing false charges of, III, 300; of Turks on Bulgars, III, 329; in Serbia, III, 351 et seq., 358, 404 et seq.; by Teuton government in Poland, III, 425 et seq.; in Mexico, IV, 61 et seq., 81; submarine, IV, 89 et seq.; in Greece, V, 226; in Russian Revolution, V, 332 et seq.; in Ukraine, VI, 19; in Czecho-Slovakia, VII, 142.

Australia, Germany hopes to win, I, 273; aids Britain, II, 361 et seq.; aids against Tsing-tau, II, 402 et seq.; German raiders on coasts of, II, 448; troops at Dardanelles, III, 252 et seq.; troops at Somme, IV, 246; aid of 1917 by, V, xxxiii; Britain loyally aided by, V, 122, 145; troops at Messines Ridge, V, 207 et seq.; in battle of Flanders, V, 277 et seq.; aids in Holy Land, V, 401 et seq.; aids in Lys battle, VI, 116 et seq.; aids to break Hindenburg Line, VI, 287 et seq.; aids in Palestine, VI, 336 et seq.; at Peace Conference, VII, 54.

Austria, early history of, I, xx; German friendship for, I, 4; war plans of, I, xxi; Germany encourages, I, xxxv; ultimatum by, I, xxxvii; forces war on Serbia, I, xxxviii et seq.; leniency to subject races, I, 61; diplomatic successes, I, 119; enfeebled in 1913, I, 129; leniency to Poles, I, 151 et seq.; many languages in, I, 161; quarrels with Balkans, I, 176 et seq.; saved by Germany, I, 186 et seq.; losses in Balkan wars, I, 231 et seq.; historical rescue by Russia, I, 365.

   Assassination of Crown Prince, I, xviii; 245 et seq.; prepares to force war on Serbia, I, 259 et seq.; secret records of, I, 276 et seq.; sends ultimatum, I, 285 et seq.; seeks to escape Great War, I, 296 et seq.; Russian opinion pictures as a dog, I, 361.

   First moves in War, I, 323 et seq.; hesitates, I, 338 et seq., 373; general course of 1914 warfare in II, xvi et seq.; first campaign and devastation in Serbia, II, 1 et seq.; sends troops against France, II, 110; crushed by Russians at Lemberg, II, 190 et seq.; artillery aids Germans, II, 294; breaks with Japan, II, 404 et seq.; in Warsaw campaign, II, 416 et seq.; expelled from Serbia, II, 430 et seq.

   General course of events in 1915 in, III, xiii et seq.; surrenders Przemysl, III, 93 et seq.; loses long struggle in the Carpathians, III, 106 et seq.; protests against American munition sales, III, 125 et seq.; escapes danger of invasion and joins German advance on Russia, III, 177 et seq.; ill-treats Italians, III, 214; protests Italy's entrance into War, III, 216 et seq.; aids in capture of Warsaw, III, 229 et seq.; her plots against America revealed, III, 274 et seq.; in Russian attack, III, 304, 320 et seq.; subordinated to Germany, III, 330; relations with Bulgaria, III, 334; aids in crushing Serbia, III, 345 et seq.; disputes with Bulgaria, III, 364; sinks to be part of "Middle Europe" empire, III, 365, 382 et seq.; takes part in exterminating Serbs, III, 404 et seq.; increasing misery in, IV, xiii et seq.; crushes Montenegro, IV, 18 et seq.; attacks Italy and is repulsed, IV, 148 et seq.; her lines again smashed by Russia, IV, 185 et seq.; loses Gorizia to Italy, IV, 294 et seq.; aided by Russian treason, IV, 315; Rumania accuses of tyranny, declares war on, IV, 324 et seq.; crushes Rumania with German aid, IV, 357 et seq.; lose Monastir to Serbs, IV, 387 et seq.; saved from disaster by Russia's breakdown, V, xxviii; seeks peace, V, xxxv; peace plans proposed, V, 4, 5; U. S. delays declaring war on, V, 115; U. S. believes war was forced upon, V, 121; army again broken by Russians, V, 250 et seq.; defeated by Italians at

holds Democracy, I, xlvi; spiritual growth in the War, I, 11;
Treitschke's view of, I, 22; American kinship to, I, 55 et seq.; aids
to European freedom, I, 63; industrial power, I, 67; Germans
suspect, I, 102; falling behind in commerce, I, 115; not opposed
to America, I, 127; opposed to Germany, I, 128; attitude toward
Serbia, I, 177; clashes with Germany, I, 193 et seq.; naval shipbuilding race, I, 204 et seq.; German scorn for, I, 230 et seq.;
German diplomacy in, I, 308 et seq.; Kaiser's fury against, I, 321,
322; seeks to prevent the War, I, 338 et seq.; would permit chas-
tising of Serbia, I, 346; her view of Russia, I, 350 et seq.; Kaiser's
schemes against, I, 358; her troubles with Russia, I, 361 et seq.;
supports France, I, 379 et seq.; enters War, I, 396 et seq.; Germany absolves of blame, I, 397; German Chancellor accuses, I,
407 et seq.

General course of War's events of 1914 in, II, xiii et seq.; seizes
control of seas, II, 20 et seq.; supposed treaty with Belgium, II,
52 et seq.; controls Mediterranean against German ships, II, 94
et seq.; joins battle in France, II, 118 et seq.; aids in defending
Paris, II, 230 et seq.; aids in Marne battle, II, 248 et seq.; aids in
Aisne battle, II, 283 et seq.; suffers from U-boats, II, 295 et seq.;
aids Antwerp, II, 304 et seq.; aids Belgians on Yser, II, 324 et
seq.; at Ypres, II, 337 et seq.; receives aid of her colonies, II,
361 et seq.; conquers German-African colonies, II, 370 et seq.;
menaced by Turkey's entrance to War, II, 391 et seq.; aids Japan
to drive Germany from East, II, 402 et seq.; drives German warships from ocean, II, 439 et seq.

Events of 1915 in, III, xiii et seq.; meets U-boat warfare, III,
49 et seq.; fights Neuve Chapelle battle, III, 65 et seq.; fails in
Dardanelles attack, III, 79 et seq.; traffic in • American munitions,
III, 126; fights second Ypres battle, III, 137 et seq.; loses
Lusitania, III, 187 et seq.; shifts from aristocracy to democracy,
III, 201 et seq.; praised by Clémenceau, III, 212; defeated at
Dardanelles, III, 252 et seq.; German spies seek to set U. S.
against, III, 298; battle of Loos, III, 302 et seq.; fails to aid
Serbia in time, III, 345 et seq.; helped in Belgium by Miss Cavell,
III, 369; German peace exactions from, III, 396.

Events of 1916 in, IV, xiii et seq.; gathering of army during
Verdun battle, IV, 46 et seq.; Germany accuses blockade by, as
illegal, IV, 96 et seq.; Germany blames for German atrocities in
France, IV, 102 et seq.; suppresses Sinn Fein revolt, IV, 114 et
seq.; loses an army in Kut siege, IV, 127 et seq.; in Jutland naval
battle, IV, 154 et seq.; upholds Arab revolt, IV, 233 et seq.; in
Somme battle, IV, 242 et seq.; American volunteers aid, IV, 259;
et seq.; protests treating submarines as merchant ships, IV, 276
et seq.; roused by Fryatt killing, protests, IV, 281 et seq.; in
Rumanian negotiations, IV, 318; aids revolution in Greece, IV,
331 et seq.; resists Bulgarian army in Greece, IV, 346 et seq., 387
et seq.; prisoners suffer in Germany, IV, 412 et seq.

Takes lead in War in 1917, V, xiii et seq.; new U-boat blockade
against, V, 6 et seq.; pursues Germans in "Hindenburg Retreat,"
V, 20 et seq.; captures Bagdad and wins Mesopotamia, V, 48 et
seq.; Germany blames, for U. S. entry into War, V, 106 et seq.;
welcomes U. S. entry into War, V, 126, 139 et seq.; wins Vimy
Ridge, V, 3 et seq.; aided by U. S. navy, V, 168 et seq.; transports
U. S. troops, V, 174 et seq.; progress in aviation, V, 198; blows
up Messines Ridge, V, 207 et seq.; aids in overthrow of autocracy
in Greece, V, 224 et seq.; accused of causing Russian breakdown,

V, 266; in battle of Flanders, V, 268 et seq.; accused by Bolshe-visits, V, 352 et seq.; aids Italy to check Teuton invasion, V, 372; in Cambrai great tank attack, V, 386 et seq.; accused of tyranny by Germans, V, 395; captures Jerusalem, V, 401 et seq.

Waning effort in 1918, VI, xiv et seq.; views on "Fourteen Points," VI, 1 et seq.; beaten back in Kaiser-battle, VI, 50 et seq.; fights at Lys, "with backs to wall," VI, 104 et seq.; navy blocks Belgian ports, VI, 126 et seq.; receives American aid, VI, 184 et seq., 193 et seq.; praises Americans, VI, 196; aids on Italian front, VI, 213 et seq.; sends troops to Arctic Russia, aids Siberia, VI, 230 et seq.; in great Ally advance, VI, 259 et seq.; aids U. S. transportation, VI, 261; breaks Hindenburg Line, VI, 281 et seq.; German blame of, VI, 310; aids in crushing Bulgaria, VI, 321 et seq.; crushes Turkey, VI, 332 et seq.; occupies Con-stantinople, VI, 341; aids in breaking Austria's front, VI, 373 et seq.; in final Ally drive, VI, 386 et seq.

During Armistice period, VII, xiii et seq.; troops enter Ger-many, VII, 1 et seq.; at Peace Conference, VII, 36 et seq.; prob-lems in Treaty, VII, 129 et seq.; at Peace signing, VII, 153 et seq.
Britons, character of, I, xxvii; liked in Russia, I, 364; gentlemanly, II, 64; soldiers as seen by Germans, II, 138 et seq.; under fire, II, 291; high resoluteness of, III, 213; as seamen, IV, 284.
Bulgaria, Teutons seek to draw into War, I, xxxvi; opposition to Serbia, I, 176 et seq.; troubles in the Ægean Sea, I, 252; aided by Pan-Germans, I, 257; in accord with Austria, I, 258; Austrian view of, I, 279; German plans for, I, 336, 340 et seq.; military strength of, II, xvii; opposed to Turkey, II, 93; Turkish diplom-acy in, II, 396 et seq.; belittles Serbian victories, II, 430 et seq.; raids Serbia, II, 433; tempted into War, III, xxix et seq.; favors Germany, III, 81; causes for joining Central Powers, III, 109; enters war, III, 328; earlier history, III, 329, 330; diplomatic maneuvers in, III, 330 et seq.; aids in crushing Serbia, III, 345 et seq.; quarrels with Austria, III, 364; submerged in "Middle Europe" empire, III, 382 et seq.; seeks to exterminate Serbs, III, 404 et seq.; her official explanations, III, 419 et seq.; Greece yields frontier to, IV, 187; attacks Allies at Salonika, IV, 316; Russian and Rumanian attitude toward, IV, 318; German praise of, IV, 322 et seq.; seeks Greek territory, IV, 331 et seq.; driven back from Monastir by Serbs, IV, 387 et seq.; events of 1917 in, V, xiii et seq.; German peace terms for, V, 4, 5; joins armistice with Russia, V, 398 et seq.; breakdown of, VI, xxxvi; Germany defends, VI, 12; signs peace with Ukrainia, VI, 18 et seq.; promised Serbian territory, VI, 47; crushed by Allies, VI, 321 et seq.; armistice with, VI, 330 et seq.; blamed by Germans for loss of War, VI, 358 et seq.; in Armistice, VI, 424; during Armistice period, VII, xiii et seq.

CAMOUFLAGE, art of, begun, II, 283 et seq.; Ally development of, VI, 272; German criticism of, VI, 366.
Canada, her share in the first six months of war, II, xiii et seq.; sends armada to Europe, II, 361 et seq.; in earlier British wars, II, 362; troops sent to France, II, 368 et seq.; compared with other colonies, II, 370; service in 1915, III, xvii; troops at Neuve Chapelle battle, III, 76 et seq.; troops meet first gas attack, III, 137; in second Ypres battle, III, 141 et seq.; official praise of troops, III, 142; troops repulse second gas attack, III, 153; has troops on *Lusitania*, III, 198, 200; German agents plot against, in

VI, 207; inspires U. S. troops in France, VI, 243; of world in War, VII, xiii.

Chosen People, the, Germans as, I, 22 et seq., 48; Hebrew idea of, I, 41; Germans rejected as, I, 114; Von Bülow's view of, III, 50; German "Intellectuals" claim to be, III, 391 et seq.

Christianity, universality of, I, 44; rejected in Germany, I, 113 et seq.; opposed to war, I, 124; progress toward, I, 296; uplift of mankind by, II, xiii; defended by Belgrade, II, 1; shown by German army, II, 185; reviving in Paris, II, 207; attacked by Mohammedans in War, II, 391 et seq.; protests in Germany, II, 424; protests against German war-practices, III, 1 et seq.; III, 40 et seq.; causes martyrdom of Armenians, III, 154 et seq.; Edith Cavell asserts devotion to, III, 379; revolts against German horrors in Poland, III, 425 et seq.; French clergy appeal to, against Germany, IV, 101 et seq., 112; condemns German destruction, V, 20; Brazil accuses Germany of deserting, V, 152.

Civilization, aided by warfare, I, 124 et seq.; denied to inland peoples, I, 188; aided by British sea power, I, 204, 217; upholds Nationalism, I, 324; appealed to, by France, I, 372 et seq.; aided by ancient Teutons, II, 179; saved by Marne battle, II, 249; threatened at Ypres battle, II, 339; devotes itself to War, III, xiii et seq.; under German domination, III, 1 et seq.; partly responsible for Armenian massacre, III, 154; Italy appeals to, III, 221; German claims to be the representative of, III, 391 et seq.; German concept of, III 425 et seq.; Belgian workmen despair of, IV, 16; Sinn Fein revolt threatens, IV, 114; U. S. volunteers enlist to save, IV, 259 et seq.; shaken to its foundations by anarchy, V, xiii et seq.; U. S. enters War for, V, 108 et seq.; U. S. as center of, V, 168; crushed in Russia, V, 243 et seq., 331 et seq.; rescued by Americans, VI, xiii et seq.; new dangers menace, VII, xxxvi.

Commerce, its influence toward war, I, xxx; growth in Germany, I, 5, 65 et seq.; in the East, I, 193 et seq.; affected by freedom of seas, and submarines, I, 204 et seq.; modern changes in, I, 222 et seq.; German ruined by the War, I, 275, 276; restrains Britain from war, I, 312; cause of the War, I, 410; losses of in 1914 warfare, II, xxxv et seq.; German blocked by Britain, II, 20 et seq.; British dependent on navy, II, 22; neutrals form trading societies, II, 35; Russian destroyed by Turkey, II, 395; Japanese threatened by Germany, II, 402 et seq.; British threatened by Germany, II, 439 et seq.; its disruption by U-boat warfare, III, xxii; Germany seeks to reëstablish, III, 37; U-boat destruction of, III, 49 et seq.; American, in munitions, III, 125 et seq., 187 et seq.; Teuton plots against, in America, III, 277 et seq.; "Middle Europe" empire founded on, III, 382 et seq.; German peace plans for, III, 397 et seq.; U-boat warfare on, IV, 89 et seq.; merchant U-boats engage in, IV, 276 et seq.; in Greece, affected by Allies, IV, 339, 342 et seq.; Germany's heaviest U-boat attack on, V, 1 et seq., 15; in the Virgin Isles, V, 9 et seq.; effect of War on, in U. S., V, 111 et seq.; historical review of, in former wars, V, 117 et seq.; effect of air-traffic on, V, 197 et seq.; renewed between Russia and Teutons, V, 393 et seq.; in "Fourteen Points," VI, 4; Teuton, profits from Russian peace, VI, 31, 40 et seq.; at Peace Conference, VII, 137; effects of Treaty on, VII, 187.

Conscription, of German populace, II, xvi et seq.; Britain driven to, III, xx; first discussed in Britain, III, 208; of Serbs by Bulgars, III, 415 et seq.; of Poles by Germany, III, 425 et seq.; under

V, 264, 265; Teutons criticize Britain for lack of, V, 395; in Ukrainia, VI, 18 et seq.; in "occupied" Germany, VII, 19; at Peace Conference, VII, 51; in Czecho-Slovakia, VII, 144.

Freedom of the Seas, upheld by Wilson, I, 58; German need for, I, 72, 128; conflicting views of, I, 204 et seq.; German demand for, II, 24 et seq.; German destruction of, III, 49 et seq.; German demand for, III, 50; Austria asks American aid to maintain, III, 128 et seq.; destroyed by *Lusitania* sinking, III, 187 et seq.; Germany demands for herself, III, 398; declares herself champion of, IV, 100; German merchant submarine boasts of possession, IV, 278; Fryatt case a test of, IV, 281 et seq.; suppressed in Greece, IV, 331 et seq.; German demand of 1917 for, V, 3; U. S. enters War for, V, 106 et seq.; "Fourteen Points" express extreme doctrine of, VI, 4 et seq.; in Peace discussion, VII, 187.

"Frightfulness," I, 16; scientifically approved, I, 27; how developed, I, 38, 132 et seq.; American judgment on, I, 133, 140; Germany's deliberate adoption of, II, xiv et seq.; Austria's use of, II, xx; shown in Serbia, II, 2 et seq.; adopted as a policy against Belgium, II, 51 et seq.; example of, II, 73 et seq.; at Louvain, II, 150 et seq.; at Tannenberg, II, 170 et seq.; in Poland, II, 424; expanded policy of, III, xxi; in northern France, III, 1 et seq.; on the ocean, III, 49 et seq., 187 et seq.; in Serbia, III, 358; in Cavell case, III, 369 et seq., 381; in northern France, IV, 102 et seq.; in U-boat warfare, IV, 283, 285; in prison camps, IV, 412 et seq.; in Hindenburg retreat, V, 20 et seq.; general review of, V, 124 et seq.; in Paris bombardment by super-gun, VI, 92 et seq.; in retreat from France, VI, 357; in suppressing revolt in Germany, VII, 115 et seq.

Gas used in War, III, xvii; for reprisals, III, 36; the first gas attack, III, 137 et seq.; French plans for, III, 138; eye-witness picture of, III, 146; at Verdun, IV, 214 et seq.; at the Somme, IV, 245; at battle of Flanders, V, 300 et seq.; effect on weapons, V, 302; on Italian front, V, 319, VI, 216, 221; in Peace-Assault, VI, 243, 250; discussed at Peace, VII, 167.

German falsehood, in the War, I, xli et seq., 2, 14; policy established, I, 23; discomfited by Harden, I, 90; admitted, I, 107; proven, I, 112 et seq.; in militarism, I, 121 et seq.; advocated by Government, I, 130, 205; employed in U. S., I, 223 et seq.; flat dishonesty of, I, 264 et seq.; self-contradictory, I, 338 et seq.; offers false evidence, I, 351 et seq.; denounced by France, I, 378; made clear in Belgium, I, 411; II, 52 et seq.; obvious official falsehoods, II, xiv, 164 et seq.; accuses French civilians, III, 34; U. S. government points out, III, 136; praises itself, III, 138; in the *Lusitania* case, III, 187, 188; against Italy, III, 214 et seq.; against U. S., III, 274 et seq.; official falsity, III, 301, 369 et seq.; in Poland, III, 430; official falsity in Belgium, IV, 9; in dealing with U. S., IV, 96 et seq.; in officially denying enslavement of French workers, IV, 102 et seq.; official in Jutland naval battle, IV, 154 et seq.; in Fryatt case, IV, 286; directed against America, V, xv et seq.; in U-boat warfare, V, 1 et seq.; in Zimmermann note, V, 42; in propaganda in Italy, V, 315 et seq.; in discussing "Fourteen Points," VI, 14; entraps Russians, VI, 31 et seq.; blames failure on her allies, VI, 358 et seq.; discussed at Peace Conference, VII, 166 et seq.

German people, character of, I, xvii, xx; sufferings of and change in, I, xxvi et seq.; faith in government, I, xli et seq.; outlook on

382; retreats before final Ally drive, VI, 386 et seq.; becomes a republic, VI, 402; accepts Armistice, VI, 415 et seq.; terms of Armistice for, VI, 421 et seq.

During Armistice days, VII, xiii et seq.; Rhineland under Allies, VII, 1 et seq.; barred from Peace Conference, VII, 36 et seq.; organizes under new Constitution, VII, 67 et seq.; loses land to Poland, VII, 94 et seq.; suppresses bolshevism, VII, 111 et seq.; loses colonies, VII, 133; in Treaty discussion, VII, 153 et seq.

God, the German concept of, I, 41, 89, 108; the old Jewish Jehovah, I, 113 et seq.; Russia also appeals to, I, 347; German intellectuals appeal to, I, 356; as a German god, II, 87, 424; rejection of, II, 185; Czar appeals to, III, 321; Irish appeal to, IV, 115; Arabs appeal to, IV, 233 et seq.; Germans learn hate from, IV, 414; Germans appeals to against America, V, ii; Czar appeals to, in abdication, V, 85; Greek king appeals to, V, 238; Austrian emperor appeals to, VI, 30; Teutons trace defeat by Italians to, VI, 213 et seq.; Kaiser appeals to, in defeat, VI, 364.

Greece, Teutons seek to lure into War, I, xxxvi; aided by Britain, I, 221; disputes with Turkey, I, 252; with Austria, I, 360; opposes Bulgaria, II, 93; threatened by Turkish ships, II, 100; protests, II, 102; influenced by Turkey's entrance into War, II, 392 et seq.; ally armies invited into, III, xxx; involved in Balkan turmoil of 1915, III, 333 et seq.; fears to oppose Germany, III, 345 et seq.; Germany and partners dispute over, III, 363; under German sway, III, 385; difficult position of, IV, xxvii; surrenders frontier to Bulgars, IV, 187; history of struggle for neutrality, revolution in, IV, 331 et seq.; drawn into War in 1917, V, xxvi, sheltered by Germany from U-boat destruction, V, 7; Ally treatment of, shocks Germany, V, 45; declaration of war by, V, 147; Allies expel king of, V, 221 et seq.; aids Allies in Salonika defense, VI, xviii; aids in overthrow of Bulgaria, VI, xxxvi, 330 et seq.; at Peace Conference, VII, 39; signs Treaty, VII, 154.

Holland, German plans against, I, 131; separated from Germany, I, 158; fought for freedom of seas, I, 217; British control over, I, 222; German plans against, I, 229 et seq.; neutrality guaranteed by Germany, I, 399; establishes commercial system for War, II, 35 et seq.; Germany threatens invasion of, II, 108; interns British marines, II, 308, and Belgians, II, 317; angered by Germany, III, xxiii; sheltered in U-boat warfare, III, 56; losses from U-boats, III, 61 et seq.; prisoners escape to, III, 372; Germany plans to absorb, III, 385; commission from, investigates Serbian miseries, III, 405, 412; Belgians appeal to, IV, 6; sheltered by Germany from U-boat destruction, V, 6; German praise of, VI, 14; Kaiser and son flee to, VI, 402 et seq.; welcomes Kaiser, VI, 410, 411; in Armistice, VI, 422 et seq.; discusses Treaty of Peace, VII, 153, 183.

Humor, German lack of, I, xxviii, 103; in Alsace, I, 169; Germany inverts, I, 339; German plunderers display, III, 22; in U-boat warfare, III, 59; of Austro-Russian fighting, III, 119; in war dispatches, III, 250, 251; of Russian revolutionists, V, xxviii; of Germans in twisting Bolshevist phrases, VI, xvii.

Hungary, early history of, I, xxi; law courts of, I, 182; brutality of, I, 185 et seq.; resemblance to Prussians, I, 187; vehement against Serbs, I, 257; claims ownership of Slavs, I, 323; employ brutality in Serbia, II, 2 et seq.; first invaded by Russians, II, 194; invaded

by Serbs, their retreat, II, 430 et seq.; campaign of 1915 in, III, xv et seq.; troops of, starve at Przemysl, III, 102; head Przemysl sortie, III, 103; threatened invasion by Russia, III, 106 et seq.; Russians repulsed from, III, 182; troops in invasion of Russia, III, 322 et seq.; military preparations in, III, 360; Germany's partner in "Middle Europe" empire, III, 382 et seq.; aids in destruction of Serbs, III, 404 et seq.; Russians again invade, IV, 185 et seq.; political effects of danger to, IV, 200; Russians withdraw from, IV, 315; faces Rumanian invasion, IV, 322 et seq.; her troops lead in Italian invasion, V, 374; prisoners in Russia oppose Czecho-Slavs, VI, 149 et seq.; suffers severely in Piave disaster, VI, 220; seeks separation from Austria, VI, 373 et seq.; during Armistice days, VII, xiii et seq.
Hypnosis, in Germany, I, xxvii; I, 12, 223 et seq.; government control of, I, 397; heedlessness of, I, 417; tragic character and consequences in Germany, II, xxi; in Verdun battles, IV, 206 et seq.; wakening from, V, 147; Germany's despair, VI, 366 et seq.; Germany's trust to, VII, 65.

IMPONDERABLES, the, Prussian neglect of, I, xxv; defiance of, I, xxxix et seq.; their resistance, I, 11; Germany values more than other States, I, 102; neglect of, I, 157; Germany confronts, I, 382 et seq.; Belgium obeys, II, 37 et seq.; U. S. recognizes, V, xv, shown in heroic examples, V, 194.
Indemnities, from France, I, 229; Germany offers Belgium, I, 384; Germany expects from Britain and U. S., III, 385 et seq.; German peace demands for, III, 399; Bolshevists declare against, V, 344; Germany receives, from Russia, VI, xviii; Pope proposes abandonment of all, VI, 1; in "Fourteen Points," VI, 4 et seq.; rejected by Ukrainia, VI, 25; Austria requires, VI, 46; in Peace arrangements, VII, xxvi et seq.; at Peace Conference, VII, 48, 159 et seq.
India, British hold roads to, I, 193 et seq.; Germany hopes to seize, I, 273; troops from, at Ypres, II, 358; loyal to Britain, II, 361; troops from, in Africa, II, 374 et seq.; summoned to "Holy War," II, 391 et seq.; troops at Neuve Chapelle, III, 69 et seq.; at Ypres battle, III, 144 et seq.; at Dardanelles, III, 253 et seq.; Germany threatens, III, 386; loses troops in Kut siege, IV, 127 et seq.; supports Arabia, IV, 234; Germany expresses sympathy for, V, 3; troops in Mesopotamian conquest, V, 48; in Palestine conquest, V, 403; in Damascus conquest, VI, 336; at Peace Conference, VII, 54.
Industrialism, German attack on, I, 8; influence against war, I, 66; organization of, I, 81; German statistics, I, 115, 163, 227; alliance with France, I, 229; German, controls Belgium, II, 63; trains French to endure, II, 208; growth of, in America, III, 128; development of, in Britain, III, 208 et seq.; development in America, III, 276 et seq.; confusion of, in Greece, IV, 331 et seq.; destruction of, in Rumania, IV, 399 et seq.; German plans against French, V, 25 et seq.; power of U, S. in, V, 418 et seq.; disorganization of, in Siberia, VI, 234 et seq.
Ireland, problems of, I, 62, 292; included in U-boat warfare, III, 51; Germany seeks to use American sympathy with, III, 283 et seq.; revolt of 1916 in, IV, xxix, 114 et seq.; troops win glory at Hulluch, IV, 119; sympathy for Sinn Fein uprising, IV, 281; Germany expresses sympathy for, V, 3; U. S. navy off coast of, V, 169; troops win at Messines, V, 210; an "Irish Day," V, 215;

KULTUR, influence under Frederick the Great, I, xxvi; growth of, I, xxix; character of, I, 2; worship of, I, 21 et seq.; opposed by Democratic culture, I, 53 et seq.; creates prosperity, I, 65 et seq.; applauded, I, 116; praised by Crown Prince, I, 141; extended to other races, I, 147 et seq.; in Alsace, I, 167 et seq.; growth in Germany, I, 226; made the excuse for massacre, II, 59; repelled by Slavs, II, 179; in China, II, 413 et seq.; made excuse for massacre, III, 2; placed above morality, III, 34; German "intellectuals" boast of, III, 391 et seq.; character of, in "Hindenburg Retreat," V, 40; final boasts of, VI, 42.

LABOR, system of, in Germany, I, 79 et seq.; French system, I, 80; needs armed protection, I, 126; dependent on Britain, I, 223; takes control of Britain, III, xx; becomes main issue of War, III, 206 et seq.; urges Italy into War, III, 215; in Bulgaria opposes War, III, 342; Teuton plans to secure from Russia, III, 394 et seq.; German exploitation of, in Poland, III, 425 et seq.; Germans enslave, in Belgium, IV, 1 et seq.; Germans enslave in France, IV, 102 et seq.; in Russian upheaval, V, xix et seq.; further enslavement by Germany, V, 23 et seq.; in U. S. endorses the War, V, 183 et seq.; always opposed to wars, V, 189; effects of aeroplane traffic on, V, 200; Bolshevism influences, V, 331 et seq.; loyal support of, in U. S., V, 418 et seq.; proclaimed in control of Ukrainia, VI, 20 et seq.; in Teuton triumph over Russia, VI, 35 et seq.; new conditions of, in new era, VII, xiii et seq.; aided to end war in Germany, VII, 15 et seq.; conditions of, in new Serbia, VII, 22 et seq.; Lloyd George's aid to, VII, 63; future of, in Germany, VII, 65; in new colonies, VII, 137; in Czech-Slovakia, VII, 148.

Labor troubles, in Germany, I, 71 et seq.; in Russia, I, 254, 300; fomented in America by Teutons, III, 276 et seq.; in Russia, IV, 307; in Petrograd in revolution, V, 72 et seq.; in German Revolution, VII, 111 et seq.

Labor unions, their growth, I, 82 et seq.; encouraged in France, I, 243; assist government in Britain, III, 208 et seq.; Germany creates in America, III, 281; resist German influence, III, 281 et seq.; Serbian report on miseries, III, 405 et seq.; protest German tyranny in Belgium, IV, 14; in Russia, IV, 309; organize in Russian Revolution, V, 79 et seq.; in Greek tumults, V, 233; take control of Russia, V, 243 et seq., 331 et seq.; approve Russia's armistice, V, 393 et seq.; in new Germany, VII, 77 et seq.

Language, comparison of various tongues, I, 145; influence on nationality, I, 146 et seq.; mixed in all countries, I, 161 et seq.; efforts to obliterate Serbian, by Bulgars, III, 414; flamboyant American use of, V, 168; French used at Russian-Teuton conference, V, 396; equal rights of, in new Serbia, VII, 24; possible twisting of, VII, 36; France demands French for Treaty, VII, 57.

Law, Austrian court methods in, I, xix; 246 et seq.; Germany plans to remake, I, 108; new military, I, 129; trial of Rosa Luxemburg, I, 134 et seq.; as the voice of Society, I, 144; influenced by language, I, 147 et seq.; rests on justice, I, 165; misused by Germans in Alsace, I, 172 et seq.; Hungarian courts, I, 182 et seq.; supreme in France, I, 240; Serbia and Austria argue over, I, 307, 332; violated by Germany, I, 378; Germans in America ignore, III, 299 et seq.; reveals Teuton crimes in America, IV, 278 et seq.; Serbia accused of abusing, in Macedonia, III, 338; in Cavell case, III,

369 et seq.; perverted in Austria, III, 384; British, in treason trial, IV, 122 et seq.

Law, International, Germany defies, I, xlii; authority on, I, 1; growth of, I, 8; trodden down by Germany, I, 16; Germany ignores, I, 108; Belgian invasion, excused by, I, 132; involved in freedom of seas, I, 204 et seq.; burlesque by Germany, I, 218; needs armed support, I, 220; Serbian respect for, I, 294; to make war impossible, I, 296; used to annex Bosnia to Austria, I, 326; appealed to by Serbia in crisis, I, 334; Belgium appeals to, I, 385; Germany admits breaking, I, 395; Britain fights for, I, 403; Germany wholly casts aside, II, xiv et seq.; Kaiser appeals to, II, 60; discarded by Germans and Turks, II, 98; German appeal to, II, 164 et seq.; Turks appeal to, II, 395 et seq.; on U-boats and blockade, III, xxii et seq.; German view of, III, 3 et seq.; German desecration of, III, 18, 49 et seq.; involved in munition trade, III, 125 et seq.; forbids poison gas, III, 137 et seq.; in *Lusitania* sinking, III, 187 et seq.; Germany appeals to, III, 363; neutrals appeal to, III, 416; Bulgaria explains, III, 423; Poles appeal to, III, 431; new encroachments on, IV, xxix; Belgians appeal to, IV, 15; U. S. opposes Germany on, IV, 88 et seq.; France protests German misuse of, IV, 104; issues roused by U-boat crossing to America, IV, 276 et seq.; Germany and neutrals appeal to in greatest U-boat destruction, V, 6 et seq.; Wilson defines in entering War, V, 109; history of, V, 117 et seq.; "Fourteen Points" appeal to, VI, 4 et seq.

League of Nations, U. S. urges upon Europe, IV, xxx; birth and early growth of the idea, V, 128; "Fourteen Points" on, VI, 5 et seq.; Peace Conference plans for, VII, xxvi et seq.; final need of, VII, xxxvi; at opening of Peace Conference, VII, 42; Poland defends on, VII, 108; disagreement on, at Conference, VII, 129 et seq.; discussion of, VII, 162 et seq.

Little nations, rights of, I, 53, 57; defended by Britain, I, 58; Germany plots against, I, 131; and tramples on, I, 144 et seq.; aided by Britain, I, 221; Britain enters War for, I, 403; Germany forces goods from, II, 35; fears of, in East, II, 392; ignored on ocean, III, 49 et seq., 187; destruction of, by Teutons, III, 416, 428 et seq.; Irish revolters join Germany against, IV, 114 et seq.; U. S. enters war for, V, 115; unite in World union against Germany, V, 147 et seq.; Greece joins Allies to defend, V, 241; Bolshevists uphold, V, 351; "Fourteen Points" discuss, VI, 3 et seq.; defended by Ukrainia, VI, 19 et seq.; in Armistice, VI, 421 et seq.

MANDATORIES, first suggested in "Fourteen Points," VI, 4 et seq.; at Peace Conference, VII, 40; dispute over, at Conference, VII, iii et seq.; practical worth of system of, VII, 135 et seq.

Marines, of U. S. organized for War, V, 431 et seq.; of Britain, storm Zeebrugge, VI, 129 et seq.; of U. S. at Belleau Wood, VI, 193 et seq.; of U. S. cited by French, VI, 201; story told by one of, VI, 201 et seq.; German, in Revolution, VI, 402; VII, 113.

Materialism, growth in Prussia, I, 3, 9 et seq.; doctrines of, I, 27 et seq.; German aids to, I, 49; runs wild in Prussia, III, 18; governs Turkey, III, 154, 174 et seq.; outspoken in Bulgaria, III, 328 et seq.; in Hindenburg retreat, V, 20 et seq.; holds Japan to Allies, V, 47; would restrain U. S. from War, V, 119; British empire rises above, V, 122; after the War, VII, xiii et seq.

Mexico, Teutons rouse, against U. S., III, 274, 283 et seq., 383; U. S. troops invade, after Villistas, IV, xxix, 61 et seq.; Carranza's protest, IV, 63; U. S. response, IV, 80 et seq.; Greek estimate of, IV, 355; Germany seeks alliance with, V, xxi, 42 et seq.

Militarism, its Prussian birth, I, xxv; William II encourages, I, xxxii; cost of, I, xxxiv; sources of, I, 3; takes control, I, 14; influence on soldiers, I, 38 et seq.; spread from Prussia, I, 47; necessary in autocracies, I, 62; effectiveness of, I, 87; necessary in Central Europe, I, 101; poisons brewed by, I, 121 et seq.; seized Alsace, I, 162; tyranny there, I, 171 et seq.; strengthens Turkey, I, 198; rejected by U. S., I, 224 et seq.; overweighs Germany, I, 228 et seq.; defended by Germans, I, 354 et seq.; Russia accused of, I, 355; power of, in opening the War, II, xiii et seq.; checked at the Jadar, II, 3; cursed by German socialist, II, 184; takes control of Austria, II, 190; German nation devoted to, III, xiii; checked by munitions trade, III, 133; Bulgaria praises, III, 340; desolates Poland, III, 425 et seq.; desolates Belgium, IV, 3 et seq.; regrets Germany's yielding to U. S., IV, 88; condemned by Arabs, IV, 233 et seq.; results of, in Germany, IV, 283; Rumania condemns, IV, 323; results of, in German prison camps, IV, 412 et seq.; condemned in U. S. declaration of War, V, 122; upholds autocracy in Greece, V, 232; in Germany, defies Russian propaganda, V, 393 et seq.; crushes Russia, VI, xvii; Wilson speech defines, VI, 1; Russia protests against, VI, 32 et seq.; last boasts of, in Germany, VI, 358 et seq.; death-blow to, VI, 402; prospects of, in new Germany, VII, 69.

"Misunderstanding," The, said to have caused the War, I, 316.

Mohammedanism, William II as protector of, I, xxxii; roused against Allies, I, 60; swayed from Egypt, I, 131; influenced by Bagdad railway, I, 193 et seq.; savage against Serbs, II, 17; loses faith in Turkey, II, 93; summoned to Holy War, II, 391; not responsible for Armenian horror, III, 155 et seq.; Russians praise, III, 330; favored in Bulgaria, III, 413; roused against Turkey, IV, xix, 222 et seq.; awed by Turkish disasters, V, xxxv; protected in British conquest of Palestine, V, 401 et seq.

Monroe Doctrine, opposition to, I, 219 et seq.; Brazil's interpretation of, V, 150; in Peace Conference, VII, xxxv.

Montenegro, lost Scutari, I, 120; Kaiser opposes union to Serbia, I, 321; aided by Russia, II, 398; invades Herzegovina, II, 430 et seq.; Serbians flee to, III, 359; fights Austrians, III, 366 et seq.; Serbs in, III, 404 et seq.; crushed by Austria, IV, xix, 18 et seq.; throws off Austrian yoke, VI, xxxvii; in "Fourteen Points," VI, 5; during Armistice period, VII, xxv; joins Serbia, VII, 22 et seq.

Mutiny, among Bavarian troops, III, 13; among Greek troops, V, 222 et seq.; among Italian troops, V, 315 et seq.; among Russian sailors, V, 333; in German navy, VI, xxxix, 358 et seq.; among German soldiers, VII, 16.

Mythology, the original science, I, 41; sources of, I, 102; in Serbia, I, 192; quoted by German plunderers, III, 26; myth of the new cross in sky, in Armenia, IV, 30; names of, used by Germans for defense lines, V, 154.

Nationalism, doctrines rejected in Germany, I, 40; War fought for, I, 59; strength of, in Germany, I, 93; power for good, I, 145; began with French Revolution, I, 156; growth in Alsace, I, 164; in the Balkans, I, 176 et seq.; encouraged by Serbian societies, I, 261; causes the War, I, 323 et seq.; opposed by Germany, I, 335 et seq.; variation in laws on, II, 34; growth in Germany, III, xiii; Turkey seeks to strengthen, II, 174; strength of, in Italy, III, 214

American desire for, V, xv et seq.; German and Ally terms of 1917 for, V, 4 et seq.; U. S. compelled to abandon efforts for, V, 106 et seq.; previous U. S. political struggle for, V, 128; desired by Russian masses, V, 243 et seq.; desired by German masses, V, 274; desired by Italian troops, V, 315 et seq.; Russian dreams of, V, 331 et seq., 393 et seq.; false form of, in Russia, VI, xvi; in Rumania, VI, xviii; efforts of 1917 toward, VI, 1; Brest-Litovsk conference for, VI, 18 et seq.; Russia and Rumania compelled to accept, VI, 31 et seq.; Bulgaria asks Allies for, VI, 321 et seq.; Allies propaganda for in Germany, VI, 284, 285; Germany sees the necessity for, VI, 358 et seq.; Austria sues for, VI, 373 et seq.; Germany uses for, VI, 402 et seq., 415 et seq.; establishment of, VII, xiii et seq., 36 et seq.; 129 et seq.; signing of, VII, 153 et seq.

Peace Conferences at the Hague, I, 209, 212, 296; encouraged by Germany, I, 296; appealed to by Serbia, I, 334; II, 13; by Belgium, II, 70; by Germany, II, 164; appealed to by Austria, III, 127 et seq.; response by America, III, 134 et seq.; forbid use of poison gas, III, 137; appealed to by Germany in *Lusitania* case, III, 196; appealed to by France, IV, 107.

Peace Leagues, in Geneva, I, 175; in Nuremberg, I, 229; Germany fosters in America, III, 281 et seq.; efforts of American, V, 128 et seq.; See League of Nations.

Peace Offers, false from Germany, I, 267; false from Austria, I, 323; from Allies, I, 374; German to Belgium, I, 383; of 1916, V, 133; false promises to Russia, by Teutons, V, 393 et seq.; from Russia and Teutons, VI, 31 et seq.; from Germany army heads, VI, 359 et seq.

Persia, foreign disputes over, I, 193 et seq.; occupied by Russians in 1915, III, 38 et seq.; Armenian massacres reach to, III, 155 et seq.; Turks and Russians battle in, IV, xvii et seq., 24 et seq., 127 et seq.; Turks drive Russians back in, IV, 187; Turks control, V, 48.

Philosophy, of the War, I, 1 et seq.; of Kultur, I, 21 et seq.; influence of German, I, 49, 84; opposed to politics, I, 103; Hegel's, I, 144 et seq.; obsolete forms of, I, 226; as shown in War, II, xiii et seq.; as applied by Hindenburg, II, 178 et seq.; of attack and defense, III, 63; of German leaders, III, 428; of Germany after War, VII, 3 et seq.

Plunder, German official, II, 157 et seq., 250; Antwerp total losses, II, 317; in Poland, II, 416 et seq., 428; in Northern France, III, 1 et seq.; in Armenia, III, 155 et seq.; Austrian and Bulgar methods of, in Serbia, III, 414; French forced to plunder French, IV, 109; Hoover condemns Teutons for, IV, 113; of prisoners by Germans, IV, 414; by Germans in Hindenburg retreat, V, 24 et seq.; broken Russian army turns to, V, 244; in Ukrainia, VI, 19; Germans in retreat from France, VI, 357; Austrians, in Italy, VI, 380; Germany escapes, VII, 1 et seq.

Poland, prefers Russia to Germany, I, 144; sufferings under Prussian rule, I, 145 et seq.; Russia fears to lose, I, 361; ravaged by Germany, II, xxxiii; in Hindenburg campaign, II, 176; previous history of, II, 191; promised freedom in War, II, 192 et seq.; Austro-Russian fighting in, II, 194 et seq.; miseries of, II, 416 et seq.; future of, II, 426; Germany conquers, III, xxv et seq.; greatness of battles in, III, 39; suffers from Przemsyl campaign, III, 93 et seq.; effect of German defeats in, III, 107 et seq.; troops of, at Dunajec, III, 179; overrun by Teutons, Warsaw captured, III, 229 et seq.; future of, III, 388; future expected by Germans, III, 395; ravaging of, by German rulers, III, 425 et seq.; weakness

of Russian aid to, V, 351; troops included in Russia's armistice
with Teutons, V, 398; declared independent by Teutons, VI, xvi;
"Fourteen Points" on, VI, 5, 12 et seq.; Russia surrenders her
share of, VI, 31; troops of, abandon Austria, VI, 379; forms republic, VII, xxiii et seq.; at Peace Conference, VII, 40; organizes
government, VII, 94 et seq.; U. S. recognizes, VII, 101; at signing of Peace, VII, 154 et seq.

Prisoners, treatment by Germans, II, 59 et seq.; German trickery
and brutality to Belgian, II, 155 et seq.; refused by German army,
II, 170 et seq.; sufferings in Russia, II, 421; French civilians
abused as, III, 33 et seq.; both sides seek to become, III, 116 et
seq.; escape of, in Belgium, III, 369 et seq.; hanged by Bulgars,
III, 418; tell horror of Verdun fight, IV, 50; French civilians
made, IV, 102 et seq.; Irish in Germany, IV, 114, 126; sufferings
of British, under Turks, IV, 143 et seq.; Russia takes huge numbers of Austrian, IV, 200; Greek army made, in peace, IV, 345;
Germans captured by Serbs, IV, 396; in German prison camps,
IV, 412 et seq.; civilians seized in France, V, 20 et seq.; German,
dazed at Messines Ridge, V, 216; in Ukranian treaty, VI, 28; freeing of Teutons in Russia, VI, 32; U. S. marines as, VI, 198; attitude of American, VI, 204; German, capture, VI, 345, 353 et seq.;
Italy, captures Austrian, VI, 380; Armistice terms for, VI, 423.

Profiteering, German, in Poland, III, 435 et seq.; Austrian in Bukowina, IV, 202 et seq.; in Greece, IV, 339 et seq.; in German prison
camps, IV, 413; in U. S. at opening of War, V, 429.

Propaganda, falsely used by Germany, I, xxxviii, 205; in U. S., I,
2, 224 et seq.; for peace, I, 124; in Serbia, I, 180, 286, 297 et seq.,
306, 329; after Potsdam conference, I, 264; Austrian in U. S., I,
324 et seq.; Austrian against Serbs, II, 7; in Belgium, II, 63; in
Turkey, III, 175, 176; in *Lusitania* case, III, 187, 188; German in
Italy, III, 214 et seq.; Teuton agency for, in U. S., III, 274 et
seq.; German in Mexico, IV, 61 et seq.; German in Ireland, IV,
114 et seq.; German against all foes, IV, 322; German in Greece,
IV, 353 et seq.; German in Russia, IV, xxv; weight of, holds U.
S. back from War, V, 127; royalist, in Greece, V, 221; German, in
Russia, V, 244, 331 et seq.; German succeeds in Italy, V, 315 et
seq.; German against Russia, VI, 36 et seq.; U. S. employs on
German soldiers, VI, 286; Germany plans to continue, VII, 189.

Prussia, creation of, I, 3; devoted to materialism, I, 10 et seq.; tyranny in, I, 17; legislation of, I, 18; control over Germany, I, 47;
love of war, I, 57; rise of, I, 92; development of power in, I, 98
et seq.; her army insulted by Socialists, I, 135; threats to Alsace,
I, 171; economic growth, I, 226; historic attitude to Austria, I,
335; sway over Russia, I, 361 et seq.; pledged to Belgium's protection, I, 416; invaded by Russians, II, 170 et seq.; Russians appeal
to, II, 185; controls occupation of France, III, 1 et seq.; organizes plunder, III, 6; accused by other Germans, III, 61; troops at
Dunajec, III, 179 et seq.; troops storm Brest-Litovsk, III, 249;
controls "Middle Europe" empire, III, 383 et seq.; methods of
compulsion used by, in Poland, III, 425 et seq.; U. S. volunteers
hope to overthrow, IV, 275; claims to be America's first friend,
IV, 278; U. S. declares her worst foe, V, 114; Europe feared for
generations, V, 140 et seq.; Kaiser vows special faith to, VI, 406;
hunger in, after War, VII, 15; new Germany repudiates, VII, 93.

Psychology, its relation to history, I, 66; German problems in, I,
99, 102, 103; changes in German, I, 113; in war, I, 351; of German
thought, II, 171; of Russians and Prussians, II, 178; military, II,

273, 417; German blunders in, III, xxv; in returned prisoners, III, 34; in government views of submarine warfare, III, 188; in Cavell case, III, 369; German view of the German mind, III, 401; of devil worship, III, 405; of German rulers, III, 427; of U-boat warfare, IV, 88; of Oriental view of Europeans, IV, 127; of execution of Captain Fryatt, IV, 284; of Americans in entering War, V, xiii et seq.; of German destructiveness in France, V, 37; of German effect on U. S., V, 42; of huge bombardments, V, 301; of German soldiers' breakdown, VI, 284; German understanding of, VII, 189.

RAILROADS, German plans for, in East, I, 193 et seq.; German boast of, I, 358; Germany plans against Belgium, II, xx; of U. S. organized for War, V, 419 et seq., 429; of France, used by Americans, V, 435 et seq.; U. S. troops break German lines of, VI, xxxv; Germans rebuild during Kaiser-battle, VI, 90; Czechs handle in Siberia, VI, 231 et seq.; Teutons lose in Bulgaria, VI, 321; in final Ally drive, VI, 394 et seq.; used for Armistice, VI, 419; Armistice terms for, VI, 422 et seq.; under new Germany, VII, 81.

Reconstruction, U. S. begins work of, in France, IV, 264; necessity of, in France and Belgium to prevent ultimate German triumph, V, 21; U. S. aids in, V, 39; Britain begins in Mesopotamia, V, 48; begun in Russia, V, 243; in Ukrania, VI, 18 et seq.; in Siberia, VI, 233, 241; Armistice terms for, VI, 421 et seq.; world efforts toward, VII, xiv et seq.; in Serbia, VII, 22 et seq.; in Peace terms, VII, 153 et seq.

Red Cross, plundered in Brussels, III, 20; used to shelter German plunder, III, 23; British accused of abusing, III, 267, 271; efforts of, in Serbia, III, 351, 352; at siege of Kut, IV, 136, 139; French, IV, 414; in U. S., V, xxiii, 122; in Canada, V, 123; in Russia's breakdown, V, 260; British in Italy, V, 303 et seq.; 315; organized for War in U. S., V, 427; in Italy, VI, 213; in Siberia, VI, 238; in Serbia, VII, 31.

Religion, early forms of, I, 24; condemned by Nietzsche, I, 27; fading in Germany, I, 37; Europe's lack of faith, I, 43; the War not religious, I, 60; mockery of appeals to, I, 114; enforced by law, I, 147 et seq.; primitive in Serbia, I, 192; Austrian rulers' views of, I, 257, 258; Lichnowsky's appeal to, I, 318; causes Balkan troubles, I, 325 et seq.; Austria's appeal to, I, 331; Ally faith in, II, xxxi; German frenzy against, II, 151 et seq.; spirit of, in Belgium, II, 325; an officer meditates on, III, 116; Germany states her devotion to, III, 220; in Cavell execution, III, 379; causes persecution in Serbia, III, 414; revival through war misery, IV, xvi; fights to save Belgians, IV, 14; causes trouble in Mexico, IV, 77; seeks to protect French civilians, IV, 105, 111; of Indian troops in siege, IV, 136 et seq.; British besieged appeal to, IV, 140; disrupts Mohammedan world, IV, 233 et seq.; upholds old systems in Russia, IV, 308; Germans malignant against, V, 38; Brazil's attitude toward, V, 151, 152; in British conquest of Palestine, V, 401 et seq.; in Ukranian constitution, VI, 19 et seq.; after the War, VII, xiii et seq.; in "occupied" Germany, VII, 19; in Greater Serbia, VII, 24 et seq., 35; at Peace Conference, VII, 40.

Revolution, its beginnings in Russia, IV, 306 et seq.; in Greece, IV, xxvii, 331 et seq.; changes course of War, V, xviii et seq.; bursts into flame in Russia, V, 68 et seq.; in Greece, V, 221 et seq.; destroys military strength of Russia, V, 243 et seq.; beginnings of, in Germany, V, 301; destroys Democracy in Russia, V,

331 et seq.; in Germany, VI, xxxix; in Ukrainia, VI, 18 et seq.;
Russia to extend, VI, 35 et seq.; in Siberia, VI, 230 et seq.; begins
in Germany, VI, 358 et seq.; makes Germany a republic, VI, 402
et seq.; during Armistice period, VII, xviii et seq.; in Germany,
VII, 67 et seq.; in Czecho-Slovakia, VII, 140 et seq.

Romanticism, rejected by moderns, I, 50; popularized in Germany,
I, 51, 84; Germans accuse Americans of, VI, 204 et seq.

Rumania, Teutons seek to draw into War, I, xxxvi; early struggles,
I, 178 et seq.; turns away from Germany, I, 231 et seq.; German
intrigue in, I, 267; Austrian judgment of, I, 277; Slav menace to,
I, 331; swayed by Turkey's entrance to War, II, 392 et seq.;
Turkish diplomacy in, II, 396; accused of aiding Turkey, III, 81;
troops serve Austria unwillingly, III, 106; but fight well, III, 111
et seq.; ensnared by Russia, IV, 305 et seq.; Russia seeks agreement with, III, 327; in Balkan turmoil of 1915, III, 345 et seq.;
relations to Hungary, III, 384; relations to Bulgaria, III, 413;
Russian treachery to, IV, xxiv; swayed by 1916 victories of
Russia, IV, 185 et seq., 200; forced into War by Russia and betrayed, IV, 305 et seq.; proclamation of war, IV, 322 et seq.; effect of entry on neutrals, IV, 350; crushed by Teutons, IV, 357
et seq.; the last defense in the mountains, IV, 399 et seq.; German
1917 plans for, V, 327; suffering of in 1918, VI, xiv et seq.; in
"Fourteen Points," VI, 5; forced to accept peace, VI, 31 et seq.;
Germans forced to withdraw from, VI, 359; Armistice terms for,
VI, 424; asserts military power during Armistice period, VII,
xxix et seq.; at Peace Conference, VII, 39, 60; at signing of
Peace, VII, 154.

Russia, rouses Slavs against Austria, I, xxix; is defiant, I, xxxvi
et seq.; German intrigue in, I, xxxviii; German ultimatum forces
War on, I, xl et seq.; charged with starting War, I, xliv; seeks
expansion, I, 60; oppresses Finns and Poles, I, 63; Germany's
use for, I, 76; helps Poles, I, 144; helps Balkans against Austria,
I, 176 et seq.; opposes Germany in East, I, 199; ruined by closing
Dardanelles, I, 222; German scorn of, I, 230 et seq.; defends
Serbia, I, 257 et seq.; Austria's secret opinion of, I, 277 et seq.;
deceived by Austria, I, 292; and involved in the turmoil of 1914,
I, 298 et seq.; unready for War, I, 314 et seq.; accused as causing War, I, 324 et seq.; forced into War by Germany, I, 338 et
seq.; policy explained, I, 359 et seq.; accused by German Chancellor, I, 409 et seq.

General course of War's events of 1914 in, II, xvi et seq.; aided
by Serb victory, II, 4; seafights of, in Black Sea, II, 32; insulted
at Constantinople, II, 102; defeated at Tannenberg, II, 170 et
seq.; crushes Austria at Lemberg, II, 190 et seq.; menaced by
Turkey, II, 391 et seq.; in Warsaw campaign, II, 416 et seq.

Main events of 1915 in, III, xiii et seq.; wins Caucasus and
north Persia, III, 38 et seq.; upheld by France and Britain, III,
66 et seq.; III, 79 et seq.; wins Przemysl and Galicia, III, 93 et
seq.; battles in Carpathians and invades Hungary, III, 106 et seq.;
aided by Armenians, III, 158; her power broken at the Dunajec,
III, 177 et seq.; receives munitions from Britain, III, 210; defeated
in Warsaw campaign, III, 229; fears of populace, III, 245; Germany invents accusations of atrocities against, III, 300; Allies
relieve, by attack in west, III, 302 et seq.; drives back Germans,
III, 320 et seq.; shocked and angered by Bulgaria's entry into
War against her, III, 328 et seq.; aids Serbs at Belgrade, III,

348; women fight for, III, 381; German peace demands from, III, 394; her part in ravaging of Poland, III, 425, 426.

Events of 1916 in, IV, xiii et seq.; victorious in Armenia, IV, 24 et seq.; army in Persia aids British, IV, 137; advances against Austria in time with Italy, IV, 149 et seq.; great Brusiloff victories over Austria, IV, 185 et seq.; praised by Joffre, IV, 231; draws Germans from French front, IV, 243; betrayed by high officials, IV, 305 et seq.; drags Rumania into War, IV, 318 et seq.; 328 et seq.; Greece fears ambitions of, IV, 334; aids Rumania feebly, IV, 357 et seq.; aids Serbians, IV, 387; aids in Rumania's final defense, IV, 399 et seq.; report on German prison camps, IV, 412 et seq.

Revolutions of 1917 in, V, xiii et seq.; aids British in East, V, 49; overthrow of the Czar, V, 68 et seq.; U. S. view of first revolution in, V, 113 et seq.; British view of, V, 142, 145; air voyages to help civilizing of, V, 205; upholds autocracy in Greece, V, 221 et seq.; Greeks avoid offending, V, 227; last military triumph of, and complete breakdown, V, 243 et seq.; Bolshevist seizure of, V, 331 et seq.; armistice with Teutons, V, 393 et seq.; effects of breakdown, V, 439.

Events of 1918 in, VI, xiv et seq.; German treatment of, as seen by Allies, VI, 2; "Fourteen Points" on, VI, 4 et seq.; consents to free Finland and Ukrainia, VI, 18 et seq.; accepts Teuton peace, VI, 31 et seq.; opposes retreat of Czecho-Slav army, VI, 144 et seq.; Allies aid democracy in, against bolshevism, VI, 230 et seq.; Armistice terms for, VI, 424; during Armistice period, VII, xiii et seq.; influence of, on new Germany, VII, 87; loses land to Poland, VII, 94 et seq.; in Peace Conference, VII, 182.

SCIENCE, chained to materialism, I, 9; opposed to religion, I, 24; helps it, I, 41; used against the weak, I, 46; German contributions to, I, 49; use in industry, I, 68 et seq.; developed in South Germany, I, 98; meets new War requirements, III, 65; leaders of, in Germany support aggression, III, 400; triumphs in merchant U-boats, IV, 276 et seq.; improves aeroplanes and submarines and explosives, V, xxiii et seq.; in German destructiveness, V, 25 et seq.; distracted by War, V, 190; British overcomes German, V, 214; organizes for War in U. S., V, 420 et seq.; invents the seventy-mile cannon, VI, 92 et seq.; develops gunnery, VI, 301; exhaustion after War, VII, xvii; at Peace Conference, VII, 40.

Secret Service, of France, I, 121, 228 et seq.; of Teutons in America, III, xxiii, 274 et seq.; in Belgium, III, 369 et seq.; German spy at Verdun, IV, 56; in Russia, IV, 307, 311; German in Greece, IV, 331 et seq., 345; Teuton in Rumania, IV, 372; of Germany, learns of French plane, V, xviii; of U. S., detects German plots, V, 42, 114; U. S. navy aids in, V, 180; of Teutons in Russia, V, 256; in Italy, VI, 216 et seq.; learns of German Peace Assault, VI, 241; in Czecho-Slovakia, VII, 145.

Serbia, accused by Austria, I, xix; early history of, I, xxii, exhaustion in 1914, I, xxx; ultimatum to, I, xxxv et seq.; threatened in 1912, I, 120, 128; oppressed by Austria, I, 176 et seq.; character of Serbs, I, 189; German policy against, I, 228; Austrian policy against, I, 232 et seq., 353 et seq.; her part in Serajevo crime, I, 245 et seq., 261, 332; previous victories, I, 266; Austria's plot against, I, 276 et seq.; receives Austrian ultimatum, I, 285 et seq.; regains world's sympathy, I, 297 et seq.; Kaiser's rage against I, 319 et seq.

xxxii; German, opposes the War, I, 17; a bar to office in Germany, I, 37; Imperialistic, I, 72, 73; State progress in, I, 82; Bülow's views on, I, 90; growth in Germany, I, 134; protests against militarism, I, 134 et seq.; defends Alsace, I, 171; aids disarmament, I, 209; views of British, I, 221; growing discontent in Germany, I, 228 et seq.; statistics of, I, 240; German advance in, I, 357; protests against German atrocities, II, 53, 57 et seq., 83 et seq., 184; German, appealed to by Poles, III, 437; encourages disruption of Russia, IV, 307 et seq.; in Germany, sneers at Rumanian suffering, IV, 371.

In Russian revolution, V, xv et seq., 68 et seq.; held France back in War, V, 122; takes control of Russia, V, 243 et seq.; almost wrecks Italian armies, V, 315 et seq.; loses control of Russia, V, 331 et seq.; rejoices in Italy's disaster, V, 366; takes control of German government, VI, xxxviii; in Ukrainia, VI, 18 et seq.; organizes revolt in Germany, VI, 359 et seq.; establishes German republic, VI, 402 et seq.; reorganizes Central Europe under Armistice, VII, xix et seq.; in Rhineland, VII, 21; Lloyd George favors, VII, 63; rules Germany, VII, 70 et seq.; in Poland, VII, 97; in Czecho-Slovakia, VII, 141 et seq.; view of Peace terms, VII, 184 et seq.

Spain, medieval intolerance of, I, 45; rights in America, I, 162; opposed by Britain, I, 204; opposed freedom of seas, I, 217; maintains neutrality at Paris, II, 206; interferes in Cavell case, II, 369 et seq., 374; Belgians appeal to, IV, 6; Ambassador joins U. S. in protest, IV, 102; favors Germany in neutrality, V, 1 et seq.; spared in U-boat blockade, V, 6; protests U-boat warfare, V, 15; remains only important neutral, V, 147; German gratitude to, VI, 14.

Statecraft, methods of, I, xvii et seq.; in Germany, I, 48; German methods in Italy, I, 75; necessity of, I, 101; falsely employed, I, 102; follies of, I, 120; in the Balkans, 1, 180 et seq.; in Asia Minor, I, 200; in the Serajevo crime, I, 245, 256, 271; its breakdown, I, 296 et seq, 339 et seq.; its folly in Russia, I, 357 et seq.; its intrigues among German officials, III, 51 et seq.; in Armenian massacres, III, 174 et seq.; seeks to keep Italy from War, III, 214 et seq.; of Teutons in America, III, 274 et seq.; in Bulgarian embroglio, III, 328 et seq.; III, 345 et seq.; trickery of, in Russia, IV, 306 et seq.; in Greece, IV, 331 et seq.; useless to America, V, 1 et seq.; 114; breaks down in Germany, VI, 402; difficulties of, in reconstruction days, VII, xiv et seq., 36 et seq.

Subject peoples, under Germany, I, 144 et seq.; under Austria, I, 176 et seq.; oppressed in Hungary, I, 187 et seq.; under Turkey, III, 154 et seq.; oppression of, in Belgium, III, 369 et seq.; in "Middle Europe" empire, III, 382 et seq.; 425 et seq.; in northern France, IV, 102 et seq.; Germany hopes for freedom of, V, 3; in Holy Land, V, 401 et seq.; "Fourteen Points" on, VI, 3 et seq. See Mandatories.

Submarines, America angered by use of, I, 204; first War uses of, by Germany, II, xxxv; legitimate attacks and successes of, II, xxxvi; German approval of, II, 20 et seq.; prevent old style blockade, II, 25; British in Baltic, II, 29; long voyages of, II, 32; successful warfare of, II, 295 et seq.; sink Japanese warship, II, 415; triumphs of, in 1915, III, xxii et seq.; undertake warfare on merchant ships, III, 49 et seq., 187 et seq.; France approves, III, 188; German success with, arouses Britain and France, III, 201; Germany plans to use against neutrals, III, 284; IV, 61; U. S. checks German use of, IV, 88 et seq.; cross Atlantic, IV, 276 et seq.; British captain executed by Germans for opposing, IV, 281 et seq.

Change course of War in 1917, V, xiv et seq.; chief blockade and destruction by, V, 1 et seq.; Germany secretly pledges herself to per-

tarism, VI, 402; rejoicings at and of, VI, 428 et seq.; disastrous results of, VII, xiii et seq.; future of, VII, xxxvi.

Women, abuse of, by Germans, I, 39; declared by Germans "biologically imbecile," I, 170; abuse of, by Hungarians, I, 185; II, 7 et seq.; used as battle screens, II, 17; abused by Germans in Belgium, II, 53 et seq.; Belgian, accused by Germans, II, 71 et seq.; sufferings of in Louvain, II, 155 et seq.; in northern France, II, 250; in Poland, II, 427; in Serbia and the East, III, xxx et seq.; Kaiser condemns, III, 2 et seq.; deportation of, III, 19; follow German army and join in plundering, III, 20; agonies of in Armenia, III, 154 et seq.; German women aid Armenians, III, 166; perish on *Lusitania*, III, 187 et seq.; aid British government by labor, III, 210 et seq.; German treatment of, in Cavell case, III, 369 et seq.; join Russian army, III, 381; in Serbian exodus, III, 406 et seq.; atrocities against in Serbia, III, 413 et seq., 420; German degradation of, III, 430 et seq.; suffering Belgium, IV, 1 et seq.; of Belgium, appeal to America, IV, 16; enslaved in France, IV, 102 et seq.; enter U. S. Congress, V, xxii; take arms and perish in Russian revolution, V, xxix; abused by Germans in Hindenburg retreat, V, 30 et seq.; in Italian retreat, V, 325; abused in Bolshevist Russia, V, 334, 360; slain in Paris by German super-gun, VI, 92 et seq.; of Germany in "occupied" region, VII, 4 et seq.; aid in Czech revolution, VII, 145; in Czech parliament, VII, 150.

World Empire, German dream of, I, 23 et seq.; boastfulness of, I, 42; commercial need of, I, 73 et seq.; plans for, I, 89 et seq.; faith in, I, 104, Germany expects, I, 108 et seq.; fears to lose, I, 232 et seq.; direct effort toward, I, 258, 259 et seq.; German rush for, I, 382 et seq.; Britain accused of seeking, I, 396 et seq.; Germany's first plan for, fails, II, xxviii; Germany despairs of, III, 62; Italy recognizes Germany's effort for, III, 227; Bulgaria believes Central Powers have won, III, 340; conquest of Serbia opens, III, 359, 382 et seq.; German methods of preserving, III, 428 et seq.; climax of hopes of, IV, xiii, 187; the last U-boat scheme toward, V, xiv; formed against Germany by entry of neutrals into War, V, 147 et seq.; Germany's last hope for, V, 432; near-roused by triumph over Russia, VI, xvi; final abandonment of, VI, 358 et seq.

World Peace, hopes for I, xviii; previous efforts at, I, 56; German doubt as to the future, I, 105 et seq.; hopes for future, I, 367; Britain's efforts toward, I, 397 et seq.; despair of, IV, xvi; France fights for, IV, 232; Germany admits necessity of, V, 3; Germany begins her "Peace Offensive" for, V, 133; Allies fight for, V, 134; Pope's efforts for, V, 151; Labor's yearning for, V, 189; development of aeroplanes to make compulsory, V, 206; bolshevists announce wild plans for, V, 395 et seq.; Armistice partly obtains, VI, xl.; "Fourteen Points" on, VI, 1 et seq.; Ukrainia seeks to aid, VI, 18 et seq.; Armistice promises, VI, 421 et seq.; difficulties of establishing, VII, xiv et seq.; signed, VII, 153 et seq.

Wounded, care of, in Serbia, I, 185; ill-treatment by Austrians, II, 8 et seq.; Belgians accused of abusing, II, 164; plundered by Germans, III, 22; in Serbian exodus, III, 409; fight madly at Verdun, IV, 224 et seq.; behavior of French and German contrasted, IV, 273; 274; neglected in German prison camps, IV, 412 et seq.; Armistice terms for, VI, 424.

GENERAL INDEX

265

troops in first gas attack, III, 148; at Peace Conference, VII, 54.

Ali Fuad, Turkish general, surrenders Jerusalem, V, 413 et seq.

Ali Riza, a soft hearted Turkish official, III, 174.

Al-Katr, in Asia, trouble at, I, 201.

Allanson, British officer, at Dardanelles, III, 261.

Allenby, British general, in Belgium, II, 126 et seq.; at Ypres, II, 340 et seq.; in Palestine, V, xxxv, 401 et seq.; on conquest of Jerusalem, V, 414; complete conquest of Palestine by, VI, xxxvii, 332 et seq.; on conquest, VI, 340.

Allenstein, in Prussia, Russian advance on, II, 171; fighting at, II, 173 et seq.; Hindenburg headquarters at, II, 185; Russian prisoners mistreated at, IV, 417.

"Allied Council of Versailles," source of, V, 372.

Alpini, Italian troops, IV, 148 et seq.; V, 374.

Alsace, Bismarck's view of, I, 4; oppression in, I, 148 et seq.; "Crime of," I, 156 et seq.; France expects attack from, II, xv; invaded by French, II, xxiii, 108 et seq.; Joffre explains campaign in, II, 119; "Fourteen Points" deal with, VI, I et seq.; Armistice terms for, VI, 421.

Alsatians, abused in German army, I, 137; confined to barracks when War opened, I, 375.

Altkirch, in Alsace, fighting at, II, 109 et seq.

Altpiano, in Italy, fighting on, IV, 151.

Altschul, American writer, work, I, 121; on militarism, I, 132.

Alviella, Count d', Belgian statesman, II, 72.

Amade, d', French general, aids British, II, 132.

Amador, Mexican official, in trouble with U. S., IV, 68.

Aman, in Holy Land, Turk retreat to, VI, 334.

Amance, in France, battle at, II, 216 et seq.

Amara, in Asia, British capture, IV, 129.

"Ambassador Morgenthau's Story," book, I, 239; III, 80.

American Escadrille, aviators in French service, IV, 261 et seq.

American Independent, newspaper in U. S. in German service, III, 298.

Amerongen, in Holland, Kaiser's refuge at, VI, 411.

Amiens, French army gathers at, II, 123; Germans capture, II, 135; retreat towards, II, 247; British base in Somme battle, IV, 242 et seq.; in Kaiser-battle, VI, 54 et seq.; in great Ally advance, VI, 272; battle of, VI, 281 et seq.

Amiral Ganteaume, French ship, torpedoed, III, 27; details of, III, 54.

Amur Railroad, in Siberia, Czechs retreat by, VI, 159.

Anafarta, in Dardenelles campaign, III, 255 et seq.

Anastasiu, Rumanian general, desperate resistance by, IV, 370.

Anatolia, French interests in I, 203; Turks, plan flight to, III, 82; Armenians suffer in, III, 159, 173; Russian advance into, IV, 24 et seq.; sympathizes with Arabia, IV, 240.

Anatolian Railway, I, 194 et seq.

Ancre River, in France, fighting on, IV, 243 et seq., 256; desolation on, V, 22 et seq.

Andechy, in France, in Kaiser-battle, VI, 71.

Andeghem, in Belgium, fighting at, II, 312.

Andenne, in Belgium, massacre at, II, 166.

Anderson, British sea-captain, on *Lusitania*, III, 194.

Andevanne, in France, Americans win, VI, 399.

Andler, French Socialist, quoted, I, 72.

Andrassy, Count, Austrian statesman, I, 178 et seq.

Andrew, Prince, of Greece, commands troops, V, 228.

Androvitze, Serbian exodus from, III, 410.

Bellicourt, on French frontier, Americans win, VI, 361 et seq.

Belloy, in France, Alan Seeger slain at, IV, 259.

Belluno, in Italy, fighting near, V, 372.

Below, von, German diplomat, I, 383, in Belgium, I, 389; quoted, I, 390, 391.

Below, von, German general, serves with Hindenburg, II, 181 et seq.; commands in East Prussia, III, 232 et seq.; in Italian 1917 campaign, V, 322, 327, 367 et seq.; in Kaiser-battle, VI, 88 et seq., 166 et seq.; superseded, VI, 263.

Belridge, Norse ship, sunk, III, 59.

Benay, in France, Germans capture, VI, 58 et seq.

Benedict, Pope, Brazil appeals to, V, 151; peace efforts of, V, 151 et seq.

Benes, Czech statesman, Poles praise, VII, 104; aids freedom, VII, 140 et seq.

Benneke, German doctor, on frightfulness, V, 37.

Benson, U. S. admiral, urges ships sent abroad, V, 176.

Bentick, Dutch count, receives Kaiser, VI, 411.

Berchtold, Austrian Chancellor, purposes of, I, 258 et seq.; urges War, I, 276 et seq.; on causes of War, I, 285; deceives ambassadors, I, 292, 293; responsible for diplomatic muddle of 1914, I, 297 et seq., 311; takes counsel with Germany, I, 319; disputes with Italy, III, 223 et seq.

Berestechko, in Russia, battle of, IV, 194.

Berg, von, German officer, on Americans, VI, 193, 204 et seq.

Berge, Major von, commands in Berlin, VI, 408.

Bergson, Henri, French author, I, 1 et seq.

Berlin, scenes in at Austrian ultimatum, I, 303; panic in at Russian invasion, II, 170; last Russian threat against, III, 177; Middle Europe railroad from, III, 382 et seq.; rejoices over Montenegro's fall, IV, 23; revolution in, VI, xxxix; hears news of retreat, VI, 280; bolshevism in, VI, 368 et seq.; new government in, VI, 402 et seq.; tumults in, VI, 408; new Constitution affects, VII, 82; battle in, VII, 111, et seq.

Berlin, treaty of, I, 286, 325 et seq., 359, 365.

Berlin University, I, 89.

Berméricourt, in France, in Kaiser-battle, VI, 166 et seq.

Bernhardi, German general, on Germany's progress, I, 23; pangermanism of, I, 110, 111; quoted, I, 115; career, I, 121; on militarism, I, 122; demands world-power, I, 205; changes tone, I, 228; on necessity of war, I, 230.

Bernhardt, Sarah, acts in Berlin, I, 170.

Bernstorff, German diplomat, III, 274; in U. S., III, 275 et seq.; his defense, III, 299; announces renewal of U-boat attacks, V, 1 et seq.; dismissed from U. S., V, 2; previous propaganda in U. S., V, 127 et seq.

Berry-au-Bac, in France, fighting at, V, 164; in Kaiser-battle, VI, 168 et seq.

Berryer, Belgian statesman, I, 390.

Bersaglieri, Italian troops, victorious, IV. 297; repulse Austrians at Sette Comuni, V, 383; in Piave battle, VI, 213 et seq.

Berthaut, French writer, VI, 164; on Kaiser-battle, VI, 180.

Berthelot, French general, in Rumania, IV, 321; in Peace Assault, VI, 246; in Ally advance, VI, 264 et seq.

Bertincourt, in France, Germans capture, VI, 66 et seq.

Bertrix, in Belgium, atrocities at, II, 91.

Berzy-le-Sec, in France, in great Ally advance, VI, 267 et seq.

Beseler, von, German general in Antwerp, II, 308 et seq.; in Poland, III, 427 et seq.

Bessarabia, Russian province, Rumanians retreat to, IV, 401; Teutons invade, V, 267.

Beth-Horon, in Palestine, British capture, V, 407 et seq.

Bremen, U-boat visits America, IV, 276.

Brennero, in Austria, Italians capture, VI, 385.

Brenta River, in Italy, campaign on, IV, 149 et seq.; in Piave rally, V, 372 et seq.; in 1918 campaign, VI, 216 et seq., 374 et seq.

Breslau, in Germany, school strikes at, I, 151.

Breslau, German warship escapes French, II, 32; escapes British, II, 94; sold to Turkey, II, 96 et seq.; stirs trouble, II, 391 et seq.; sortie by, VI, 341.

Brest, French port, Americans at, VII, 129.

Brest-Litovsk, in Russia, in 1915 warfare, III, xxvi; campaign for, III, 229 et seq.; capture of, III, 249; negotiations at, V, xxx, 393; peace convention at, VI, xvi et seq., 2 et seq., 18 et seq., 31; Czecho-Slovaks condemn peace of, VI, 148; Siberians reject peace of, VI, 241; Armistice cancels peace terms of, VI, 424.

Breton, French colonel, at Marne battle, II, 261.

Brialmont, Belgian general, built forts, II, 39.

Briand, French statesman, as Premier, IV, xxxi; on deportations from France, IV, 102, 104; aids Rumania, IV, 316; Germany criticizes, IV, 330; leaves office, V, 106.

Bridgeport, in U. S., German agency at, III, 280.

Brie, in France, seat of Marne battle, II, 253.

Brienne, in Marne battle, II, 260.

Brieuilles, in France, Americans win, VI, 346 et seq.

Briey, in Lorraine, iron mines in, I, 74, 164; Germany fights for, IV, 208; U. S. troops threaten, V, 434; VI, 400.

Brilliant, British ship, in Zeebrugge raid, VI, 139.

Brincken, German officer, plots in U. S., III, 286 et seq.

Brindisi, in Italy, naval base at, V, 370.

Bristol, British warship, II, 445.

Britain, See Subject Index.

British East Africa, fighting in, II, 374 et seq.

Brits, British colonel, in Africa, II, 384 et seq.

Brockdorff - Rantzau, German statesman, confesses defeat, VI, 393; made Foreign Minister, VII, 75; protests at Treaty, VII, 153, 159 et seq.

Brod, in Serbia, fighting at, IV, 395.

Brody, in Galicia, captured, IV, 194; advance from, IV, 199; Russian break near, V, 253.

Broenbeek, in Belgium, fighting along, V, 290 et seq.

Broodseinde, in Ypres campaign, III, 145; in Flanders battle, V, 285 et seq.

Brookings, American official, aids in organizing U. S., V, 422.

Broqueville, de, Belgian statesman, I, 394; quoted, I, 395; not anti-German, II, 64; on "Fourteen Points," VI, 1, 17.

Brown, U. S. colonel, in Mexican intervention, IV, 63.

Brownsville, in Texas, Mexican attack on, IV, 82.

Bruges, in Belgium, German treatment, of, I, 20; deportations from, IV, 3; Fryatt trial in, IV, 288 et seq.; in Zeebrugge raid, VI, 126 et seq.; freed, VII, 62.

Brumowsky, Austrian aviator, VI, 222.

Brunehilde Line, of German defense, in Ally drive, VI, 389 et seq.

Brunswick, Duke of, leads plundering, III, 22.

Brusiloff, Russian general, in Lemberg campaign, II, 191 et seq.; extricates army from Carpathians, III, 177 et seq.; great 1916 victories of, IV, xxiv, 185 et seq.; his report of victory, IV, 196; advance blocked by treason, IV, 305; retreats, IV, 315; heads 1917 attack, V, xxviii; supports Democracy in Russia, V, 76; on Russia's breakdown, V, 243, 250; sneered at by Russian bolshevists, V, 261; commends valor of Czecho-Slovaks, VI, 147.

Brussels, Belgians abandon, II, xxii; German schedule for capture of, II, 39; receives news of massacres, II, 53 et seq.; Germans enter, II, 137; Germans advance from, II, 304 et seq.; Cavell case in, III, 369 et seq.; deportations from, IV, 3; Kaiser at, VI, 406.

Brussels, British ship, rams submarine, IV, 285 et seq.

Bryan, American statesman, in *Lusitania* case, III, 188; leads pacifist forces, V, 138.

Bryant, British colonel, in Africa, II, 371 et seq.

Bryce, British statesman, on Armenian massacre, III, 154.

Brzezany, on Austrian frontier, in 1917 campaign, V, 251 et seq.

Buchan, British writer, V, 365; on Italy's rally at the Piave, V, 366; on Lys battle, VI, 105, 123; on Aisne battle, VI, 164; on Peace Assault, VI, 244; on Ally triumph, VI, 259.

Buchanan, Sir G., British diplomat, quoted, I, 257, 410; sees German propaganda in Russia, IV, 314.

Bucharest, Rumanian capital, Teuton intrigue at, II, 396 et seq.; agitated for war, IV, 319 et seq.; menaced by Teuton armies, IV, 357 et seq.; panic in, IV, 360; capture of, IV, 399 et seq.; restored, VI, 424.

Bucharest, treaty of, I, 176, 374; revision of treaty, I, 258; real cause of Great War, I, 266.

Buczacz, in Galicia, Russians capture, IV, 192, 196; in 1917 campaign, V, 255.

Budapest, men of, make poor troops, III, 11; revolution in, VII, xxi.

Buenz, German agent in New York, III, 295 et seq.

Bug River, on Russian front, fighting on, II, 195, in Warsaw campaign, III, 232 et seq.

Buissy, in France, British win, VI, 294 et seq.

Bukoba, in East Africa, British capture, II, 389.

Bukowina, Austrian province, attacked, III, 108, 186; Brusiloff

campaign conquers, IV, 185 et seq.; Rumanian claims on, IV, 319, 327; lost to Russian armies, V, 255 et seq.

Bukri, in Serbia, fighting at, IV, 395.

Bulfin, British general, at Ypres, II, 350 et seq.

Bulgaria, See Subject Index.

Bulgarian Peace Commission, article by, III, 404, 419.

Bull, newspaper in U. S. in German pay, III, 298.

Bullard, U. S. general, in great Ally drive, VI, 271; in Argonne, VI, 349 et seq.

Bullecourt, in France, fighting at, V, 164, 386 et seq.

Bülow, von, German general, commands Second Army, II, 123; attacks Namur, II, 147 et seq.; forces weakened, II, 231; commands army next von Kluck, II, 239 et seq.; advances along Oise River, II, 249; in Marne battle, II, 256 et seq.; German defense of, II, 267 et seq.; attacks Rheims, II, 290; on Russian front, III, 324 et seq.

Bülow, Prince von, article on Germany's progress, I, 89; sought world-power, I, 206; sought big navy, I, 210; denies thoughts of war, I, 339, 354; wins diplomatic triumph, I, 359; approves U-boat attacks, III, 50; heads propagandist work in Italy, III, 215; denounced by Italy, III, 227, 228.

Bundy, U. S. general, at Château-Thierry, VI, xxiii, 193.

Bunsen, De, British diplomat, I, 258; in Vienna, I, 285; on causes of War, 292.

Bunz, German agent in America, "honored," III, 300.

Burgas, in Bulgaria, industrial needs of, III, 337.

Burgundy, Germany covets, I, 132; threatened in Marne battle, II, 262.

Burian, Hungarian statesman, protests American munitions, III, 125; aids Teuton plots in America, III, 279; continues in power, IV, xxxii.

Burkah, in Palestine, British capture, V, 404.

Burke, Edmund, upheld liberty, I, 55.

Burney, British admiral, in Jutland battle, IV, 174 et seq.

Burniaux, Belgian family, slaughtered, II, 76 et seq.

Busch, German statesman, quoted, I, 35.

Busche, von dem, German secretary, VI, 408.

Bussche, von der, German officer, on peace, VI, 358, 359.

Bussche - Haddenhausen, German diplomat, in Rumania, IV, 319, 329.

Buzancy, in France, Americans win, VI, 388 et seq., 398.

Buzeu, in Rumania, fighting at, IV, 411 et seq.

Byers, Boer general, fights British, II, 378 et seq.

Byng, British general, at Ypres battle, II, 344 et seq.; at Cambrai, V, xxxiii, 386 et seq.; in Kaiser-battle, VI, 54; in British drive, VI, 299.

Bystrzyca River, in Galicia, IV, 195.

Bzura River, in Poland, fighting on, II, 418 et seq.

Cabrilovic, assassin, I, xix, 246 et seq.

Cadore, in Italy, retreat from, V, 371.

Cadorna, Italian general, operations of 1916 under, IV, xxii; commands in Asiago campaign, IV, 148 et seq.; in capture of Gorizia, IV, 294; retired, V, xxxii; commands Isonzo attack, V, 303 et seq., 306; on Caporetto disaster, V, 315, 318; directs Italian retreat, V, 318 et seq.; replaced by Diaz, V, 365 et seq.

Caen, Germans in, I, 74.

Caillaux, French diplomatist, troubles of, I, 120, 254.

Caillette Woods, in Verdun battle, IV, 57 et seq., 221.

Cairo, in Egypt, base at, VI, 333.

Calabar, in West Africa, fighting at, II, 372.

Calais, German advance threatens, II, 325 et seq.; battle of, II, 337

et seq.; Canada defends, II, 361; Germany threatens, VI, 108.

Calcutta, in India, German sea raids near, II, 448.

Callaris, Greek general, deposed, V, 228.

Callimassiotis, Greek official, aids U-boats, V, 233.

Calthorp, British admiral, at Constantinople, VI, 332 et seq.

Calvinia, in Africa, fight at, II, 381.

Cambon, Jules, French statesman, I, 228; article by, I, 235; character, I, 288; report by, I, 303; British dealings of, I, 311, 315; quoted, I, 318; signs Peace Treaty, VII, 158.

Cambrai, first fighting at, II, 132; battle at, II, 149; in 1917 campaign, V, xxxiii; German retreat to, V, 28; great tank assault at, V, 386 et seq.; U. S. engineers at, V, 438; goal in Kaiser-battle, VI, 51; British recapture, VI, 299 et seq.

Cameron, U. S. general, at St. Mihiel, VI, 318; at Argonne, VI, 349.

Cameroon River, in Africa, fighting on, II, 373.

Cameroons, in Africa, conquered, II, 370 et seq.

Camp des Romains, French fortress, captured, II, 290, 291.

Campbell - Bannerman, British statesman, I, 209, 212; quoted, I, 214.

Campenhout, in Belgium, atrocities at, II, 155, 169.

Campobasso, Italian brigade, heroism of, V, 306.

Cana, British historian, III, 65; on Neuve Chapelle battle, III, 67.

Canada, See Subject Index.

Canadian War Records, V, 153, 158 et seq.

Canale, on Italian front, fighting at, V, 308.

Candler, British writer, IV, 127; on siege of Kut, IV, 130; on fall of Bagdad, V, 48, 64.

Canopus, British warship, II, 441 et seq.

Cantigny, in France, Americans

capture, VI, xxxi, 169, 184 et seq.; results of battle, VI, 193.

Cape Colony, loyal to Britain, II, 370 et seq.

Capelle, von, German admiral, IV, 154; on Jutland battle, IV, 165.

Capello, Italian general, commands on Isonzo front, V, 307 et seq., 366 et seq.

Caporetto, on Italian frontier, disaster of, V, xxxi, 303, 308, 315 et seq., 365 et seq.; effects of, V, 439.

Capper, British general, at Ypres, III, 343 et seq.

Caprile, Italian mountain pass, fight for, V, 376.

Caracalu, Rumanians surrender at, IV, 370.

Carden, British admiral, at Dardanelles, III, 85 et seq.

Carency, in France, heroic French attack at, V, 167.

Carey, British general, in Kaiserbattle, VI, 50, 69 et seq., 77.

Carigan, in France, Americans win, VI, 346 et seq.

Carillo, Spanish author, II, 209; on Nancy battle, II, 219.

Carlos, King of Rumania; his purposes, I, 279; resolves on War, IV, 327; announces War, IV, 328.

Carlowitz, von, German general, resists American advance, VI, 276.

Carlsruhe, in Germany, bombed, I, 377.

Carlyle, Thomas, quoted, I, 225.

Carmen Sylva, Rumanian queen, IV, 399.

"Carnegie Inquiry," in Balkans, III, 419 et seq.

Carnia, on Austrian frontier, advance from, V, 369 et seq.

Carol, King of Rumania, See Carlos.

Caron, French general, in Germany, VII, 7.

Carpathian Mountains, fighting in, II, 194; Austrian advance through, II, 419; terrible winter campaign in, III, xv, 106 et seq.; Russians escape disaster in, III, 177 et seq.; Austrian retreat to, IV, 200; Rumanian

claims to, IV, 323; Rumanian campaign in, IV, 357 et seq.

Carpenter, British naval officer, commands Zeebrugge raid, VI, 126.

Carranza, Mexican statesman, Germany confers with, III, 284; in U. S. intervention, IV, 61 et seq.; his protest, IV, 63; indirectly approached by Germany, V, 44.

Carrizal, in Mexico, U. S. troops attacked at, IV, 62 et seq.

Carso, Austro-Italian battles on, IV, 295 et seq.; in 1917 campaign, V, 320, 367 et seq.

Carson, British statesman, in *Lusitania* inquiry, III, 191.

Cary, de, French general, retreating to Marne, II, 249, 252; in Marne battle, II, 255 et seq.; in Aisne battle, II, 290; commands in Argonne, IV, 41.

Casement, Irish leader, aids Germany in U. S., III, 289; aids revolt in Ireland, IV, 114 et seq.; his dying speech, IV, 122.

Caspian Sea, Germany seeks base on, VI, 230.

Cassel, in Prussia, prisoners sent to, II, 55.

Cassel, on Belgian frontier, German goal, VI, 105; attack on, VI, 108.

Cassin, U. S. destroyer, torpedoed, V, 176.

Cassorie, in Hungary, people flee from, III, 122.

Castagnevizza, in Austria, Italians capture, IV, 300.

Castelgomberto, Mount, in Italy, fighting on, V, 374 et seq.

Castelnau, French general, in Lorraine, II, 115 et seq.; victor at Nancy, II, 209 et seq.; value of victory, II, 226, 248; aids Marne battle, II, 255 et seq.; in Race to Sea, II, 305; commands Champagne attack, III, 305 et seq.

Catala, Spanish priest at Louvain, II, 167 et seq.

Catalaunian Plains, near the Marne, I, 46.

Catt, Mrs., U. S. leader, aids in War work, V, 423.

Cattaro, Austrian seaport, IV, 19.

Cattier, Belgian professor, II, 72.

Caubone, French general, in Greek tumults, V, 229 et seq.

Caucasia, threatened by Germany, I, 200; leads Turkey into War, II, 398; Russia accused of attacking, II, 399; campaign in, III, 38 et seq.; surrendered to Turkey by treaty, VI, 32.

Caucasus Mountains, campaign of 1915 in, III, xv; area of, III, 38; fighting in, III, 40 et seq.; Duke Nicholas takes Russian command in, III, 320, 321; great campaign in, IV, 24 et seq.

Cavan, Lord, British general, on Piave battle, VI, 213, 226; in final Italian victory, VI, 375 et seq.

Cavell, Edith, British nurse, execution of, III, xxxi, 369 et seq.; results of, IV, 281, 292.

Cecil, British statesman, IV, 114; on Irish revolt, IV, 125; on entry of U. S. into War, V, 124.

Celliers, British leader in Africa, II, 382 et seq.

"Central Europe," book by Naumann, I, 65.

Cephalonia, Greek island, Allies seize, IV, 343.

Cerisy, in France, in Kaiser-battle, VI, 73 et seq.

Cerizy, in France, battle at, II, 134.

Cerna River, on Serbian frontier; Allies advance on, III, 363 et seq.; campaign on, IV, 390 et seq.; Ally victory on, VI, 323 et seq.

Cernavoda, in Rumania, campaign for, IV, 359 et seq.

Cernay, in Alsace, fighting at, II, 110 et seq.

Cerny, in Aisne battle, II, 293 et seq.

Cettinje, Montenegrin capital, captured, IV, xix, 18 et seq.

Ceylon, German sea raids near, II, 448.

Chaban-Dede, Armenian fort, IV, 32 et seq.

Chabarovsk, in Siberia, fighting at, VI, 151.

Chailak Dere, in Dardanelles campaign, III, 254.

Châlons, in France, first German advance on, II, 124; in Ourcq battle, II, 245; in Peace Assault, VI, 244 et seq.

Chambrettes, in Verdun battle, IV, 375.

Champagne, Marne battle in, II, 253 et seq.; assault of 1915 in, III, xxviii, 65 et seq.; great September assault in, III, 302 et seq.; fighting of 1916 in, IV, 48; consequences of, IV, 254; assault of 1917 in, V, 153 et seq.; Guynemer serves in, V, 193; French losses in, V, 219; advance of 1918 in, VI, 357.

Champenoux, in France, fighting at, II, 219 et seq.

Chanak, in Turkey, attacked, III, 86 et seq.; British take possession of, VI, 342, 343.

Chantilly, near Paris, Germans reach, II, 229; conference at, VI, 312.

Chapin, U. S. volunteer in France, IV, 263.

Chapman, British hero, in Africa, II, 376.

Chapman, U. S. volunteer in France, IV, 261; hero deeds of, IV, 267.

Charleroi, in Belgium, battle of II, xxiv, 149; atrocities at, II, 54 et seq.; deportations from, IV, 3.

Charles, Emperor of Austria, a court favorite, I, 255; character of, I, 257; ascends throne, IV, xxxi; as Archduke leads attack on Italy, IV, 53; seeks peace, V, xxxv; rouses German quarrel, V, 327 et seq.; seeks peace, VI, xxx; congratulates people on Ukranian peace, VI, 18, 30; praised as peacemaker, VI, 42; abdicates, VI, 373, 385, 406; VII, xxi; spies watch, VII, 146.

Charlotte Amalia, in Virgin Isles, harborage at, V, 95.

Charmes, in France, battle at, II, 210 et seq.

Charost, French bishop, IV, 102; on enslaving labor, IV, 111.

Charpentry, in France, Americans win, VI, 350.

Château-Thierry, first German advance on, II, 123, 237 et seq.; plundering at, III, 22; Germans and Americans meet at, VI,

fears of coming of Ally fleet in, III, 79 et seq.; discussion of Armenian massacres in, III, 157; Bulgaria aspires to own, III, 334; German railroad to, III, 382 et seq.; religious leadership of, IV, 233; Russian-Rumanian dispute over, IV, 318; Russia plans seizure of, V, 351; saves itself by surrender, VI, xxxvii, 332 et seq.; British occupation of, VI, 343, 344.

Constanza, Rumania's seaport campaign for, IV, 357 et seq.; scenes in, IV, 407.

Contalmaison, in Somme battle, IV, 246 et seq.

Contich, in Belgium, surrender at, II, 317.

Contrisson, in France, fighting at, II, 261.

Cooreman, Belgian judge, II, 72.

Corada, Monte, Italian front, V, 310.

Coral Bay, in Virgin Isles, harbor at, V, 95.

Corbeny, in France, fighting at, V, 164; aeroplane combat at, V, 195, 196.

Corcovado, in Constantinople, II, 96.

Corfu, Greek island, Serbs escape to, III, xxx; Allies seize for Serb refuge, IV, 343, 387; U. S. navy at, V, 169; Serb union begun at, VII, 22.

Corfu, Declaration of, VII, 23.

Cormicy, in France, in Kaiser-battle, VI, 167 et seq.

Cormontreuil, in Aisne battle, II, 292.

Cormoran, German raider, interned, II, 446.

Cornulier, French general, leads cavalry raid, II, 242.

Cornwall, British warship, II, 445.

Coronel, battle of, II, 32, 412, 439 et seq.

Cortemark, in Belgium, French advance to, II, 330.

Costa Rica, severs relations with Germany, V, 147.

Coucy, in France, devastation of, V, 38; in Kaiser-battle, VI, 181.

Coulommiers, in France, Germans in, II, 229; British retake, II, 233; German account of, II, 244; contour of, II, 253; atroci-

ties at, III, 31; Americans defend, VI, 212.

Courcelette, in France, in Somme battle, IV, 258; Canadian assault at, V, 158.

Courcelles, in France, in Kaiser-battle, VI, 173 et seq.

Courchamps, in France, Americans win, VI, 267.

Courcy, in France, plundered, III, 24.

Courland, in Russia, Germans invade, III, 232 et seq.; conquer, III, 243; made a German dependency, VI, xvi; Germany announces freedom of, VI, 12, 31; German plans for, VI, 40; Poland fears, VII, 100.

Courtacon, in France, burned, III, 24.

Courtrai, in Belgium, Kaiser at, II, 332; fighting at, II, 356 et seq.

Coutanceau, French general, II, 262.

Covington, U. S. transport, sunk, V, 175, 180.

Cowdin, U. S. volunteer in France, IV, 262; deeds of, IV, 265, 267.

Cowley, British hero in Kut siege, IV, 140.

Cracow, Poles study at, I, 151; gives money for War, II, 191; in Lemberg campaign, II, 192 et seq.; Russians threaten, II, 417; III, 108; German advance from, III, 177 et seq.

Craddock, British admiral, slain, II, 470 et seq.

Craiova, in Rumania, captured, IV, 370.

Cramon, von, German general, with Austrians, III, 345; on Serbian expedition, III, 366; in Italian campaign, IV, 148; article by, IV, 152; in Russian campaign, IV, 185, 197; on Italian defeat, V, 315; diplomatic services of, V, 326 et seq.

Craônne, in France, in 1917 campaign, V, 164; in Kaiser-battle, VI, 166 et seq.

Creel, American writer, V, 168; on U. S. navy, V, 181.

Crefeld, in Germany, prison camp at, IV, 415 et seq.

on German revolution, VI, 368;
on Berlin battle, VII, 111, 112.

Delo Naroda, Russian newspaper,
quoted, V, 337, 339.

Delpeuche, U. S. volunteer in
France, IV, 262.

Demange, French family, slaughtered, III, 25.

Demir Hissar, in Greece, Bulgars
seize, IV, 347, 348.

Denikine, Russian general, V, 243;
on Russian breakdown, V, 260;
Siberia seeks aid of, VI, 233.

Denmark. See Subject Index.

Deprez, Mme., French lady
abused by Germans, V, 33.

Deraa, in Palestine, British capture, VI, 335 et seq.

Der-el-Zor, Asiatic desert, Armenians driven to, III, 156.

Derfflinger, German warship, sunk
in Jutland battle, IV, 165 et seq.

Deschanel, French statesman, V,
191; on air victories, V, 191 et
seq.

Destrée, French writer, on munitions crisis, III, 201.

Detroit, in U. S., German plotting
in, III, 286 et seq.

Detwiller, the cock of, I, 169.

Deutsche Bank, the Imperial, I,
268 et seq.; loans by, I, 273;
greatness of, I, 357.

Deutschland, U-boat, visits America, IV, 276 et seq.; effect of, V,
129.

"*Deutschland über Alles,*" sung
by troops, II, 221, 222; sung at
Somme battle, IV, 251.

Deve-Boyun, Armenian mountains, fighting in, IV, 27 et seq.

De Wet, Boer general, fights British, II, 378 et seq.; his aid to
Germany, II, 386.

Dhaheriyeh, in Palestine, fighting
at, V, 405.

Diala, in Mesopotamia, battle of,
V, 49, 60 et seq.

Diala River, in Mesopotamia,
fighting on, V, 60 et seq.

Diaz, Armando, Italian general,
in command, V, xxxii; directs
Piave rally, V, 365 et seq.; in
Piave victory, VI, 216 et seq.; in
final victory, VI, 373, 374.

Diaz, Porfirio, Mexican president,
friendly to Germany, V, 45.

Dickman, U. S. general, at St.
Mihiel, VI, 318; in Argonne,
VI, 353.

Diderichs, Czecho-Slovak general,
commands in Siberia, VI, 148 et
seq.

Diedrichs, German admiral, II,
412 et seq.

Dielette, Germans occupy, I, 74;
use as base, I, 76.

Diepenbrock, Dutch neutral, investigates horrors, III, 416.

Diericx, Aline, Belgian lady, tells
sufferings, II, 73 et seq.

Diest, Belgian armies gather at,
II, 39.

Dieulet, in France, Americans
win, VI, 399.

Dieuze, in Lorraine, fighting at,
II, 114 et seq.

Dijon, University of, I, 65.

Dimitrieff, Russian general, II,
192; invades Hungary, III, 108
et seq.

Dinant, in Belgium, fighting at,
II, xxiv; massacre at, II, 55, 57,
166.

Disforth, German general, II, 51
et seq.; article by, II, 82.

Disraeli, British statesman, quoted, I, 95, 253.

Dittman, German Socialist leader,
VII, 113.

Dixmude, in Belgium, retreating
Allies occupy, II, 325 et seq.;
357 et seq.; in battle of Flanders V, 273; in drive by Belgian, VI, 300.

Dixon, British scholar, on naval
battles, II, 439; on Jutland battle, IV, 154.

Djavid Bey, Turkish statesman,
II, 103 et seq.

Djelli-Gel, Armenian mountain,
fighting on, IV, 27 et seq.

Djemal Bey, Turkish statesman,
opposes Germany, II, 103; aids
in control of Turkey, III, 83;
receives massacre orders, III,
174; commands at Dardanelles,
III, 269 et seq.; tyranny in
Syria, IV, 233; Arabs defy, IV,
235; abandons Egyptian campaign, V, 402; cruelty to Jews,
V, 413.

"Djemet," Young Turk committee, III, 174 et seq.

I, 209, 210; his opinion of Kaiser, I, 358; policy of, I, 380.

Egelhaaf, German historian, on Verdun, IV, 208.

Egypt. See Subject Index.

Eichhorn, German general, in East Prussian campaign, III, 233, 239 et seq.

Eichner, Bavarian leader, slain, VII, 126.

Einem, von, German general, repels Champagne assault, III, 315 et seq.; in Peace Assault, VI, 245 et seq.; in Ally drive, VI, 263 et seq.

Einicke, German legal writer, quoted, III, 136.

Einville, German advance from, II, 218.

Eisner, German Socialist, quoted, VI, 368.

Eitel Fritz, Prince of Prussia, plunders French, III, 22; at Dunajec, III, 181.

Eje-Milkovski, Polish leader, quoted, II, 425.

El Arish, in Palestine, British capture, V, 402.

Elbing, German warship, sunk in Jutland battle, IV, 170.

El Garbi, in Mesopotamia, British base at, IV, 129.

El Gussa, in Mesopotamia, British capture, IV, 129.

El Hannah, in Mesopotamia, British defeat at, IV, 132 et seq.

Elincourt, in France, in Kaiser-battle, VI, 173.

Elizabeth, Czarina of Russia, I, 365.

Elkin, William, American teacher, I, 21.

Elliot, British colonel, in Zeebrugge raid, VI, 130.

Ellis, British general, commands tanks, V, 387, et seq.

El Paso, in U. S., conference with Mexicans at, IV, 65 et seq.

El Pino, in Mexico, U. S. troops occupy, IV, 64.

Elst, van der, Belgian diplomat, I, 389; quoted, I, 391.

Elswick, British manufactories at, III, 207.

Embermenil, in France, atrocity at, III, 28.

Embros, Greek newspaper, quoted, V, 233.

Emden, German warship, lost, II, 32; raids of, II, 439 et seq.; her career, II, 447 et seq.; III, 52; fairness of, III, 53.

Emmich, von, German general, commands in Belgium, II, 38; interviews Gen. Leman, II, 48; advances against French, II, 113; captures Liege, II, 147.

Engerand, French economist, on iron mines, IV, 208.

England. See Britain in Subject Index.

English Channel, barred to Germans, II, xv, 24 et seq.; battle for the, II, 335 et seq.; German peace plans to possess, III, 393; U-boat destruction in, IV, 91; U. S. navy aids in defense of, V, 168 et seq.; German advance threatens, VI, 108; Zeebrugge raid protects, VI, 126 et seq.

Enver Pasha, Turkish leader, I, 260; his career, II, 93; openly joins Germans, II, 103 et seq.; leads Turkey into War, II, 391 et seq.; in Caucasus campaign, III, xv, 42 et seq.; in Dardanelles defense, III, 79 et seq.; aids Armenian massacres, III, 169; helps create "Middle Europe," III, 382; in Armenian campaign, IV, 28 et seq.; Arabs defy, IV, 235; abandons Palestine, V, 412; flees from Turkey, VI, 333.

Eparges, les, in France, Americans in, VI, 318.

Epehy, in France, in Kaiser-battle, VI, 57 et seq., 84.

Eperjes, in Hungary, people flee from, III, 122.

Epernay, in France, break in German line at, II, 244 et seq.; historic fighting at, II, 253; in Peace Assault, VI, 242 et seq.

Epieds, in France, Americans win, VI, 276.

Epinal, French fortifications at, II, 108; fighting at, II, 116; army base at, II, 215; in Nancy campaign, II, 219 et seq.; effects on Ourcq battle, II, 245.

Epinouville, in France, Americans win, VI, 350.

Erivan, in Armenia, struggle for, III, 38 et seq.

Ermenonville, in Marne battle, II, 278.

Erquinghem, in France, British retreat to, VI, 113.

Ervillers, in France, Germans capture, VI, 89.

Erzberger, Mathias, German statesman, denies thoughts of war, I, 339, 354; leads revolters, VI, 405; heads Armistice commission, VI, 415 et seq.; leads new party, VII, 69.

Erzerum, in Armenia, campaign for, III, 41 et seq.; Russians capture, IV, 24 et seq.; Turks advance against, IV, 187.

Erzingan, in Armenia, troops at, III, 42; Turks retreat to, IV, 37.

Esperey, D', French general, at battle of Ourcq, II, 229 et seq.; Kluck comments on, II, 246; in retreat to Marne, II, 252; in Marne battle, II, 255 et seq.; in Aisne battle, II, 290; in Champagne attack, III, 67 et seq.; commands against Bulgaria, VI, xxxvii; in Kaiser-battle, VI, 166 et seq.; crushes Bulgaria, VI, 321 et seq., 328; Austria fears, VI, 373; Germans criticize, VI, 420.

Essad Effendi, II, 391; article by, II, 400.

Essad Pasha, Turkish general, at Dardanelles, III, 268.

Essen, van der, Belgian scholar, II, 150; article by, II, 151.

Essen, factories of, I, 77, 269.

Estaires, in France, in Lys battle, VI, 106 et seq.

Esté, Italian royal family, I, 256.

Esthonia, Russian province, German plan to annex, III, 395; made a German dependency, VI, xvi; Germany promises independence of, VI, 12, 32; German views for, VI, 40.

Etalon, in France, Germans capture, VI, 90.

Etavigny, in France, fighting at, II, 232.

Ethé, in France, atrocity at, III, 28.

Etienne, Eugene, French statesman, I, 121; statement by, L, 128.

Etrépilly, French victory at, II, 228; Americans capture, VI, 276.

Eulenburg, German dramatist, assails Belgians, II, 72.

Euphrates River, Turks retreat to, III, 38; campaign on upper, IV, 27 et seq.; Kut siege on, IV, 127 et seq.; in Bagdad campaign, V, 48 et seq.

Evan-Thomas, British admiral, in Jutland battle, IV, 157 et seq.

Evans, Major, American, in Belleau Woods fight, VI, 193; account by, VI, 201.

Evegnée, Fort, in Belgium, II, 38 et seq.

Evert, Russian general, in 1916 campaign, IV, 188; in revolution, V, 76.

Eyschen, Luxemburg statesman, II, 63.

Fabeck, von, German general, in Flanders, II, 331, 345 et seq.

Fagaras, in Austria, Rumanians from, III, 106 et seq.

Faille, De la, Dutch neutral, investigates horrors, III, 416.

Fair Play, American newspaper, in German pay, III, 297.

Faiti, Mount, in Austria, Italians capture, IV, 300.

Falaba, British ship, atrocious attack on, III, 61 et seq., 196, 199; details of, IV, 285.

Falkenhausen, German diplomat, in Brussels, III, 377.

Falkenhayn, von, German general, his leadership criticized by Kluck, II, 217 et seq.; chief-of-staff, II, 304; bulletin on Antwerp, II, 317; on Yser battle, II, 324; article by, II, 334; directs Serbian campaign, III, 345, 360; upholds Greece, III, 367, 368; directs Verdun assault, IV, 38; his account of Verdun, IV, 46; opposes attack on Italy, IV, 152; praises Austrians, IV, 153; retired from command of staff, IV, 206; in Rumanian campaign,

et seq.; Canadians at, II, 368; renewed, V, 268 et seq.

Fleck, von, German general, plunders French, V, 33.

Flemings, Germanizing of, II, 63 et seq.; character of, II, 324; Germans claim kinship with, III, 394.

Fleron, Fort, in Belgium, II, 38 et seq.

Flesquières, in France, British repulse at, V, 388 et seq.

Fleurbaix, in France, heroic defense of, VI, 113.

Fleury, in Verdun battles, IV, 206 et seq., 374, 378.

Flora, Dutch ship, saves lives, II, 302.

Florence Brigade, Italian, heroism of, V, 306.

Florina, in Macedonia, Bulgars seize, IV, 349; Serbs regain, IV, 388.

Flotow, von, Austrian statesman, III, 222.

Flotwell, German statesman, I, 149.

Foch, marshal, at battle of Nancy, II, xxiii et seq.; at Marne battle, II, 231, 248 et seq.; quoted, II, 276; in Aisne battle, II, 290; commands in Flanders, II, 324 et seq.; commands French in second Ypres battle, III, 143 et seq.; commands in Loos battle, III, 307 et seq.; in Somme battle, IV, xxiii; made chief of staff, V, 166; in council over Italian invasion, V, 372; made Commander in Chief of Allies, VI, xxi; directs 1918 campaigns, VI, xxi et seq.; dictates Armistice, VI, xxxix; directs opening of Kaiser-battle, VI, 65 et seq.; given command of all Allies, VI, 97 et seq.; British praise of, VI, 103; in Lys battle, VI, 104 et seq., 119; in Aisne battle, VI, 165 et seq.; asks American aid, VI, 184 et seq.; resists Peace Assault, VI, 244 et seq.; begins great Ally drive, VI, 259 et seq.; appeal to U. S. troops, VI, 260; Ludendorff's opinion of, VI, 279; approves U. S. attack on St. Mihiel, VI, 313; on Argonne, VI, 346 et seq.; orders Italian

advance, VI, 373; on final Ally drive, VI, 386, 400; Germans forced to surrender to, VI, 402; in Armistice conference, VI, 415 et seq.; controls "occupied" Germany, VII, 18; Clemenceau aids, VII, 62.

Fogare, in Italy, Austrians win at, V, 374 et seq.

Folina, in Italy, fighting at, V, 374 et seq.

Ford, Sir C., British diplomat, quoted, I, 92.

Foreign Legion, of France, U. S. volunteers in, IV, 259 et seq.

Forgac, Austrian statesman, I, xix; treachery of, I, 184, 246 et seq.; warns Allies, I, 292.

Formidable, British warship, sunk, III, xxii.

Forstner, Captain von, German naval expert, quoted, VI, 368.

Forstner, von, Prussian hero, I, 171 et seq.; recalled, II, 114.

Fortescue, British author, article by, II, 416.

Fortune, British war vessel, sunk at Jutland, IV, 164.

Foss, German admiral, II, 439; on German sea fights, II, 447.

Fossé, in France, plundered and burnt, III, 21.

Fossoy, in France, in Peace Assault, VI, 244, Americans defend, VI, 245.

Fothi, Rumanian soldier, fights Russians, III, 115 et seq

Fournes, in Belgium, bombarded, II, 332.

"Fourteen Points," peace basis, proclaimed, VI, xv, 1 et seq.; basis of Armistice, VI, 415 et seq.; causes of dissatisfaction with, VII, xxvii et seq.; at Peace Conference, VII, 36; dispute over, VII, 129 et seq.

Fox, American writer, spreads German falsehoods, III, 299.

Fox, British writer, V, 207; on Messines explosion, V, 213.

France. See Subject Index.

Francis Joseph, Emperor of Austria, seeks quiet, I, xxiii; opposed in Hungary, I, 187; opposes his heir, I, 245 et seq.; quoted, I, 255; out of sympathy with his heir, I, 256 et seq.;

War, I, 317; blamed by Kaiser, I, 322; receives Kaiser's pledge, I, 353; receives Belgium's appeal, I, 391; praises British navy, II, 21; reviews navy, II, 23; welcomes Canadian troops, II, 368; letter to Captain Fryatt's widow, IV, 287.

George Washington, U. S. transport, at Brest, VII, 129.

Gera, in Germany, bolshevists at, VI, 371.

Gerard, U. S. diplomat, in Germany, IV, 102; on enslaving labor, IV, 103; on prison camps, IV, 430; summoned home, V, 2, 135.

Gerbéviller, in France, fighting at, II, 210; ravage of, III, 25 et seq.

Gergogne River, in France, fighting on, II, 242.

Gerlache, De, Belgian soldier, I, 382; article by, I, 389; services of, II, 304; article by, II, 311.

"German Bolshevik Conspiracy, The," American pamphlet, V, 355.

"German Chauvinism," book by Nippold, I, 12.

German East Africa, fighting in, II, 370 et seq.

"German Empire's Hour," book by Frobenius, I, 111.

"German Military Code," book, quoted, III, 372.

German South West Africa, I, 29; fighting in, II, 384.

"German War Book," III, 3 et seq.; discusses sea warfare, III, 58.

Germany. See Subject Index.

"Germany in Arms," book by Crown Prince, I, 122.

Gessner German law-writer, quoted, III, 57.

Gey Dag, Armenian mountain, fighting on, IV, 28 et seq.

Gheluvelt, in Belgium, fighting at, II, 331; 338 et seq.; in "battle of Flanders," V, 272 et seq.

Ghent, German treatment of, I, 20; British retreat by, II, 309 et seq.; in Antwerp campaign, II, 315; deportations from, IV, 3; recaptured, VI, xxxv, 387 et seq.; German review at, VI, 406.

Gibbon, British writer, V, 313; on Caporetto disaster, V, 322.

Gibbs, British writer, II, 253; on Somme battle, II, 254; on Vimy Ridge battle, V, 153; quoted, V, 298; on 1918 drive, VI, 281, 297; on occupying Germany, VII, 1, 9.

Gibraltar, U. S. naval forces at, V, 169.

Gibson, American diplomat, in Brussels, III, 369; on Cavell case, III, 376.

Giesl, von, Austrian diplomat, quoted, I, 253; opens War, I, 293.

Gill, U. S. naval officer, V, 168; on navy in War, V, 177.

Gillespie, British colonel, in Dardanelles campaign, III, 258.

Gilsa, German officer, in revolution, VII, 123, 124.

Giolitti, Italian statesman, reveals Austrian trickery, I, 184.

Gironde, French cavalry officer, in raid, II, 243.

Giurgevo, on Danube, Teutons capture, IV, 371.

Givenchy, in France, battle at, III, 76; attack on, III, 309; in Lys battle, VI, 115 et seq.

Givet, in Belgium, French approach, I, 383; recaptured, VI, 398 et seq.

Gladstone, British statesman, quoted, I, 195, 408.

Glasgow, British warship, II, 440 et seq.

Gleaves, U. S. admiral, commands transport service, V, 168 et seq.

Glen Springs, in U. S., Mexican raid on, IV, 67 et seq.

Glitra, first merchant ship sunk by U-boat, III, 53.

Gloucester, British ship, pursues Germans, II, 94 et seq.

Gneisenau, German statesman, quoted, I, 105.

Gneisenau, German warship, II, 440 et seq.

Gnesen, on Polish frontier, German base at, II, 422.

Gobineau, French author, I, 8, 21.

Godley, British general, at Dardanelles, III, 256.

Goeben, German ship, escapes French, II, 32; escapes British,

II, 94; sold to Turkey, II, 96 et
seq.; brings Turkey into War,
II, 391; bombards Russian
coast, II, 397; et seq.; defends
Dardanelles, III, 82; sortie by,
VI, 341.

Goethe, teachings of, I, 51, 93;
disliked Prussia, I, 98; quoted,
I, 106, 234; America admires, I,
354.

Golitzin, Russian statesman, opposes people, V, xix, 75 et seq.

Goltz, von der, German general,
quoted, I, 198; denies thoughts
of war, I, 339, 354; commands
Turks at Dardanelles, III, 92;
journeys to Bagdad, III, 170; as
governor of Belgium, IV, 9 et
seq.; commands in Mesopo-
tamia, IV, 129.

Goltz, von der, German agent in
America, III, 289 et seq.

Gombosh, Austrian colonel, in
Carpathian campaign, III, 120.

Gomez, Mexican general, attacks
U. S. troops, IV, 62.

Gompers, American labor leader,
V, 183; on draft law, V, 189;
aids in organizing U. S. for
War, V, 423.

Gonnelieu, in France, British attack at, V, 388.

Gonzaga, Prince, Italian general,
heroic deeds of, V, 309.

Good Hope, British warship, II,
440 et seq.

Gordon, J. W., British author, I,
321.

Gordon, Winifred, authoress, IV,
357; on Rumanian defeat, IV,
363.

Gordon Highlanders, at Ypres,
II, 343.

Goremykin, Russian prime minister, V, 71.

Gorges, British colonel, in Africa,
II, 374.

Gorizia, in Austria, Italians storm,
IV, 294 et seq.; in 1917 campaign, V, 303 et seq., 319; Austrians recapture, V, 367.

Gorlice, in Galicia, battle of, III,
xviii, 177 et seq.; results of, III,
231; German estimate of, III,
316.

Gornichevo Pass, on Greek fron-

tier, Serbs recapture, IV, 388 et
seq.

Gorringe, British general, in Kut
campaign, IV, 129 et seq.; in
Kaiser-battle, VI, 65.

Goschen, Sir Edward, British
statesman, quoted, I, 75; seeks
reduction of armaments, I, 209;
acts in Berlin in 1914, I, 303;
warns Britain, I, 305; argues
with Germans, I, 397 et seq.;
quoted, I, 399; article by, I, 404;
Bethman interview, I, 407 et
seq.

Gotha, in Germany, bolshevists at,
VI, 371.

Goudberg Spur, in Flanders battle,
V, 299 et seq.

Gough, British general, defeats
Germans on Somme, II, 134; in
Ypres battle, II, 338 et seq.; in
Loos battle, III, 307 et seq.;
loses battle of Picardy, VI, xx,
50 et seq.

Gougnies, in Belgium, atrocities
at, II, 55 et seq.

Gounaris, Greek statesman, in
power, IV, 336, 337; leader of
pro-Germans against Allies, V,
222 et seq.

Gouraud, French general, checks
"Peace-battle," VI, xxv; aids
Americans in Argonne, VI,
xxxv; on Peace Assault, VI,
242, 243, 245 et seq.; in Ally
drive, VI, 265 et seq.; in Argonne, VI, 345 et seq.; in final
Ally drive, VI, 387, et seq.

Gourko, Russian general, II, 170;
article by, II, 185.

Gouy, in France, Americans capture, VI, 306 et seq.

Graberk River, on Austrian frontier, fighting on, V, 258 et seq.

Grabez, Serbian conspirator, I,
248 et seq.

Gradishte, in Serbia, bombarded,
II, 5.

Grado, in Italy, retreat from, V,
369.

Grahame-White, British aviator,
V, 191; on "air age," V, 197.

Grand Couronné, in France, retreat to, II, 115 et seq.; battle
of, II, xxvi, 209 et seq.; result
of, II, 226.

"Grand Fleet," British, II, 21 et seq.

"Grand Fleet," German, refuses to fight, VI, 359 et seq.

Grand Morin River, Germans advance over, II, 124, 148, 227.

Grand Pré, in France, Americans capture, VI, xxxv, 345 et seq.

Grant, British general, in Kaiser-battle, VI, 69.

Grappa, Mount, in Italy, fortified, V, 330; fighting for, V, 371 et seq.; in 1918 campaign, VI, 215 et seq., 376 et seq.

Gratz, Lichnowsky at, I, 309.

Graudenz, Prussian fortress, in Tannenberg campaign, II, 176 et seq.; in Warsaw campaign, II, 423.

Gravenstafel, in Belgium, British capture, V, 288 et seq.

Graziani, French general, in Italy, VI, 229.

"Great Pillage, The," III, 1 et seq.

Greece. See Subject Index.

Grelling, German author, career of, I, 89, 90; on Germany's guilt, I, 109.

Gressaire Wood, in France, Americans win, VI, 272.

Grewe, British historian, III, 320; on Russia's rally, III, 323; on Verdun, IV, 209; on Isonzo campaign, IV, 294, 296.

Grey, Sir Edward, opposes war, I, xxxvii et seq.; accepts war, I, xlvi; sought German friendship in East, I, 194 et seq.; sought Turkey's friendship, I, 201; quoted, I, 206; reduced armaments, I, 209 et seq.; quoted, I, 214; seeks peace, I, 296, 303, 305; article by, I, 305; seeks German agreement, I, 310; defends France, I, 311; quoted, 316, 317; Kaiser's opinion of, I, 321, 322; Germany admits his fair dealing, I, 344; quoted, I, 379; plans world harmony, I, 397; praised by Asquith, I, 398 et seq.; quoted, I, 401; called "Peace Maker of Europe," I, 402; promises aid to Serbia, III, 357; upholds Venizelos in Greece, IV, 335 et seq.

Grimm, Swiss socialist, aids Lenine, V, 345.

Grisnez, Cape, scene of U-boat assault, III, 53.

Grisolera, in Italy, Hungarians capture, V, 374.

Grobovoye, Armenian mountain, Russians win, IV, 36.

Grodek, in Galicia, Austrian advance on, III, 94; Russians defend, III, 185; Germans capture, III, 231 et seq.

Grodno, Russian fortress, in Warsaw campaign, III, xxvi, 229 et seq.; in Russia's rally, III, 320 et seq.

Grondys, Dutch witness of Louvain sack, II, 157.

Groner, German general, urges abdication, VI, 407, 408.

Grosetti, French general, in Yser battle, II, 341.

Grouitch, Mme., Serbian writer, VII, 22; on Serbia, VII, 28.

Grunnel, von, German general, seeks Armistice, VI, 416 et seq.

Guatemala, U. S. attitude toward, V, 119; severs relations with Germany, V, 147; at Peace Conference, VII, 39; signs Treaty, VII, 154.

Guchevo Hills, in Serbia, campaign in, II, 432 et seq.

Guchkov, Russian statesman, in Revolution, V, xxvii, 68 et seq.; secures Czar's abdication, V, 83 et seq.; appeals to people, V, 243, 244.

Gué, in Belgium, massacre at, III, 35.

Guémappe, in France, Canadians win, VI, 290 et seq.

Guépratte, French admiral, at Dardanelles, III, 92.

Guerrero, in Mexico, U. S. victory at, IV, 61 et seq.

Gueshoff, Bulgarian statesman, III, 340 et seq.

Guidicaria, Italian valley, in 1918 campaign, VI, 215 et seq.

Guillaume, Belgian diplomat, II, 93; article by, II, 104.

Guillerville, French writer, VII, 140; on Czecho-Slovakia, VII, 145.

Guiscard, in France, sacking of, V, 33; in Kaiser-battle, VI, 68 et seq.

357; in battle of Flanders, V, 273; in Lys battle, VI, 114.

Hollinshead, U. S. volunteer in France, IV, 270, 271.

Hollond, British writer, quoted, II, 22.

Holstein, German consul, reports on Armenian horror, III, 167.

Holy Land, William II visits, I, xxxii, 197. See also Palestine.

Honduras, severs relations with Germany, V, 147; at Peace Conference, VII, 39; signs Treaty, VII, 154.

Hood, British admiral, slain in Jutland battle, IV, 158 et seq.

Hooge, in Belgium, fighting at, II, 341 et seq.; in 1917 campaign, V, 209, 277.

Hoover, American statesman, in Belgium, IV, 102; on enslavement by Germans, IV, 113; results gained in Belgium, IV, 263; aids in organizing U. S. for War, V, 423; in Poland, VII, 94; quoted, VII, 106; on Poland, VII, 109.

Horn, Werner, German agent in America, III, 293.

Horn Reef, in Jutland battle, IV, 163.

Horne, British general, in Kaiser-battle, VI, 65; in Lys battle, VI, 111; in drive on Cambrai, VI, 299.

Horodenka, in Galicia Russians attack, III, 183; Russians capture, IV, 195; Austrians flee from, IV, 201.

Hortstein, Austrian general, II, 19.

Houghton, U. S. volunteer in France, IV, 275.

House, U. S. diplomat, Poland praises, VII, 106; signs Treaty, VII, 158.

Houston, U. S. Secretary of Agriculture, on organizing for War, V, 418.

Howard, British admiral, quoted, II, 26.

Howe, American economist, on "occupation" of Germany, VII, I, 11.

Howze, U. S. major, on Mexican border, IV, 63.

Hoyos, Count, Austrian diplomat, I, 276; reports on War, I, 284.

Huber, German official, reports Armenian horrors, III, 165.

Huddleston, British writer, on Peace Conference, VII, 36, 49, 129.

Huebner, German writer, in battle, II, 118; article by, II, 137.

Hueffer, German scholar, quoted, I, 37.

Huene, Baron von, German governor of Antwerp, IV, 9, 10.

Huerta, Mexican general, Germans plot with, III, 283.

Hughes, Canadian general, II, 362 et seq.

Hughes, U. S. statesman, in presidential campaign, V, 128.

Huj, in Palestine, British capture, V, 404.

Hull, Canadian general, in first gas attack, III, 144.

Hulluch, in France, fighting at, III, 308 et seq.; Irish glory at, IV, 119.

Humbert, French writer, I, 301.

Humbert, French general, in Marne battle, II, 258 et seq.; 277; in Kaiser-battle, VI, 82 et seq.

Hungary. See Subject Index.

Huns, first invaded Europe, I, xx; devastations of, I, 46.

Hussein, King of Arabia, IV, 232 et seq.; at capture of Damascus, VI, 333.

Hutier, von, German general, in Kaiser-battle, VI, 80 et seq.; 172 et seq.; in Ally drive, VI, 263.

Huy, in Belgium, protected, II, 162; Germans slay Germans at, III, 36.

Hymans, H., Belgian statesman, I, 390.

Hymans, Paul, Alsatian writer, quoted, I, 168.

"Hymn of Hate." I, 396; quoted, I, 417.

"I Accuse," book by Grelling, I, 90.

Id, in Caucasia, Turks seize, III, 43.

Igel, German agent in America, III, 278 et seq.

Ikom, in Africa, fighting at, II, 372.

102 et seq.; Germans driven from, VI, xxxiv, 300 et seq.; freedom of, VII, 62.

Limanova, in Poland, battle at, III, 230.

Lincoln, Abraham, quoted, V, 120; VII, 143.

Linsingen, German general, under Kluck's command, II, 242 et seq., 247; sent to aid Austria, III, 111; defeats Russians in Carpathians, III, 231 et seq.; checks 1916 advance of Russians, IV, 193 et seq.; in chief command against Russia, IV, 198.

Lipa River, on Russian frontier, fighting on, IV, 194 et seq.

Lissauer, German writer, I, 396; poem by, I, 417.

List, German economist, his ideas, I, 226.

Lithuania, Germans conquer, III, 243; people oppose Germans, III, 249 et seq.; German plan to annex, III, 395; Russian treason surrenders, V, 70; troops of, in Bolshevist service, V, 364; made a German dependency, VI, xvi; promised independence, VI, 12, 31; German views on, VI, 40; Poland's desire for, VII, 100, 101.

Little Russia, VI, 18; See Ukrainia in Subject Index.

Litzman, German general, in Kovno capture, III, 239.

Liubliana, new name for Laibach, VII, 22.

Livaditza, in Serbia, Teutons capture, III, 340.

Livenza River, in Italy, fighting on, V, 365 et seq.

Liverpool, *Lusitania* bound for, III, 190.

Livieratos, Greek labor leader, aids Pro-Germans, V, 233.

Livonia, Russian province, made a German dependency, VI, xvi; promised independence, VI, 12, 32; German views for, VI, 40.

Lizerne, in Ypres campaign, gas attack at, III, 142; recaptured, III, 146.

Lizy, in Marne battle, II, 242, 276 et seq.

Lloyd George, David, British

statesman, quoted, I, 59; warns Germany, I, 310; explains Britain's course, I, 396; on source of War, I, 415; takes lead in Britain, III, xx, 201 et seq.; quoted, III, 211; made Prime Minister, IV, xxxi, 106; on U. S. entry into War, V, 139; listens for Messines explosion, V, 207; decides fate of Greece, V, 230; in conference on Italy's disaster, V, 372; urges unified command, VI, xxi, 97, 101; praises Czecho-Slovaks, VI, 151; asks U. S. aid, VI, 184, 187; difficulties in Armistice days, VII, xxix; at Peace Conference, VII, 36; speech of, VII, 44; policies of, VII, 49; early career of, VII, 63; quoted, VII, 63, 66; at signing of Treaty, VII, 158; quoted, VII, 168.

Lochow, von, German general, in Ourcq battle, II, 247.

Locker-Lampson, British officer in Russia, V, 256.

Locre, on Belgian frontier, in Kaiser-battle, VI, 122.

Lodz, in Poland, battle of, II, 416 et seq.; results of, III, 230; horrors in, III, 434 et seq.; riots at, III, 436.

Loetzener Lake, in Prussia, Russian defeat at, II, 183.

Lohmann, German official, builds U-boats, IV, 277.

Loisy, in France, fighting at, II, 223.

Lomax, British general, wounded, II, 338; at Ypres, II, 348 et seq.

Lombardy, Italian province, invaded, IV, 149; V, 315 et seq.

Lome, in Africa, British capture, II, 371.

Lomnica River, on Austrian frontier, Russian victory on, V, 254.

Lomza, Polish fortress, in Warsaw campaign, III, 229 et seq.

Loncin, Fort, at Liége, II, 38; bombardment of, II, 43 et seq.

London, bombed by aircraft, III, xxi; celebrates U. S. entry into War, V, xxiv; Pershing welcomed in, V, 431.

London Convention, rejected, II, 34.

London Pact, established, II, 395.

Marcelcave, in France, in Kaiser-battle, VI, 70 et seq.

Marchand, French general, in Champagne assault, III, 310.

Marchevolette, Fort, at Namur, bombarded, II, 148.

Marcoing, in France, British capture, V, 389, 390; in final drive, VI, 302.

Marcovitch, Serbian scholar, I, 323; article by, I, 332.

Mareuil, in France, Kluck's headquarters at, II, 245 et seq.

Marfée, in France, battle at, II, 119, 122.

Maricourt, in France, Somme battle, begins at, IV, 256.

Marie, Queen of Rumania, British birth of, IV, 322; as Rumania's idol, IV, 399; on sufferings of her people, IV, 404.

Marienburg, in East Prussia, II, 179.

Marigny, in Marne campaign, II, 242.

Marincovich, Mme., in Serbia, II, 429; on reconquest of Belgrade, II, 435.

Maritch, Serbian official, II, 14.

Maritz, Boer leader, II, 379 et seq.

Maritza River, expansion of Bulgaria on, III, 339.

Markoff, Russian author, I, 338; on Russian statecraft, I, 359.

Marks, British seaman hero, II, 301.

Marlborough, British warship, in Jutland battle, IV, 163 et seq.

Marmora, Sea of, fighting in, III, 88 et seq.

Marne River, ancient battle of Attila at, I, 46; French plans for, II, 37; Germans checked at, II, 115; British retreat across, II, 136; Germans reach, II, 143 et seq.; Germans beyond, II, 227 et seq., 244; retreat across, II, 232 et seq.; Germany again fights along, VI, xxiii; again driven back from, VI, xxxii; in Kaiser-battle, VI, 164 et seq., 186, 193 et seq.; in Peace Assault, VI, 242 et seq.; in Ally drive, VI, 259 et seq.

Marne, Battle of the, importance of, II, 118; regarded as a miracle, II, 209 et seq.; dependent on victory at Nancy, II, 214; part of Britons in, II, 226; dependent on Ourcq victory, II, 229 et seq.; German official statement about, II, 241; German recognition of failure, II, 246 et seq.; details of, II, 248 et seq.

"Marne, Retreat to the," II, xxiv et seq., 118 et seq.; British heroism in, II, 227.

Marne Salient, Germans create in 1918, VI, xxiii et seq., 164 et seq.; wiped out, VI, 259 et seq.

Marne, Second Battle of the, VI, 259 et seq.

Marre Ridge, in Verdun battle, IV, 47, 48.

Maros River, in Hungary, invaders fail to reach, IV, 364.

Marquéglise, in France, massacre at, III, 27; in Kaiser-battle, VI, 173 et seq.

Marschall, Baron, German diplomat, I, 199; died in London, I, 308.

Marschall, Bishop, Austrian diplomat, I, 258.

Marseillaise, sung at Verdun, IV, 44; sung at deportations, IV, 106; at Verdun, IV, 228; in Russian uprisings, V, 332.

Marseilles, German bombs found at, III, 285; U. S. warport at, V, 436.

Marshall, British general, in Mesopotamia, V, 49 et seq.

Marshall, U. S. vice-president, signs declaration of war, V, 107.

Martin, French writer, VII, 129; on Peace Conference, VII, 138.

Martoff, Russian Menshevik leader, V, 354.

Martson, Russian general, II, 187.

Marwitz, von der, German general, II, 228 et seq.; in Ourcq battle, II, 244 et seq.; sent to Austria, III, 111; in Kaiser-battle, VI, 88 et seq., 263; on Argonne, VI, 345, 357.

Marx, Karl, ideas of, I, 86; real founder of bolshevism, V, 350; influence on bolshevist revolution, V, 354 et seq.

Masaryk, Czecho-Slovak leader, VI, 144; on Czech independence,

265 et seq.; superseded by Falkenhayn, II, 304, 317.

Moltke, Count D. von, attends Kaiser, VI, 402; article by, VI, 405.

Moltke, German warship, flagship in Jutland battle, IV, 168, 180.

Mombosa, in East Africa, British base, II, 388.

Momchiloff, Bulgarian statesman, on atrocities, III, 358.

Monastir, in Serbia, Bulgarians advance to, III, 365; Serbian rebirth at, III, 405; recapture of, IV, xxvii, 387 et seq.; Ally defense of, VI, xviii; Ally advance from, VI, 322 et seq.

Monceau, in Belgium, atrocities at, II, 55; burned, III, 25, 26.

Monchy, in France, massacre at, III, 28; in Kaiser-battle, VI, 86; Canadians capture, VI, 290 et seq.

Mondement, in Marne battle, II, 258.

Monesi, Italian general, VI, 228.

Monfalcone, in Austria, Italians attack, IV, 296 et seq.; retreat from, V, 368 et seq.

Monfenera, in Italy, fighting around, V, 380.

Monmouth, British warship, II, 440 et seq.

Monro, British general, at Ypres, II, 349 et seq.

Mons, in Belgium, battle at, II, xxiv, 119, 125 et seq.; German view of battle, II, 138.; advance from, II, 149; fugitives from, II, 203; British again fight at, II, 337 et seq.; deaths at, IV, 4; prisoners abused at, IV, 414; recapture of, VI, 387 et seq.; British triumphal entry into, VI, 392.

Montauban, in Somme battle, IV, 244 et seq.

Montbertoin, in France, fighting at, II, 244, 246.

Montceaux, in France, German account of, II, 238 et seq.; British account of, II, 279.

Montdidier, in France, Germans capture, VI, xx; advance from VI, xxiv, 55 et seq.; in Kaiser-battle, VI, 173 et seq., 184.

Montello, in Italy, fighting on, V, 371 et seq.; in 1918 campaign, VI, 215 et seq., 375 et seq.

Montenegro. See Subject Index.

Montereau, Germans in, I, 74.

Monte Santo, See Santo.

Montfaucon, in Verdun battle, IV, 41; in Argonne battle, VI, 346 et seq.

Monthyon, in France, fighting at, II, 231.

Montigny, in France, in Kaiser-battle, VI, 173 et seq.

Montmedy, in France, German headquarters at, VI, 386; in final drive, VI, 388 et seq.

Montmirail, in France, Germans capture, II, 146; French regain, II, 234; in Ourcq battle, II, 242 et seq.; in Marne battle, II, 256 et seq.; afterwards, II, 292.

Montsec, in France, Americans win, VI, 317 et seq.

Montuori, Italian general, commands Asiago front, VI, 229.

Moraht, German military critic, III, 106, on Carpathian battles, III, 124.

Morava River, Austria's goal, I, 337; campaign on, II, 432 et seq.; in Serbia, fighting on, III, 348 et seq.; Teuton possession of, III, 403; Bulgarian atrocities by, III, 419 et seq.

Morbede, in Belgium, fighting at, II, 308.

Morel, in France, Kaiser at, II, 221.

Morgan, von, German general, in Russia, II, 421.

Morgenthau, Henry, American diplomat, I, 259; on causes of War, I, 260; work at Constantinople, II, 93; article by, II, 94; on Dardanelles disaster, III, 79 et seq.; as seen by Turks, III, 175.

Morhange, battle of, II, xxiii, 108 et seq.; effect of battle, II, 210 et seq., 223.

Morlaincourt, French general, II, 263.

Morley, British writer, quoted, I, 41.

Morley, Lord, British statesman, I, 201.

Morocco, German need of, I, 69; quarrels over, I, 111; trouble

"On the Biological Imbecility of Women," German book, I, 170.

Ontario, Canadian province, troops of, V, 300.

Oosttaverne, in Belgium, fighting at, V, 209 et seq.

Orah, in Mesopotamia, British defeat at, IV, 132.

Orange Free State, II, 382 et seq.; receives munitions, III, 131.

Orange River, in Africa, fighting on, II, 386 et seq.

Oranienbaum, in Russia, troops at, join Revolution, V, 77.

Orany, in Russia, fighting at, III, 324 et seq.

Orkhanieh, Fort, defends Dardanelles, III, 85.

Orlando, Italian statesman, made prime minister, V, 366 et seq.; seeks U. S. aid, VI, 184, 187; quoted, VII, 168.

Orlovski, Bolshevist writer, quoted, V, 349.

Ornain River, in France, fighting on, II, 254 et seq.

Orne River, in France, German success at, IV, 47.

Oropos, in Greece, king expelled from, V, 237.

Orsova, on the Danube, in Serbian campaign, III, 357; German feints at, III, 360; Serb victory at, III, 361.

Orsetti, French family, plundered III, 23.

Ortelsburg, in Tannenberg campaign, II, 175; fighting at, II, 181, 183.

O'Ryan, U. S. general, aids British, VI, 308.

Osborn, German writer, on Flanders battle, V, 268, 273; on Piave battle, VI, 213, 221.

Osborne, British investigator, at prison camp, IV, 430.

Oslavia, in Austria, Italians capture, IV, 296 et seq.

Osmanli, royal family of Turkey, IV, 233 et seq.

Ossovetz (or Ossowiec), Russian fortress, bars German advance, II, 428; heroic defense of, III, 229 et seq.

Osten Sacken, Von der, German writer, V, 207; on 1917 campaign, V, 218; on Russian breakdown, V, 243, 266.

Ostend, route to India, I, 198; British retreat to, II, 308; Belgian retreat to, II, 312 et seq.; Belgians secure at, II, 317; British ships bombard, III, 303; goal of Flanders battle, V, 270; British block port of, VI, xxii, 126 et seq.; freed, VII, 62.

Osterode, in East Prussia, II, 183.

Ostrolenka, in Poland, Germans capture, III, 233.

Ostrovo, Lake, in Macedonia, Bulgars advance to, IV, 349; Serbs recapture, IV, 387 et seq.

Ostruznica, in Serbia, battle at, III, 347.

Ostwald, German chemist, I, 24; quoted, I, 67.

Otago, British colonial battalion, at Dardanelles, III, 256, 259.

Otavi, in South West Africa, British base at, II, 388.

Otavifonstein, in South West Africa, fighting at, II, 388.

Otranto, Gulf of, British fleet in, II, 97.

Otranto, Strait of, British fleet in, II, 97.

Otranto, British merchant ship, in battle, II, 440.

Ottignies, in France, sacked, III, 24.

Ottynia, on Russian frontier, captured, IV, 195.

"Our Future," book by Bernhardi, I, 121.

Ourcq River, battle of, II, xxvii, 226 et seq.; character of country, II, 253; in Kaiser-battle, VI, 168 et seq.; in Ally drive, VI, 266 et seq.

Ourfa, in Asia Minor, atrocities at, III, 167 et seq.

Ouritski, Bolshevist leader, controls Assembly, V, 362 et seq.

Overton, U. S. officer, heroism of, VI, 203.

Ovillers, in Somme battle, IV, 245 et seq.

Owen, British writer, VI, 332; on Turkey's surrender, VI, 341.

Oxford University, I, 204, 312.

Pabst, German Major, suppresses revolt, VII, 124.

Paddebeek, in Flanders battle, V, 299.
Paderewski, Polish leader, aids sufferers, III, 426; leads Poland, VII, 94 et seq.; on Poland's hopes, VII, 102.
Page, American ambassador, in Rome, III, 408.
Painlevé, French statesman, V, 153; on Champagne failure, V, 166; in Italian consultation, V, 372.
Palacky, Czech former statesman, quoted, VII, 152.
Palan-Teken, Armenian mountains, fighting in, IV, 27 et seq.
Palestine, early fighting in, IV, xviii; campaign of 1917 in, V, xxxv, 401 et seq.; British conquest of, VI, xxxvii; German and British views for, VI, 12 et seq.; British victories in, VI, 332 et seq.
Pallavicini, Austrian diplomat, in Turkey, I, 261 et seq.; II, 95; III, 79 et seq.
Palmer, U. S. war-correspondent, quoted, IV, 263; on Cantigny, VI, 184, 191.
Panama, joins in War, V, 147; at Peace Conference, VII, 39; signs Peace, VII, 152.
Panama Canal, importance of Virgin Isles to, V, 94; threatened by War, V, 149.
Pangani, in East Africa, British capture, II, 389.
Papen, German agent in America, III, 278 et seq.; his deeds official, III, 301.
Papp, Austrian general, retreats, from Russians, IV, 204.
Paraschnitza, in Serbia, fighting at, II, 12.
Parchim, in Germany, prisoners abused at, III, 33.
Pargny, in France, fighting at, II, 261.
Paris, British general, at Antwerp, II, 306 et seq.
Paris, first fears of attack, II, xxv, 124; German march toward, II, 142; government leaves, II, 198 et seq.; saved by battle of the Ourcq, II, 226; Kluck plans against, II, 238 et seq.; in Marne battle, II, 248 et

seq.; not the German goal, II, 266 et seq.; bombed by aircraft, III, xxi; celebrates U. S. entry into War, V, xxiv; Pershing reaches, V, 431; Germans threaten in 1918, VI, xiii, xxiii; bombarded by long-distance gun, VI, xxv; Czecho-Slovakia proclaimed at, VI, xxx; menaced by Kaiser-battle, VI, 79 et seq.; bombarded by great guns, VI, 92 et seq.; German advance approaches, VI, 164 et seq.; populace withdraw from, VI, 184, 186, 193 et seq.; approach of despair in, VI, 209 et seq.; final threat and repulse from, VI, 244; Peace Conference at, VII, 36 et seq.; scenes in, VII, 50; Polish exiles in, VII, 94; Czech government in, VII, 140.
Parral, in Mexico, U. S. troops fight at, IV, 62 et seq.
Parroy, on Lorraine frontier, French retreat to, II, 116.
Parsifal, Germans like, I, 20.
Parux, in France, burned, III, 26.
Pascal, French philosopher, quoted, I, 102, 103.
Paschendaele, in Ypres campaign, II, 333; Canadians win at, V, xxxiii, 268 et seq., 294 297, 387; in Lys battle, VI, 107; Belgians recapture, VI, 300.
Pas-de-Calais, Germany covets, I, 229.
Pashitch, Serbian statesman, aids Russia, I, 179 et seq.; praised, I, 190; condemns Serajevo crime, I, 254 et seq.; seeks peace, I, 315; absence delays diplomacy, I, 333; proclaims Serbia's glory and death, III, 352; protests Bulgarian destruction, III, 415; treats with Greece, IV, 333; leads new Serbia, VII, 22 et seq.; at Peace Conference, VII, 52, 54.
Passaga, de, French general, at Verdun, IV, 379.
Passan, Armenian district, fighting in, IV, 27 et seq.
Passchendaele. See Paschendale.
Passenheim, in East Prussia, Russian defeat at, II, 183.
Passubio, Mount, in Italy, fighting on, IV, 148.

55 et seq.; upheld statecraft, I, 101.

Pittsburg, in U. S., German plotting in, III, 280.

Plancy, in France, Foch headquarters at, II, 257.

Planima, Monte, on Italian front, V, 310.

Plaskavitza, on Bulgar frontier, Greeks capture, VI, 328.

Platten, Swiss pacifist, aids Russians, V, 346.

Plato, influence on Germany, I, 22.

Plava, in Austria, Italian advance from, IV, 299; in 1917, campaign, V, 310 et seq.

Plavtchitch, Serb guerilla, deeds of, III, 421, 422.

Plehanoff, Russian statesman, rejected by voters, V, 361.

Plehve, Russian general, in Carpathian campaign, III, 108.

Plock, in Poland, battle at, II, 418.

Ploegsteert, in Belgium, in Kaiserbattle, VI, 114.

Ploesci, in Rumania, battles near, IV, 401 et seq.

Plumer, British general, in Loos battle, III, 305 et seq.; commands British in Italy, V, 372 et seq.; in Battle of Picardy, VI, 66; in Lys battle, VI, 111; in final drive, VI, 300.

Pluschow, German aviator, II, 410.

Plymouth, in England, Canadians land at, II, 366.

Podbrozie, in Russia, battle at, III, 325.

Podgora Plateau, in Austria, Italians storm, IV, 296 et seq.

Podgoritze, Serbian retreat through, III, 410.

Podolia, in Russia, Teutons invade, V, 267; included in Ukrainia, VI, 20.

Podunavlie, Serbian region, fighting in, III, 357.

Poelcapelle, in Ypres campaign, II, 333; in Flanders battle, V, 271, 289 et seq.

Pohl, von, German admiral, orders U-boat war, III, 51 et seq.

Poincaré, President of France, in Russia, I, xxxvi; accused by Socialists, I, xliv; visits Russia, I, 298; Germany distrusts, I,

320; defends France, I, 368; on entry into War, I, 370; prepares abandonment of Paris, II, 198 et seq.; rejoices over Marne victory, II, 248; letter by, II, 282; at Peace Conference, VII, 36 et seq.; speech of, VII, 37.

Poincaré, Mme., reception by, VII, 12.

Pojarevatz, in Serbia, battle at, III, 356; insurrection at, III, 418.

Pola, in Austria, British block ships from, II, 98 et seq.; naval base in invasion of Italy, V, 369 et seq.

Poland. See Subject Index.

Polena, in Hungary, sufferings of troops at, III, 120.

Polivanof, Russian statesman, quoted, III, 237.

Pollock, British writer, V, 68; on Russian Revolution, V, 69.

Pollock, U. S. naval officer, at transfer of Virgin Isles, V, 104.

Polygone Wood, in Ypres battle, II, 349; in Flanders battle, V, 285 et seq.

Pomerania, in East Prussia, character of, III, 15.

Pommer, German soldier, quoted, I, 140.

Pommern, German warship, sunk in Jutland battle, IV, 162 et seq.

Ponevyezh, in Russia, negotiations near, V, 397.

Pont-a-Mousson, in France, bombarded, II, 115; fighting at, II, 215 et seq.; in St. Mihiel battle, VI, 311.

Poperinghe, in Ypres campaign, II, 357.

Popoff, Bulgar colonel, crimes of, III, 421.

Popovitch, Serbian statesman, quoted, III, 420.

Portland, in England, fleet at, II, 22 et seq.

Port Stanley, in Falkland Isles, battle of, II, 444.

Portugal, in South African war, II, 390; troops of, in 1918 campaign, VI, xxi; in Lys battle, VI, 110 et seq.; British praise of, VI, 122; at Peace Conference, VII, 39.

Posen, oppression in, I, 148 et

VI, 280; Armistice surrenders, VI, 422; France seeks expansion to, VII, xiv; Allies take control of, VII, 1 et seq.

Rhodesia, in South African campaign, II, 390.

Rhododendron Spur, in Dardanelles assault, III, 259 et seq.

Rjaesan, Russian steamer, captured, II, 448.

Ribar, Austrian official, on Serbia's sufferings, III, 420.

Ribemont, on French frontier, British retreat to, II, 149.

Ribot, French prime minister, protests at German destructiveness, V, 38; welcomes U. S. entry into War, V, 106, 146; decides fate of Greece, V, 230.

Riddell, British general, slain, III, 145.

Riga, Russian city, in Warsaw campaign, III, 229, 232; Germans expelled from, III, 251, 304; pillar of 1915 defense, III, 320 et seq.; defense of 1916 in, IV, 186, 188; capture of, V, xxviii, 439.

Rintelen, German agent in America, III, 279 et seq.

Rio Grande, U. S. border river, in Mexican trouble, IV, 67 et seq.

Robeck, de, British admiral, at Dardanelles, III, 88 et seq.

Roberts, British general, address to Canadians, II, 367.

Robertson, U. S. hero in Boureshes, VI, 201.

Robilant, de, Italian general, in Piave battle, V, 371 et seq.

Rockwell, Kiffin, U. S. volunteer in France, IV, 261; deeds of, IV, 266, 268.

Rockwell, Paul, U. S. volunteer in France, IV, 260.

Rocquigny, in France, Germans capture, VI, 65 et seq.

Rodzianko, Russian leader, directs Duma, IV, 308; leads Duma in Revolution, V, 75 et seq.

Roehl, von, German general, quoted, I, 30.

Roeux, in France, fighting at, V, 162.

Rohne, German general, on great guns, VI, 92, 96.

Rohr, Austrian general, in Isonzo campaign, IV, 296.

Rohrbach, German author, quoted, I, 37, 198; on Peace Treaty, VII, 153, 189.

Roisel, in France, in Kaiser-battle, VI, 85.

Rojische, in Russia, battle of, IV, 191.

Rokitno, Polish marshes, Germans capture, III, 238.

Romagne, in France, Americans win, VI, 346 et seq.

Romanones, Spanish prime minister, V, 1; on U-boat warfare, V, 15.

Romanos, Greek diplomat, II, 206.

Rome, ancient teachings of, I, 99; reports of victory reach, V, 305.

Rominter Heath, in Prussia, Russian defeat at, II, 183.

Rommel, German author, quoted, I, 30.

Ronarch, French admiral, at Yser battle, II, 345.

Ronssoy, in France, Germans capture, VI, 57 et seq.

Roosevelt, U. S. statesman, Kaiser seeks friendship of, I, 358; urges U. S. entry into War, V, 128.

"Roots of the War," book by Davis, I, 156 et seq.

Roques, French general, in Marne battle, II, 260.

Rose, J. H., British historian, I, 193; article by, I, 197.

Rosières, in France, in Kaiser-battle, VI, 72 et seq.

Rosner, German writer, on Hindenburg retreat, V, 20, 21; on Germany's failure, VI, 259; Kaiser's personal reporter, VI, 276.

Ross, British sea-captain, in Jutland battle, IV, 174.

Rostock, German warship, in Jutland battle, IV, 160.

Rosztoki Pass, in Carpathians, Russians win, III, 110, 123.

Roubaix, on French frontier, deportations from, IV, 103 et seq.; freed, VII, 62.

Roulers, in Belgium, Germans advance from, II, 326; French reach, II, 330 et seq.; in Flan-

Stambulivski, Bulgarian leader, III, 340 et seq.

Stampher, German writer, VII, 126.

Stanck, Czech leader, in cabinet, VII, 145.

Stanislau, on Russian frontier, fighting at, IV, 194, 200; Russian victory at, V, 252 et seq.

Stanza, Austrian leader in massacre, II, 16.

Starr, U. S. volunteer in France, IV, 263; deeds of, IV, 269, 270.

Staszkowka, in Galicia, battle at, III, 179.

Stead, British statesman, I, 221.

Steenbeek River, in Belgium, fighting on, V, 272 et seq.

Steenstraate, in Ypres battle, III, 142 et seq.

Stefanik, Czech leader, VII, 140 et seq.

Stegler, German agent in America, III, 294 et seq.

Stein, German doctor, III, 382; on Middle Europe, III, 402.

Steinacher, Freiherr von, German general, II, 108; article by, II, 115; authority of, II, 118; on "Frontiers battle," II, 147; on Somme battle, IV, 242, 254.

Steinbach, Ervin von, German patriot, I, 166.

Steinberg, German officer, plots against U. S., III, 285 et seq.

Stendal, in Germany, prison camp at, IV, 419.

Stengel, von, German teacher, quoted, I, 48.

Stepanovic, Serbian general, II, 3.

Stephen, ancient king of Rumania, IV, 327.

Stettin, German army center, VII, 82.

Steuben, General von, American patriot, I, 55.

Stewart, U. S. volunteer in France, IV, 263; deeds of, IV, 275.

Stirling, British sea-captain, in Jutland battle, IV, 176, 177.

Stokhod River, in Russia, fighting on, IV, 193 et seq.

Stol, Monte, on Italian frontier, fighting on, V, 323.

Stone, U. S. volunteer in France, IV, 261.

Stopnica, in Poland, Austrian advance in, III, 182.

"Storks, The," French aeroplane escadrille, V, 191 et seq.

Strachan, Canadian hero, V, 389.

Stranz, von, German general, II, 217.

Strassburg, seized by Bismarck, I, 163 et seq.; German fortifications at, II, 108; German army of, II, 113 et seq.

Stresemann, German leader, directs Liberals, VII, 69.

Stropka-Polena, in Hungary, III, 120; Russians capture, III, 121.

Struma River, in Macedonia, Bulgars control, IV, 346 et seq.; Allies capture, VI, 327 et seq.

Strumitza, in Bulgaria, raid from, II, 433; Allies repelled near, III, 361; Allies capture, VI, 322 et seq.

Stryi, in Galicia, Austrian advance on, III, 124, 186.

Strypa River, in Galicia, campaign on, IV, 190 et seq.; Czechs retreat along, VI, 147.

Studt, Prussian statesman, I, 150; quoted, I, 155.

Sturdee, British admiral, destroys German fleet, II, 443 et seq.

Sturgkh, Austrian statesman, aids in plotting War, I, 276 et seq.; slain, IV, xxxi; spies watched, VII, 145.

Sturmer, German diplomat, on Dardanelles attack, III, 91; on Armenian massacres, III, 172.

Sturmer, Russian statesman, prime minister, IV, xxv, 185; attacked as traitor, IV, 305 et seq.; betrays Rumania, IV, 366; betrays Russia, V, xix; flees from Revolutionists, V, 78.

Styr River, in Russia, campaign on, IV, 191 et seq.

Suez Canal, I, 193; threatened in War, II, 394; fighting on, V, 401.

Sugana, Val, in Italy, fighting in, V, 371 et seq.

Suhotine, Russian officer, in Rasputin plot, V, 87.

Sukhomlinoff, Russian general and statesman, revelations at trial of, I, xliv; aids mobilization, I, 332; menaces Germany,

Trajan Wall, in Rumania, fighting by, IV, 350 et seq.

Transcaucasia, threatened by War, II, 394; volunteers of, aid Russia, III, 158; Russian victories in, IV, 24 et seq.

Transvaal, in Africa, II, 380, 382 et seq.; receives munitions, III, 131.

Transylvania, Hungarian province, in Austrian war plans, I, 284; Rumania threatens, IV, 317; invaded, IV, 322.

Travers, British general, at Dardanelles, III, 258.

Tree Sante, in Austria, fighting for, V, 304 et seq.

Trebizond, in Armenia, massacre at, III, 157; Russians capture, IV, 24.

Treitschke, German lecturer, themes of, I, xxix; influence of, I, 22 et seq.; quoted, I, 31; teaching War, I, 89 et seq.; quoted, I, 90; scorned small States, I, 97; Pan-Germanism of, I, 110; quoted, I, 124; his lectures, I, 156; article by, I, 165.

Trembowla, on Russian frontier, troops flee to, V, 255 et seq.

Trentino, offered Italy by Austria, III, 217 et seq.; campaign in, IV, xxii, 148 et seq.; influence on Russian attack, IV, 186; Cadorna's report on, IV, 294; in 1918 campaign, VI, 216 et seq., 374 et seq.

Tretiakov, Russian prisoner, abused, IV, 418.

Trevelyan, G., British author, I, 176; on Serbia, I, 184; on capture of Monte Santo, V, 303, 310; on Caporetto disaster, V, 315, 318; on Piave victory, VI, 213, 223; on final Italian triumph, VI, 373, 375.

Treves, in Germany, Americans occupy, VII, 1.

Treviso, in Italy, in 1918 campaign, VI, 216 et seq.

Triaucourt, in France, atrocities at, III, 21.

Trieste, value to Germany, I, 336; under Austrian rule, III, 215; offered to Italy, III, 217 et seq.; Italian advance against, IV, 294

et seq.; in 1917 campaign, V, 303; fears for, V, 326; Italians capture, VI, xxxviii; in 1918 campaign, VI, 216; Italians enter, VI, 373.

Triple Alliance, its members, I, xxxi; threatens Europe, I, 110; internal weakness of, I, 119; needed Turkey, I, 231 et seq.; breaking down, I, 300, 309; Italy's duties under, III, 214; Italy breaks, III, 215 et seq.

Triple Entente, its origin, I, xxxi; attacks Germany, I, 109; in danger, I, 200; character of, I, 213; opposed Turkey, I, 231 et seq.; deceived by Austria, I, 256; increased power before War, I, 380; attitude in Balkans, II, 392; urges Italy into War, III, 217 et seq.

Tripoli, seized by Italy, I, 119.

Triumph, British warship, II, 409, 415.

Trocy, in France, in Ourcq battle, II, 242 et seq.

Troesnes, in France, in Kaiserbattle, VI, 171.

Trompczynski, Polish leader, III, 425; protest of, III, 431.

Tronquoy Tunnel, in France, fighting for, VI, 301 et seq.

Trotsky, Russian bolshevist, returns to Russia, V, 345; in revolution, V, 348 et seq.; in armistice, V, 393 et seq.; on Teuton peace, VI, 31 et seq.; opposes Czechs, VI, 149 et seq.

Troupakis, Greek official, expelled in revolution, IV, 349.

Troy, in Asia Minor, British at, III, 85.

Troyon, in Marne battle, II, 263 et seq.

Trumbic, Slavic statesman, aids reconstruction, VII, 22 et seq.

Truppel, German governor, in China, II, 414.

"Truth about the War," German pamphlet, II, 61 et seq.

Trysten, in Russia, battle at, IV, 193.

Tsarkoe Selo, in Russia, troops join Revolution, V, 75 et seq.

Tsavo, in Africa, fight at, II, 375.

Tschirschky, German diplomat, I, 292; ambassador at Vienna, I,

296; reproved for pacifism, I, 313; reports by, I, 319 et seq.

Tseretelli, Russian Socialist leader, in Revolution, V, 90; loses control, V, 361.

Tsi-nan, in China, trade at, II, 406.

Tsing-tau, Japanese capture of, II, 402 et seq.; *Emden* at, II, 447.

Tsumeb, in Southwest African campaign, II, 387, 388.

Tucholka, in Carpathian campaign, III, 124.

Tufta, Armenian fort, Russians win, IV, 33 et seq.

Tunis, French seized, II, 398.

Turbulent, British destroyer, sunk in Jutland battle, IV, 164.

Turin, in Italy, riots at, V, 321.

Turka, in Galicia, fighting at, III, 183.

Turkestan, source of Turks, I, 61.

Turkey. See Subject Index.

Turner, British sea-captain, on *Lusitania,* III, 189 et seq.

Turner, Canadian general, in first gas attack, III, 149.

Turnu-Severin, in Rumania, ceded to Austria, VI, 44.

Tuslagol, in Dardanelles campaign, III, 269 et seq.

Turtukai, in Rumania, captured, IV, 329.

Tutrakan, in Rumania, fighting at, IV, 358 et seq.

Twinhout, in Antwerp campaign, II, 319.

Tyrol, in Austria, concessions in Italy, III, 217 et seq.; fighting in, IV, 148 et seq.; censequences of, IV, 197; feint attack from, V, 329.

Tyrrell, British diplomat, I, 316.

Tysmienitsa, on Galician frontier, Russians capture, IV, 195.

Tzer Mountain, in Serbia, battle of, II, 1 et seq.

Udine, in Italy, Austrians capture, V, 324, 325, 365.

Udinsk, in Siberia, Czechs seize, VI, 150.

Ufa, in Siberia, center of revolution, VI, 232 et seq.

Uganda, in Africa, II, 374; railroad destroyed by Germans, II, 388.

Uhland, Ludwig, German liberal, I, 99.

Uknoff Regiment, of Russia, gallantry of, V, 253.

Ukoko, in Africa, capture of, II, 373.

Ukraine. See Subject Index.

Ulema, Mohammedan priesthood, upholds War, II, 391; in protest, IV, 233.

Ulianoff, birth name of Lenine; See Lenine.

Ulster, in Ireland, tumults in, IV, 123 et seq.

Underwood, U. S. Senator, tariff by, I, 265; quoted by German official, V, 45.

United States. See Subject Index.

Urmia, Lake, on Persian border, Russians reach, IV, 26.

Uruguay, severs relations with Germany, V, 147; signs Peace, VII, 154.

Usambara, in East Africa, campaign for, II, 388 et seq.

Usciezko, on Austrian frontier, Russians capture, IV, 195.

Usdau, in Germany, fighting at, II, 173 et seq.

Usedom, von, German admiral, at Dardanelles, III, 92.

Ushitze. See Uzhitse.

Uskub, in Serbia, Teutons capture, III, 358; Serbs' reconquest of, VI, xxxvii, 327.

Uszok Pass, in Carpathians, Russians lose, III, 111 et seq.; retreat from, III, 182.

Uzhitse, in Serbia, II, 5; cholera at, II, 436; Austrians seize, III, 353.

Uzun-Ahmet, Armenian fort, Russians win, IV, 32.

Vaal River, in South Africa, II, 384, 390.

Vachereauville, in Verdun battle, IV, 375.

Valcartier, in Canada, camp at, II, 364 et seq.

Valdez, Panama statesman, on entering into War, V, 147.

Valenciennes, British retreat to, II, 121, 127; fighting at, II, 149; recapture of, VI, xxxvi, 386 et seq.

Valievo, in Serbia, disease at, III, 351.

Vallone River, in Austria, Italian attacks on, IV, 295 et seq.; retreat from, V, 367.

Valona, offered by Austria to Italy, III, 217.

Valparaiso, seafight near, II, 440.

Valyevo, in Serbia, II, 5; hospital at, II, 10; fighting at, II, 431 et seq.

Van, in Armenia, Turkish troops at, III, 42; Turks retreat to, III, 48; Russians capture, IV, 26.

Vanceboro, in U. S., German bomb crime at, III, 293.

Vendeleur, British major, IV, 412; on German abuse of prisoners, IV, 414.

Vendervelde, Belgian liberal, I, 395; at Peace Conference, VII, 53.

Vendeventer, British colonel, in Africa, II, 381.

Vanilla, British trawler, sunk, III, 63, 64.

Vanrensburg, Boer prophet, II, 380.

Vardar River, in Macedonia, Austria's goal, I, 336; in 1915 campaign, III, 361 et seq.; Allies advance by, IV, 340; Allies win, VI, 322 et seq.

Vareddes, in France, fighting at, II, 232 et seq.; in Ourcq battle, II, 242.

Varennes, in France, Americans win, VI, 350.

Varna, in Bulgaria, industrial needs of, III, 337; armies advance from, IV, 358 et seq.

Vassé, French civilian, slaughtered, III, 29.

Vassitch, Serbian hero, III, 352; commands Serbian army in Monastir campaign, IV, 387.

Vauthier, French general, II, 232.

Vaux, in France, Americans fight at, VI, xxiv, 193 et seq., 245.

Vaux, Fort, in Verdun battle, IV, 45 et seq., 206 et seq., 225, 373 et seq.

Vedegrange, in France, fighting at, III, 311 et seq.

Velaine, in France, German victory at, II, 221.

Veldhoek, in Ypres campaign, II, 348 et seq.; in Flanders battle, V, 284.

Veles, in Serbia, Bulgars capture, III, 349, 358; fighting at, III, 361 et seq.; deportations from, III, 412; Allies recapture, VI, 322 et seq.

Velika Plenina, in Serbia, battle at, III, 350.

Veliselo, in Serbia, fighting at, IV, 393, 394.

Vendhuile, in France, Americans win, VI, 303.

Venetia, Italian province, invaded, IV, 149; Austrian plans for, VI, 214.

Venice, Austrians threaten, V, xxxii, 321; campaign to save, V, 370;; ultimate relief of, VI, 373 et seq.

Venizelos, Greek statesman, supports Allies, III, 352; overthrown by Greek king, III, 353; German view of, III, 367; leads in revolution, IV, xxvii, 332 et seq.; overthrows king, V, xxvi; power restored throughout Greece, V, 221 et seq.; on Greek victory over Bulgars, VI, 321, 329; at Peace Conference, VII, 52.

Verdun, early treaty at, I, 104; became French, I, 158; Germany demands possession of, I, 369; France fortifies, II, xv, 108; German first advance toward, II, 113 et seq., II, 215 et seq.; Germans admit themselves held back by, II, 245; in Marne battle, II, 247 et seq.; siege of, begun, II, 290, 291; German assault on, IV, xiii, 38 et seq.; influences Italy, IV, 152; influence on Allies, IV, 193, 197; climax of battle at, IV, 206 et seq.; U. S. volunteers at, IV, 270 et seq.; final counterattacks at, IV, 373 et seq.; effects of, V, xiv; Guynemer serves at, V, 192; German gains of 1917 at, V, 219; French success of 1917 at, V, 298; U. S. troops based on, V, 434; U. S. troops defend, V, 440; VI, 300 et seq.

Vereeniging, Treaty of, II, 379.

Verguier, le, in France, in Kaiserbattle, VI, 57 et seq.

Wiatrowka, in Galicia, Hungarians capture, III, 179.

Wiazowinca, in Galicia, fighting at, III, 181.

Widzy, in Russia, battle at, III, 325.

Wieprz River, in Poland, fighting on, III, 233 et seq.

Wiesbaden, in Germany, French occupy, VII, 13.

Wiesbaden, German warship, sunk in Jutland battle, IV, 164 et seq.

Wilbrandt, German dramatist, quoted, I, 100.

Wilcox, British writer, V, 331; on Bolshevist movement, V, 344.

"Wilhelm Meister," novel by Goethe, I, 93.

Wilhelmina, Queen, receives Kaiser, VI, 410, 411.

Wilhelmina, American ship, seized by British, III, 56.

Wilhelmshaven, in Germany, II, 196, 300; U-boat warfare ordered from, III, 51; German losses secreted in, IV, 162; revolution in, VI, 369.

Willard, U. S. organizer, aids in War work, V, 418, 423; on U. S. railroads, V, 429.

Willcocks, British general, at Neuve Chapelle battle, III, 69.

Willenberg, in Germany, fighting at, II, 173 et seq.

William I, Emperor, his wisdom, I, 91; beloved in Russia, I, 364; distrusted, I, 365.

William II, Emperor, his early reign, I, xxxi; prepares for War, I, xxxv et seq.; praise of, I, 17; quoted, I, 30, 37, 57, 58, 89; his wisdom in peace, I, 95; his people devoted to, I, 101; denies responsibility for War, I, 109; political morality of, I, 158; quoted, I, 169, 171; wins Turkey"s support, I, 195; quoted, I, 197; sought naval power, I, 206 et seq.; quoted, 210, 213, 227; becomes warlike, I, 228 et seq.; visits Austrian prince, I, 245; quoted, I, 253; Austrian prince resembled, I, 257; in the "Potsdam Plot," I, 259 et seq.; quoted, I, 269, 270, 274; urges War on Austria, I, 277 et seq.;

comments on reports, I, 296; fears assassins, I, 298, 299; approves London ambassador, I, 308; regrets Archduke, I, 312; comments by, I, 319 et seq.; telegraphic correspondence with Czar, I, 347 et seq.; Harden's picture of, I, 357 et seq.; his former Russian policy, I, 360; present at great 1914 battles of Nancy and Ypres, II, xxxi; accuses Belgians, II, 51 et seq.; article by, II, 60; scorns British army, II, 136; Belgians condemn, II, 158; defeated by Hindenburg, II, 170; at battle of Grand Couronné, II, 210 et seq.; French opinion of, II, 218; withdraws from France, II, 235; at Ypres battle, II, 346 et seq.; confers with Boer leaders, II, 379; congratulates Hindenburg, II, 425; condemns French to extermination, III, 1 et seq.; orders U-boat warfare, III, 51; at battle of Dunajec, III, 181; pledges word to Greece, III, 367; loss of control by, IV, xxxii; boasts of naval victory at Jutland, IV, 162; congratulates troops on Verdun "victory," IV, 209; relation to Greek royal family, IV, 331; Hindenburg appeals to, IV, 376; stops Verdun battle, IV, 378; condemned by Americans for Hindenburg devastation, V, 40; Rasputin praises, V, 87; on battle of Arras, V, 153, 163; in dispute with Austrians, V, 327, 328; compared to Lenine, V, 332; did not influence Lenine, V, 357; relation to his people, V, 394; proclaims people's sovereignty, VI, xxxviii; abdicates, VI, xxxix; orders Kaiser-battle, VI, 51, 52; interviews generals, VI, 276; is told of defeat, VI, 305; proclaims constitutional government, VI, 358, 364; abdication of, VI, 402, 403 et seq.; Allies demand surrender of, VII, xxix; Germans regard as helpless tool of Junkers, VII, 11; Peace Conference discusses, VII, 48; Czech spies watch,

Wotan Line, of German defenses in France, V, 154.

Woyrsch, German general, defends Silesian frontier, II, 423; in Warsaw campaign, III, 231 et seq.

Wrisberg, von, Prussian general, quoted, VI, 411.

Wuri River, in Africa, fighting on, II, 374.

Wurms, Austrian general, in Piave battle, VI, 218.

Wurtemberg, revolution in, VI, 402; new constitution affects, VII, 82.

Wyrall, British writer, II, 37; article by, II, 38.

Wyssokie, in Russia, fighting at, III, 248.

Wytschaete, in Ypres campaign, II, 333 et seq.; in 1917 campaign, V, 207 et seq., 277; in Kaiser-battle, VI, 106, 114.

Y. M. C. A., V, xxiii.

Yale University, Law expert from, VII, 129.

Yamada, Japanese general, II, 411.

Yankovitch, Serb guerilla, crimes of, III, 422.

Yarmuk valley, in Palestine, British seize, VI, 335.

Yashenin, Russian prisoner, abused, IV, 422.

Yebnah, in Palestine, British capture, V, 405.

Yekaterinberg, in Russia, Czechs seize, VI, 150.

Yekaterinoslav, Russian province, in Ukrainia, VI, 20.

Young, British writer, on Berlin revolts, VII, 111, 114.

"Young Turks," influence in East, I, 199; rule in Turkey, II, 93 et seq., 391 et seq.; responsible for Armenian horror, III, 173; order massacres, III, 174 et seq.; Arabia condemns and defies, IV, 233 et seq.; V, 401.

Younger, British investigator, IV, 412; on prison camps, IV, 424.

Younghusband, British general, in Asia, IV, 130.

Yovanovitch, Serbian diplomat, I, 254, 255, 257.

Ypres, center of British warfare, II, xxx; Belgian resistance aids, II, 310; causes of fighting at, II, 324 et seq., 332; battle of, II, 337 et seq.; influences Polish campaign, II, 424; gas attack and second battle of, III, 137 et seq.; great bombardment of, III, 148; resembles Verdun, IV, 53; fourth battle of, V, xvii, 207 et seq.; battle of Flanders starts from, V, 268 et seq.; results of, V, 386, 439; in 1918 campaign, VI, xxii; in Kaiser-battle, VI, 104, 107 et seq.; in final drive, VI, 300; ruins of, VII, 11.

Yser River, main line of Belgian resistance, II, xxix et seq.; Belgian retreat to, II, 311; battle of the, II, 324 et seq.; Ypres on, II, 337; fresh fighting on, II, 355 et seq.; in 1917 campaign, V, 209 et seq., 273 et seq.; in Kaiser-battle, VI, 124.

Ytres, in France, in Kaiser-battle, VI, 65 et seq.

Yudenitch, Russian general, in Caucasus victory, III, 47; on Armenian campaign, IV, 24.

Yuruk, Turkish warship, conference on, III, 81.

Yussuf Izzedin, Turkish prince, slain, IV, 240.

Yusupoff, Russian prince, in Rasputin plot, V, 86 et seq.

ZABERN, incident of 1913 at, I, 171 et seq.; German plan for, I, 229; recalled, II, 114.

Zaecar, in Serbia, retreat from, III, 338.

Zagora, on Italian front, fighting near, V, 308.

Zagreb, new name given Agram, VII, 22.

Zaimas (or Zaïmis), Greek prime minister, IV, 341; leads pro-Germans, V, 231 et seq.

Zalesczyki, on Galician frontier, Russians capture, IV, 195.

Zalocostas, Greek statesman, opposes Allies, V, 228 et seq.

Zameczyka, Mount, in Galicia, captured, III, 179.

Zandvoorde, in Ypres campaign, II, 341 et seq.

Zane, U. S. officer, heroism of, VI, 202.

OFFICIAL SUMMARY

OF

AMERICA'S PART IN THE WAR

THE
WAR WITH GERMANY

A STATISTICAL SUMMARY

By

LEONARD P. AYRES

Colonel, General Staff

CHIEF OF THE STATISTICS BRANCH OF THE GENERAL STAFF

WASHINGTON

ISSUED BY AUTHORITY

CONTENTS

CONTENTS

CONTENTS

DIAGRAMS

DIAGRAMS

TABLES

MAPS

Chapter I

FOUR MILLION MEN

THE MEN WHO SERVED

ABOUT 4,000,000 men served in the Army of the United States during the war (Apr. 6, 1917 to Nov. 11, 1918). The total number of men serving in the armed forces of the country, including the Army, the Navy, the Marine Corps, and the other services, amounted to 4,800,000. It was almost true that among each 100 American citizens 5 took up arms in defense of the country.

During the Civil War 2,400,000 men served in the northern armies or in the Navy. In that struggle 10 in each 100 inhabitants of the Northern States served as soldiers or sailors. The American effort in the war with Germany may be compared with that of the Northern States in the Civil War by noting that in the present war we raised twice as many men in actual numbers, but that in proportion to the population we raised only half as many.

It would be interesting and instructive to make comparisons between the numbers in the American armies during the war and those of France, Great Britain, Italy, and Germany, but unfortunately this is most difficult to do fairly and truly. The reason for the difficulty lies in the diverse military policies of the nations.

It was the policy of France, for example, to mobilize and put into uniform most of the able-bodied men in the population who were not beyond middle age. Some of these were sent into the combatant forces and services of supply of the active armies. Thousands of others were put at work in munitions factories. Others worked on railroads or cultivated their farms. In general, it was the policy of the Government to put its available man power into uniform and then assign these soldiers to the work that had to be done, whether it was directly military in nature or not.

In the United States it was the policy to take into the Army only those men who were physically fit to fight and to assign them, save in exceptional cases, only to work directly related to the ordinary duties of a soldier. The work of making munitions, running railroads, and building ships was done by men not enrolled in the armed forces of the Nation.

THE AMERICAN EXPEDITIONARY FORCES AND THE BRITISH EXPEDITIONARY FORCES

There is, however, one comparison which may fairly be made. This is the comparison between the American Expeditionary Forces and the British Expeditionary Forces. Both

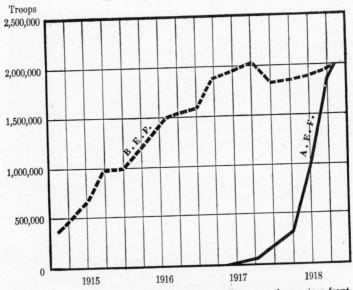

Diagram 1.—British and American Expeditionary Forces on the western front.

countries devoted their major efforts to building up and maintaining their armies in France. The results are set forth in diagram 1, which shows the strength of the two forces at different dates.

The British curve mounts rapidly at first and falls off in the latter part of the period. The American starts slowly and then shoots up very rapidly. The British curve is in general convex in shape and the American is concave.

The British sent to France many more men in their first year in the war than we did in our first year. On the other hand, it took England three years to reach a strength of

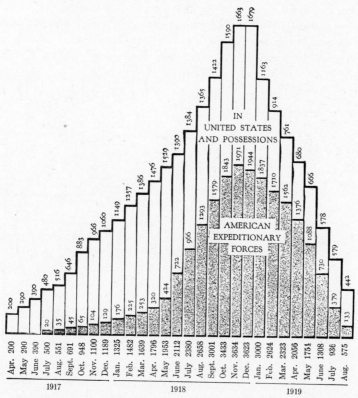

Diagram 2.—Thousands of soldiers in the American Army on the first of each month.

2,000,000 men in France and the United States accomplished it in one-half of that time.

It must, however, be borne in mind that the British had to use men from the beginning to fill gaps caused by casualties, while the American forces were for many months built up in strength by all the new arrivals.

ARMY AT HOME AND IN FRANCE

The most difficult feature of the American undertaking is to be found in the concentration of the major part of the effort into the few months of the spring and summer of 1918. When the country entered the war it was not anticipated in America, or suggested by France and England, that the forces to be shipped overseas should even approximate in numbers those that were actually sent.

It was not until the German drive was under way in March, 1918, that the allies called upon America for the supreme effort that carried a million and a half soldiers to France in

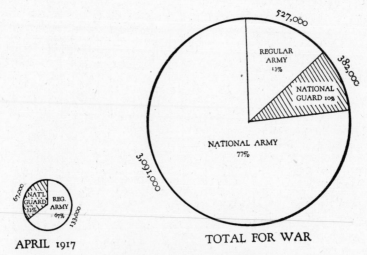

APRIL 1917   TOTAL FOR WAR

Diagram 3.—Sources of the Army.

six months. Diagram 2 shows the number of soldiers in the American Army each month from the beginning of the war, and the number of them who were overseas.

When war was declared there were only 200,000 in the Army. Two-thirds of these were Regulars and one-third National Guardsmen who had been called to Federal service for duty along the Mexican border. When the war ended this force had been increased to 20 times its size and 4,000,000 men had served.

After the signing of the armistice, demobilization of troops was begun immediately. As diagram 2 indicates, more than 600,000 were discharged during December. Forces in this country were at once cut to the lowest point consistent with carrying on the storage of equipment and settlement of contracts, and the discharge of men returning from overseas. In spite of the time necessary for return of overseas forces, demobilization was caried forward more rapidly in proportion to the number under arms than in any previous American war.

Diagram 3 shows the three sources from which the Army came.

More than half a million came in through the Regular Army. Almost 400,000 more, or nearly 10 per cent, entered through the National Guard. More than three-quarters of all came in through the selective service or National Army enlistments. Of every 100 men 10 were National Guardsmen, 13 were Regulars, and 77 belonged to the National Army, or would have if the services had not been consolidated and the distinctions wiped out on August 7, 1918.

THE SELECTIVE SERVICE

The willingness with which the American people accepted the universal draft was the most remarkable feature in the history of our preparation for war.

It is a noteworthy evidence of the enthusiastic support given by the country to the war program that, despite previous hostility to the principle of universal liability for military service, a few months after the selective service law was passed, the standing of the drafted soldier was fully as honorable in the estimation of his companions and of the country in general as was that of the men who enlisted voluntarily. Moreover, the record of desertions from the Army shows that the total was smaller than in previous wars and a smaller percentage occurred among drafted men than among those who volunteered. The selective service law was passed on May 19, 1917, and as subsequently amended it mobilized all the man power of the Nation from the ages of 18 to 45, inclusive. Under this act, 24,234,021 men were registered and slightly more than 2,800,000 were inducted into the military service.

All this was accomplished in a manner that was fair to the men, supplied the Army with soldiers as rapidly as they could be equipped and trained, and resulted in a minimum of disturbance to the industrial and economic life of the Nation.

The first registration, June 5, 1917, covered the ages from 21 to 31. The second registration, one year later (June 5, 1918 and Aug. 24, 1918), included those who had become 21 years old since the first registration. The third registration (Sept. 12, 1918), extended the age limits downward to 18 and upward to 45. The total number registered with the proportion who were actually inducted into the service is shown in Table 1.

TABLE 1.—*Men Registered and Inducted.*

Registration	Age Limits	Registered	Inducted	Per Cent Inducted
First and second..............	21 to 31	10,679,814	2,666,867	25
Third......................	{ 18 to 20 } { 32 to 45 }	13,228,762	120,157	1
Alaska, Hawaii, and Porto Rico....	18 to 45	325,445	23,272	7
Total......................	18 to 45	24,234,021	2,810,296	12

At the outbreak of the war, the total male population of the country was about 54,000,000. During the war some 26,000,000 of them, or nearly half of all, were either registered under the selective-service act or were serving in the Army or Navy without being registered. Diagram 4 shows the percentages of the male population who were included in each of the registrations and the proportion who were not registered.

The experience of the Civil War furnishes a basis for comparing the methods used and the results obtained in the two great struggles. This comparison is strikingly in favor of the methods used in the present war. During the Civil War large sums were paid in bounties in the hope that by this means recourse to the draft might be made unnecessary. This hope was frustrated and the draft was carried through by methods which were expensive and inefficient. This may be summed

up by noting that during the War with Germany we raised
twice as many men as we raised during the Civil War, and at
one-twentieth of the cost. This does not mean one-twentieth of
the cost per man, but that 20 times as much money was actually
spent by the Northern States in the Civil War in recruiting
their armies as was spent for the same purpose by the United
States in the War with Germany. In this war 60 per cent
of all armed forces were secured by the draft, as compared
with 2 per cent in the case of the Civil War. Diagram 5

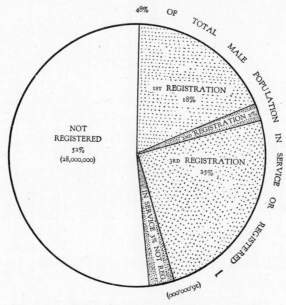

Diagram 4.—Male population registered and not registered.

shows the number of men inducted through the draft each
month.

   The columns and the figures of the diagram illustrate the
manner in which the men came into the service. In the fall
of 1917 the first half million came in rapidly. During the
winter the accessions were relatively few, and those that did
come in were largely used as replacements and for special
services. In the spring of 1918 came the German drive and
with it urgent calls from France for unlimited numbers of

men. Then over a period of several months the numbers of
new men brought into the service mounted into the hundreds
of thousands, and reached their highest point in July, when

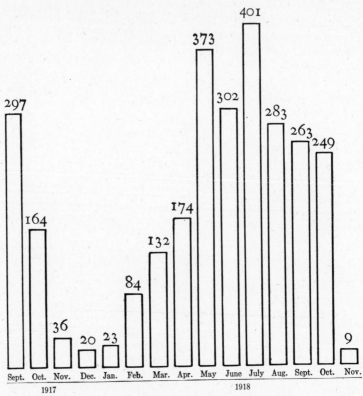

Diagram 5.—Thousands of men drafted each month.

400,000 were inducted. During the succeeding months the
numbers fell off considerably on account of the epidemic of
influenza, and with November the inductions ceased entirely
due to the unexpected ending of the war.

REJECTIONS FOR PHYSICAL REASONS

Under the operation of the draft, registrants were given
physical examinations by the local boards in order that those
men who were not of sufficient physical soundness and vigor

for military life might be sorted out. After those who were found to be qualified for service had been sent to camp, they were given another examination by the Army surgeons, and additional men were rejected because of defects which had not been discovered in the first examination.

An attempt has been made to compute from the records of these two sets of physical examinations data which will show how the men from the different States compared in their

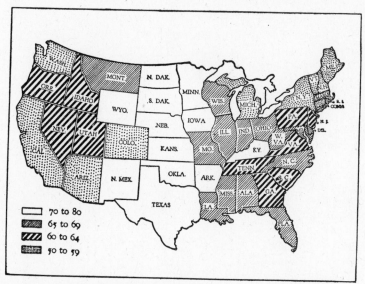

Map 1.—Per cent of drafted men passing physical examination, by States.

physical qualifications. Results are presented in map 1 on this page which shows four classifications of the States.

First come those States which are indicated in outline. These are the States which sent men of so high an order of physical condition that from 70 to 80 per cent of them survived the two examinations and were accepted into the military service. It is noteworthy that these States constitute about one-quarter of all, and are mostly located in the Middle West. Next come the States from which 65 to 69 per cent of the applicants were accepted, and these are indicated by light diagonal lines. This group is about equal in numbers with the first, and most of them are contiguous to the first group either on the east or west. The third group makes still poorer records. Here from 60 to 64 per cent of the young men passed the tests. The States are indicated by heavy diagonal bars. Most of them were in the South and far West. Finally, there is a group of States, including, like each of the other groups, about one-quarter of all, and indicated on the map by dotted lines. Here are the States from which 50 to 59 per cent of the candidates were accepted. They are found in the Northeast and the far West, especially in those portions of the West which have in recent years become popular as health resorts and so have attracted large numbers of physically subnormal people. In general, it is noteworthy that the best records are made by those States that are agricultural rather than industrial, and where the numbers of recently arrived immigrants are not large. Conversely, most of the States making low records are preeminently manufacturing States and also have in their populations large numbers of recently arrived immigrants.

Further analysis of the records of physical examinations shows that the country boys made better records than those from the cities; the white registrants better than the colored; and native-born better records than those of alien birth. These differences are so considerable that 100,000 country boys would furnish for the military service 4,790 more soldiers than would an equal number of city boys. Similarly, 100,000 whites would furnish 1,240 more soldiers than would an equal number of colored. Finally, 100,000 native-born would yield 3,500 more soldiers than would a like number of foreign-born. The importance of these differences may be appreciated by noting that 3,500 men is equivalent to an infantry regiment at full war strength.

200,000 OFFICERS

About 200,000 commissioned officers were required for the Army. Of this number, less than 9,000 were in the Federal service at the beginning of the war. Of these, 5,791 were Regulars and 3,199 were officers of the National Guard in the Federal service. Diagram 6 shows with approximate accuracy the sources of the commissioned strength of the Army.

The figures show that of every six officers one had had previous military training in the Regular Army, the National Guard, or the ranks. Three received the training for their commissions in the officers' training camps. The other two went from civilian life into the Army with little or no military training. In this last group the majority were physicians, a few of them were ministers, and most of the rest were men of special business or technical equipment, who were taken into the supply services or staff corps.

THE SHARE OF EACH STATE

A summary of the results attained is shown in diagram 7 on page 21, which gives the number of soldiers (not including officers) furnished by each State. The bars are proportionate in length to the total number of men furnished, whether by volunteering in the Regular Army, coming in through the National Guard, or being inducted through the draft.

SUMMARY

1. The number of men serving in the armed forces of the Nation during the war was 4,800,000, of whom 4,000,000 served in the Army.

2. In the War with Germany the United States raised twice as many men as did the Northern States in the Civil War, but only half as many in proportion to the population.

3. The British sent more men to France in their first year of war than we did in our first year, but it took England three years to reach a strength of 2,000,000 men in France, and the United States accomplished it in one-half of that time.

4. Of every 100 men who served, 10 were National Guardsmen, 13 were Regulars, and 77 were in the National Army (or would have been if the services had not been consolidated).

5. Of the 54,000,000 males in the population, 26,000,000 were registered in the draft or were already in service.

6. In the physical examinations the States of the Middle

West made the best showing. Country boys did better than city boys; whites better than colored; and native-born better than foreign-born.

7. In this war twice as many men were recruited as in the Civil War and at one-twentieth of the recruiting cost.

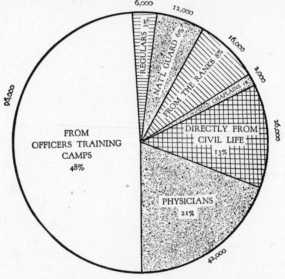

Diagram 6.—Sources of the commissioned personnel.

8. There were 200,000 Army officers. Of every six officers, one had previous military training with troops, three were graduates of officers' training camps, and two came directly from civil life.

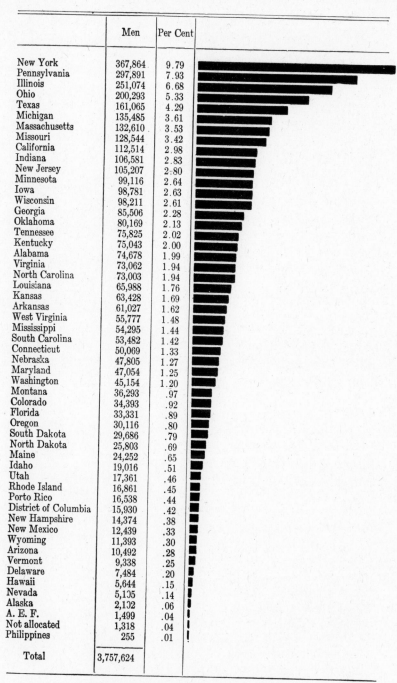

	Men	Per Cent
New York	367,864	9.79
Pennsylvania	297,891	7.93
Illinois	251,074	6.68
Ohio	200,293	5.33
Texas	161,065	4.29
Michigan	135,485	3.61
Massachusetts	132,610	3.53
Missouri	128,544	3.42
California	112,514	2.98
Indiana	106,581	2.83
New Jersey	105,207	2.80
Minnesota	99,116	2.64
Iowa	98,781	2.63
Wisconsin	98,211	2.61
Georgia	85,506	2.28
Oklahoma	80,169	2.13
Tennessee	75,825	2.02
Kentucky	75,043	2.00
Alabama	74,678	1.99
Virginia	73,062	1.94
North Carolina	73,003	1.94
Louisiana	65,988	1.76
Kansas	63,428	1.69
Arkansas	61,027	1.62
West Virginia	55,777	1.48
Mississippi	54,295	1.44
South Carolina	53,482	1.42
Connecticut	50,069	1.33
Nebraska	47,805	1.27
Maryland	47,054	1.25
Washington	45,154	1.20
Montana	36,293	.97
Colorado	34,393	.92
Florida	33,331	.89
Oregon	30,116	.80
South Dakota	29,686	.79
North Dakota	25,803	.69
Maine	24,252	.65
Idaho	19,016	.51
Utah	17,361	.46
Rhode Island	16,861	.45
Porto Rico	16,538	.44
District of Columbia	15,930	.42
New Hampshire	14,374	.38
New Mexico	12,439	.33
Wyoming	11,393	.30
Arizona	10,492	.28
Vermont	9,338	.25
Delaware	7,484	.20
Hawaii	5,644	.15
Nevada	5,135	.14
Alaska	2,132	.06
A. E. F.	1,499	.04
Not allocated	1,318	.04
Philippines	255	.01
Total	3,757,624	

Diagram 7.—Soldiers furnished by each State.

Chapter II

SIX MONTHS OF TRAINING

THE AVERAGE MAN

THE average American soldier who went to France received six months of training in this country before he sailed. After he landed overseas he had two months of training before entering the battle line. The part of the battle line that he entered was in a quiet sector and here he remained one month before going into an active sector and taking part in hard fighting.

The experiences of thousands of soldiers differ widely from the typical figures just presented, but a careful study of the training data of nearly 1,400,000 men who actually fought in France gives the average results shown above. In summary they are that the average American soldier who fought in France had six months of training here, two months overseas before entering the line, and one month in a quiet sector before going into battle.

THE DIVISIONS

The Infantry soldier was trained in the division, which was our typical combat unit. In the American Army it was composed of about 1,000 officers and 27,000 men. Training and sorting organizations of about 10,000 men, known as depot brigades, were also utilized, but as far as possible, the new recruits were put almost immediately into the divisions which were the organizations in which they would go into action.

Before the signing of the armistice there were trained and sent overseas 42 American divisions. The training of 12 more was well advanced, and there were 4 others that were being organized. The plans on which the Army was acting called for 80 divisions overseas before July, 1919, and 100 divisions by the end of that year.

TABLE 2.—*Place of Organization of Divisions and Sources by States.*

Division	Camp	States from Which Drawn
Regulars:		
1st	France	Regulars.
2nd	France	Regulars.
3rd	Greene, N. C.	Regulars.
4th	Greene, N. C.	Regulars.
5th	Logan, Tex.	Regulars.
6th	McClellan, Ala	Regulars.
7th	MacArthur, Tex.	Regulars.
8th	Fremont, Calif.	Regulars.
9th	Sheridan, Ala	Regulars.
10th	Funston, Kans.	Regulars.
11th	Meade, Md	Regulars.
12th	Devens, Mass.	Regulars.
13th	Lewis, Wash.	Regulars.
14th	Custer, Mich.	Regulars.
15th	Logan, Tex.	Regulars.
16th	Kearny, Calif.	Regulars.
17th	Beauregard, La.	Regulars.
18th	Travis, Tex.	Regulars.
19th	Dodge, Iowa	Regulars.
20th	Sevier, S. C.	Regulars.
National Guard:		
26th	Devens, Mass.	New England.
27th	Wadsworth, S. C.	New York.
28th	Hancock, Ga.	Pennsylvania.
29th	McClellan, Ala.	New Jersey, Virginia, Maryland, District of Columbia.
30th	Sevier, S. C.	Tennessee, North Carolina, South Carolina.
31st	Wheeler, Ga.	Georgia, Alabama, Florida.
32nd	MacArthur, Tex.	Michigan, Wisconsin.
33rd	Logan, Tex.	Illinois.
34th	Cody, N. Mex.	Nebraska, Iowa, S. Dakota, Minnesota, N. Dakota.
35th	Doniphan, Okla.	Missouri, Kansas.
36th	Bowie, Tex.	Texas, Oklahoma.
37th	Sheridan, Ohio.	Ohio.
38th	Shelby, Miss.	Indiana, Kentucky, West Virginia.
39th	Beauregard, La.	Arkansas, Mississippi, Louisiana.
40th	Kearny, Calif.	California, Colorado, Utah, Arizona, New Mexico.
41st	Fremont, Calif.	Various States.
42nd	Mills, N. Y.	Various States.
National Army:		
76th	Devens, Mass.	New England, New York.
77th	Upton, N. Y.	New York City.
78th	Dix, N. J.	Western New York, New Jersey, Delaware.
79th	Meade, Md.	Northeastern Pennsylvania, Maryland, District of Columbia.
80th	Lee, Va.	Virginia, West Virginia, Western Pennsylvania.
81st	Jackson, S. C.	North Carolina, S. Carolina, Florida, Porto Rico.
82nd	Gordon, Ga.	Georgia, Alabama, Tennessee.
83rd	Sherman, Ohio.	Ohio, Western Pennsylvania.
84th	Zachary Taylor, Ky.	Kentucky, Indiana, Southern Illinois.
85th	Custer, Mich.	Michigan, Eastern Wisconsin.
86th	Grant, Ill.	Chicago, Northern Illinois.
87th	Pike, Ark.	Arkansas, Louisiana, Mississippi, Southern Alabama.
88th	Dodge, Iowa	North Dakota, Minnesota, Iowa, Western Illinois.
89th	Funston, Kans.	Kansas, Missouri, South Dakota, Nebraska.
90th	Travis, Tex.	Texas, Oklahoma.
91st	Lewis, Wash.	Alaska, Washington, Oregon, California, Idaho, Nebraska, Montana, Wyoming, Utah.
92nd	Funston, Kans.	Colored, various States.
93rd	Stuart, Va.	Colored, various States.

Table 2 lists the divisions that were organized and trained before the signing of the armistice. The different columns show the number by which each division was designated, the camp where it was trained, and the States from which its mem-

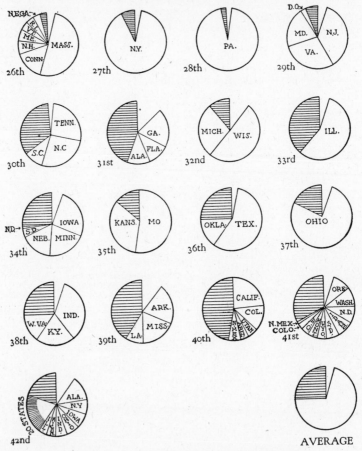

Diagram 8.—Composition of National Guard divisions.

bers came at the time of organization. In many cases the original composition was afterwards greatly changed by bringing in replacements to make up for losses.

The divisions are in three groups. The Regular Army divisions, numbered from 1 to 20, were originally made up from Regular Army units plus voluntary enlistments and selective-service men. The National Guard divisions, numbered from 26 to 42, came in largely from the militia of the several States. The National Army divisions, numbered from 76 to 92, were made up almost wholly of men called in by the selective-service law. As an aid to memory it may be helpful to note that the Regular Army divisions were numbered below 25, the National Guard divisions from 25 to 50, and the National Army divisions between 50 and 100.

All the divisions shown in the table reached France except the 12 Regular Army divisions numbered from 9 to 20. The divisions being organized at the time of the signing of the armistice were numbered 95, 96, 97, and 100.

The sources of the National Guard divisions are shown in diagram 8. The white portion of each circle shows the part of each division drawn from the National Guard; the shaded portion represents troops drawn from the National Army and other sources; and the unfilled gap in each circle represents the number of troops that the division was short of its authorized strength when it sailed.

Reference to the lower right-hand circle in the diagram shows that the average composition of these National Guard divisions was one made up of about two-thirds State troops and one-third other troops. This illustrates the noteworthy fact that one tendency of the methods of divisional organization was to produce composite divisions made up of men from most varied sources.

The Forty-second Division, called because of its composite character the "Rainbow Division," was made up of selected groups from over the entire country and sent to France early. The Forty-first, called the "Sunset Division," was a composite of troops from many Western States. Four divisions were made up from one State each: the Twenty-seventh, Twenty-eighth, Thirty-third, and Thirty-seventh.

CAMPS AND CANTONMENTS

To carry forward the training program, shelter was constructed in a few months for 1,800,000 men. For the

National Guard and National Army divisions, 16 camps and 16 cantonments were built. National Guard units being organized rapidly during the summer of 1917 were put under canvas in camps throughout the South. The cantonments were largely in the North for the National Army called in the fall of 1917. The location of these 32 training areas is shown in map 2 on this page.

One National Guard division, the "Rainbow," required no training field, for it was assembled directly at Camp Mills for early transportation to France. Two National Army divi-

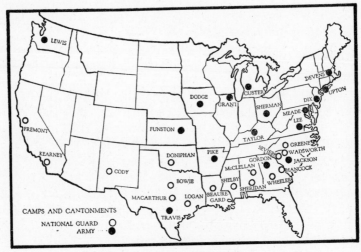

Map 2.—Camps and cantonments.

sions, the Ninety-second (colored) and the Ninety-third (colored), were trained in separate units at various camps. The headquarters of the Ninety-second were at Camp Funston and those of the Ninety-third at Camp Stuart. The remaining 16 National Guard and 16 National Army divisions began their training in the camps and cantonments in the summer and fall of 1917.

The building of the cantonments was authorized in May, 1917; the last site was secured on July 6, and on September 4 accommodations were ready for 430,000 men. This capacity was shortly increased to 770,000, an average capacity per cantonment of 48,000. Construction of the camps went forward at the same rapid pace. Although tents were provided for housing the soldiers, a considerable number of wooden buildings were necessary, as well as water supply, sewerage, electric light, and roadway construction. The capacity of the camps reached 684,000, giving a total camp and cantonment capacity of nearly a million and a half.

The Regular Army divisions were trained in part at one or another of these 32 centers, in part as separate units at various Army posts.

Troops had to be accommodated at many other points besides the 32 camps and cantonments. There were schools for training men for special services, such as the Artillery, Aviation, Engineer Corps, Chemical Warfare, Tank Corps, Quartermaster Corps. There were proving grounds and testing fields. There were also large embarkation camps at New York and Newport News. For these purposes housing was constructed with a capacity for more than 300,000 men.

INSTRUCTORS FOR TRAINING 4,000,000 MEN

In the American Army there is one officer for each 20 men. This means that 200,000 officers were required for the army of 4,000,000 men. But when war was declared there were only 6,000 officers in the Regular Army. The National Guard divisions were fortunately able to furnish most of their own officers. After this source of supply had been exhausted, however, it was still necessary to secure some 180,000 officers elsewhere.

The officers' training camp was the instrumentality that really solved the problem of securing the commissioned personnel of the American Army. The successful precedents of the Plattsburg camps were followed. Candidates for the camps were selected after rigid tests as to physical and mental qualifications, many Reserve Corps officers being included. Three months of intensive training put the prospective officers through all the tasks required of the enlisted man and the duties of the platoon and company commander. This type of training camp furnished the Army with nearly half its total number of officers and more than two-thirds of those for line service. Diagrams 9 and 10 show some details about the graduates of these training camps.

Diagram 9 shows the ranks of the commissions granted.

Rank	Number Commis- sioned	Per Cent	
Colonels	2		
Lieutenant-Colonels	1		
Majors	294	1.4	
Captains	5,429	6.7	
First Lieutenants	12,397	15.4	
Second Lieutenants	62,445	77.5	
Total	80,568		

Diagram 9.—Officers commissioned from training camps, by ranks.

By far the largest number of graduates were given the grade of second lieutenant, but exceptional ability, coupled with previous military training, was singled out in the first series of camps for more advanced commissions.

Branch of Service	Number Commis- sioned	Per Cent	
Infantry	48,968	60.7	
Field Artillery	20,291	25 2	
Quartermaster	3,067	3.8	
Coast Artillery	2,063	2.6	
Cavalry	2,032	2.5	
Engineer	1,966	2.4	
Signal	1,262	1.6	
Ordnance	767	1.0	
Statistical	152	.2	
Total	80,568		

Diagram 10.—Officers commissioned from training camps, by services.

Diagram 10 shows the number of officers commissioned in each branch of the service. Infantry and Artillery absorbed seven-eighths of the graduates with the Infantry taking more than twice as many as the Artillery. The total of 80,568 is not the grand total of graduates of officers' training schools but only of schools training officers for line duty. After the close of the second series of schools in November, 1917, it was found desirable for various staff corps and departments to conduct separate specialized schools for training their officers and many commissions were granted in these staff schools in addition to those shown in the diagram. The Quartermaster, Engineer, Signal, Ordnance, and Statistical officers shown in diagram 10 were all graduated from the first two series of schools.

FRENCH AND BRITISH INSTRUCTORS

Shortly after the first of the new camps were established France and England sent to the United States some of their ablest officers who had seen service on the western front to

Subject of Instruction	Number of Instructors	Per Cent	
Artillery	71	24.9	
Liaison	43	15.0	
Minor tactics	31	10.8	
Fortifications	29	10.1	
Automatic rifles	29	10.1	
Hand grenades	29	10.1	
Field and staff officers' course	27	9.5	
Miscellaneous	27	9.5	
Total	286		

Diagram 11.—French instruction officers.

bring to our training approved methods developed in the war. These instructors were not numerous but the aid they rendered was of the first importance. Diagrams 11 and 12 show how the subjects of instruction were divided among them.

Diagram 11 gives the information for the French officers, who were 286 in number. Their major specialties were Artillery and staff work. Corresponding details for the English officers are shown in diagram 12. These military specialists were 261 in number and much of their effort was devoted to instruction in gas and physical training.

In addition to the officers shown, the British also detailed 226 non-commissioned officers as instructors, who were as-

Subject of Instruction	Number of In- structors	Per Cent	
Gas	59	22.6	
Physical training and bayonet	58	22.2	
Machine gun	38	14.6	
Sniping	36	13.8	
French mortar	34	13.0	
Company commanders' course	21	8.0	
Miscellaneous	14	5.4	
Artillery	1	.4	
Total	261		

Diagram 12.—British instruction officers.

signed to different subjects in about the same ratio as the officers. These groups of foreign instructors attached to training schools, divisions, and other units, rendered service out of all proportion to their number. They were a significant contribution to our training program.

LENGTH OF TRAINING

Of the 42 American divisions which reached France, 36 were organized in the summer and early autumn of 1917. The other 6 were organized as divisions by January, 1918, but had been in training as separate units months before that time.

Although the average American soldier who fought in France had been under training only six months before sailing, the figure for the training of the divisions is greater than that. The main reason for the difference is that gaps in the divisions were filled by men who had received much less training than the original troops of the organization.

The average division had been organized eight months before sailing for France and its period of training was fur-

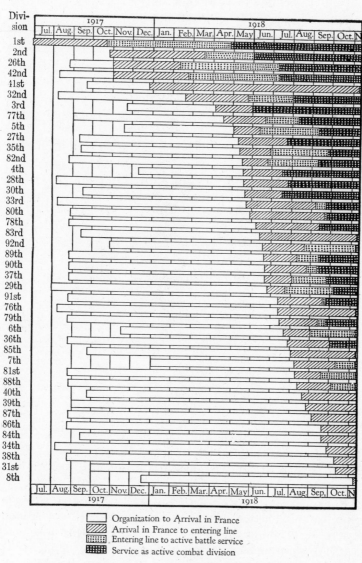

Diagram 13.—Time from organization of divisions to entering line.

ther lengthened by a two months' interim between the time the division landed in France and the time it entered the line. Diagram 13 shows these periods for each of the 42 divisions. Each division is represented by a horizontal bar. The unshaded part shows the period from organization to arrival of headquarters in France; the diagonal-lined part, the time in France before entering line; the part with black dots on white ground, the time between entering the line for the first time and engaging in combat in an active sector, and the solid portion with white dots, the length of service as an active battle organization.

The First and Second Divisions left this country as separate units and were organized in France. The troops of which they were composed were mostly thoroughly trained men of the Regular Army. The Second Division also included two regiments of Marines. The next three, while their stay in this country as organized divisions was short, were composed of selected units of the National Guard, most of which had seen service on the Mexican border and could be counted as well-trained bodies of troops. All the other divisions show extended periods of training in this country. The Regular Army divisions show the shortest periods, but were made up of the most experienced soldiers.

It is noticeable that all but two of the National Guard and National Army divisions were organized in August and September, 1917. The two exceptions to the rule were the Twenty-ninth, whose records show that it started the process of reorganization a few days ahead of schedule, and the Ninety-second (colored) Division which for a number of months trained in separate units at a number of different camps.

The conclusion to be drawn from the diagram would seem to be that the average American division entered battle only after 10 or 11 months of thorough training. This is true of the skeletons of divisions, but it is not true of all the men who made up their strength. There are two reasons for this. In the first place, some weeks or even months usually elapsed from the time a division was organized to the time when it reached full strength. In the second place, troops were frequently taken from one division to bring up to strength another which was sailing, or to be sent overseas to replace losses. The training of individual enlisted men was therefore less than for the divisions as organizations.

The length of training of the men can be got at in another way. By September, 1917, we had 500,000 men in this country training for overseas duty. We did not have 500,000 men in France until May, 1918, or eight months later. It is probable that the millionth man who went overseas began training in December, 1917. He did not reach France until July, 1918, after seven months of training. Evidence of this character goes to show that for our first million men the standard of seven months' training was consistently maintained as an average figure.

In June with the German drives in full swing, the Allies called on us to continue the extraordinary transportation of troops begun in April. The early movement had been met by filling up the divisions that sailed with the best trained men wherever they could be found. Divisions embarked after July 1 had to meet shortages with men called to the colors in the spring. By November the average period of training in the United States had been shortened to close to four months, and the average for the period July 1 to November 11 was probably five months.

Seven months may then be taken as the average training figure for the first million men, five months for the second million, an average of six months before reaching France. After reaching France an average of two months' training before going into front-line trenches was maintained, although the experience of divisions used as replacements in the last months was under this figure.

There were of course many cases in which the training was under these averages. To make these cases as few as possible a number of safeguards were set up. In this country a careful system of reporting on training was arranged so that only the better trained divisions might be sent forward. At the replacement centers in France the men who had slipped through without sufficient training were singled out and put through a 10 days' course in handling the rifle,

In the last months of the war, the induction of men was carried forward at top speed and every device was used for hastening training. The result fully justified the effort. Into the great Meuse-Argonne offensive we were able to throw a force of 1,200,000 men while we had many thousands of troops engaged in other parts of the line. Our training-camp officers stood up to the test; our men, with their intensive drilling in open-order fighting, which has characterized American training, routed the best of the German divisions from the Argonne Forest and the valley of the Meuse.

SUMMARY

1. The average American soldier who fought in France had six months of training here, two months overseas before entering the line, and one month in a quiet sector before going into battle.

2. Most soldiers received their training in infantry divisions which are our typical combat units and consist of about 1,000 officers and 27,000 men.

3. Forty-two divisions were sent to France.

4. More than two-thirds of our line officers were graduates of the officers' training camps.

5. France and England sent to the United States nearly 800 specially skilled officers and noncommissioned officers who rendered most important aid as instructors in our training camps.

CHAPTER III

TRANSPORTING 10,000 MEN A DAY

SENDING THE TROOPS OVERSEAS

DURING the 19 months of our participation in the war more than 2,000,000 American soldiers were carried to France. Half a million of them went over in the first 13 months and a million and a half in the last 6 months. Within a few weeks of our entrance into the war we began, at the earnest request of our cobelligerents, to ship troops overseas. At first the movement was not rapid. We had only a few American and British troop ships chartered directly from their owners. During the early winter, as the former German liners came into service, embarkations increased to a rate of nearly 50,000 per month, and by the end of 1917 had reached a total of 194,000.

The facts as to the transportation of troops to France and back to the United States are presented in diagram 14, in which the upright columns show the number carried each month.

Early in 1918 negotiations were entered into with the British Government by which three of its big liners and four of its smaller troop ships were definitely assigned to the service of the Army. The results of this are shown in the increased troop movement for March. It was in this month that the great German spring drive took place in Picardy, with a success that threatened to result in German victory. Every ship that could be secured was pressed into service. The aid furnished by the British was greatly increased. It was in May and the four following months that the transport miracle took place. The number of men carried in May was more than twice as great as the number for April. The June record was greater than that of May, and before the 1st of July 1,000,000 men had been embarked.

35

The record for July exceeded all previous monthly totals, the number of troops carried being more than 306,000. Before the end of October the second million men had sailed from our shores. During many weeks in the summer the number carried was more than 10,000 men a day, and in July the

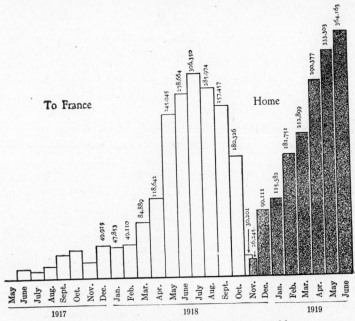

Diagram 14.—Men sailing each month to France and home.

total landed averaged more than 10,000 for every day of the month.

No such troop movement as that of the last summer had ever been contemplated, and no movement of any such number of persons by water for such a distance and such a time had ever previously occurred. The record has been excelled only by the achievement in bringing the same men back to the shores of the United States. The monthly records of this return are shown by the stippled columns of the same diagram, which indicate the even more rapid increase of totals from month to month and the attainment of higher monthly accomplishments. The total number of soldiers brought home in

June was nearly 360,000. If we add to this the sailors and marines, the total is more than 364,000.

GROWTH OF THE TRANSPORT FLEET

The necessity for creating a great transport fleet came just at the time when the world was experiencing its most acute shortage of tonnage. The start was made by chartering a few American merchant steamers and by the 1st of July there

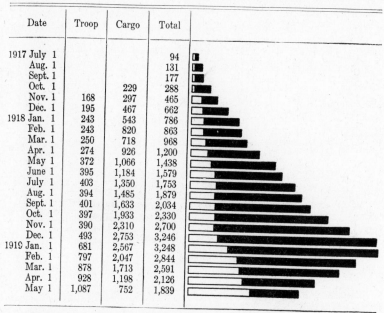

Date	Troop	Cargo	Total
1917 July 1			94
Aug. 1			131
Sept. 1			177
Oct. 1		229	288
Nov. 1	168	297	465
Dec. 1	195	467	662
1918 Jan. 1	243	543	786
Feb. 1	243	820	863
Mar. 1	250	718	968
Apr. 1	274	926	1,200
May 1	372	1,066	1,438
June 1	395	1,184	1,579
July 1	403	1,350	1,753
Aug. 1	394	1,485	1,879
Sept. 1	401	1,633	2,034
Oct. 1	397	1,933	2,330
Nov. 1	390	2,310	2,700
Dec. 1	493	2,753	3,246
1919 Jan. 1	681	2,567	3,248
Feb. 1	797	2,047	2,844
Mar. 1	878	1,713	2,591
Apr. 1	928	1,198	2,126
May 1	1,087	752	1,839

Diagram 15.—The trans-Atlantic fleet in thousands of dead-weight tons.

were in service seven troop ships and six cargo ships with a total dead-weight capacity of 94,000 tons.

Diagram 15 shows how there was developed from these small beginnings a great transport fleet which aggregated by the end of 1918 three and one-quarter million dead-weight tons of shipping. The size of the fleet each month is shown by the figures in the bars of the diagram. It will be noted that each bar is divided in two parts, the portion on the left showing the dead-weight tonnage of the troop ships and that on the right the tonnage of the cargo ships.

During these same months another great American transport fleet, of which little has been said in the public press, was created with an almost equally striking rapidity. This was our cross-Channel fleet, which carried cargo and men from England to France. Its growth is pictured in the bars of diagram 16, in which the figures also represent the number of dead-weight tons from month to month. Beginning with

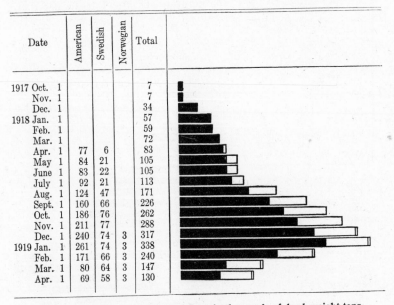

Date	American	Swedish	Norwegian	Total
1917 Oct. 1				7
Nov. 1				7
Dec. 1				34
1918 Jan. 1				57
Feb. 1				59
Mar. 1				72
Apr. 1	77	6		83
May 1	84	21		105
June 1	83	22		105
July 1	92	21		113
Aug. 1	124	47		171
Sept. 1	160	66		226
Oct. 1	186	76		262
Nov. 1	211	77		288
Dec. 1	240	74	3	317
1919 Jan. 1	261	74	3	338
Feb. 1	171	66	3	240
Mar. 1	80	64	3	147
Apr. 1	69	58	3	130

Diagram 16.—The cross-Channel fleet, in thousands of dead-weight tons.

7,000 tons in October, 1917, this fleet consisted of more than a third of a million tons by the end of 1918. About one-fourth of the vessels were Swedish or Norwegian, while the rest were American. This service utilized large numbers of small wood and steel vessels built by the Emergency Fleet Corporation at the yards of the Great Lakes and along the coast.

WHERE THE SHIPS CAME FROM

In building up our trans-Atlantic and Channel fleets every possible source of tonnage had to be called on for every ship that could be secured. The first great increment was the

seized German vessels, which came into service during the
fall of 1917.   The taking over of Dutch steamers in the spring
of 1918 and the chartering of Scandinavian and Japanese

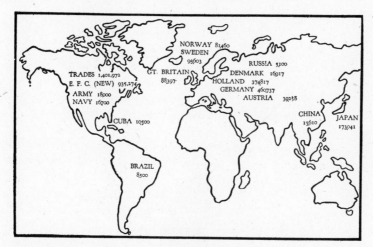

NORWAY 81,460
SWEDEN 98,603
RUSSIA 5,500
TRADES 1,401,972
GT. BRITAIN 88,397
DENMARK 16,917
E. F. C. (NEW) 935,274
HOLLAND 374,817
ARMY 18,000
GERMANY 460,737
NAVY 16,700
AUSTRIA 39,258
CUBA 10,500
CHINA 15,610
JAPAN 173,041
BRAZIL 8,500

**Map 3.—Dead-weight tons of American Army shipping secured from different
countries.**

tonnage accounted for great increases in the cargo fleet.   Map
3 shows the amounts of tonnage that were secured for our
Army fleet from the different countries of the world.

The most ample credit must be given to the Emergency
Fleet Corporation, which turned over nearly a million tons
of new ships, and to the Shipping Control Committee, which
stripped bare of all suitable vessels our import and export
trades and turned over for Army use nearly a million and a
half tons of ships.   The Army vessels also came from 12 other
nations well scattered over the globe and shown in the figures
of the map already referred to.

EMBARKATION AND DEBARKATION

Most of the troops who sailed for France left from New
York.   Half of them landed in England and the other half
in France.   Most of those who landed in England went directly to Liverpool and most of those who landed in France
went to Brest.   While these statements are valid generaliza-

tions, they fall short in showing what happened in detail. The principal facts of the eastward troop movement are shown in map 4, on page 41.

Troops left America from 10 ports, as shown in the little table in the left of the map. In this table the several ports of Hoboken, New York, and Brooklyn have all been included in one, and the same thing is true of the different ports at Hampton Roads, which have been shown under the heading of Newport News.

While 10 American ports were used, including 4 in Canada, more than three-quarters of all the men went from New York. The ports of arrival are given in the tables on the right of the map, which show that the ports of debarkation in Europe were even more numerous than those of embarkation in America.

HELP FROM THE ALLIES

Credit for the troop movement must be shared with the Allies, and with the British in particular, since approximately half of the troops were carried in their ships. This is shown by the figures of diagram 17.

Among every hundred men who went over, 49 went in British ships, 45 in American ships, 3 in those of Italy, 2 in French, and 1 in Russian shipping under English control. Part of the explanation for the large numbers of troops carried in American ships is to be found from the fact that under the pressure of the critical situation on the western front, ways were found to increase the loading of our own transports by as much as 50 per cent. In addition, our transports exceeded those of the Allies in the speed of their "turnarounds." The facts as to the average number of days taken by the ships to go to Europe, discharge their cargo and troops, come back, take on another load, and start for France once more, are shown in diagram 18.

The cycle of operations is termed a "turnaround," and it is not complete until the vessel has taken its load over, discharged it, returned, reloaded, and actually started on another trip. When our ships began operations in the spring of 1917 the average turnaround for the troop ships was 52 days, and that

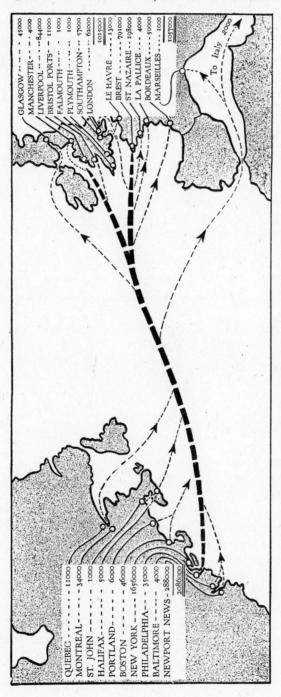

Map 4.—Troops sailing from American ports and landing in France and England.

for the cargo ships 66 days. These performances were improved during the summer months, but became very much longer during the exceptionally cold winter of 1917. During the spring, summer, and fall of 1918 the performances of both cargo and troop ships became standardized at about 70 days for cargo ships and 35 days for troop ships.

In noting these facts, as presented in the figures of the

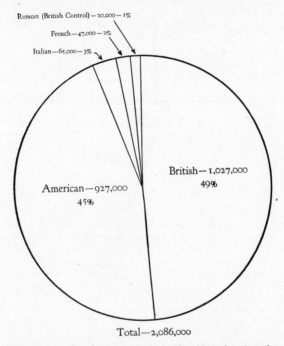

Russian (British Control) — 20,000 — 1%

French — 47,000 — 2%

Italian — 65,000 — 3%

British — 1,027,000
49%

American — 927,000
45%

Total — 2,086,000

Diagram 17.—American troops carried by ships of each nation.

diagram, it is to be borne in mind that the figures refer to the lengths of the turnarounds of all the ships sailing from American ports in one month. Thus the high figure of 109 days for the cargo ships means that 109 days was the average time required for all the cargo ships leaving American ports in November to complete their turnarounds and start on their next trips. These vessels made their trips in the exceptionally cold months of December, January, and February.

The fastest ships have averaged under 30 days. During

the spring and summer of 1918 the *Leviathan*, the former
Vaterland, has averaged less than 27 days, as has the *Mount
Vernon*, the former *Kronprinzessen Cecelie*.   These turnarounds, made under the embarrassment of convoy, are much
quicker than anything attained in commercial operation.   During the summer the *Leviathan* has transported troops at the

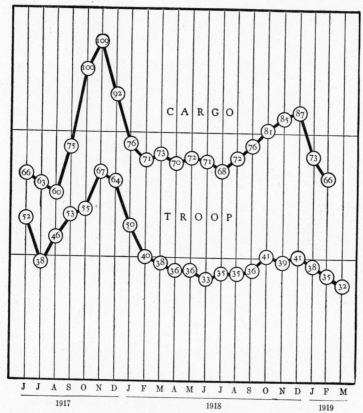

Diagram 18.—Average turnarounds of troop and cargo transports in days.

rate of over 400 a day, and so has landed the equivalent of a
German division in France each month.   Two American ships,
the *Great Northern* and *Northern Pacific*, have averaged 25
and 26 days, respectively, and have each made turnarounds
in 19 days.

CARGO MOVEMENT

The first shipment of cargo to support the forces abroad was made in June, 1917, and amounted to 16,000 tons. After the first two months the shipments grew rapidly and steadily

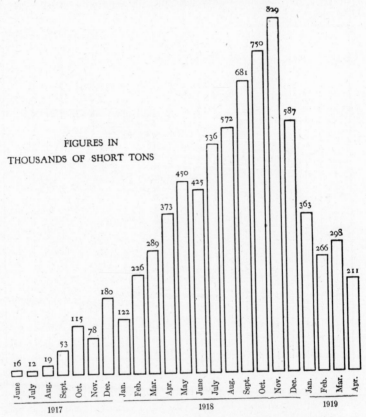

FIGURES IN
THOUSANDS OF SHORT TONS

Diagram 19.—Tons of Army cargo shipped to France each month.

until they were in excess of 800,000 tons in the last month of the war. These facts are shown in diagram 19.

The shipment of cargo differs from that of troops in that it was done almost entirely by American ships. Less than 5 per cent of the cargo carried was transported in allied bottoms. The great bulk of the cargo was carried in the cargo ships shown in diagram 15 on page 37. Relatively small amounts were carried in the troop ships. After the signing of the armistice every ship was withdrawn from the service as soon as it could be spared and put back into trades or the carrying of food for relief work in Europe. By April the total cargo fleet was only a third as large as it had been five months before.

The cargo carried for the American Army consisted of

	Short Tons	Per Cent	
Quartermaster	3,606,000	48.39	
Engineer	1,506,000	20.21	
Ordnance	1,189,000	15.96	
Food relief	285,000	3.82	
Motor Transport	214,000	2.87	
French material	208,000	2.79	
Signal Corps	121,000	1.62	
Medical	111,000	1.49	
Aviation	61,000	.82	
Red Cross	60,000	.81	
Y. M. C. A.	45,000	.60	
Miscellaneous	35,000	.47	
Chemical Warfare	11,000	.15	
Total	7,452,000		

Diagram 20.—Tons of cargo shipped for each Army supply service to April 30, 1919.

thousands of different articles of the most varied sort. Something of this variety is revealed by diagram 20, which shows the number of short tons carried for each of the Army supply services and for the special agencies. Nearly one-half of all consisted of quartermaster material, largely composed of food and clothing. The next largest elements were engineering and ordnance supplies. All together, from our entrance into the war through April, 1919, the Army shipped from this side of the Atlantic nearly seven and a half million tons of cargo.

Included in the cargo shipment were 1,791 consolidation locomotives of the 100-ton type. Of these, 650 were shipped set up on their own wheels, so that they could be unloaded on the tracks in France and run off in a few hours under their own steam. Shipment of set-up locomotives of this size had never been made before. Special ships with large hatches were withdrawn from the Cuban ore trade for the purpose and the hatches of other ships were specially lengthened, so that when the armistice was signed the Army was prepared to ship these set-up locomotives at the rate of 200 a month.

The Army also shipped 26,994 standard-gauge freight cars,

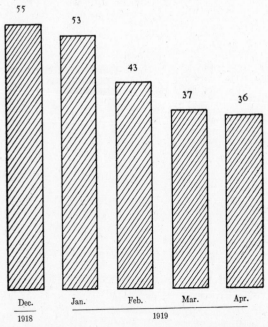

Diagram 21.—Average days required to convert cargo ships to troop transports.

and at the termination of hostilities was preparing to ship flat cars set up and ready to run. Motor trucks to the number of 47,018 went forward, and when fighting ceased were being shipped at the rate of 10,000 a month. Rails and fittings for the reinforcing of French railways and for the construction of our own lines of communications aggregated 423,000 tons. In addition to the tons of cargo mentioned above the Army shipped 68,694 horses and mules, and at the cessation of hostilities was shipping them at the rate of 20,000 a month.

The increase in the shipment of cargo from the United States was consistently maintained from the start of the war, and at its cessation was undergoing marked acceleration.

Aside from the cargo shipped across the Atlantic, Gen. Pershing imported large amounts from European sources, the chief item being coal from England. In October he brought into France by means of his cross-Channel fleet a total of 275,000 tons of coal and other commodities.

LOSSES AT SEA

During the whole period of active hostilities the Army lost at sea only 200,000 dead-weight tons of transports. Of this total 142,000 tons were sunk by torpedoes. No American troop transport was lost on its eastward voyage. For this splendid record the Navy, which armed, manned, and convoyed the troop transports, deserves the highest commendation.

RETURN OF TROOPS

In diagram 14, on page 36, figures are presented showing the number of troops brought back to the United States from France each month since the signing of the armistice. The figures mount even more rapidly and reach higher totals than those of the eastward journeys.

As soon as the armistice was signed preparations were made for returning the troops to the United States in the shortest possible time. This was rendered difficult by the fact that for the eastward movement we had relied largely on the British, who carried approximately half of all the troops. After the signing of the armistice the British needed these ships for the return of their own colonial troops, to Canada, Australia, and South Africa.

This situation was met by the Army Transport Service, which immediately began the conversion of our large cargo ships into troop-carrying vessels. Diagram 21 shows the number of days that were required to convert cargo ships into troop-carrying transports. The upright columns of the diagram are proportional to the number of days required. The ships upon which work was begun in December were not ready for the first trips as troop carriers until 55 days later. During the following months the work went forward more and more rapidly, as is shown by the shortening lengths of the columns in the diagram. By April the time required for converting cargo ships to troop carriers had been almost cut in two and was approximately one month. By means of these converted cargo ships, by the assignment of German liners, and also by the great aid rendered by the Navy, which put at the Army's disposal cruisers and battleships, the Army was brought back home even more rapidly than it was taken to France.

SUMMARY

1. During our 19 months of war more than 2,000,000 American soldiers were carried to France. Half a million of these went over in the first 13 months and a million and a half in the last 6 months.

2. The highest troop-carrying records are those of July, 1918, when 306,000 soldiers were carried to Europe, and June, 1919, when 364,000 were brought home to America.

3. Most of the troops who sailed for France left from New York. Half of them landed in England and the other half landed in France.

4. Among every 100 Americans who went over 49 went in British ships, 45 in American ships, 3 in Italian, 2 in French, and 1 in Russian shipping under English control.

5. Our cargo ships averaged one complete trip every 70 days and our troop ships one complete trip every 35 days.

6. The cargo fleet was almost exclusively American. It reached the size of 2,700,000 dead-weight tons and carried to Europe about 7,500,000 tons of cargo.

7. The greatest troop-carrier among all the ships has been the *Leviathan*, which landed 12,000 men, or the equivalent of a German division, in France every month.

8. The fastest transports have been the *Great Northern* and the *Northern Pacific*, which have made complete turnarounds, taken on new troops, and started back again in 19 days.

CHAPTER IV

FOOD, CLOTHING, AND EQUIPMENT

THE PROBLEM OF PURCHASE

I N the spring of 1917 there were in the United States some 4,000,000 young men who were about to become soldiers, although they little suspected the fact. Before they entered the Army, as well as after they were in it, these men consumed such ordinary necessities of life as food, coats, trousers, socks, shoes, and blankets.

These simple facts lead directly to the mistaken conclusion that the problem of supplying the necessities of life for the soldiers in the Army was the comparatively simple one of diverting into the camps substantially the same amounts of food and clothing as these young men would have used in their homes if there had been no war.

These men constituted about one twenty-fifth of the population of the country and undoubtedly consumed before the war more than one twenty-fifth of the food and clothing used in the United States. But after every possible allowance has been made for the requirements of youth and the wastefulness of war, the figures of Army purchases still present surprising contrasts with those of civilian use in normal times.

Some of these contrasts are shown in diagram 22, which compares total American production of blankets, wool gloves, wool socks, and men's shoes in 1914, as given in the census of manufacturers, with Army purchases of the same articles in 1918.

The first two columns of the diagram relate to blankets. They show that the Army purchases in 1918 were two and one-quarter times as great as the entire American production in 1914. To put it another way, the figures mean that the blankets bought in one year for the use of 4,000,000 or 5,000,000 soldiers would have been sufficient to make good

the actual normal consumption of blankets by 100,000,000
American civilians for two and a quarter years. From the
data of the other columns of the same diagram similar, if not
equally surprising, comparisons may be made.

The reasons for the enormous figures of Army purchases

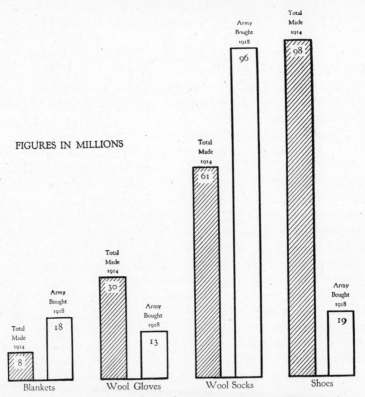

FIGURES IN MILLIONS

Diagram 22.—Total American production of four articles compared with Army
purchases.

are not far to seek. In the first place, men who went to camp
received complete equipment of new articles, whereas ordinary
production in peace time goes mainly to replace articles that
have been worn out. In the second place, the supplies required for an army increase in proportion to the distance that
separates the army from its home base. In the third place,
the consumption in action is three or four times the peace rate.

The stream of supplies going forward to an army may be likened to the water delivered against a fire by an old-fashioned bucket brigade. For every pailful thrown on the fire there must be many that have been taken from the source of supply and are on the way. As the distance from the source increases this supply in transit constantly grows. When an army is 3,000 or 4,000 miles from its sources of supply the amounts of supplies in reserve and in transit are enormous as compared with the quantities actually consumed each month.

The rule generally followed for clothing was that there should be for each man at the front a three months' reserve in France, another two or three months' reserve in the United States, and a third three months' supply continuously in transit. Wool coats, for example, last about three months in active service. Hence for every coat on a man's back at the front there had to be a coat in reserve in France, a coat in transit, and a coat in reserve in the United States. For every man at the front four coats were needed, and needed as soon as he went overseas. Two million men overseas required something like 8,000,000 coats, and required them immediately.

The same thing was true for other supplies and munitions. The need for reserves and the time required for transportation called for the supply of enormous quantities and called for it at once. The immediate needs for each man sent forward were in fact far in excess of the later requirements. For munitions difficult to manufacture, such as artillery and ammunition, the problem presented by this necessity for reserves and large amounts in transit, in addition to the actual equipment of troops, was almost insuperable. The initial need is so great in a situation of this character that it can only be met in one of two ways; either by having the initial equipment available at the outbreak of war, or by immediately securing such an enormous productive capacity that it is larger than is required for maintaining the establishment later.

In supplying food and clothing and other articles which are matters of common commercial production, the problem was not as difficult as with ordnance, but the large needs for initial equipment did put an enormous strain upon the industries concerned. A list of the total deliveries during the war of some of the common articles of clothing shows the size of the task. They are given in Table 3. The cost of the articles listed was more than $1,000,000,000.

All these garments could be made in ordinary commercial factories, but their quantity was so enormous that at a number of times during the war it was feared that the demand would run ahead of the supply. When the troop movement was speeded up in the spring of 1918 the margin on woolen clothing was dangerously narrow. To secure these and other

TABLE 3.—*Clothing Delivered to the Army April 6, 1917, to May 31, 1918.*

Articles	Total Delivered	Articles	Total Delivered
Wool stockings........pairs	131,800,000	Blankets.................	21,700,000
Undershirts...............	85,000,000	Wool breeches............	21,700,000
Underdrawers.............	83,600,000	Wool coats..............	13,900,000
Shoes...............pairs	30,700,000	Overcoats...............	8,300,000
Flannel shirts.............	26,500,000		

articles in sufficient quantity it was found necessary in many cases for the Army to take control of all stages of the manufacturing process, from assembling the raw material to inspecting the finished product. For many months preceding the armistice the War Department was owner of all the wool in the country. From September, 1918, to June, 1919, if the troop movement had continued, Army needs were estimated at 246,000,000 pounds of clean wool, while the amount allotted to civilian needs was only 15,000,000 pounds. The British Army had in a simliar way some years before taken control of the English wool supply in order to meet army and navy needs. Their requirements were, however, less than ours, to the extent that they did not need such a large reserve in France and practically none in transit. Their requirements per man for equipment were for this reason about two-thirds as great as ours.

Somewhat the same story might be told for about 30,000 kinds of commercial articles which the Army purchased. Purchases included food, forage, hardware, coal, furniture, wagons, motor trucks, lumber, locomotives, cars, machinery, medical instruments, hand tools, machine tools. In one way or another the Army at war drew upon almost every one of the 344 industries recognized by the United States Census. In some cases readjustments of machinery for a slightly modified product were necessary. In many an improved product was demanded. In practically all an enormous production was required. In the cases of some articles all the difficulties of quantity production were combined with the problems of making something not before manufactured. Typical instances are the 5,400,000 gas masks and the 2,728,000 steel helmets produced before the end of November, 1918.

MACHINERY OF DISTRIBUTION

For those supplies that were to a certain degree articles of commercial manufacture, the problem of distribution was fully as difficult as procurement. For production, machinery already in existence could be utilized; for distribution, a new organization was necessary. In this country the problem was not hard for there were ample railway facilities; an abundance of motor transportation could be requisitioned if necessary; and the troops were near the sources. In France, a complete new organization was necessary whose main duty it was to distribute munitions and supplies. It was called the Services of Supply, the S. O. S., and had its headquarters at Tours. It was an army behind the Army. On the day the armistice was signed, there were reporting to the commanding general of the Services of Supply, 386,000 soldiers besides 31,000 German prisoners, and thousands of civilian laborers furnished by the Allies. At the same time there were in the zone of the armies 160,000 noncombatant troops, the majority of whom were keeping in operation the lines of distribution of supplies to the troops at the front. The proportion of noncombatants in the American Army never fell below 28 per cent. In the British Army it often ran higher. Even when there was the greatest pressure for men at the front, the work back of the lines took roughly one man out of every three.

Distributing supplies to the American forces in France was in the first place a problem of ports, second a problem of railroads, third a problem of motor and horse-drawn transportation, and fourth a problem of storage.

The ports and railroads of France were crowded with war traffic and fallen into disrepair. It was not necessary to build new ports, but American engineers added 17 new berths, together with warehouses and dock equipment. It was not

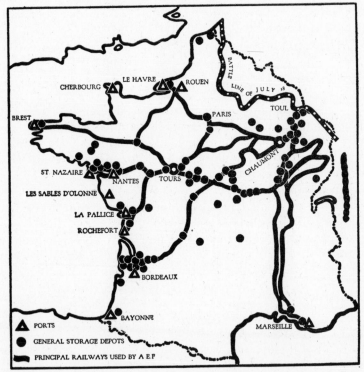

Map 5.—Seaports, storage points, and supply lines of the American Army in France.

necessary to build new railroads, for France already had a railway net denser per square mile than that of the United States, but it was desirable to increase the carrying capacity by nearly 1,000 miles of new trackage, and by switching facilities at crucial points, by new repair shops and round-houses, and by new rolling stock. These things were done

by the Engineers.   The problems were not wholly solved.
There were never enough docks to prevent some loss of time
by vessels waiting to dock, but the capacity for handling
American cargo was tripled from 10,000 tons per day in the
spring of 1918 to 30,000 tons by November 11 and the waiting
time of ships was shorter than in commercial practice.   There
were never wholly adequate railway facilities, but with the
help of locomotives and freight cars shipped from this side
freight was carried inland about as fast as it was landed.
Map 5 shows the main railway lines used by the overseas
forces.   They connect the principal ports at which the Army
fleet docked with the headquarters of the Services of Supply
at Tours and with the Toul-Verdun sector, where the American armies operated.   The dots represent the principal storage
depots of the transportation service.

NARROW-GAUGE RAILWAYS AND MOTOR TRUCKS

Railroads carried American supplies from the ports in
France to intermediate or advance depots.   As map 5 shows,
railroad lines roughly paralleled the front.   Spurs led up to
the front, but beyond a certain distance the standard-gauge
railroad did not go.   Where the danger of shelling began or
where the needs changed rapidly as the battle activity shifted
from this front to that, the place of the heavy railway was
taken by other means of distributing supplies.   First came
the narrow-gauge railroad, with rails about 2 feet apart,
much narrower than the usual narrow-gauge road in this
country.   American engineers built 538 miles of these roads,
for which 406 narrow-gauge locomotives and 2,385 narrow-
gauge cars were shipped from this country, in addition to
the standard-gauge equipment.

Beyond the range of the narrow-gauge railway came the
motor truck.   The truck could go over roads that were under
shell fire.   It could retire with the Army or push forward
with advancing troops.   Trucks were used on a larger scale
in this war than was ever before thought possible.   The
American Infantry division on the march with the trucks,
wagons, and ambulances of its supply, ammunition, and sanitary trains stretches for a distance of 30 miles along the road.

The 650 trucks which the tables of organization of the division provide are a large factor in this train. The need for trucks increased moreover during the latter months of the war as trench warfare gave place to a war of movement. As the forces moved forward on the offensive away from their railway bases, more and more trucks were demanded.

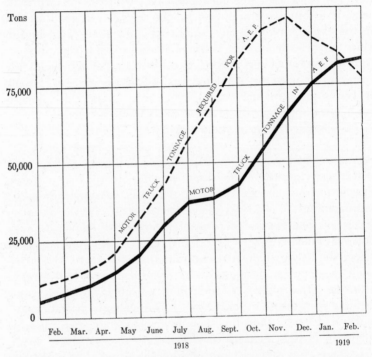

Diagram 23.—Motor-truck tonnage needed and available in the American Expeditionary Forces.

The Army overseas never had all the trucks it needed during the period of hostilities. Diagram 23 shows how the supply, month by month, measured up to the numbers called for in the tables of organization. The broken line shows the truck tonnage needed and the heavy line the amount available.

The supply was least adequate during the last four months of the war, when the shipment of trucks fell behind the accelerated troop movement. The difficulty was almost entirely a shortage of ships. At practically all times there were quantities of trucks at the ports of embarkation, but trucks take enormous amounts of cargo space on ships. It is slow and difficult work to load them, and time after time embarkation officials were forced to leave the trucks standing at the ports and load their ships rapidly with supplies needed still more urgently overseas. In October and November more ships were pulled out of the trades and the trucks were shipped even at the expense of other essential supplies. The shipment kept pace with the troop movement, but the initial shortage could not be overcome until February. The number of trucks sent overseas prior to the armistice was 40,000 and of these 33,000 had been received in France. The trucks ranged in size from three-quarters of a ton to 5 tons.

Beyond the range of the motor truck the horse and wagon were the means of supply distribution. Here again the American armies made an inadequate equipment do the work that was required. The shipment of animals overseas was discontinued early in 1918 on the information that horses could be purchased overseas. Then in the fall when every ton of shipping was precious, the supply of foreign horses proved inadequate and 23 of the best of the Army's cargo vessels had to be converted to animal transports. About 500 horses and mules were embarked in September and 17,000 in October. The shipments could not, however, be started soon enough to prevent a shortage. A horse uses as much ship space as 10 tons of cargo, but in the latter months the need for animals was so great that this sacrifice was made.

In general, it may be said that the Army overseas never had enough means of transportation. It may also be said that they had very large quantities and that they produced remarkable results with the supply they had.

47,000 TELEGRAMS A DAY

In order to operate the transportation of supplies in France, a new system of communication had to be set up; so the Signal Corps strung its wires over nearly every part of France. This is shown in map 6.

The heavy lines indicate telephone and telegraph lines

wholly constructed by Americans or wires strung on French poles. The light lines are wires leased from the French or taken over from the Germans. Trunk lines led from all the principal ports to Paris, to Tours, and to general headquarters (G. H. Q.) back of the American battle areas. The lines running to Coblenz for the army of occupation were taken

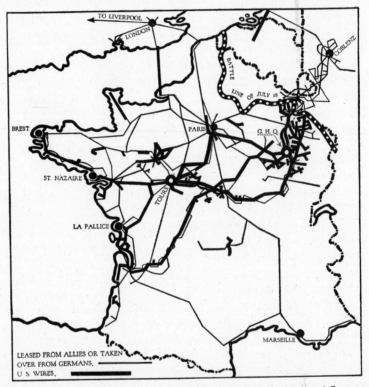

Map 6.—American telephone and telegraph lines in France, England, and Germany.

over from the Germans. At the time of the signing of the armistice the Signal Corps was operating 282 telephone exchanges and 133 complete telegraph stations. The telephone lines numbered 14,956, reaching 8,959 stations. More than 100,000 miles of wire had been strung. The peak load of operation reached was 47,555 telegrams a day, averaging 60 words each.

CONSTRUCTION IN THE UNITED STATES

To build factories and storage warehouses for supplies, as well as housing for troops, 200,000 workmen in the United States were kept continuously occupied for the period of the war. The force of workers on this single activity was larger than the total strength of both southern and northern armies in the Battle of Gettysburg. The types of construction in-

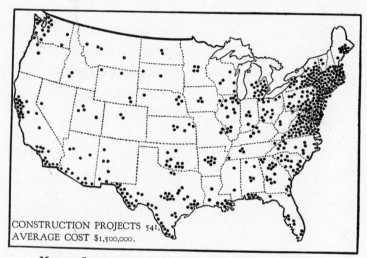

CONSTRUCTION PROJECTS 541,
AVERAGE COST $1,500,000.

Map 7.—Construction projects of the Army in the United States.

cluded cement piers and warehouses, equipment for proving grounds, plants for making powder and explosives, repair shops, power plants, roads, and housing for troops. Building was required in every State of the Union, as shown in map 7. Each dot represents a construction project.

The region of greatest activity was the Northeast, at once the most densely populated section and the center of munitions production.

Housing constructed had a capacity of 1,800,000 men, or more than the entire population of Philadelphia. The operations of the Construction Division constituted what was probably the largest contracting business ever handled in one office.

The total expenditures in this enterprise to November 11,

1918, were, in round numbers, $800,000,000, or about twice the cost of the Panama Canal. The per cent of the total which was allotted to various purposes is shown in diagram 24. The largest single item is the cost of National Army cantonments which was nearly one-quarter of the total.

	Millions of Dollars	Per Cent of Total	
National Army cantonments	199	24	
Ordnance Dept. projects	163	20	
Miscel. camps and cantonments	139	17	
Quartermaster Corps projects	137	16	
National Guard camps	74	9	
Hospitals	23	3	
Regular Army posts	22	3	
Coast Artillery posts	13	2	
Aviation and Signal Corps projects	8	1	
Other construction	40	5	
Total	818		

Diagram 24.—Costs of construction projects in the United States.

Ordnance Department projects, including the building of enormous powder, high-explosive, and loading plants, come second.

The costs of construction were probably higher than they would have been for slower work. The outstanding feature of the accomplishment was its rapidity. Each of the cantonments was completed in substantially 90 days. It was this speed that made it possible to get the draft army under training before the winter of 1917 set in and made it available just in time for the critical action of the summer of 1918.

CONSTRUCTION IN THE A. E. F.

The conduct of the war in France necessitated a construction program comparable in magnitude and number of projects

with that in the United States. Less new building was required for shelter and for the manufacture of munitions, but
more for the development of port and railroad facilities and
for the repair and operation of the complicated equipment
of a modern army.

The storage space constructed in France was more than
nine-tenths as large as the amount built at home. Hospital

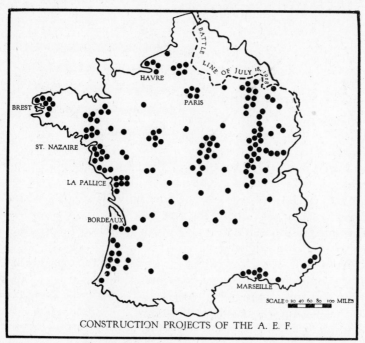

CONSTRUCTION PROJECTS OF THE A. E. F.

Map 8.—Construction projects of the Army in France.

capacity constructed in France was twice the new capacity
at home.

All construction work in France was performed by the
Corps of Engineers under the Services of Supply. The labor
force consisted largely of American soldiers and German
prisoners, although French and English civilians and Chinese
coolies were used wherever available. To economize tonnage
materials were obtained in Europe as far as possible, sometimes at high prices. The Engineer Corps ran its own quar-

ries and its own logging camps and sawmills. Only such materials as could not be obtained abroad—chiefly machinery and steel products—were purchased in the United States.

Up to the signing of the armistice construction projects had been undertaken by the Corps of Engineers to the number of 831. Their distribution over France is shown in map 8, in which every dot represents a place at which one or sometimes several projects were undertaken. The A. E. F. left its trail in the shape of more or less permanent improvements over the greater part of France. The projects cluster most thickly around the ports used by American forces and the American area on the southern end of the battle line.

FOOD AND CLOTHING AT THE FRONT

The real test of the efficiency of the supply service comes when an army engages in battle. Measured by that test the work of feeding, clothing, and equipping the American Army was well done for, in the main, the expeditionary forces received what they needed. Within the limits of this report no account can be given in detail of how fully the supplies received overseas met the needs of the troops. A few typical and fundamentally important items only can be selected. Food and clothing are the most essential.

At no time was there a shortage of food in the expeditionary forces. Soldiers sometimes went hungry in this as in all other wars, but the condition was local and temporary. It occurred because of transportation difficulties during periods of active fighting or rapid movement when the units outran their rolling kitchens. The stocks of food on hand in depots in France were always adequate. This is illustrated in diagram 25. The columns show the stocks of food in depots on the first of each month in terms of how many days they would last the American forces then in France.

During the winter and spring of 1918 the amounts on hand rose steadily. On May 1, about the time when American troops were entering active fighting for the first time, they were well over the 45-day line, which was considered the required reserve during the latter months of the war. For a time efforts were made to build up a 90-day supply in order that the overseas forces might continue to operate for some months, even if the lines of supply across the ocean were cut. As the menace of the submarine became less acute, and as the need of ship tonnage for other supplies became more pressing, the required reserve was cut to 45 days. It will be seen from the diagram that at no time during the period of active operations did the reserve fall below this line.

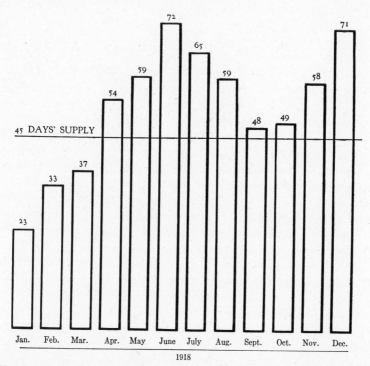

Diagram 25.—Days' supply of Army rations on hand in the American Expeditionary Forces each month.

In the matter of clothing also, the supply services rose to the emergency of combat.

There were periods in the history of many individual units when needed supplies could not be immediately obtained but, as in the case of food, the difficulty was one of local transportation.

The records of the Quartermaster show that during the six

months of hard fighting, from June to November, the enlisted man in the A. E. F. received on the average:

Slicker and overcoat, every 5 months.
Blanket, flannel shirt, and breeches, every 2 months.
Coat, every 79 days.
Shoes and puttees, every 51 days.
Drawers and undershirt, every 34 days.
Woolen socks, every 23 days.

SUMMARY

1. The problems of feeding and clothing the Army were difficult because of the immense quantities involved rather than because of the difficulty of manufacturing the articles needed.

2. Requirements for some kinds of clothing for the Army were more than twice as great as the prewar total American production of the same articles.

3. To secure the articles needed for the Army the Government had to commandeer all the wool and some other staple articles in the United States and control production through all its stages.

4. The distribution of supplies in the expeditionary forces required the creation of an organization called the Services of Supply, to which one-fourth of all the troops who went overseas were assigned.

5. American Engineers built in France 17 new ship berths, 1,000 miles of standard-gauge track, and 538 miles of narrow-gauge track.

6. The Signal Corps strung in France 100,000 miles of telephone and telegraph wire.

7. Prior to the armistice 40,000 trucks were shipped to the forces in France.

8. Construction projects in the United States cost twice as much as the Panama Canal, and construction overseas was on nearly as large a scale.

9. The Army in France always had enough food and clothing.

CHAPTER V

SPRINGFIELDS, ENFIELDS, AND BROWNINGS

RIFLES

DURING the years immediately preceding our entrance into the war there was much discussion within the War Department, as well as in the country at large, of the need for increased military preparedness. Reference to the department reports for 1914, 1915, and 1916 shows that what was then considered as the best military and civilian opinion was agreed that the army that would have to be called into the field in any large emergency was one of 500,000 men.

In these reports attention was called to the fact that while our available resources in trained men, in airplanes, and in machine guns were entirely inadequate, our reserve stocks of rifles and small-arms ammunition were sufficient for even a larger Army than the half million suggested.

On the outbreak of hostilities there were on hand nearly 600,000 Springfield rifles of the model of 1903. This arm is probably the best Infantry rifle in use in any army, and the number on hand was sufficient for the initial equipment of an army of about 1,000,000 men. What no one foresaw was that we should be called upon to equip an army of nearly 4,000,000 men in addition to furnishing rifles for the use of the Navy.

The emergency was met in several different ways. The available Springfields were used to equip the Regular Army and National Guard divisions that were first organized. In addition to these rifles we also had in stock some 200,000 Krag-Jörgensen rifles that had been stored for an emergency and were in sufficiently good condition to be used for training purposes. In addition, efforts were made to speed up the manufacture of new Springfields.

It was soon found, however, that manufacturing difficulties would make it impossible to increase the output of Springfields to much beyond 1,000 per day, which was clearly insufficient. At this juncture decision was reached to undertake the manufacture of an entirely new rifle to meet the deficiency.

Fortunately, there were in this country several plants which were just completing large orders for the Enfield rifle for the British Government. A new rifle—the model 1917—was

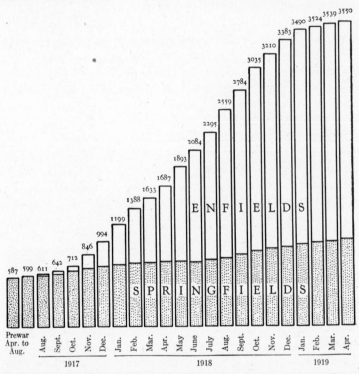

Diagram 26.—Thousands of Springfields and Enfields accepted to the end of each month.

accordingly designed. This rifle resembled the British Enfield sufficiently so that the plants equipped for Enfield production could be rapidly converted to its manufacture, but it was chambered to use the same ammunition as is used in the Springfield and in the machine guns and automatic rifles of American manufacture.

Diagram 26 shows the number of Springfields and Enfields accepted to the end of each month from the beginning of the war up to the end of April, 1919. The figures include the prewar stock of Springfields.

Beginning with slightly less than 600,000 Springfields at the outbreak of the war, the total at the end of the war had increased to nearly 900,000. The Enfields first came into production in August, 1917. After their manufacture had actually begun the output increased rapidly until it totaled at the end of the war, in November, 1918, nearly 2,300,000.

During the entire period the production of spare parts for the Springfield rifles was continued at an increased rate. The first divisions sent to France were equipped with this rifle. It is a fact that about half the rifle ammunition used against the enemy by United States troops was shot from Springfield rifles. The test of battle use has upheld the high reputation of the Springfield, and has demonstrated that the American Enfield is also a weapon of superior quality. The American troops were armed with rifles that were superior in accuracy and rapidity of fire to those used by either their enemies or the Allies.

MACHINE GUNS

The use of machine guns on a large scale is a development of the European war. This is demonstrated by the records of every army. In the case of the American forces the figures are particularly impressive. In 1912 Congress sanctioned the allowance of the War Department of four machine guns per regiment. In 1919, as a result of the experience of the war, the new Army plans provide for an equipment of 336 machine guns per regiment. The second allowance is 84 times as great as the one made seven years earlier.

In the annual report of the Secretary of War for 1916, transmitted in the fall of that year, attention was called to the efforts then being made to place our Army on a satisfactory footing with respect to machine guns. The report says:

Perhaps no invention has more profoundly modified the art of war than the machine gun. In the European War this arm has been brought into very great prominence. * * * When the Congress at the last session appropriated $12,000,000 for the procurement of machine guns, it seemed important, for obvious reasons, to free the air of the various controversies and to set at rest in as final a fashion as possible the conflicting claims of makers and inventors. A board was therefore created. * * * A preliminary report has been made by this board, selecting the Vickers-Maxim type for heavy machine guns, recommending the purchase of a large supply of them, and fixing a date in May at which time exhaustive tests to determine the relative excellence of various types of light machine guns are to be made.

In accordance with these recommendations, 4,000 Vickers machine guns were ordered in December, 1916. By the end of the next year 2,031 of them had been delivered. In further accord with the recommendations of the board, careful tests were held in May, 1917, of various types of heavy machine guns, and also of light machine guns, which have come to be known as automatic rifles. Rapidity of fire, freedom from stoppage and breakage, accuracy, weight, ease of manufacture, and other factors were all carefully examined.

The Vickers gun justified the good opinion previously formed of it, but it was clear that it could not be put on a quantity-production basis because of technical difficulties in manufacture. Fortunately, a new gun well adapted to quantity production was presented for trial. This gun, the heavy Browning, performed satisfactorily in all respects and was adopted as the ultimate standard heavy machine gun. The light Browning, designed by the same expert, was easily in the lead as an automatic rifle, weighing only 15 pounds. The Lewis gun, too heavy for satisfactory use as an automatic rifle and not capable of the long-sustained fire necessary in a heavy gun, was very well suited, with slight modification, for use as a so-called flexible gun on aircraft. A small number (2,500) of these guns were ordered for training purposes for ground use, but the bulk of the possible production of this gun was assigned to aircraft purposes. In addition to the flexible type, airplanes require also a synchronized gun; that is, a gun whose time of firing is so adjusted that the shots pass between the propeller blades. The Vickers gun had been used successfully for this purpose in Europe and the call was insistent for their diversion to this use, both for our own planes and for those of the French. After many trials and adjustments, however, the Marlin gun, a development of the old Colt, was adapted to this purpose, releasing part of the early production of Vickers guns for ground use. A subsequent development was the design of a modified form of the heavy Browning for aircraft use as a synchronized gun.

Production of all the types mentioned was pressed and the advantages of preparedness illustrated. The placing of the order for 4,000 Vickers in 1916 enabled 12 of our early

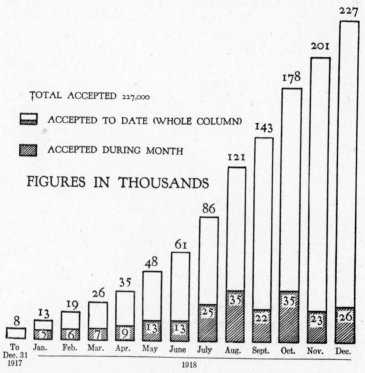

Diagram 27.—Thousands of American machine guns produced to the end of each month.

divisions to receive that weapon as their heavy machine gun. The thorough trial given in May, much earlier than would have been possible except for previous plans, made possible a selection of suitable types for every purpose and the completion of the first light Brownings in February, 1918, and the first heavy Brownings in April of the same year.

The remarkable rise in the rate of production is shown by

months in diagram 27.   The rise was broken only in September, the month of the influenza epidemic.

The earliest needs of our troops in France were met by French Hotchkiss machine guns and Chauchat automatic rifles.   A little later, divisions going over were provided with Vickers heavy guns and Chauchat automatic rifles.   After July 1, divisions embarking were equipped with light and heavy Brownings.   Both Browning guns met with immediate success and with the approval of foreign officers as well as with that of our own.

Although the light and the heavy Browning guns were brought into production in February and April of 1918, they were not used in battle until September.   This was not because of any shortage of supply in the later summer months but because of a deliberate and most significant judgment on the part of Gen. Pershing.   After careful tests of the new weapons had been made in Europe the American commander in chief decided that the two new Brownings were so greatly superior to any machine guns in use by any of the armies on either side that the wisest course would be to wait until several divisions could be equipped with them and a plentiful future supply assured before using them in battle at all.

What he feared was that if the first of the guns to reach the expeditionary forces were used in battle there would always be some chance that one might be captured by the Germans.   If this should happen it was possible that with their quick recognition of the importance of any military improvement and the demonstrated German industrial capacity for quantity production, they might begin the immediate manufacture of German Brownings.   In this event the advantage of the possession of large numbers of greatly improved types of machine guns and automatic rifles would be partly lost to the American forces.

For these reasons the Brownings were not used in combat until they were used in large numbers in the Meuse-Argonne battle.   There they amply justified the faith of the American commander and the Ordnance Department in their superior qualities.

The total number of machine guns of American manufacture

produced to the end of 1918 is shown in Table 4. In addition there were secured from the French and British 5,300 heavy machine guns, of which nearly all were French Hotchkiss guns, and 34,000 French Chauchat automatic rifles.

TABLE 4.—*Machine Guns Produced to the End of 1918.*

Heavy Browning field	56,612
Vickers field	12,125
Other field	6,366
Lewis aircraft	39,200
Browning aircraft	580
Marlin aircraft	38,000
Vickers aircraft	3,714
Light Browning	69,960
Total	226,557

RIFLES AND MACHINE GUNS USED IN FRANCE

When troops embarked for France they carried with them their rifles, and sometimes their machine guns and automatic rifles. If appropriate allowance is made for such troop property in addition to what was shipped in bulk for replacement and reserves, it is found that about 1,775,000 rifles, 29,000 light Brownings, and 27,000 heavy Brownings, and 1,500,-000,000 rounds of rifle and machine-gun ammunition were shipped to France from this country before November 1. These supplies were supplemented by smaller amounts recieved from the French and British, as already mentioned. The actual use of American-made machine guns and automatic rifles in France is summarized in Table 5.

TABLE 5.—*Use of American-made Automatic Arms in France*

	Used at the Front	Total Including Training
Light Browning	4,608	17,664
Heavy Browning	1,168	3,528
Vickers ground gun	2,340	2,860
Lewis aircraft	1,393	3,930
Marlin aircraft	1,220	3,084
Vickers aircraft	1,320	1,625

PISTOLS AND REVOLVERS

From the beginning of the war the call for pistols was insistent. In this case the American Army was fortunate in having in the Browning-Colt a weapon already in production and more effective than the corresponding weapon used by any other army. But while there never was any question as to the quality of the pistol, there was much trouble in securing them in numbers adequate to meet the demands. To help meet the situation a revolver was designed using the same ammunition, and placed in production in October, 1917. As a result the troops in France who were likely to require them for close combat were supplied with one or the other of these weapons so far as possible, but full equipment was never secured.

SMALL-ARMS AMMUNITION

A sufficient supply of small-arms ammunition has always been available to provide for troops in service. The complication due to the use of machine guns and automatic rifles of French caliber has been successfully met. To meet the special needs of the Air Service and of antiaircraft defense, new types of ammunition have been designed and produced, the purposes of which are indicated by their names—armor piercing, tracer, and incendiary. Before the end of the war American production of small arms ammunition amounted to approximately 3,500,000,000 rounds, of which 1,800,000,000 were shipped overseas. In addition, 200,000,000 rounds were secured from the French and British.

ARMS AND THE MEN

Diagram 28 is an attempt to answer in graphic form the question "To what degree did the different elements of our troop program and our small-arms program move forward in company front?" The solid black ribbon represents the number of men in the American Army from month to month. The lower black dotted ribbon represents similarly the strength of the Army in France.

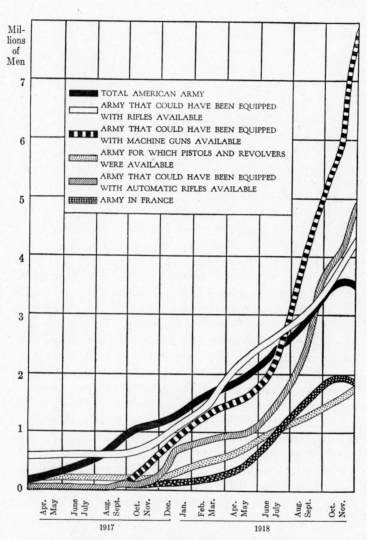

Diagram 28.—Small arms available each month.

On the same scale are drawn four other ribbons indicating widely fluctuating quantities for the different months. The lower white dotted ribbon represents the size of army that could have been equipped, according to the tables of organization, with the number of pistols and revolvers actually on hand each month. The diagram shows that we never had nearly enough of these weapons to equip fully our entire Army, and only during part of the months of the war were there enough for the full equipment of the troops in France even if all the pistols and revolvers had been there and issued.

The ribbon for automatic rifles shows an adequate supply for all troops only in the last two months of the war. That for machine guns shows inadequate supplies up to July and then so enormous a production as to be sufficient before the end of the war for an army of nearly 8,000,000 men. The ribbon for rifles shows relatively close agreement during the entire period. There was an initial surplus, then a deficit for six months, and after that a consistent surplus.

In the cases of automatic rifles, machine guns, and rifles there was always a supply on hand in excess of what would have been required for the equipment of the expeditionary forces alone.

In making the computations for all these comparisons an appropriate allowance has been made in every case for reserves, wastage, and time lost in transit. The curves represent as nearly as it has been possible to make them the actual balance each month between the number of men and the total equipment available. They can not, of course, take into account any shortages that may have resulted in specific localities through failures in distribution.

Only the Springfield and Enfield rifles are included in the computation of available rifles, although hundreds of thousands of Krag-Jörgensen and Russian rifles and some Canadian Ross rifles were used for training purposes.

The rapid rise of the lines representing the men that could have been equipped with machine guns and automatic rifles in the later months is due to the heavy production of Brownings. In fact, this production was one of the striking features of our war effort. It would have resulted, if the fighting had been prolonged, in a greatly increased volume of fire on the part of the American troops.

PREPARING FOR THE CAMPAIGN OF 1919

At this point it is appropriate to comment on the fact that there were many articles of munitions in which American production reached great amounts by the fall of 1918 but which were not used in large quantities at the front because the armistice was signed before big supplies of them reached France. In the main, these munitions were articles of ordnance and aviation, equipment involving such technical difficulties of manufacture that their production could not be improvised or even greatly abbreviated in time.

As the production figures are scrutinized in retrospect, and it is realized that many millions of dollars were spent on army equipment that was never used at the front, it seems fair to question whether prudent foresight could not have avoided some of this expense.

Perhaps the best answer to the question is to be found in the record of a conference that took place in the little French town of Trois Fontaines on October 4, 1918, between Marshal Foch and the American Secretary of War.

In that conference the allied commander in chief made final arrangements with the American Secretary as to the shipment of American troops and munitions in great numbers during the fall and winter preparatory for the campaign of 1919.

This was one day before the first German peace note and 38 days before the end of the war, but Marshal Foch was then calling upon America to make her great shipments of munitions and her supreme contribution of man power for the campaign of the following year.

SUMMARY

1. When war was declared the Army had on hand nearly 600,000 Springfield rifles. Their manufacture was continued, and the American Enfield rifle designed and put into production.

2. The total production of Springfield and Enfield rifles up to the signing of the armistice was over 2,500,000.

3. The use of machine guns on a large scale is a development of the European war. In the American Army the allowance in 1912 was four machine guns per regiment. In 1919 the new Army plans provide for an equipment of 336 guns per regiment, or eighty-four times as many.

4. The entire number of American machine guns produced to the end of 1918 was 227,000.

5. During the war the Browning automatic rifle and the Browning machine gun were developed, put into quantity production, and used in large numbers in the final battles in France.

6. The Browning machine guns are believed to be more effective than the corresponding weapons used in any other army.

7. American production of small arms ammunition amounted to approximately 3,500,000,000 rounds, of which 1,800,-000,000 were shipped overseas.

8. Attention is directed to diagram 28, on page 73, comparing numbers of men under arms each month with numbers for which equipment of pistols, rifles, automatic rifles, and machine guns were available.

Chapter VI

TWO THOUSAND GUNS ON THE FIRING LINE

ARTILLERY

IT was true of light artillery as it was of rifles, that the United States had, when war was declared, a supply on hand sufficient to equip the Army of 500,000 men that proponents of preparedness had agreed might have to take the field in the event of a large emergency. There were 900 pieces of field artillery then available. The gun on hand in largest quantities was the 3-inch fieldpiece, of which we had 544. As 50 of these are required for one division, this was a sufficient number to equip 11 divisions. When the emergency arrived, however, it was far larger than had been foreseen even by those who had been arguing that we needed an army several times as large as the one we then had. The initial plans called for the formation of 42 divisions, which would require 2,100 3-inch fieldpieces almost at once. In addition, these divisions would require for active operations in France a repair shop reserve, a replacement reserve, and a stream of guns in transit which would increase their initial requirements to about 3,200. To keep this army going would require only a production of about 100 guns per month, but to get it going within a reasonable length of time would have required a productive capacity of 300 or 400 guns per month, depending on how soon it would be imperative for the army to be in action. The great difference between the manufacturing output necessary to get an army going quickly, and that required to keep it going after it has been equipped, explains the enormous industrial disadvantage suffered by a nation which enters a war without its stocks of military supplies for initial equipment already on hand.

To meet the situation the decision was made in June, 1917, to allot our own guns to training purposes and to equip our forces in France with artillery conforming to the French and British standard calibers. The arrangement was that we should purchase from the French and British the artillery needed for our first divisions and ship to them in return equivalent amounts of steel, copper, and other raw materials so that they could either manufacture guns for us in their own factories or give us guns out of their stocks and proceed to replace them by new ones made from our materials.

The plans then formulated further provided that, with our initial requirements taken care of in this way, we should at once prepare to manufacture in our own plants artillery of these same calibers for the equipment of later divisions. In general, it may be truly said that these plans were carried through successfully along the lines originally laid down. With no serious exceptions, the guns from British and French sources were secured as needed, but our own plants were slower in producing complete units ready for use than had been hoped and planned.

In our factories the 3-inch guns of improved model which had been ordered in September, 1916, were changed in caliber to use standard French ammunition, and became known as 75 mm. guns, model 1916. The British 18-pounder then being produced in this country was similarly redesigned, and became known as the 75 mm. gun, model 1917. Work was immediately begun also on the plans for the French 75 mm. gun so as to make it possible to produce it in American factories. For this gun, however, it was necessary to develop new manufacturing capacity.

In the case of other calibers of artillery, the same means in general were taken to secure a supply. Material previously on order was adapted to meet the new conditions; capacity actually engaged on production for the French and British was utilized to as great an extent as possible, and foreign plans were adapted to American practice and new plants erected to push production. It was necessary, of course, in all this work not to interfere with American production for the Allies. Of the enormous amount of equipment made necessary by the expansion of the Army from its first strength to the contemplated force of 5,000,000 men, the artillery and artillery ammunition could be improvised with the least facility, for the necessary processes of its manufacture involved irreducible periods of time. In spite of all these handicaps, the record of actual production on United States Army orders only, is 1,642 complete units of artillery before the armistice was signed. The total production of complete units of artil-

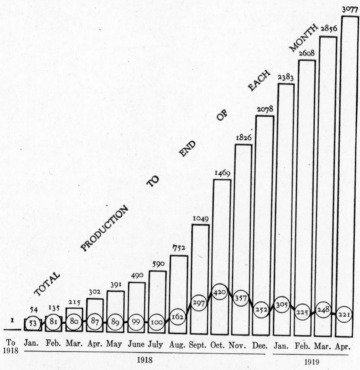

Diagram 29.—Complete units of artillery made in America.

lery in American plants is shown by the figures of diagram 29. The data are exclusive of production for the Navy and for the Allies.

In point of fact the figures showing the number of complete units produced are somewhat unfair to the American record. The difficult problem of planning the production of the different component parts was not satisfactorily solved until about the end of the war. The result was that by the production of a single component, after the armistice was signed, hundreds of units were completed, and the totals for the months after the armistice are as large as those before October, although the work actually done in those months was very much less. These facts are revealed by the monthly

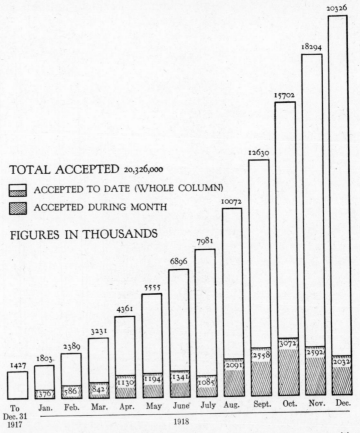

TOTAL ACCEPTED 20,326,000

▨ ACCEPTED TO DATE (WHOLE COLUMN)

▨ ACCEPTED DURING MONTH

FIGURES IN THOUSANDS

Diagram 30.—Thousands of complete rounds of American artillery ammunition produced

and total figures of the diagram. Up to the end of April, 1919, the number of complete artillery units produced in American plants was more than 3,000, or equal to all those purchased abroad from the French and British up to the signing of the armistice.

ARTILLERY AMMUNITION

In the magnitude of the quantities involved the Artillery ammunition program was the biggest of all. Copper, steel, high explosives, and smokeless powder were all required by the hundreds of millions of pounds. As no firms were prepared to manufacture complete rounds, it was necessary for the Ordnance Department to make contracts for each component and to assume the burden of directing the distribution of these components between manufacturers. For the shrapnel it was possible to use the design substantially the same as that which had previously been used in this country, but the high explosive and gas shell proved more troublesome. A large supply of American shell was produced, however, before the signing of the armistice, and shipment to Europe in quantity had begun. The ammunition actually used against the enemy at the front was nearly all of French manufacture, but the approaching supply from America made possible a more free use of the French and British reserves. As shown in diagram 30, our monthly production of artillery ammunition rose to over 2,000,000 complete rounds in August and over 3,000,000 rounds in October if we include United States calibers. By the end of 1918 the number of rounds of complete artillery ammunition produced in American plants was in excess of 20,000,000, as compared with 10,000,000 rounds secured from the French and British.

BRITISH AND AMERICAN ARTILLERY PRODUCTION

One mode of measuring our accomplishments in the way of artillery production is to compare what we succeeded in producing in our own plants in the first 20 months after the declaration of war with what Great Britain produced in the first 20 months after her entry into the war. This comparison is made in diagram 31, which compares for that period of time American and British production of complete units of light and heavy artillery and rounds of light and heavy shells. Antiaircraft artillery (a small item) is not included in either class. Canadian production of machined shell for Great Britain and the United States is included in each case.

In each of the comparisons of diagram 31 the bar in outline represents British production over the first 20 months, and the one in solid black the American output over the first 20 months. The figures show that the British did better than

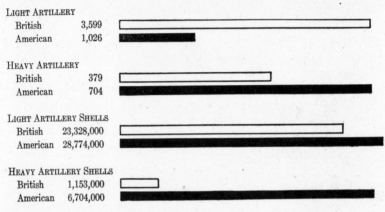

LIGHT ARTILLERY
British   3,599
American   1,026

HEAVY ARTILLERY
British   379
American   704

LIGHT ARTILLERY SHELLS
British   23,328,000
American   28,774,000

HEAVY ARTILLERY SHELLS
British   1,153,000
American   6,704,000

Diagram 31.—British and American production of artillery and ammunition in the first 20 months of war.

we did in the production of light artillery, but that we excelled their record in heavy artillery and in both sorts of shell production.

SMOKELESS POWDER AND HIGH EXPLOSIVES

One of the striking contributions of the United States to the cause of the Allies was the enormous quantity of smokeless powder and high explosives produced. From April 1, 1917, to November 11, 1918, the production of smokeless powder in the United States was 632,000,000 pounds, which was almost exactly equal to the combined production of France and Great Britain. This was not all for our own use. About half the British supply in 1917 was drawn from this country, and in 1918 over a third of the French supply was American made. This large supply was made possible in part by plants erected for the British in this country, but the American Ordnance Department also added new plants. As a result, the estab-lished rate of production in this country by the close of the war was 45 per cent greater than the combined French and British rate.

The American production of high explosives — T.N.T., ammonium nitrate, picric acid, and others—was not established, when we declared war, on so large a scale as that of smokeless powder. It was necessary, therefore, to erect new plants. This need, by the way, was the main reason for the restrictions on the sale of platinum, which is necessary at one point in the process of manufacture. As a result of the efforts that were made, our established rate of production of high explosives at the close of the war was over 40 per cent larger than Great Britain's, and nearly double that of France. The averages for August, September, and October for the three countries were:

Great Britain	30,957,000
France	22,802,000
United States	43,888,000

The result of the high rate of production of both smokeless powder and high explosives was that the artillery ammunition program was never held up for lack of either the powder which hurls the bullet or shell from the gun or the high explosive which makes the shell effective when it reaches its destination.

TOXIC GASES

When the clouds of chlorine suddenly enveloped the British and French lines in the Ypres salient, early in 1915, a new weapon was introduced into the war. That it was a powerful weapon is evidenced by the fact that during the year 1918 from 20 to 30 per cent of all our battle casualties were due to gas.

At the time we entered the war we had had practically no experience in manufacturing toxic gases, and no existing facilities which could be readily converted to such use. At the signing of the armistice, we were equipped to produce gas at a more rapid rate than France, England, or Germany.

In the early days of our participation in the war it was hoped that concerns engaged in chemical manufacture could be put into this new field. There were many valid objections, however, to such a plan. Many of these concerns were already crowded with war work. Entirely new equipment would have to be installed, which, in all likelihood, would be practically worthless at the close of the war. Exhaustive investigation and experimentation would mean delay in securing quantity production. The element of danger would mean diffi-

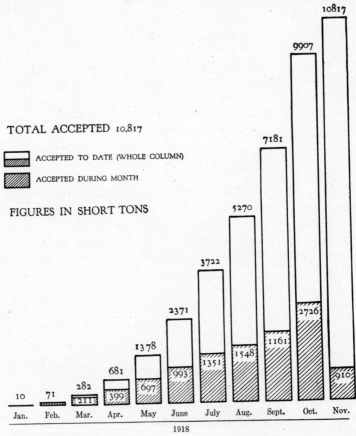

Diagram 32.—Tons of toxic gases manufactured each month.

culty in securing and retaining adequate labor forces. For these reasons the Government found it necessary to build its own chemical plants and to finance certain private firms. The majority of these producing plants, together with plants for filling shells with gas, were built on a tract of land in the Aberdeen Proving Ground, Md., which came to be known as the Edgewood Arsenal. The auxiliary plants were also known as Edgewood Arsenal. The columns of diagram 32 show the number of short tons of toxic gases produced in American plants each month. The increase in production was rapid and steady during 1918 and, before the armistice, more than 10,000 tons had been manufactured.

Production of gas and the capacity for filling were at all times well ahead of the supply of shell containers to be filled. In June, 1918, considerable quantities of mustard gas, chlorpicrin, and phosgene were shipped overseas for filling gas shells produced by the French. By the end of July no more French shells were available for this purpose and the surplus gas was sold to the French and British.

TRACTORS AND TANKS

An innovation in this war, development of which in the future promises to be even more important, was the increased use of motor transportation. As applied to the artillery, this meant the use of caterpillar tractors to haul the big guns, especially over rough ground. When we entered the war no suitable designs existed for caterpillar tractors of size appropriate for the medium heavy artillery. But new 5-ton and 10-ton types were perfected in this country, put into production, and 1,100 shipped overseas before November 1. About 300 larger tractors were also shipped and 350 more secured from the French and British.

The tank was an even more important application of the caterpillar tractor to war uses. In the case of the small 6-ton tanks, the efforts of this country were largely concentrated on improvement of design and on development of large scale production for the 1919 campaign. Up to the time of the armistice 64 had been produced in this country, and the rate at which production was getting under way is shown by the fact that in spite of the armistice the total completed to March 31, 1919, was 799. The burden of active service in France was borne by 227 of these tanks received from the French.

The efforts of this country in the case of heavy 30-ton

tanks were concentrated on a cooperative plan, by which this country was to furnish Liberty motors and the rest of the driving mechanism, and the British the armor plate for 1,500 tanks for the 1919 campaign. It has been estimated that about one-half the work on the American components for this project had been completed before November 11, and the work of assembly of the initial units was well under way. For immediate use in France, this country reecived 64 heavy tanks from the British.

OUR ARTILLERY IN FRANCE

The most important single fact about our artillery in France is that we always had a sufficient supply of light artillery for the combat divisions that were ready for front-line service. This does not mean that when the divisions went into the battle line they always had their artillery with them, for in a number of cases they had not.

The statement does mean, however, that when divisions went into line without their artillery this was not because of lack of guns but rather because it takes much longer to train artillery troops than it does infantry and so, under the pressure of battle needs in the summer and fall of 1918, American divisions were put into line a number of times supported by French and British artillery or without artillery.

When the armistice came in November the American forces not only had a sufficient number of 75's for the 29 combat divisions, but in addition enough over for 12 other divisions.

A careful study of the battle records of all the divisions shows that if all the days in the line of all the combat divisions are added together, the total is 2,234. The records further show the number of days that each division was in line with its own artillery, with British artillery, with French, or without any.

The result of the compilation is to show that in every 100 days that our combat divisions were in line they were supported by their own artillery for 75 days, by British artillery for 5 days, by French for 1½ days, and were without artillery for 18½ days out of the 100. Of these 18½ days, however, 18 days were in quiet sectors and only one-half of one day in active sectors. There are only three records of American divisions being in an active sector without artillery support. The total of these three cases amounts to one-half of 1 per cent, or about 14 hours out of the typical 100 days just analyzed.

The most significant facts about our artillery in France are presented in summary in Table 6, which takes into account only light and heavy field artillery and does not include either the small 37 mm. guns or the trench mortars.

TABLE 6.—*American Artillery in France—Summary.*

Total pieces of artillery received to November 11	3,499
Number of American manufacture	477
American-made pieces used in battle	130
Artillery on firing line	2,251
Rounds of artillery ammunition expended	8,850,000
Rounds of ammunition of American manufacture expended	208,327
Rounds of American-made ammunition expended in battle	8,400

The facts of the table can be summarized in round numbers with approximate accuracy by saying that we had in France 3,500 pieces of artillery, of which nearly 500 were made in America, and we used on the firing line 2,250 pieces, of which over 100 were made in America.

GUNS NEEDED VS. GUNS AVAILABLE

Diagram 33 shows the degree of balance which existed each month throughout the war between the men under arms and the artillery that was available for them. The number of men in the entire American Army is shown by the upper black ribbon, and the number of these who were in France is shown by the lower black-barred ribbon.

The upper white ribbon shows the size of army that could have been fully equipped each month with the pieces of light artillery, consisting of 75 mm. and 3-inch field guns, that were then actually available. If the supply had been fully ample this line would run somewhat above the upper black ribbon, to allow for an adequate reserve and for the retirement of the less satisfactory types of guns. Actually the white ribbon runs below the black one from September, 1917, to Sep-

tember, 1918, and indicates a slight deficiency in training
equipment, which was relieved in the fall of 1918 by large
deliveries of the 1917 model.

In a similar way the lower lined ribbon shows for each month
the size of army that could have been equipped with the proper

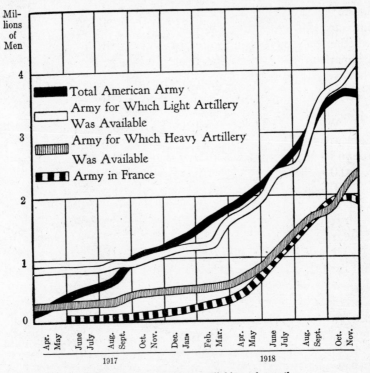

Diagram 33.—Artillery available each month.

number of pieces of heavy artillery of calibers greater than
3 inches. The measure of full equipment is based on the
tables of organization adopted early in the war. These tables
call for more heavy artillery for a given number of men than
the French, British, or Germans actually used, and much more
than had ever been thought advisable before this war.

If all our heavy field artillery had been of types suitable for
use in France, we should have had enough, even on this high
standard, to meet the needs of the expeditionary forces. How-

ever, as we had some types that were considered suitable only for training the shortage indicated by the diagram was a real one. The rapid rise in the latter months of the war shows that the great difficulties of manufacture of this type of material were being overcome toward the end of the war. In considering the facts presented by this diagram it is to be borne in mind that all suitable pieces of artillery are taken into account from the date they were produced or secured whether they were then located in America or in France. The comparison is between the men that we had and the guns that we had each month.

SUMMARY

1. When war was declared the United States had sufficient light artillery to equip an army of 500,000 men, and shortly found itself confronted with the problem of preparing to equip 5,000,000 men.

2. To meet the situation it was decided in June, 1917, to allot our guns to training purposes and to equip our forces in France with artillery conforming to the French and British standard calibers.

3. It was arranged that we should purchase from the French and British the artillery needed for our first divisions and ship them in return equivalent amounts of steel, copper, and other raw materials so that they could either manufacture guns for us in their own factories or give us guns out of their stocks and replace them by new ones made from our materials.

4. Up to the end of April, 1919, the number of complete artillery units produced in American plants was more than 3,000, or equal to all those purchased from the French and British during the war.

5. The number of rounds of complete artillery ammunition produced in American plants was in excess of 20,000,000, as compared with 10,000,000 rounds secured from the French and British.

6. In the first 20 months after the declaration of war by each country the British did better than we did in the production of light artillery, and we excelled them in producing heavy artillery and both light and heavy shells.

7. So far as the Allies were concerned, the European war was in large measure fought with American powder and high explosives.

8. At the end of the war American production of smokeless powder was 45 per cent greater than the French and British production combined.

9. At the end of the war the American production of high explosives was 40 per cent greater than Great Britain's and nearly double that of France.

10. During the war America produced 10,000 tons of gas, much of which was sold to the French and British.

11. Out of every hundred days that our combat divisions were in line in France they were supported by their own artillery for 75 days, by British artillery for 5 days, and by French for 1½ days. Of the remaining 18½ days that they were in line without artillery, 18 days were in quiet sectors, and only one-half of 1 day in each hundred was in active sectors.

12. In round numbers, we had in France 3,500 pieces of artillery, of which nearly 500 were made in America, and we used on the firing line 2,250 pieces, of which over 100 were made in America.

Chapter VII

AIRPLANES, MOTORS, AND BALLOONS

PREWAR EQUIPMENT

WHEN war was declared in April, 1917, the United States had two aviation fields and 55 serviceable airplanes. The National Advisory Committee on Aeronautics, which had been conducting a scientific study of the problems of flight, advised that 51 of these airplanes were obsolete and the other 4 obsolescent.

This judgment was based on the operations in Mexico, which had demonstrated serious defects in the designs of American planes used there. It was well known that improved types had been developed in the European conflict, but the details of their design were carefully guarded and withheld from neutrals.

Immediately following the declaration of war, the Allied Governments, particularly the French, urged the necessity of sending 5,000 American aviators to France during the first year, if superiority in the air were to be insured. This request emphasized the need of speed. The European instructors who came over later to assist in the training work made no pretense that the 5,000 schedule was practicable. The problem was to approximate it as nearly as possible. Public expectation was greatly exaggerated, due to the general ignorance, shared by even the best informed American authorities on aviation, as to the requirements, other than simple flying ability, which this service exacts.

There were three primary requisites for bringing into existence an elementary aviation service. These were training planes, aviators, and service planes. All of them had to be created.

TRAINING

For the task of training, as well as that of securing the necessary planes and motors, there existed in our Army no

91

adequate organization of qualified personnel. Before the war
our air service had been small, struggling, and unpopular.
Aviation was restricted to unmarried officers under 30 years
of age, and offered no assured future as a reward for success.
It had made its greatest appeal to the younger and more daring
types of line officers, and was not an organization on which

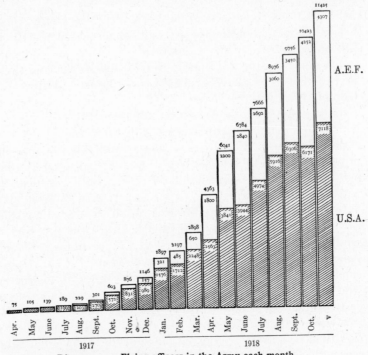

Diagram 34.—Flying officers in the Army each month.

a great industrial expansion could be built, or from which
any large number of qualified instructors could be drawn.

Training for aviation divides itself into three stages—elementary, advanced and final. Elementary training, given to
all candidates alike, includes physical training, hygiene, various
practical and theoretical military subjects, the study of the
structure and mechanism of airplanes and engines, signaling,
observation, ground gunnery, and elementary flying to the
point of doing simple flying alone.

Advanced training consisted in the specialized work necessary to qualify the student as a well-prepared all-around pilot or observer, as the case might be, ready to take up and master quickly any type of machine or any kind of observation or bombing duty which the exigencies of the service might necessitate.

Final training, given in Europe, was a short intensive specialization on the particular type of machine, or the particular military problem to which the pilot or observer was finally assigned.

The initial shortage of instructors and the opening of new fields made it necessary to retain a considerable proportion of the early graduating classes as instructors. At the date of the armistice there were 27 fields in operation, with 1,063 instructors; 8,602 men had been graduated from elementary training, and 4,028 from advanced training. There were then actually in training 6,528 men, of whom 59 per cent were in elementary, and 41 per cent in advanced training schools.

There had been sent to the expeditionary forces more than 5,000 pilots and observers of whom, at the date of armistice, 2,226 were still in training, and 1,238 were on flying duty at the front.

Diagram 34 shows the number of flying officers in the Army from month to month.

The columns show the whole number in service each month and the upper portions the numbers of those who were in service overseas. The total personnel of our Air Service, including flying and nonflying officers, students, and enlisted men, increased from about 1,200 at the outbreak of the war to nearly 200,000 at the close.

TRAINING PLANES AND ENGINES

With 5,000 aviators demanded and only 55 training planes on hand, the production of training planes was the problem of greatest immediate concern. A few planes provided for in the 1917 fiscal appropriation were on order. Other orders were rapidly placed. Deliveries of primary training planes were begun in June, 1917. To the date of the armistice over

5,300 had been produced, including 1,600 of a type which was abandoned on account of unsatisfactory engines.

Advanced training planes reached quantity production early in 1918; up to the armistice about 2,500 were delivered. Approximately the same number were purchased overseas for training the units with the expeditionary force. Diagram 35 shows the production of training planes and engines by months.

European experience had demonstrated that the maintenance of a squadron, whether in training or in service, requires more engines than planes for replacements. Pending the results of American experience, British figures, requiring an average production of two engines per plane, were adopted as standard for American computations. Extensive orders were placed for two types of elementary and three types of advanced training engines.

The upper line in the diagram shows that quantity production of training engines was reached in 1917, and that by the end of November, 1918, a total of nearly 18,000 training engines and more than 9,500 training planes had been delivered. Of the engines, all but 1,346 were built in the United States; and of the 9,500 training planes, more than 8,000 were of American manufacture.

SERVICE PLANES

As soon as war was declared it became possible for American officers and engineers to learn the secrets of the great improvements that had been developed during the war in the design of airplanes used in battle service. A commission was immediately sent abroad to select types of foreign service planes for production in the United States.

A controlling factor in their selections was the necessity of redesigning the models so as to take American-made motors, as foreign engine production was insufficient to meet even the needs of the Allies.

Because of this and because of the rapidity with which the designs of the smaller planes were changing, the best allied authorities urged the concentration of American production on the more stable observation and bombing machines, leaving the production of pursuit planes to the European factories, which were in closer contact with the front.   In the case of any plane selected only an estimate could be made as to its probable adaptability to a new type of motor, this engineering risk being less in the more conservative types of design.   This

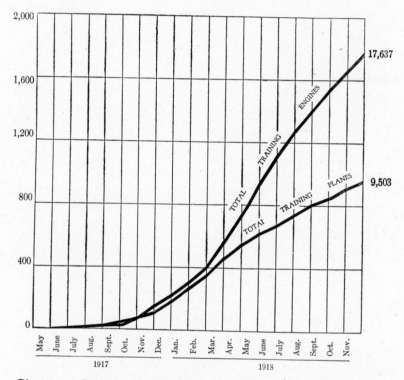

Diagram 35.—Production of training planes and engines to the end of each month.

consideration, together with the imperative need for quick large-scale production, led to the selection of four types for this experiment: The De Havilland–4 (British) observation and day-bombing machine, the Handley-Page (British) night bomber, the Caproni (Italian) night bomber, and the Bristol (British) two-seat fighter.   This selection was approved by the French and British authorities.

The redesigned De Havilland–4 proved to be a good, all-round plane of rather poor visibility, with a tank design which increased the danger in case of a crash, but with these defects more than compensated by unusually good maneuvering ability, and great speed. The De Havillands were acknowledged to be the fastest observation and bombing planes on the western

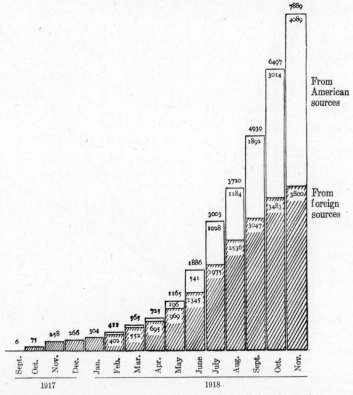

Diagram 36.—Production of service planes to the end of each month.

front. At the time of the armistice this plane was being produced at a rate of over 1,100 per month. A total of 3,227 had been completed, 1,885 had been shipped to France, and 667 to the zone of the advance. The Handley-Page was re-designed to take two high-powered American motors, passed its tests, and on the date of the armistice, parts for 100 had been shipped abroad for assembly.

Delay in the receipt of plans for the Caproni greatly retarded the redesign of this machine. Successful tests of the new model were, however, completed previous to the armistice. The Bristol fighter was a failure. The changes necessary to accommodate the American engine so increased the total weight as to render the machine unsafe.

Diagram 36 shows the production of service planes from American and foreign sources. The total at the end of November, 1918, was nearly 7,900, of which nearly 4,100 were of American manufacture, and remaining 3,800 were of foreign manufacture. In other words, of every 100 battle planes which we received up to the end of November, 1918, 52 were of American manufacture and 48 were made in foreign factories.

Two new models—the Le Pere two-seat fighter, and the Martin bomber—were designed around the standard American motor, and in tests prior to the armistice each showed a performance superior to that of any known machine of its class. Neither, however, was completed in time for use in actual service.

SERVICE ENGINES

The rapid development of the heavier types of airplane, together with the pressing need for large scale production, made necessary the development of a high-powered motor adaptable to American methods of standardized quantity production. This need was met in the Liberty 12-cylinder motor which was America's chief contribution to aviation. After this standardized motor had passed the experimental stage production increased with rapidity, the October output being over 3,850. The total production of Liberty engines to the date of the armistice was 13,574. Of this production 4,435 were shipped overseas to the expeditionary forces and 1,025 were delivered to the British, French, and Italian air services.

Other types of service engines, including the Hispano-Suiza 300 horsepower, the Bugatti, and the Liberty 8-cylinder, were under development when hostilities ceased. The Hispano-Suiza 180 horsepower had reached quantity production; 469 of this type were produced, of which about one-half were shipped overseas for use in foreign-built pursuit planes.

The columns of diagram 37 indicate the total number of service engines produced for the Army to the end of each

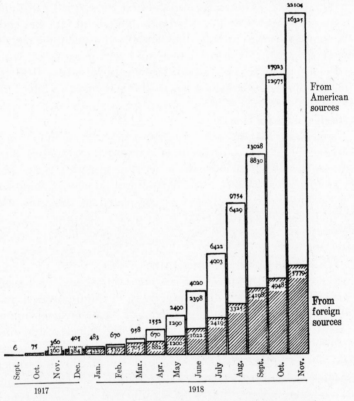

Diagram 37.—Production of service engines to the end of each month.

month, and show how many of them came from American factories and how many from foreign ones.

Up to the end of November, 1918, the total number of service engines secured was in excess of 22,000. Of this number more than 16,000, or 73 per cent, were from American sources and less than 6,000 from foreign sources.

RAW MATERIALS

The American and allied airplane programs called for quantities of certain raw materials, which threatened to exhaust the supply. This was true of spruce and fir, lubricating oils, linen, "dopes," and mahogany.

In order to meet the spruce and fir shortage labor battalions were organized and placed in the forests of the west coast, loyal organizations of civilian labor were fostered, new kiln processes were developed which seasoned the lumber rapidly, without loss of strength and resiliency. These methods solved the problem. Approximately 174,000,000 feet of spruce and fir were delivered, of which more than two-thirds went to the Allies.

Castor oil was at first the only satisfactory lubricant for airplane motors. The limited supply was far short of the prospective demand, but the situation was met by planting a large acreage of castor beans and the development of a mineral oil substitute.

To meet an acute shortage of linen for the wings of planes a fabric of long fiber cotton was developed which proved superior to linen.

The standard "dope" used by the Allies to cover the wings of their planes, making them air and water tight, was limited in supply and highly inflammable. A substitute dope, far less inflammable and of more plentiful basic materials, was produced.

Mahogany for propellers was partially replaced by walnut, oak, cherry, and ash, and by improved seasoning processes excellent results were secured.

ACCESSORIES

Few facilities and little experience existed at the beginning of the war for the development of many of the delicate instruments and intricate mechanisms required in the equipment of service planes. Intensive research brought some notable results, of which several deserve especial mention. These are:

The oxygen mask, equipped with telephone connections which enabled the flyer to endure the rarified air at any altitude which his plane could reach without losing speaking contact with his companions.

The military parachute, which was developed to unprecedented safety. This was used principally for escape from burning balloons, and was improved so that it would bring down safely the entire balloon basket with its load. During the entire war there was not an American casualty due to parachute failure.

The electric-heated clothing for aviators on high altitude work. The electric suit, developed in the latter months of the war and used at the front, was lined with insulated coils through which current was driven by means of a small dynamo actuated by a miniature propeller driven by the rush of the plane through the air.

Long-focus, light filtration cameras by which good photographs could be taken through haze from altitudes of 3 miles or more. Primary credit for this belongs to Europe, but America improved the mechanism and standardized the design for quantity production.

The wireless telephone, by which the aviator is enabled to converse easily with other planes and with ground stations. This development came too late to be of any substantial use at the front, but its value for peace as well as for any future war is obvious.

BALLOONS

Diagram 38 shows the total number of observation balloons manufactured and the number that were shipped overseas.

In no field did American manufacturing capacity achieve a greater relative success. Before the armistice we had produced 642 observation balloons and had received 20 from the French. Forty-three of our balloons had been destroyed and 35 given to the French and British.

This left us with 574 balloons at the end of the war. On the same date the Belgian Army had 6, the British 43, the French 72, and the Germans 170 on the western front. These figures mean that at the end of the war we had nearly twice as many observation balloons as the enemy and the Allies combined had at the front.

FORTY-FIVE SQUADRONS AT THE FRONT

The American pilots of the Lafayette Escadrille were transferred from the French to the American service December 26, 1917, flying as civilians until formally commissioned in late January, 1918.   They were then attached to and served with the French Fourth Army, operating over Rheims.

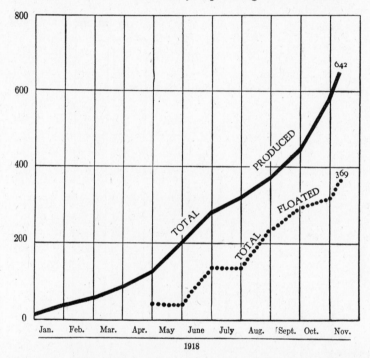

Diagram 38.—Observation balloons produced and shipped overseas each month.

In addition to the purely American operations, two full squadrons were attached to the British Royal Air Force in March and June, respectively, of 1918, remaining with the British throughout the war, and participated in the following engagements: The Picardy drive, Ypres, Noyon-Montdidier, Viellers, Bray-Rosieres-Roye, Arras, Bapaume, Canal du Nord, and Cambrai.

The strictly American aviation operations started in the

middle of March, 1918, with the patrolling of the front from
Villeneuve-les-Vertus by an American pursuit squadron using
planes of the French-built Nieuport-28 type. These operations were in the nature of a tryout of the American trained
aviators, and their complete success was followed by an immediate increase of the aerial forces at the front, with en-

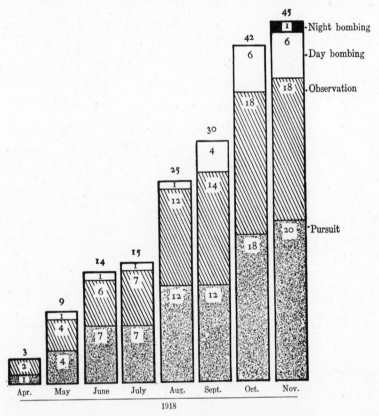

Diagram 39.—American air squadrons in action each month.

largement of their duties and field of action. By the middle
of May squadrons of all types—pursuit, observation, and
bombing—as well as balloon companies were in operation
over a wide front. These squadrons were equipped with the
best available types of British- and French-built service planes.

The rapid increase in American air forces is shown in diagram 39. The height of the columns shows the number of squadrons in action each month. The squadrons were of four types: Observation squadrons, whose business was to make observations, take photographs, and direct artillery fire;

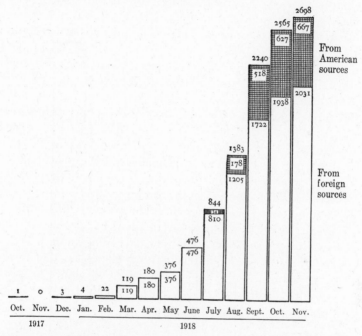

Diagram 40.—Service planes sent to zone of advance by end of each month.

pursuit squadrons, using light fighting planes to protect the observation planes at their work, to drive the enemy from the air, or to "strafe" marching columns by machine-gun fire; the day bombers, whose work was the dropping of bombs on railways or roads; and the night bombers, carrying heavier bomb loads for the destruction of strategic enemy works.

In April the American forces just going into active sectors had three squadrons, two for observation and one for pursuit. Their strength totaled 35 planes. In May, as the diagram shows, the squadrons were increased to nine. The most rapid growth occurred after July, when American De Havilland planes were becoming available in quantity for observation and day bombing service, and by November the number of squadrons increased to 45, with a total of 740 planes in action.

The equipment of American squadrons was in the early months entirely of French and British manufacture. American De Havilland-4 planes were first used at the front on August 7, and the number in service increased rapidly from that time on.

The total number of service planes that had been sent to the zone of advance by the end of each month for the use of American airmen with our armies is shown in diagram 40. The upper portion of the columns represents planes of American make, and the lower portion planes of foreign make. Of the total 2,698 planes sent to the zone of advance, 667, or one-quarter, were of American make and the proportion was rapidly increasing at the time of the signing of the armistice.

Of the 2,031 planes from foreign sources sent forward about nine-tenths were French. The planes sent to the zone of advance were approximately one-half of the service planes received by the A. E. F., the other half being in back areas.

The rapid rate of destruction of planes at the front is illustrated by the fact that out of the 2,698 planes dispatched to the zone of advance about 1,100 remained at the time of the signing of the armistice.

IMPORTANT OPERATIONS

Three major operations, marking the critical points in American participation in the war, also furnish a comparison indicating the growth of American air forces in action. These are: The Second Battle of the Marne, St. Mihiel, and the Meuse-Argonne.

CHATEAU-THIERRY—JULY

On the Chateau-Thierry-Soissons front the Germans had at the start a pronounced superiority in the air. The American Air Service succeeded, however, in establishing the lines of contact with enemy airmen from 3 to 10 miles within the enemy's lines, photographed the entire front and the terrain deep behind the lines, and played an important part in putting German air forces on the defensive. The German concentration for the attack of July 15 was reported in detail and the location of the German reserves established, while the secrecy of the allied mobilization for the counterattack was maintained and the Germans surprised. The American force employed consisted of four pursuit squadrons, three observation squadrons and three balloon companies.

ST. MIHIEL—SEPTEMBER

In capturing the St. Mihiel salient the American first army was aided and protected by the largest concentration of air force ever made, of which approximately one-third were American and the other two-thirds were French, British, and Italian squadrons operating under American command. Throughout this operation the German back areas were kept under bombardment day and night; their reserves and ammunition dumps were located for the American long-range artillery; propaganda designed to disaffect enemy personnel was dropped; record was made by photograph of every movement of the enemy's lines and reserves, such information being frequently delivered to headquarters in finished photographs within half an hour of its occurrence; and fast pursuit planes armed with machine guns flew low over the German lines, firing directly into his infantry.

Day bombers and corps and artillery observers were forced to fly low on account of the fog which hampered all the day operations, greatly reduced the visibility, and made liaison especially difficult. This accounts for the fact that some trouble was experienced by the Infantry with German "strafing" planes.

The American air force employed consisted of 12 pursuit squadrons, 11 observation squadrons, 3 bombing squadrons, and 14 balloon companies. This large force performed an amount of flying approximately three times as great as was done during the Chateau-Thierry operations. Diagram 41 shows the number of hours spent in the air each week by American service planes at the front. During the last two

weeks of July the flying time was more than 1,000 hours per
week. The week of the St. Mihiel offensive it rose to nearly
4,000 hours.

MEUSE-ARGONNE—SEPTEMBER TO NOVEMBER

Because the Meuse-Argonne engagement covered a wider
front and a more extended period of time, against an enemy

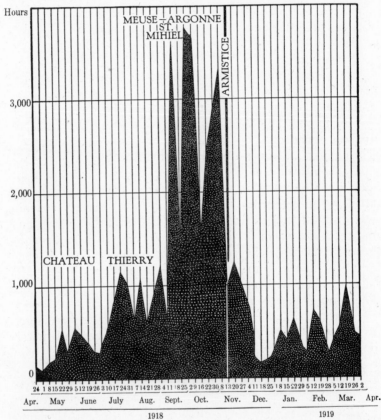

Diagram 41.—**Hours spent in the air each week by American service planes at
the front.**

who had improved his distribution of air force along the
entire southern section of the front, no such heavy instan-
taneous concentration of planes as was made at St. Mihiel was
possible. In this operation, moreover, less assistance was ren-

dered by French and British flyers. The American force used during the engagement was considerably larger than at St. Mihiel.

AIRPLANES

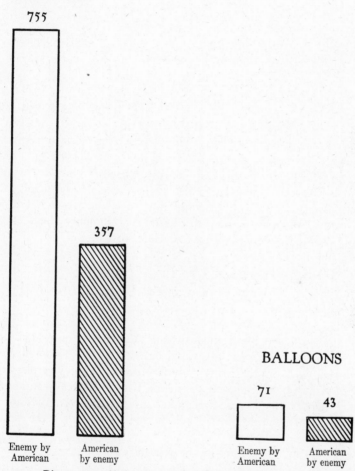

Diagram 42.—Airplanes and balloons brought down in action.

During the six weeks' struggle, the losses were heavy, but replacements were brought forward so rapidly that at the last stage of the action the available American strength was greater than at the start. As shown by diagram 41, American air activities continued during the Argonne fighting on the same scale as during the St. Mihiel offensive.

STRENGTH AT ARMISTICE

At the signing of the armistice, there were on the front 20 pursuit squadrons, 18 observation squadrons, and 7 squadrons of bombers; with 1,238 flying officers and 740 service planes. There were also 23 balloon companies.

THE TEST OF BATTLE

The final test of the American Air Service is the test of battle. The final record is the record of the results of combat. Casualty figures are an important part of the record. American aviators brought down in the course of their few months of active service 755 enemy planes. Our losses in combat were 357 planes. This is illustrated in diagram 42. The record of our balloon companies shows a somewhat less favorable comparison between our own and enemy losses, the figures being 43 American and 71 German balloons destroyed.

SUMMARY

1. On the declaration of war the United States had 55 training airplanes, of which 51 were classified as obsolete and the other 4 as obsolescent.

2. When we entered the war the Allies made the designs of their planes available to us and before the end of hostilities furnished us from their own manufacture 3,800 service planes.

3. Aviation training schools in the United States graduated 8,602 men from elementary courses and 4,028 from advanced courses. More than 5,000 pilots and observers were sent overseas.

4. The total personnel of the Air Service, officers, students, and enlisted men, increased from 1,200 at the outbreak of the war to nearly 200,000 at its close.

5. There were produced in the United States to November 30, 1918, more than 8,000 training planes and more than 16,000 training engines.

6. The De Havilland—4 observation and day bombing plane

was the only plane the United States put into quantity production. Before the signing of the armistice 3,227 had been completed and 1,885 shipped overseas. The plane was successfully used at the front for three months.

7. The production of the 12-cylinder Liberty engine was America's chief contribution to aviation. Before the armistice 13,574 had been completed, 4,435 shipped to the expeditionary forces, and 1,025 delivered to the Allies.

8. The first flyers in action wearing the American uniform were members of the Lafayette Escadrille, who were transferred to the American service in December, 1917.

9. The American air force at the front grew from 3 squadrons in April to 45 in November, 1918. On November 11 the 45 squadrons had an equipment of 740 planes.

10. Of 2,698 planes sent to the zone of the advance for American aviators 667, or nearly one-fourth, were of American manufacture.

11. American air squadrons played important rôles in the battles of Chateau-Thierry, St. Mihiel, and the Meuse-Argonne. They brought down in combat 755 enemy planes, while their own losses of planes numbered only 357.

CHAPTER VIII

TWO HUNDRED DAYS OF BATTLE

TWO OUT OF THREE

TWO out of every three American soldiers who reached France took part in battle. The number who reached France was 2,084,000, and of these 1,390,000 saw active service in the front line.

American combat forces were organized into divisions, which, as has been noted, consisted of some 28,000 officers and men. These divisions were the largest on the western front, since the British division numbered about 15,000 and those of the French and Germans about 12,000 each. There were sent overseas 42 American divisions and several hundred thousand supplementary artillery and service of supply troops. Diagram 43 shows the numerical designations of the American divisions that were in France each month. The numbers in the columns are the numbers of the divisions in France each month, and in every case the numbers of those arriving during the month are placed at the top of the column, while those designating the divisions already there are shown below.

Of the 42 divisions that reached France 29 took part in active combat service, while the others were used for replacements or were just arriving during the last month of hostilities. The battle record of the United States Army in this war is largely the history of these 29 combat divisions. Seven of them were Regular Army divisions, 11 were organized from the National Guard, and 11 were made up of National Army troops.

American combat divisions were in battle for 200 days, from the 25th of April, 1918, when the first Regular division after long training in quiet sectors, entered an active sector on the Picardy front, until the signing of the armistice. During these 200 days they were engaged in 13 major operations, of which 11 were joint enterprises with the French, British, and Italians, and 2 were distinctly American.

At the time of their greatest activity in the second week

Diagram 43.—**Numerical designations of American divisions in France each month.**

of October all 29 American divisions were in action. They then held 101 miles of front, or 23 per cent of the entire allied battle line. From the middle of August until the end of the war they held, during the greater part of the time, a front longer than that held by the British. Their strength tipped the balance of man power in favor of the Allies, so that from the middle of June, 1918, to the end of the war the allied forces were superior in number to those of the enemy.

The total battle advances of all the American divisions

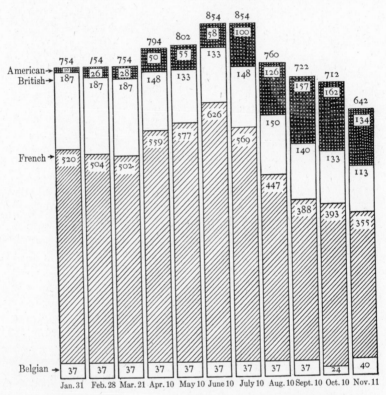

Diagram 44.—Kilometers of front line held by armies of each nation.

amount to 782 kilometers, or 485 miles, an average advance for each division of 17 miles, nearly all of it against desperate enemy resistance. They captured 63,000 prisoners, 1,378 pieces of artillery, 708 trench mortars, and 9,650 machine guns. In June and July they helped to shatter the enemy advance toward Paris and to turn retreat into a triumphant offensive.   At St. Mihiel they pinched off in a day an enemy salient which had been a constant menace to the French line for four years.   In the Argonne and on the Meuse they carried lines which the enemy was determined to hold at any cost, and cut the enemy lines of communication and supply for half the western battle front.

The maps and diagrams in this chapter show in more detail the part American troops played in the allied endeavor, something of the scale and character of their operations, and several comparative records of the 29 combat divisions.

TIPPING THE BALANCE OF POWER

The place American troops took in the allied undertaking is illustrated in diagram 44, which shows in kilometers the length of front line held by the armies of each nation on the allied side during the year 1918.   In January American troops were holding 10 kilometers, or 6¼ miles of front in quiet sectors.   In April their line had lengthened to 50 kilometers. In July this figure was doubled and in September tripled.   The high point was reached in October, with 29 divisions in line, extending over a front of 162 kilometers, or 101 miles, nearly one-quarter of the entire western front.   These changes are shown on the diagram in the upper portions of the columns in solid black with white stipple.

The length of front shown as occupied by the French includes the lines held by the Italian Second Army Corps.   On November 11, 1918, the Italians held 14 kilometers, or 2⅓ per cent of the western front.

The fluctuations in the heights of the columns show how the allied lines gradually lengthened as the five German offensives bellowed them out in big salients and rapidly shortened as the German retreats began.

Another measure of American participation is the effect caused by the rapid arrivals of American troops on the rifle strength of the allied armies.   One of the best indexes of effective man power is the number of riflemen ready for front line service.   For example, there are 12,250 rifles in an American division and smaller numbers in those of other armies.

Diagram 45 shows the rifle strength of the allied and German armies on the western front from April 1 to November 1, 1918.

The broken line shows the German rifle strength at the beginning of each month and the solid line the allied strength. On the 1st of April the Germans had an actual superiority of 324,000 riflemen on the western front. Their strength increased during the next two months but began to drop during June. At the same time the allied strength, with the con-

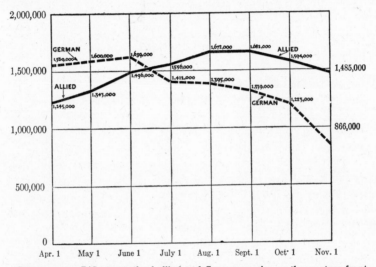

Diagram 45.—Rifle strength of allied and German armies on the western front.

stantly growing American forces, was showing a steady increase, so that the two lines crossed during June. From that time on allied strength was always in the ascendency and since the French and British forces were weaker in October and November than they were in April and May, this growing ascendency of the Allies was due entirely to the Americans. By November 1 the allied rifle strength had a superiority over the German of more than 600,000 rifles.

THIRTEEN BATTLES

American troops saw service on practically every stretch of the western front from British lines in Belgium to inactive sectors in the Vosges.   On October 21, 1917, Americans entered the line in the quiet Toul sector.   From that date to the armistice American units were somewhere in line almost continuously.

It is difficult to cut up the year and 22 days which inter-

TABLE 7.—*Thirteen Major Operations in Which Americans Participated.*

Operation	Approximate Number of Americans Engaged
West front—Campaign of 1917:	
Cambrai, Nov. 20 to Dec. 4	2,500
West front—Campaign of 1918:	
German offensives, Mar. 21 to July 18—	
Somme, Mar. 21 to Apr. 6	2,200
Lys, April 9 to 27	500
Aisne, May 27 to June 5	27,500
Noyon-Montdidier, June 9 to 15	27,000
Champagne-Marne, July 15 to 18	85,000
Allied offensives, July 18 to Nov. 11—	
Aisne-Marne, July 18 to Aug. 6	270,000
Somme, Aug. 8 to Nov. 11	54,000
Oise-Aisne, Aug. 18 to Nov. 11	85,000
Ypres-Lys, Aug. 19 to Nov. 11	108,000
St. Mihiel, Sept. 12 to 16	550,000
Meuse-Argonne, Sept. 20 to Nov. 11	1,200,000
Italian front—Campaign of 1918:	
Vittorio-Veneto, Oct. 24 to Nov. 4	1,200

vened into well-defined battles, for in a sense the entire war on the western front was a single battle.   It is possible, however, to distinguish certain major operations or phases of the greater struggle.   Thirteen such operations have been recognized in which American units were engaged, of which 12 took place on the western front and 1 in Italy.   Battle clasps will be awarded to the officers and men who participated in these engagements.   These battles are named and the number of Americans engaged is shown in Table 7, on this page.

The first major operation in which American troops were engaged was the Cambrai battle at the end of the campaign of 1917.   Scattering medical and engineering detachments, serving with the British, were present during the action but sustained no serious casualties.

GERMAN OFFENSIVES

The campaign of 1918 opened with the Germans in possession of the offensive. In a series of five drives of unprecedented violence the imperial Great General Staff sought to break the allied line and end the war. These five drives took

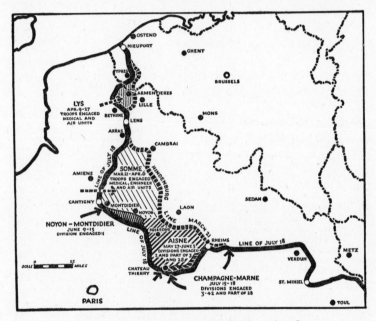

Map 9.—The five great German offensives of 1918.

place in five successive months, beginning in March. Each drive was so timed as to take advantage of the light of the moon for that month. Map 9, on this page, shows the ground won by the Germans in each of the offensives. The arrows indicate the points at which American troops went into the battle, and the small numbers are the numerical designations of the American divisions taking part.

The first drive opened on March 21, on a 50-mile front across the old battlefield of the Somme. In 17 days of fighting the Germans advanced their lines beyond Noyon and Montdidier and were within 12 miles of the important railroad center of Amiens with its great stores of British supplies. In this battle, also known as the Picardy offensive, approximately 2,200 American troops, serving with the British and French, were engaged.

The attack upon Amiens had been but partially checked when the enemy struck again to the north in the Armentieres sector and advanced for 17 miles up the valley of the Lys. A small number of Americans, serving with the British, participated in the Lys defensive.

For their next attack (May 27) the Germans selected the French front along the Chemin des Dames north of the Aisne. The line from Rheims to a little east of Noyon was forced back. Soissons fell, and on May 31 the enemy had reached the Marne Valley, down which he was advancing in the direction of Paris. At this critical moment our Second Division, together with elements of the Third and Twenty-eighth Divisions, was thrown into the line. By blocking the German advance at Chateau-Thierry, they rendered great assistance in stopping perhaps the most dangerous of the German drives. The Second Division not only halted the enemy on its front but also recaptured from him the strong tactical position of Bouresches, Belleau Wood, and Vaux.

The enemy had by his offensives established two salients threatening Paris. He now sought to convert them into one by a fourth terrific blow delivered on a front of 22 miles between Montdidier and Noyon. The reinforced French Army resisted firmly and the attack was halted after an initial advance of about 6 miles. Throughout this operation (June 9–15) the extreme left line of the salient was defended by our First Division. Even before the drive began the division had demonstrated the fighting qualities of our troops by capturing and holding the town of Cantigny (May 28).

There followed a month of comparative quiet, during which the enemy reassembled his forces for his fifth onslaught. On July 15 he attacked simultaneously on both sides of Rheims, the eastern corner of the salient he had created in the Aisne drive. To the east of the city he gained little. On the west he crossed the Marne, but made slight progress. His path was everywhere blocked. In this battle 85,000 American troops were engaged—the Forty-second Division to the extreme east in Champagne, and the Third and Twenty-eighth to the west, near Chateau-Thierry.

ALLIED OFFENSIVES

The turning point of the war had come. The great German offensives had been stopped. The initiative now passed from

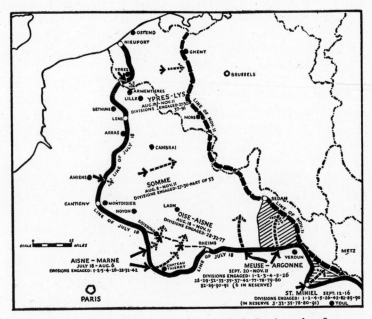

Map 10.—American participation in the allied offensives of 1918.

Ludendorff to Marshal Foch, and a series of allied offensives began, destined to roll back the German armies beyond the French frontier. In this continuous allied offensive there may be distinguished six phases or major operations in which the American Expeditionary Forces took part.

These six operations are shown on map 10, on this page, in which the solid arrows indicate points where American divisions entered the line, and the broken arrows the distances over which they drove forward. In four of the six operations the American troops engaged were acting in support of allied divisions and under the command of the generals of the Allies.

The moment chosen by Marshal Foch for launching the first counteroffensive was July 18, when it was clear that the German Champagne-Marne drive had spent its force. The place chosen was the uncovered west flank of the German salient from the Aisne to the Marne. The First, Second, Third, Fourth, Twenty-sixth, Twenty-eighth, Thirty-second, and Forty-second American Divisions, together with selected French troops, were employed. When the operation was completed (August 6) the salient had been flattened out and the allied line ran from Soissons to Rheims along the Vesle.

Two days later the British struck at the Somme salient, initiating an offensive which, with occasional breathing spells, lasted to the date of the armistice. American participation in this operation was intermittent. From August 8 to 20 elements of the Thirty-third Division, which had been brigaded for training with the Australians, were in the line and took part in the capture of Chipilly Ridge. Later the Twenty-seventh and Thirtieth Divisions, which served throughout with the British, were brought over from the Ypres sector and used in company with Australian troops to break the Hindenburg line at the tunnel of the St. Quentin Canal (Sept. 20–Oct. 20).

In the meantime simultaneous assaults were in progress at other points on the front. On August 18 Gen. Mangin began the Oise-Aisne phase of the great allied offensive. Starting from the Soissons-Rheims line, along which they had come to rest August 6, the French armies advanced by successive stages to the Aisne, to Laon, and on November 11 were close to the frontier. In the first stages of this advance they were assisted by the Twenty-eighth, Thirty-second, and Seventy-seventh American Divisions, but by September 15 all of these were withdrawn for the coming Meuse-Argonne offensive of the American Army.

The day after the opening of the Oise-Aisne offensive the British launched the first of a series of attacks in the Ypres sector which continued with some interruptions to the time of the armistice and may be termed the "Ypres-Lys offensive." Four American divisions at different times participated in this operation. The Twenty-seventh and Thirtieth were engaged in the recapture of Mount Kemmel (August 31 to September 2). The Thirty-seventh and Ninety-first were withdrawn from the Meuse-Argonne battle and dispatched to Belgium, where they took part in the last stages of the Ypres-Lys offensive (Oct. 31 to Nov. 11).

With the organization of the American First Army on August 10, under the personal command of Gen. Pershing, the history of the American Expeditionary Forces entered upon a new stage. The St. Mihiel (Sept. 12–16) and Meuse-Argonne (Sept. 26–Nov. 11) offensives were·major operations planned and executed by American generals and American troops. The ground won in each is shown by the shaded areas in map 10.

In addition to the 12 operations above mentioned, American troops participated in the Battle of Vittorio-Veneto (Oct. 24 to Nov. 4), which ended in the rout of the Austrian Army.

THE BATTLE OF ST. MIHIEL

The first distinctly American offensive was the reduction of the St. Mihiel salient carried through from September 12 to September 15, largely by American troops and wholly under the orders of the American commander in chief. The positions of the various American divisions at the beginning of the offensive and on each succeeding day are shown on map 11 on page 121. The arrows indicate the advance of each division. In the attack the American troops were aided by French colonial troops, who held the portion of the front line shown by broken lines on the left of the map. The Americans were also aided by French and British air squadrons.

The attack began at 5 a.m., after four hours of artillery preparation of great severity, and met with immediate success. Before noon about half the distance between the bases of the salient had been covered and the next morning troops of the First and Twenty-sixth Divisions met at Vigneulles, cutting off the salient within 24 hours from the beginning of the movement.

Two comparisons between this operation and the Battle of Gettysburg emphasize the magnitude of the action. About

550,000 Americans were engaged at St. Mihiel; the Union forces at Gettysburg numbered approximately 100,000. St. Mihiel set a record for concentration of artillery fire by a four-hour artillery preparation, consuming more than 1,000,000 rounds of ammunition. In three days at Gettysburg Union artillery fired 33,000 rounds.

The St. Mihiel offensive cost only about 7,000 casualties,

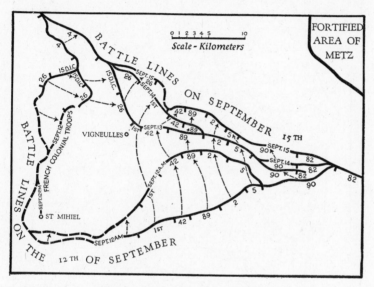

Map 11.—The Battle of St. Mihiel.

less than one-third the Union losses at Gettysburg. There were captured 16,000 prisoners and 443 guns. A dangerous enemy salient was reduced, and American commanders and troops demonstrated their ability to plan and execute a big American operation.

THE BATTLE OF THE MEUSE-ARGONNE

The object of the Meuse-Argonne offensive, said Gen. Pershing in his report of November 20, 1918, was "to draw the best German divisions to our front and to consume them." This sentence expresses better than any long description not only the object but also the outcome of the battle. Every

available American division was thrown against the enemy.
Every available German division was thrown in to meet them.
At the end of 47 days of continuous battle our divisions had
consumed the German divisions.

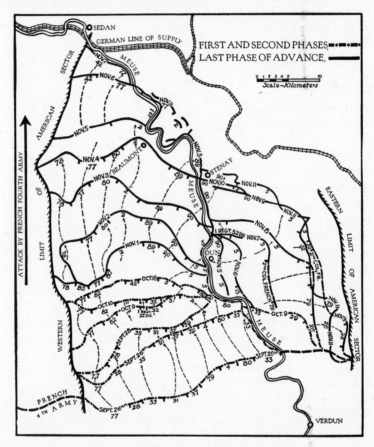

Map 12.—The Battle of the Meuse-Argonne.

The goal of the American attack was the Sedan-Meziéres
railroad, the main line of supply for the German forces on
the major part of the western front. If this line were cut,
a retirement on the whole front would be forced. This retirement would include, moreover, evacuation of the Briey iron

fields, which the Germans had been using to great advantage to supplement their iron supply. The defense of the positions threatened was therefore of such importance as to warrant the most desperate measures for resistance. When the engagement was evidently impending the commander of the German Fifth Army sent word to his forces, calling on them for unyielding resistance and pointing out that defeat in this engagement might mean disaster for the fatherland.

Map 12 shows the progress of the American action, giving the lines held by division on different days. On the first day, the 26th of September, and the next day or two after that, the lines were considerably advanced. Then the resistance became more stubborn. Each side threw in more and more of its man power until there were no more reserves. Many German divisions went into action twice, and not a few three times, until, through losses, they were far under strength. All through the month of October the attrition went on. Foot by foot American troops pushed back the best of the German divisions. On November 1 the last stage of the offensive began. The enemy power began to break. American troops forced their way to the east bank of the Meuse. Toward the north they made even more rapid progress, and in seven days reached the outskirts of Sedan and cut the Sedan-Meziéres railroad, making the German line untenable.

In the meantime (Oct. 2 to 28) our Second and Thirty-sixth Divisions had been sent west to assist the French who were advancing in Champagne beside our drive in the Argonne. The liaison detachment between the two armies was for a time furnished by the Ninety-second Division.

In some ways the Meuse-Argonne offers an interesting resemblance to the Battle of the Wilderness, fought from May 5 to 12, 1864, in the Civil War. Both were fought over a terrain covered with tangled woods and underbrush. The Wilderness was regarded as a long battle, marked by slow progress, against obstinate resistance, with very heavy casualties. Here the similarity ends. The Meuse-Argonne lasted six times as long as the Battle of the Wilderness. Twelve times as many American troops were engaged as were on the Union side. They used in the action ten times as many guns and fired about one hundred times as many rounds of artillery ammunition. The actual weight of the ammunition fired was greater than that used by the Union forces during the entire Civil War. Casualties were perhaps four times as heavy as among the Northern troops in the Battle of the Wilderness.

The Battle of the Meuse-Argonne was beyond compare the greatest ever fought by American troops, and there have been few, if any, greater battles in the history of the world. Some of the more important statistics of the engagement are presented in Table 8.

TABLE 8.—*American Data for the Meuse-Argonne Battle.*

Days of battle 47
American troops engaged 1,200,000
Guns employed in attack 2,417
Rounds of artillery ammunition fired 4,214,000
Airplanes used 840
Tons of explosives dropped by planes on enemy lines......... 100
Tanks used 324
Miles of penetration of enemy line, maximum 34
Square kilometers of territory taken 1,550
Villages and towns liberated 150
Prisoners captured 16,059
Artillery pieces captured 468
Machine guns captured 2,864
Trench mortars captured 177
American casualties 120,000

RECORD OF 29 COMBAT DIVISIONS

Twenty-nine combat divisions achieved the successes and bore the losses of active operations. The story of their achievements can not be told within the limits of this account. There are, however, certain fundamental records which give us a picture of the accomplishments of these divisions. They tell us how long each division served in the front line; how far each advanced against the enemy; how many prisoners each captured; and how heavily each suffered.

The length of service of each division in quiet and in active sectors of the line is shown in diagram 46. The First Division was the first in line and the first to enter an active sector. It reached France in June, 1917, went into line in October and into an active sector in April, 1918. The next three divisions in order of length of service all reached France in 1917.

Three of the 29 divisions were still serving their apprenticeship and had not seen much severe battle service at the time of

Division	Quiet	Active	Total	Quiet Active
1st	127	93	220	
26th	148	45	193	
42nd	125	39	164	
2nd	71	66	137	
77th	47	66	113	
5th	71	32	103	
82nd	70	27	97	
35th	92	5	97	
32nd	60	35	95	
3rd	0	86	86	
89th	55	28	83	
29th	59	23	82	
28th	31	49	80	
90th	42	26	68	
37th	50	11	61	
33rd	32	27	59	
27th	0	57	57	
30th	0	56	56	
92nd	51	2	53	
79th	28	17	45	
4th	7	38	45	
6th	40	0	40	
78th	17	21	38	
7th	31	2	33	
81st	31	0	31	
91st	15	14	29	
88th	28	0	28	
36th	0	23	23	
80th	1	17	18	
Total	1,329	905		

Diagram 46.—Days spent by each division in quiet and active sectors.

the signing of the armistice. They were the Sixth, the Eighty-first, and the Eighty-eighth. It is interesting that of the total of 2,234 days which American divisions spent in line, four-tenths were in active sectors.

Diagram 47 pictures the accomplishments of different divisions by showing the number of kilometers each advanced against the enemy, and in graphic form the percentage of the total kilometers advanced which was carried through by each division. The length of the advance depends in each case on the length of service of the division, the duty assigned to it (whether offensive or defensive), the nature of the terrain to be covered, the strength and effectiveness of opposing

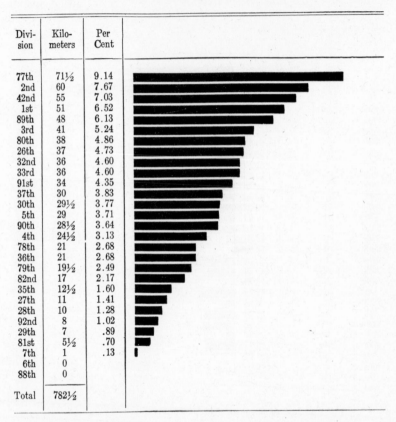

Division	Kilometers	Per Cent
77th	71½	9.14
2nd	60	7.67
42nd	55	7.03
1st	51	6.52
89th	48	6.13
3rd	41	5.24
80th	38	4.86
26th	37	4.73
32nd	36	4.60
33rd	36	4.60
91st	34	4.35
37th	30	3.83
30th	29½	3.77
5th	29	3.71
90th	28½	3.64
4th	24½	3.13
78th	21	2.68
36th	21	2.68
79th	19½	2.49
82nd	17	2.17
35th	12½	1.60
27th	11	1.41
28th	10	1.28
92nd	8	1.02
29th	7	.89
81st	5½	.70
7th	1	.13
6th	0	
88th	0	
Total	782½	

Diagram 47.—Kilometers advanced against the enemy by each division.

enemy forces, artillery support, etc. Hence, conclusions as to the relative efficiency of divisions can not be drawn from these figures alone.

The Seventy-seventh National Army Division, composed largely of troops from New York City, made the greatest advance—a total of 71½ kilometers, or nearly 45 miles. This was more than 9 per cent of the ground gained by the divisions.

If the advances are turned into miles the total advance is 485 miles, and the average gain for each division 17 miles.

Diagram 48 on the number of German prisoners captured is subject to the same qualifications as the preceding diagram. The figures for number of prisoners taken are from the official

Division	Men Captured	Per Cent	
2nd	12,026	19.07	
1st	6,469	10.26	
89th	5,061	8.02	
33rd	3,987	6.32	
30th	3,848	6.10	
26th	3,148	4.99	
4th	2,756	4.37	
91st	2,412	3.82	
27th	2,357	3.74	
5th	2,356	3.74	
3rd	2,240	3.55	
29th	2,187	3.47	
32nd	2,153	3.41	
90th	1,876	2.97	
80th	1,813	2.87	
37th	1,495	2.37	
42nd	1,317	2.09	
79th	1,077	1.71	
28th	921	1.46	
82nd	845	1.34	
35th	781	1.24	
77th	750	1.19	
36th	549	.87	
78th	432	.68	
81st	101	.16	
7th	69	.11	
92nd	38	.06	
6th	12	.02	
88th	3	.00	
Total	63,079		

Diagram 48.—German prisoners captured by each division.

records of the different divisions. The total is somewhat higher than the rolls of American prisoner stockades have shown, but the difference is probably in prisoners turned over to the French or British. The total number of Americans taken prisoner by Germans was 4,480.

The price paid for these achievements was 256,000 battle

casualties; a heavy price when counted in terms of the individuals who gave their lives or suffered from wounds; a small price when compared with the enormous price paid by the nations at whose sides we fought. Diagram 49 gives the roll of honor of the divisions for battle casualties.

Division	Battle Deaths	Wounded	Total	Total Casualties
				Killed Wounded
2nd	4,478	17,752	22,230	
1st	4,411	17,201	21,612	
3rd	3,177	12,940	16,117	
28th	2,551	11,429	13,980	
42nd	2,644	11,275	13,919	
26th	2,135	11,325	13,460	
32nd	2,915	10,477	13,392	
4th	2,611	9,893	12,504	
77th	1,992	8,505	10,497	
27th	1,785	7,201	8,986	
30th	1,629	7,325	8,954	
5th	1,976	6,864	8,840	
82nd	1,298	6,248	7,546	
89th	1,433	5,858	7,291	
35th	1,067	6,216	7,283	
90th	1,392	5,885	7,277	
33rd	989	6,266	7,255	
78th	1,384	5,861	7,245	
79th	1,419	5,331	6,750	
80th	1,132	5,000	6,132	
91st	1,414	4,364	5,778	
37th	977	4,266	5,243	
29th	951	4,268	5,219	
36th	600	1,928	2,528	
7th	296	1,397	1,693	
92nd	176	1,466	1,642	
81st	251	973	1,224	
6th	93	453	546	
88th	29	89	118	
Total	47,205	198,056		
Others	3,075	7,634		
Grand Total	50,280	205,690		

Diagram 49.—Casualties suffered by each division.

The figures given were corrected to June 3 and constitute the final record of the office of the adjutant general of the expeditionary forces. Battle deaths include both killed in action and died of wounds. Under wounded are included many slightly injured.   Artillery brigade losses are included in the figures of the divisions to which they were originally assigned.

Under "others" are grouped the casualties of several different kinds of units.   These are the following:

Others	Killed	Wounded	Total
Troops not in divisions.	1,019	3,496	4,515
Ninety-third Division.	584	2,582	3,166
Replacement and depot divisions.	690	1,556	2,246
Divisional deaths not distributed.	782	. . . .	782
Total.	3,075	7,634	10,709

The troops not in divisions were largely artillery, headquarters, train, and other special services attached to groups of divisions operating together in corps and armies.

The Ninety-third Division is worthy of special comment. It has not been listed among the combat divisions because it was always incomplete as a division.   It was without its artillery and some other units, and was brigaded with the French from the time of its arrival in France in the spring of 1918 until the signing of the armistice.   Its service in the line was fully as long as that of many of the so-called combat divisions. This is indicated by a comparison of its casualties with those in the other divisions.   The division was made up of colored soldiers from National Guard units of various States.

Casualties in replacement and depot divisions are partly accounted for in two ways.   In the first place the artillery of a number of these divisions went into action separately. Secondly, some replacement units joining combat divisions suffered casualties before the papers involved in their transfer had been completed.   Hence they were reported in their original organizations.

Among the 10,709 "other" casualties there is one most interesting and not inconsiderable group, some of the members of which are included in "troops not in divisions," and the rest among the casualties of replacement and depot divisions. These are the men who deserted to the front.   They went

A. W. O. L. (absent without official leave) from their organizations in the zone of supplies or in the training areas, and found their way up to the battle line, where many of them took part in the fighting and some of them were killed or wounded. These cases were so numerous that Gen. Pershing made special arrangements by which trained men who had rendered good service behind the lines, could, as a reward, secure opportunity to go to the front and take part in the fighting.

In the next chapter a more careful analysis is made of American casualties, and the battle and disease deaths in this war are compared with the records of the United States and other nations in previous wars.

SUMMARY

1. Two out of every three American soldiers who reached France took part in battle. The number who reached France was 2,084,000, and of these 1,390,000 saw active service at the front.

2. Of the 42 divisions that reached France 29 took part in active combat service. Seven of them were Regular Army divisions, 11 were organized from the National Guard, and 11 were made up of National Army troops.

3. American divisions were in battle for 200 days and engaged in 13 major operations.

4. From the middle of August until the end of the war the American divisions held during the greater part of the time a front longer than that held by the British.

5. In October the American divisions held 101 miles of line, or 23 per cent of the entire western front.

6. On the 1st of April the Germans had a superiority of 324,000 in rifle strength. Due to American arrivals the allied strength exceeded that of the Germans in June and was more than 600,000 above it in November.

7. In the Battle of St. Mihiel 550,000 Americans were engaged, as compared with about 100,000 on the Northern side in the Battle of Gettysburg. The artillery fired more than 1,000,000 shells in four hours, which is the most intense concentration of artillery fire recorded in history.

8. The Meuse-Argonne Battle lasted for 47 days, during which 1,200,000 American troops were engaged.

9. The American battle losses of the war were 50,000 killed and 206,000 wounded. They are heavy when counted in terms of lives and suffering, but light compared with the enormous price paid by the nations at whose sides we fought.

Chapter IX

HEALTH AND CASUALTIES

THE DEADLIEST WAR

OF every 100 American soldiers and sailors who took part in the war with Germany, 2 were killed or died of disease during the period of hostilities. In the Northern Army during the Civil War the number was about 10. Among the other great nations in this war, between 20 and 25 in each 100 called to the colors were killed or died. To carry the comparison still further, American losses in this war were relatively one-fifth as large as during the Civil War and less than one-tenth as large as in the ranks of the enemy or among the nations associated with us.

TABLE 9.—*Battle Deaths in Armies Engaged in Present War*, 1914-1918.

Russia	1,700,000
Germany	1,600,000
France	1,385,300
Great Britain	900,000
Austria	800,000
Italy	364,000
Turkey	250,000
Serbia and Montenegro	125,000
Belgium	102,000
Roumania	100,000
Bulgaria	100,000
United States	50,300
Greece	7,000
Portugal	2,000
Total	7,485,600

The war was undoubtedly the bloodiest which has ever been fought. One possible competitor might be the Crimean War, in which the casualty rate per 100 men was equally heavy. The British forces in the Crimean War lost 22 of every 100 men, the French 31, the Turkish 27, and the Russian 43. More than four-fifths of the losses were, however, deaths from disease, while in the recent war with Germany disease deaths were inconsiderable as compared with battle deaths. The forces engaged in the Crimean War were, moreover, much smaller.

The total battle deaths in the recent war were greater than

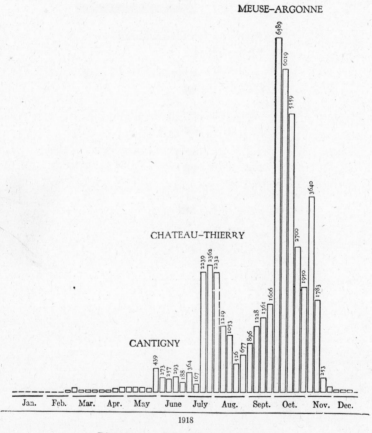

Diagram 50.—Battle deaths each week.

all the deaths in all wars for more than 100 years previous. From 1793 to 1914 total deaths in war may safely be estimated at something under 6,000,000. Battle deaths alone from 1914 to 1918 totaled about 7,500,000. An estimate of the losses of the principal nations engaged is shown in Table 9.

The table shows that Russia had the heaviest losses, in spite of the fact that she withdrew from the war after the fall of 1917. American losses are third from the bottom of the list. German losses were thirty-two times as great as the losses of

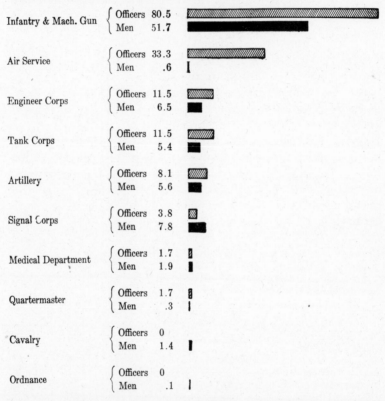

Infantry & Mach. Gun	Officers	80.5
	Men	51.7
Air Service	Officers	33.3
	Men	.6
Engineer Corps	Officers	11.5
	Men	6.5
Tank Corps	Officers	11.5
	Men	5.4
Artillery	Officers	8.1
	Men	5.6
Signal Corps	Officers	3.8
	Men	7.8
Medical Department	Officers	1.7
	Men	1.9
Quartermaster	Officers	1.7
	Men	.3
Cavalry	Officers	0
	Men	1.4
Ordnance	Officers	0
	Men	.1

Diagram 51.—Battle deaths among each thousand officers and men who reached France.

the United States, the French twenty-eight times, and the British eighteen times as large.

That American losses were not more severe is due to the fact that our armies were only in heavy fighting for 200 days. Diagram 50 shows the number of battle deaths occurring each week through 1918. The first rise in the columns, the last part of May, reflects the battle of Cantigny. The second rise, in July, indicates the heavy losses which took place when American divisions were thrown in along the Marne salient at the beginning of the allied offensive. The heaviest losses were in the Meuse-Argonne drive from the last week of September until November 11. The weekly deaths during a part of that period were around the 6,000 mark.

BATTLE DEATHS BY SERVICES

The chances of death are much heavier in the Infantry than in any other branch of the service. Diagram 51 compares the various services in respect to the chances of death in each. The bars show how many battle deaths there were among each 1,000 men in the various services who reached France. Of each 1,000 enlisted men in the Infantry 52 were killed in action or died of wounds. The officers show a higher rate. The most striking difference between the death rates of officers and men appears in the Air Service. Here the casualties among officers are much higher than among men because in our service all aviators are officers.

WOUNDED, PRISONERS, AND MISSING

For every man who was killed in battle, six others were wounded, taken prisoner, or reported missing. The total

TABLE 10.—*Battle Casualties in the American Expeditionary Forces.*

Killed in action	35,560
Died of wounds	14,720
Total dead	50,280
Wounded severely	90,830
Wounded slightly	80,480
Wounded, degree undetermined	34,380
Total wounded	205,690
Missing in action (Aug. 1, 1919).....................	46
Taken prisoner	4,480
Grand total	260,496

battle casualties in the expeditionary forces are shown in Table 10. The number who died of wounds was only 7 per cent as large as the number who were wounded. The hospital records show that about 85 per cent of the men sent to hospitals on account of injuries have been returned to duty. About half the wounded were reported as slightly wounded and many of them would not have been recorded as casualties in previous wars. Except for 373 who died, all the prisoners shown in the table have now been returned.

The number of men reported as missing has been steadily reduced from a total of 78,000 to the figure 46 shown in

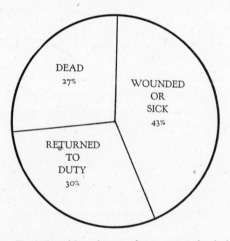

Diagram 52.—Final disposition of cases of men reported missing in action.

the table. This reduction has gone on without clearing any case as dead except on evidence establishing the fact of death. The total number of cases cleared as presumed dead will be about 1,550. The results of clearing up the records of more than 21,000 cases, exclusive of prisoners, which were reported in the casualty cables to this country, are shown in diagram 52. The largest number have been found in hospitals, while a considerable number have returned to duty after being lost from their units.

The work of the Central Records Office of the American Expeditionary Forces in clearing up the cases of men listed as missing has been more successful than that done in any of the other armies or in any previous great war. The missing lists of the other nations still run into the hundreds of thousands. The most recent figures for France and Great Britain are 264,000 and 121,000, respectively.

BATTLE AND DISEASE LOSSES

The total number of lives lost in both Army and Navy from the declaration of war to July 1, 1919, is 125,500. Deaths in the Army, including marines attached to it,. were 115,660. About two-thirds of these deaths occurred overseas. Diagram 53 shows the proportion which occurred in the United States and overseas, and also the proportion which

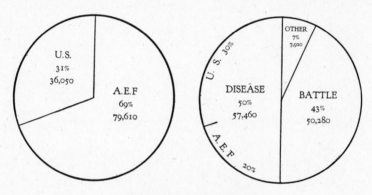

Diagram 53.—Total deaths.

disease deaths bore to battle deaths. Under "Other" are included deaths from accident. There were 768 lost at sea, of whom 381 are included under battle deaths, since their loss was the direct result of submarine activity. Almost exactly half the losses were from disease. If the comparison between disease and battle losses is limited to the expeditionary forces, battle losses appear more than twice as large as deaths from disease.

This is the first war in which the United States has been engaged that showed a lower death rate from disease than from battle. In previous wars insanitary conditions at camps and the ravages of epidemic diseases have resulted in disease deaths far in excess of the number killed on the battle field. The facts are shown in diagram 54. In order to make a fair comparison the figures used are the numbers of deaths each year among each 1,000 troops. Since the time of the Mexican War a steady improvement has been made in the health of troops in war operations. The death rate from disease in the Mexican War was 110 per year in each 1,000 men; in the Civil War this was reduced to 65; and in the Spanish War to 26; while the rate in the expeditionary forces in this war was

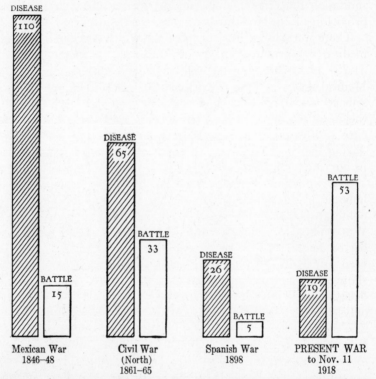

Diagram 54.—Disease and battle deaths. Figures show proportion of deaths per year in each 1,000 men.

19. The battle rate of 53 for the overseas forces is higher than in any previous war. It is higher than in the Civil War because all of the fighting was concentrated in one year, while in the Civil War it stretched over four years. The rates in this war for the total forces under arms both in the United States and France from the beginning of the war to May 1, 1919, were 13 for battle and 15 for disease.

THE CONTROL OF DISEASE

Some of the outstanding causes of the remarkably low disease death rate in the war against Germany are: (1) A highly trained medical personnel, (2) compulsory vaccination of the entire Army against typhoid fever, (3) thorough camp sanitation and control of drinking water, and (4) adequate provision of hospital facilities.

There were at the beginning of the war 2,089 commissioned medical officers, including the Reserves. During the war 31,251 physicians from civil life were commissioned in the Medical Corps. This number included leaders of medical science who have not only made possible the application of the most recent advances of medicine in the prevention and cure of disease, but have themselves made new discoveries during the course of the war, resulting in great saving of life in our own and other armies.

The intestinal diseases such as dysentery, the typhoids, bubonic plague, cholera, and typhus, have ravaged and even obliterated armies in the past. During the Spanish-American War typhoid fever alone caused 85 per cent of the total number of deaths. In the War with Germany these diseases have been practically eliminated as causes of death. Diagram 55 shows the relative proportion of deaths caused by principal diseases. During the entire war up to May 1, 1919, a total of only 2,328 cases of typhoid fever were reported and only 227 deaths from this cause. The result is due to the compulsory vaccination of every man who entered the Army and to excellent sanitary conditions. The other intestinal diseases are similarly of little effect as causes of death or have not occurred at all.

It was to be expected that with careful control exercised, epidemics of these diseases would be avoided in the United States; but in the Expeditionary Forces, where troops were quartered in temporary camps, billeted with civilians, or actively engaged in prolonged battle, the reduction of these diseases is a notable achievement in sanitary control.

It is evident from the diagram that pneumonia has been the greatest cause of death. More than 40,000 died of the disease.

Of these, probably 25,000 resulted from the influenza-pneu-
monia epidemic which swept through every camp and cantonment in this country and caused thousands of deaths in the
expeditionary forces. Up to September 14, 1918, only 9,840
deaths from disease had occurred in the Army, and the death
rate for the period of the war up to that time was only 5 per

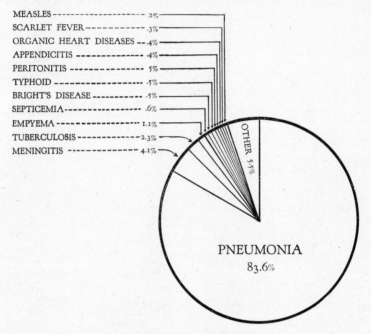

Diagram 55.—Deaths by principal diseases.

year for each 1,000 men. During the eight weeks from
September 14th to the 8th of November, 316,089 cases of
influenza and 53,449 of pneumonia were reported among
troops in this country. The explosive character of the epidemic is shown in diagram 56. The curve in the diagram
shows the weekly death rate for each 1,000 troops in this
country during the year 1918. The curve starts to rise sharply
during the third week in September. It reached its high point
the second week in October, when 4 out of each 1,000 troops
under arms in this country died. The rate subsided at the

end of October, but during the succeeding months remained somewhat higher than it had been previous to the epidemic.

Two other diseases which offered difficult problems for the medical force were measles and spinal meningitis.   Measles

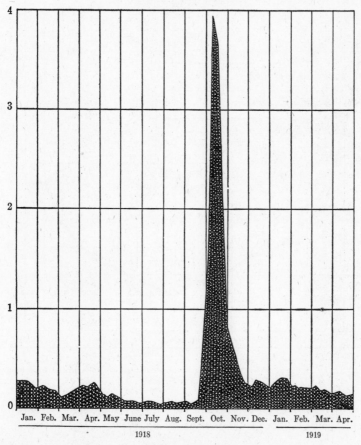

Diagram 56.—Deaths per 1,000 soldiers each week in the United States, showing effect of influenza epidemic.

was prevalent during the first year of the war, and was particularly dangerous as the predecessor of pneumonia.   After vigorous efforts to control it, the number of cases was greatly reduced.   Meningitis has caused nearly 2,000 deaths, ranking next to pneumonia as shown in diagram 55.   Both of these

contagious diseases were largely the result of bringing numbers of men together in the confinement of camps and cantonments where the control of contagion is difficult.   In the case

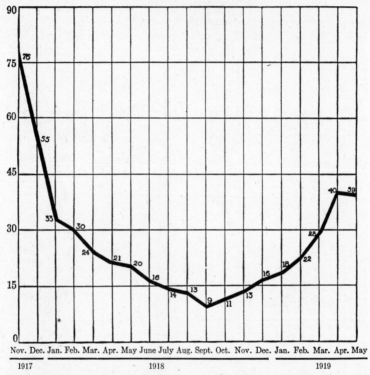

Diagram 57.—Venereal cases in hospitals among each 10,000 men in the American
Expeditionary Forces.

of measles, men from rural communities who had not been
immunized by previous exposure were particularly susceptible.

VENEREAL DISEASE

Great success has also been experienced in the control of the
venereal diseases. A comprehensive program of education,
together with medical prophylaxis, has produced unusual results. While these diseases have continued to be the most
frequent cause of admissions to the sick report, and the greatest source of noneffectiveness in the Army, a large proportion

of the cases were contracted before entering the Army. A special study of all new cases of venereal diseases reported at five large cantonments—Lee, Va.; Dix, N. J.; Upton, N. Y.; Meade, Md., and Pike, Ark.—during the year ended May 21, 1919, shows that of 48,167 cases treated, 96 per cent were contracted before entering the Army and only 4 per cent after.

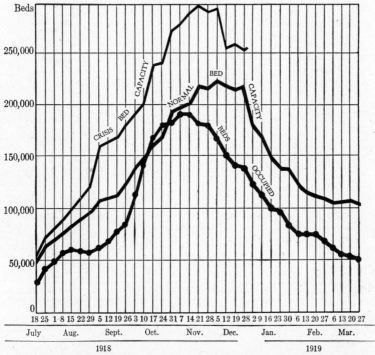

Diagram 58.—Beds available and occupied in the American Expeditionary Forces.

The record for the forces overseas has been particularly noteworthy. There, few fresh recruits entered the Army from civil life, and hence the conditions more accurately show the effects of the Army control exercised.

Up to September, 1918, there was steady reduction of non-effectiveness from venereal diseases in the Army overseas. At the beginning of that month there was less than one venereal patient in hospitals among each 1,000 men. Diagram 57 shows

the number of venereal patients in hospitals at the beginning
of each month per 10,000 troops in the expeditionary forces.
While the relative number of patients has increased since hostilities stopped, the record is still excellent. Regular weekly
inspections, covering about 85 per cent of the total number of
troops overseas, have disclosed during six months since the
armistice less than one new case in each thousand men examined weekly. The actual average was one new case each week
among each 2,630 men examined.

HOSPITALIZATION

At the beginning of the war what was then considered an
extravagant program of hospital construction was entered
upon, with the intent that in no case should the Army lack
facilities for the care of its sick. Table 11 summarizes the
hospital construction in the United States.

TABLE 11.—*Army Hospital Construction in the United States.*

	Number	Normal Bed Capacity
New hospitals..	62	88,468
Leased buildings and converted Army posts......................	39	29,383
Post hospitals remodeled...	48	6,056
Total..	̇49	123,907

The figures are exclusive of very numerous small hospitals
already in Army use. In addition more than 200 hospitals
were put in operation overseas. On December 1, 1918, there
were available in Army hospitals 399,510 beds, or 1 bed to
every 9 men in the Army. Of these, 287,290 were overseas
and 112,220 were in this country.

Diagram 58 shows the number of patients at the end of
each week in the American Expeditionary Forces compared
with the beds available. The hospital capacity was exceeded
in this country only during the influenza epidemic, when it
became necessary to take over barracks for hospital purposes.
The overseas record was even better. Except during two

weeks in October, at the height of the attack on the Hindenburg line, the number of patients did not exceed the normal bed capacity of the hospitals, and at that time there were approximately 60,000 unused emergency beds.

Over 130,000 patients were evacuated from the expeditionary forces to hospitals in this country. They were distributed to hospitals in this country in accordance with a twofold plan permitting the specialization of hospitals for the most efficient treatment of the various kinds of cases and placing the convalescents near their homes.

SUMMARY

1. Of every 100 American soldiers and sailors, who served in the war with Germany, two were killed or died of disease during the period of hostilities.

2. The total battle deaths of all nations in this war were greater than all the deaths in all the wars in the previous 100 years.

3. Russian battle deaths were 34 times as heavy as those of the United States, those of Germany 32 times as great, the French 28 times, and the British 18 times as large.

4. The number of American lives lost was 125,500, of which about 10,000 were in the Navy, and the rest in the Army and the marines attached to it.

5. In the American Army the casualty rate in the Infantry was higher than in any other service, and that for officers was higher than for men.

6. For every man killed in battle, six were wounded.

7. Five out of every six men sent to hospitals on account of wounds were cured and returned to duty.

8. In the expeditionary forces battle losses were twice as large as deaths from disease.

9. In this war the death rate from disease was lower, and the death rate from battle was higher, than in any other previous American war.

10. Inoculation, clean camps, and safe drinking water practically eliminated typhoid fever among our troops in this war.

11. Pneumonia killed more soldiers than were killed in battle. Meningitis was the next most serious disease.

12. Of each 100 cases of venereal disease recorded in the United States, 96 were contracted before entering the Army, and only 4 afterwards.

13. During the entire war available hospital facilities in the American Expeditionary Forces have been in excess of the needs.

CHAPTER X

A MILLION DOLLARS AN HOUR

TOTAL WAR EXPENDITURES

FOR a period of 25 months, from April, 1917, through April, 1919, the war cost the United States considerably more than $1,000,000 an hour. Treasury disbursements during the period reached a total of $23,500,000,000, of which $1,650,-000,000 may be charged to the normal expenses which would have occurred in time of peace. The balance may be counted as the direct money cost of the war to the end of April, 1919, a sum of $21,850,000,000. The figure is 20 times the prewar national debt. It is nearly large enough to pay the entire cost of our Government from 1791 up to the outbreak of the European war. Our expenditure in this war was sufficient to have carried on the Revolutionary War continuously for more than a thousand years at the rate of expenditure which that war actually involved.

In addition to this huge expenditure, loans were advanced to the Allies at the rate of nearly half a million dollars an hour. Congress authorized for this purpose $10,000,000,000, and there was actually paid to various Governments the sum of $8,850,000,0000.

Of the United States Government war costs, the Army was responsible for the expenditure of 64 per cent, or just short of two-thirds of the entire amount. Through April 30, 1919, there had been withdrawn from the Treasury on the Army account $14,244,061,000. If there is deducted from this figure what would be the normal expenditure for a peace-time Army for a similar period there remains a total of $13,930,-000,000 directly chargeable to the war.

The rate of expenditure for the Army and for the entire Government increased rapidly as the war progressed. This

147

is illustrated in diagram 59, which compares the daily rates of expenditure for the first three months of the war, the fiscal year entirely included in the war, and the first 10 months of the following year. The total height of the columns shows the daily rate of expenditure for the whole Government and the shaded portion of the column the rate for the Army.

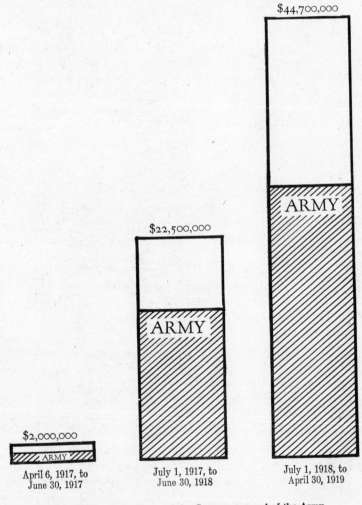

Diagram 59.—Cost per day of the Government and of the Army.

During the first three months war expenditures were at the rate of $2,000,000 per day. During the next year they averaged more than $22,000,000 a day. For the final 10 months of the period the daily total reached the enormous sum of over $44,000,000. The very high daily average in the last period, most of which is in the months after the termination of hostilities, is surprising until we consider that the building of ships for the Emergency Fleet Corporation, the construction and operation of naval vessels, the food, clothing, pay, and land and ocean transportation of the Army have had to go forward at about the same rate as during the war. The great flow of munitions and supplies for the Army and Navy could not, out of regard for the industrial balance of the country, be stopped with too great abruptness. A considerable number of wartime activities and purchases had still to be paid for as well.

ARMY EXPENDITURES

Table 12 shows the amounts expended by each important Army bureau. The Quartermaster Corps, which paid the soldiers and furnished them with food, clothing, equipment, and miscellaneous supplies, spent the most. The Ordnance

TABLE 12.—*Expenditures by Army Bureaus.*

	Expended to April 30, 1919	Per Cent
Quartermaster Corps:		
Pay of the Army, etc............................	$1,831,273,000	12.9
Other Quartermaster Corps appropriations...........	6,242,745,000	43.8
Ordnance Department.............................	4,087,347,000	28.7
Air Service.....................................	859,291,000	6.0
Engineer Corps..................................	638,974,000	4.5
Medical Department..............................	314,544,000	2.2
Signal Corps....................................	128,920,000	.9
Chemical Warfare Service.........................	83,299,000	.6
Provost Marshal General..........................	*24,301,000	.17
Secretary's office and miscellaneous.................	*33,367,000	.23
Total......................................	$14,244,061,000	100.00

*Figures are for Dec. 31, 1918. Expenditures since that date for these purposes have been small compared with other items in table.

Department was next in order, with over $4,000,000,000 for munitions, more than half of its expenditure being for artillery ammunition.

The total of our Army expenditures shown in Table 12 about equals the value of all the gold produced in the whole world from the discovery of America up to the outbreak of the European war. The single item of pay for the Army is larger than the combined salaries of all the public-school principals and teachers in the United States for the five years from 1912 to 1916.

WHERE THE DOLLAR WENT

Diagram 60 shows the relative amount of the Army expenditures spent for different purposes. It does this by dividing the typical dollar into sectors, showing the number of cents of each dollar that went for each purpose.

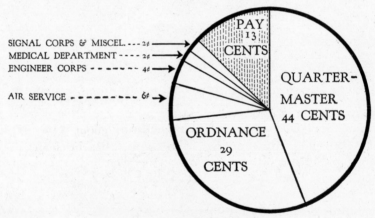

SIGNAL CORPS & MISCEL. ---- 2¢
MEDICAL DEPARTMENT ---- 2¢
ENGINEER CORPS -------- 4¢

AIR SERVICE --------- 6¢

PAY 13 CENTS

QUARTER-MASTER 44 CENTS

ORDNANCE 29 CENTS

Diagram 60.—Where the Army dollar went.

PERMANENT ASSETS

As a result of the war efforts large quantities of munitions, supplies, and equipment have been secured which will be of value for many years to come. The Army now owns some of the finest docks in the world. The 16 National Army cantonments and 3 of the National Guard camps will be retained permanently as training camps. A number of first-class aviation fields and depots and balloon schools will be a permanent asset. We have stocks of most articles of clothing sufficient to last our Army for a number of years. There is a large supply of standardized trucks.

As to rifles and machine guns and their ammunition, light and heavy artillery and ammunition, tanks and tractors, of these we have a supply more than sufficient to equip fully an army of a million men and maintain them in active combat for six months. These munitions are of the best quality and latest design—Springfield and Enfield rifles; Browning machine guns and automatic rifles; field guns and howitzers of tried French design. Articles of miscellaneous equipment are available in like quantity and quality.

Thousands of Liberty motors and service planes are immediately available for any emergency. Engineer, signal, and medical equipment is on hand to the value of millions of dollars.

All these are lasting assets which we have as a result of war expenditures. They give us a most valuable equipment for preparedness in the Military Establishment.

WAR EXPENDITURES OF ALL NATIONS

Table 13 gives the figures showing the war expenditures of all nations up to May, 1919.

The total direct war costs amount to about $186,000,-000,000, and of this sum the enemy countries spent about one-third and those on the allied side about two-thirds. Germany spent more than any other nation, and was closely followed by Great Britain, whose expenditures include those of her colonies. The figure for France is $12,000,000,000 less than that for Great Britain, and our own figure is below that for France. The Austrian expenditure was almost equal to that of the United States. It is noteworthy that the United States spent about one-eighth of the entire cost of the war and something less than one-fifth of the expenditures on the allied side.

SUMMARY

1. The war cost the United States considerably more than $1,000,000 an hour for over two years.

TABLE 13.—*Estimated Total War Expenditures of Principal Nations to April 30, 1919.*

[All figures in billions of dollars and excluding normal expenses and loans to allies.]

Country	Billions of Dollars
Great Britain and Dominions.....................................	38
France..	26
United States...	22
Russia..	18
Italy...	13
Belgium, Roumania, Portugal, Jugo-Slavia......................	5
Japan and Greece...	1
Total allies and United States............................	123
Germany...	39
Austria-Hungary...	21
Turkey and Bulgaria..	3
Total Teutonic allies.....................................	63
Grand total..	186

2. The direct cost was about $22,000,000,000, or nearly enough to pay the entire cost of running the United States Government from 1791 up to the outbreak of the European war.

3. Our expenditures in this war were sufficient to have carried on the Revolutionary War continuously for more than 1,000 years at the rate of expenditure which that war actually involved.

4. In addition to this huge expenditure nearly $10,000,-000,000 have been loaned by the United States to the Allies.

5. The Army expenditures have been over $14,000,000,000, or nearly two-thirds of our total war costs.

6. During the first three months our war expenditures were at the rate of $2,000,000 per day. During the next year they averaged more than $22,000,000 a day. For the final 10 months of the period, from April, 1917, to April, 1919, the daily average was over $44,000,000.

7. Although the Army expenditures are less than two-thirds of our total war costs, they are nearly equal to the value of

all the gold produced in the whole world from the discovery of America up to the outbreak of the European war.

8. The pay of the Army during the war cost more than the combined salaries of all the public-school principals and teachers in the United States for the five years from 1912 to 1916.

9. The total war costs of all nations were about $186,000,-000,000, of which the Allies and the United States spent two-thirds and the enemy one-third.

10. The three nations spending the greatest amounts were Germany, Great Britain, and France, in that order. After them come the United States and Austria-Hungary, with substantially equal expenditures.

11. The United States spent about one-eighth of the entire cost of the war, and something less than one-fifth of the expenditures of the allied side.

SOME INTERNATIONAL COMPARISONS

By Diagrams and Tables

DURATION OF THE WAR

Allied and Associated Nations	War Declared by Central Powers	War Declared Against Central Powers	DURATION OF WAR		
			Years	Months	Days
1. Serbia	July 28, 1914	Aug. 9, 1914	4	3	14
2. Russia*	Aug. 1, 1914	Nov. 3, 1914	3	7	3
3. France	Aug. 3, 1914	Aug. 3, 1914	4	3	8
4. Belgium	Aug. 4, 1914	Apr. 7, 1917	4	3	7
5. Great Britain	Nov. 23, 1914	Aug. 4, 1914	4	3	7
6. Montenegro	Aug. 9, 1914	Aug. 6, 1914	4	3	5
7. Japan	Aug. 27, 1914	Aug. 23, 1914	4	2	19
8. Portugal	Mar. 9, 1916	Nov. 23, 1914	3	11	19
9. Italy		May 23, 1915	3	5	19
10. San Marino		June 6, 1915	3	5	4
11. Roumania †	Aug. 29, 1916	Aug. 27, 1916	1	6	10
12. Greece		Nov. 23, 1916	1	11	18
13. United States		Apr. 6, 1917	1	7	5
14. Panama		Apr. 7, 1917	1	7	4
15. Cuba		Apr. 7, 1917	1	7	4
16. Siam		July 22, 1917	1	3	20
17. Liberia		Aug. 4, 1917	1	3	8
18. China		Aug. 14, 1917	1	2	28
19. Brazil		Oct. 26, 1917	1	..	16
20. Guatemala		Apr. 21, 1918	..	6	21
21. Nicaragua		May 6, 1918	..	6	5
22. Haiti		July 12, 1918	..	3	30
23. Honduras		July 19, 1918	..	3	23

*Treaty Mar. 3, 1918.   †Treaty Mar. 6, 1918.

COSTS OF THE WAR AT A GLANCE

COST IN HUMAN LIFE

Army deaths... 8,000,000
Civilian deaths... 8,000,000
Permanent human wrecks from wounds, etc.................. 6,000,000

    Total human loss (chiefly of vigorous males)...............22,000,000

COST IN PROPERTY DESTROYED

France (factories, farms, public works, etc.)............$10,000,000,000
Belgium (factories, farms, public works, etc.)........... 5,000,000,000
Other surviving countries............................... 13,000,000,000
Russia (losses really incalculable)..................... 20,000,000,000
Ships (chiefly British)................................ 3,500,000,000
Cargoes.. 4,500,000,000

    Total direct property loss...........................$56,000,000,000

COST IN MONEY

Government expenditure by Allies......................$105,000,000,000
Government expenditure by Central Powers........... 65,000,000,000
Increased charitable expenditures....................   2,000,000,000
Loss by bankruptcy of Russia, Turkey, etc............ 30,000,000,000

    Total direct money loss..........................$202,000,000,000

TOTAL FINANCIAL ESTIMATES OF COST

Human life (as based on life insurance figures)......... $70,000,000,000
Direct property destruction.......................... 56,000,000,000
Money loss... 202,000,000,000
Indirect property and money loss (through lack of usual
  peace time products)............................... 150,000,000,000

    Final Total......................................$478,000,000,000

Note: As a basis for valuing this enormous sum of almost half a trillion dollars, take the fact that the total wealth of the United States, the richest country in the world, was valued at $220,000,000,000 in 1916. In other words, if the United States and another country equally wealthy had been engulfed in some vast earthquake, without loss of human life, the financial loss would have scarce equaled that of the War.

HUMAN LIFE COSTS

From the latest official figures supplied by each Government.

TOTAL CASUALTIES OF ARMED FORCES

	Population	Mobilized	Dead	Wounded	Prisoners
BritishEmpire[1]	440,000,000	8,654,280	873,980	2,525,927	279,357
United States	98,800,000	4,165,483	123,547	231,722	4,994
France	39,840,000	7,500,000	1,385,300	3,000,000	446,300
Italy	36,000,000	5,615,000	496,921	949,576	485,458
Belgium	7,645,000	267,000	20,000	60,000	10,000
Serbia	3,094,000	707,343	322,000	28,000	100,000
Montenegro	437,000	50,000	3,000	10,000	7,000
Rumania	7,508,000	750,000	200,000	120,000	80,000
Greece	4,820,000	230,000	15,000	40,000	45,000
Portugal	6,100,000	100,000	4,000	15,000	200
Japan	54,000,000	800,000	300	907	3
Russia	178,379,000	12,000,000	1,700,000	4,950,000	2,500,000
Totals	876,623,000	40,839,106	5,144,048	11,931,132	3,958,312
German Empire	68,166,000	11,000,000	1,718,246	4,350,122	1,073,620
Austria-Hungary	61,039,000	6,500,000	800,000	3,200,000	1,211,000
Turkey	21,274,000	1,600,000	300,000	570,000	130,000
Bulgaria	4,400,000	400,000	201,224	152,399	10,825
Totals	154,879,000	19,500,000	3,019,470	8,272,521	2,425,445
Final Totals	1,031,502,000	60,339,106	8,163,518	20,203,653	6,383,757

[1] Exact figures of losses among the Indian and Negro troops in the British army are unavailable. Their mobilized number was 1,524,197; so their numbers have been here included and their losses estimated proportionally with other British forces.

CIVILIANS SLAIN

Armenians[1]	1,100,000	Rumanians	275,000
Greeks (in Turkey)[1]	900,000	French	40,000
Syrians[1]	150,000	Belgians	30,000
Serbians	650,000	British (by U-boats)	20,620
Poles and Lithuanians	500,000	Neutrals (by U-boats)	7,500

[1] The first three items, which represent the total of official Turkish massacres, were estimated by the Eastern relief commissions in 1920 at almost double these figures.

These form the closest available approximations to the number of civilians massacred, starved or dying from privation as a direct result of the War's ravage. They do not include deaths from privation in uninvaded regions. These were especially heavy in Austria-Hungary and Russia.

FINANCIAL COSTS

From the latest official figures supplied by each Government.

NATIONAL DEBTS[1]

	1913	1918	1920
France	$6,346,000,000	$30,000,000,000	$46,000,000,000
Britain	3,485,000,000	36,391,000,000	39,218,000,000
United States	1,028,000,000	17,005,000,000	24,974,000,000
Italy	2,921,000,000	12,000,000,000	18,102,000,000
Belgium	825,000,000	3,500,000,000	4,000,000,000
Russia	4,537,000,000	25,000,000,000[2]	....
Germany	5,048,000,000	44,341,000,000	53,052,000,000
Austria	2,152,000,000	16,475,000,000	17,668,000,000
Hungary	1,731,000,000	8,513,000,000	9,412,000,000
Bulgaria	135,000,000	800,000,000	2,158,000,000

[1] The debt at the end of 1913 shows the pre-War debt. That of 1918 shows the debt incurred up to the armistice. Hence the difference might be figured as the actual War debt. The increase through 1920, however, more nearly represents the true War debt as the 1920 figures include the first gigantic effort toward restoration and reconstruction after the War.

[2] This is Russia's debt as announced in 1917. After that her leaders repudiated her debts. In other words she became bankrupt, and whatever she had owed became lost to her creditors whether at home or abroad.

NET FINANCIAL LOSSES OF THE ALLIES

	Gross War Cost[1]	Possible Profit[2]	Net Loss
Great Britain	$51,052,634,000	$10,000,000,000	$41,052,634,000
France	54,272,915,000	30,000,000,000	24,272,915,000
United States	34,414,000,000	2,300,000,000	32,114,000,000
Italy	18,680,847,000	6,500,000,000	12,180,847,000
Belgium	8,174,731,000	5,700,000,000	2,474,731,000
Japan	481,818,000	250,000,000	231,818,000

[1] The Gross War Cost here includes increased national debt, abnormal war taxes already collected, funds distributed in war-charities, pension accounts, and direct losses of civilian property.

[2] The Possible Profit figures include German territory acquired, German shipping coal, etc., partly given and partly promised, and future indemnities promised.

FINANCIAL LOSSES OF EASTERN EUROPE

German increased national debt	$48,000,000,000
German territorial losses (estimated)[1]	30,000,000,000
German indemnity to be paid	40,000,000,000
Losses of German people (estimated)	10,000,000,000
German Total	$128,000,000,000

[1] Germany has surrendered all her many colonies, and by direct treaty 25,000 square miles of her European territory. By plebiscite she has already lost, or will probably lose, over 11,000 miles more.

The losses of Russia, Austro-Hungary and the Turkish Empire are beyond estimate, as two, or perhaps all three, of these empires have completely disintegrated. "A dead man loses nothing." The natural resources of these eastern regions remain very nearly as rich as before; but the accumulated property or developed wealth, which formerly amounted to perhaps fifty billion dollars, now probably amounts to scarce a fifth of that amount; and the human energy or labor power of the regions is also tragically depleted.

PROPERTY COSTS

From the latest official figures supplied by each Government.

PROPERTY LOSS ON LAND[1]

France.........	$10,000,000,000	Poland.........	$1,500,000,000
Belgium.......	7,000,000,000	Russia..........	1,250,000,000
Italy...........	2,750,000,000	Rumania........	1,000,000,000
Serbia.........	2,000,000,000	Germany........	1,750,000,000
Britain........	1,750,000,000	Austria-Hungary..	1,000,000,000

Total..........$30,000,000,000

[1] This includes only damage inflicted by the enemy by invasion, air-raids, etc. In Russia and in the subject lands of the Turkish Empire there was also vast damage inflicted by the constituted authorities or by civil war.

MERCHANT SHIPPING LOST

	Tons		Tons
Great Britain........	7,757,000	Neutrals.............	1,990,000
United States........	395,000	Central Powers........	1,965,000
Other Allies.........	2,603,000		

Total.............14,710,000

LOSS BY YEARS

1915 = 1,299,700   1916 = 2,362,800   1917 = 6,202,800   1918 = 2,637,400

U-BOATS SUNK[1]

1915 = 21   1916 = 28   1917 = 67   1918 = 89   Total = 205

[1] These are "confirmed" sinkings. More than twice this number were reported sunk.

WARSHIP LOSSES[1]

	Tons		Tons
British................	550,000	German................	350,000
Other Allies...........	253,000	German Allies..........	65,000
Totals...............	803,000	Total................	415,000

[1] The warships rated at over 15,000 tons each, which were lost in the war, were: by Britain, Queen Mary 27,000, Audacious 24,000, Indefatigable 18,750, Invincible 17,250, King Edward VII 16,350; by Italy, L. da Vinci 22,000; by Germany, Lutzow 28,000, Blucher 15,550.

SHIPPING OF THE WORLD IN TONS

	June, 1914	June, 1919[1]	June, 1920
Great Britain...................	18,892,000	16,345,000	18,111,000
British Dominions..............	1,632,000	1,863,000	2,032,000
United States..................	4,287,000[2]	11,933,000	14,525,000
France.......................	1,922,000	1,962,000	2,963,000
Norway.......................	1,957,000	1,597,000	1,980,000
Japan........................	1,708,000	2,325,000	2,996,000
Holland......................	1,472,000	1,574,000	1,773,000
Italy.........................	1,430,000	1,238,000	2,118,000
Germany.....................	5,135,000	3,247,000	419,000

[1] Immediately after June, 1919, Germany was deprived by the Peace Treaty of most of the shipping which was still nominally hers. This reduced her total at once to below 700,000 tons, and that of the chief Allies was correspondingly increased.

[2] This includes not only transatlantic but also lake and river shipping as well.

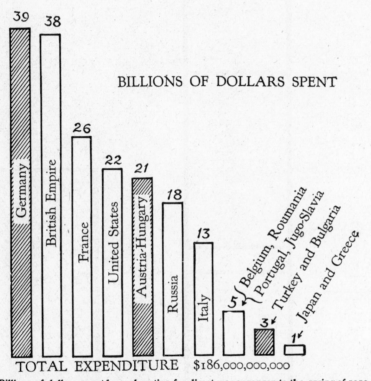

BILLIONS OF DOLLARS SPENT

39   38

26

22   21

18

13

5

3

1

Germany

British Empire

France

United States

Austria-Hungary

Russia

Italy

Belgium, Roumania
Portugal, Jugo-Slavia

Turkey and Bulgaria

Japan and Greece

TOTAL EXPENDITURE $186,000,000,000

Billions of dollars spent by each nation for direct war expenses to the spring of 1919.

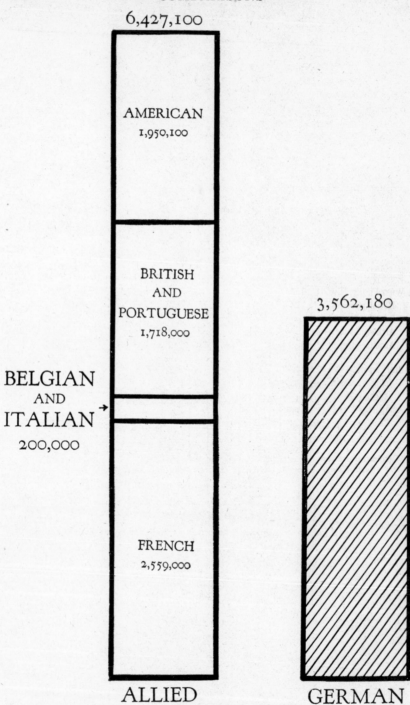

COMPARISONS

6,427,100

AMERICAN
1,950,100

BRITISH
AND
PORTUGUESE
1,718,000

3,562,180

BELGIAN
AND
ITALIAN
200,000

FRENCH
2,559,000

GERMAN

ALLIED

Ration strength of the allied and enemy forces on the Western front at the time
of the armistice

	Per Cent of Total for Three Naions			
	French	British	American	
WEST FRONT, NOV. 11, 1918				
Ration strength	41	28	31	
Length of front held	59	19	22	
Artillery in batteries	54	32	14	
Airplane strength	57	30	13	
ALL FRONTS, YEAR 1918				
Artillery ammunition fired,				
including training	51	43	6	
Small arms ammunition				
fired, including training	37	46	17	

Comparative strength of French, British, and American Armies at the signing of the armistice and comparative expenditures of ammunition during 1918.

COMPARISONS

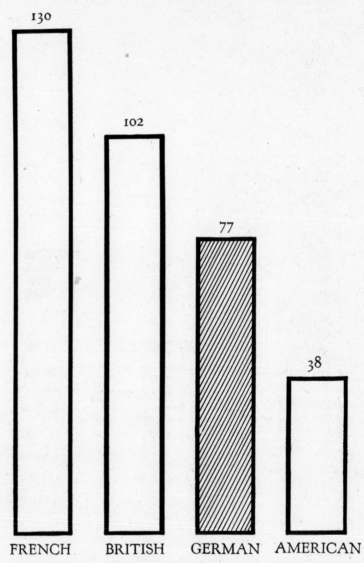

Number of battle airplanes per each 100,000 men in each army at the date of
the armistice.

COMPARISONS

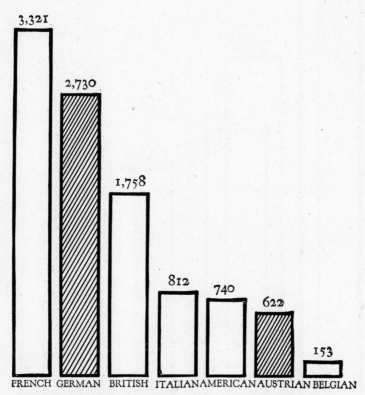

Number of battle airplanes in each army at the date of the armistice.

COMPARISONS

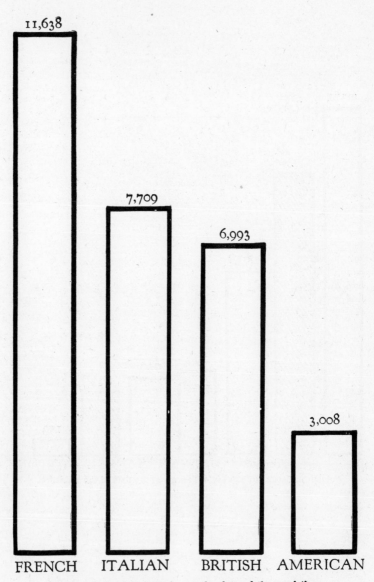

Guns organized in batteries at the date of the armistice.

	Belgian	French	British	American	
Jan. 31	5	69	25	1	
Feb. 28	5	67	25	3	
Mar. 21	5	66	25	4	
Mar. 30	5	72	19	4	
Apr. 10	5	70	19	6	
Apr. 20	5	72	17	6	
Apr. 30	5	72	17	6	
May 10	5	71	17	7	
May 20	5	74	17	4	
May 30	4	75	16	5	
June 10	4	73	16	7	
June 20	4	68	16	12	
June 30	4	69	16	11	
July 10	4	67	17	12	
July 20	4	67	18	11	
July 30	5	63	18	14	
Aug. 10	5	58	20	17	
Aug. 20	5	58	19	18	
Aug. 30	5	56	19	20	
Sept. 10	5	54	19	22	
Sept. 20	5	56	20	19	
Sept. 30	6	58	18	18	
Oct. 10	3	55	19	23	
Oct. 20	6	53	22	19	
Oct. 30	4	60	17	19	
Nov. 11	6	55	18	21	

Per cent of Western front held by each army during 1918. The Italian troops are included with the French and the Portuguese with the British.

COMPARISONS

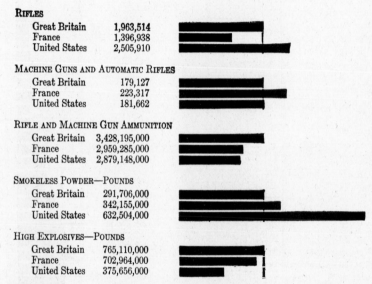

RIFLES

Great Britain	1,963,514
France	1,396,938
United States	2,505,910

MACHINE GUNS AND AUTOMATIC RIFLES

Great Britain	179,127
France	223,317
United States	181,662

RIFLE AND MACHINE GUN AMMUNITION

Great Britain	3,428,195,000
France	2,959,285,000
United States	2,879,148,000

SMOKELESS POWDER—POUNDS

Great Britain	291,706,000
France	342,155,000
United States	632,504,000

HIGH EXPLOSIVES—POUNDS

Great Britain	765,110,000
France	702,964,000
United States	375,656,000

Production of articles of ordnance by Great Britain, France, and the United States during the 19 months of American participation from Apr. 6, 1917, to Nov. 11, 1918.

COMPARISONS

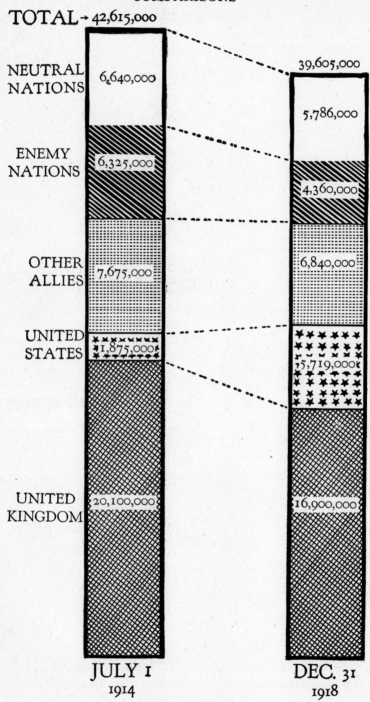

TOTAL → 42,615,000

NEUTRAL NATIONS — 6,640,000

ENEMY NATIONS — 6,325,000

OTHER ALLIES — 7,675,000

UNITED STATES — 1,875,000

UNITED KINGDOM — 20,100,000

JULY 1
1914

39,605,000

5,786,000

4,360,000

6,840,000

5,719,000

16,900,000

DEC. 31
1918

Seagoing merchant shipping of the world measured in gross tons on July 1, 1914, and Dec. 31, 1918.

CENTRAL EUROPE
SHOWING
NEW STATES

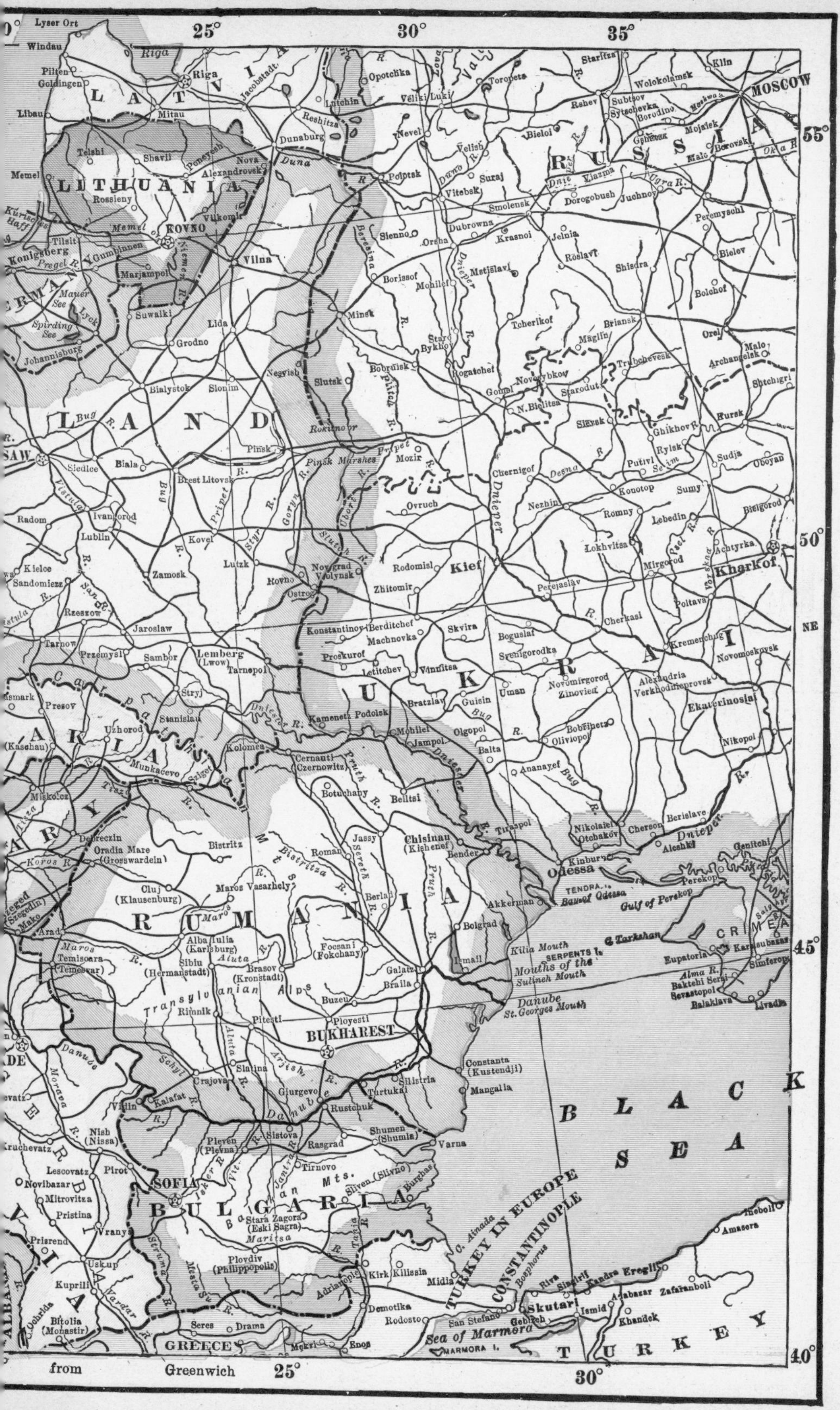

25°
30°
35°
55°
50°
45°
40°
NE
from Greenwich 25°
30°
LATVIA
LITHUANIA
POLAND
GERMANY
RUSSIA
UKRAINE
RUMANIA
BULGARIA
SERBIA
HUNGARY
GREECE
TURKEY IN EUROPE
TURKEY
BLACK SEA
CRIMEA
CONSTANTINOPLE
Sea of Marmora
MARMORA I.
Gulf of Perekop
Bay of Odessa
TENDRA I.
SERPENTS I.
C. Tarkhan
Kilia Mouth
Mouths of the Danube
Sulineh Mouth
St. Georges Mouth
Bosphorus
C. Ainada
Transylvanian Alps
Balkan Mts.
Carpathian Mts.
Pinsk Marshes
Riga
Kurisches Haff
Mauer See
Spirding See
Lyser Ort
Windau
Pilten
Goldingen
Libau
Mitau
Jacobstadt
Dunaburg
Reshitza
Lutchin
Opotchka
Veliki Luki
Toropets
Staritza
Wolokolamsk
Klin
MOSCOW
Rshev
Subtsov
Sytschevka
Borodino
Gshatsk
Mojaisk
Borovsk
Malo
Bieloi
Velish
Nevel
Telshi
Shavli
Poneyesh
Nova Alexandrovsk
Memel
Rossieny
Vilkomir
KOVNO
Tilsit
Konigsberg
Gumbinnen
Marjampol
Vilna
Suwalki
Lida
Grodno
Johannisburg
Polotsk
Vitebsk
Suraj
Smolensk
Viazma
Dorogobush
Juchnov
Peremyshl
Sienno
Orsha
Dubrowna
Krasnoi
Jelnia
Roslavl
Shisdra
Bielev
Borissof
Mohilef
Mstislavl
Bolchof
Minsk
Tcherikof
Briansk
Orel
Stary Bykhov
Maglin
Trubchevsk
Malo Archangelsk
Bobruisk
Rogatchef
Novozybkov
Starodub
Shtchigri
Negvish
Slutsk
Gomel
N. Bielitsa
Kursk
Bialystok
Slonim
Rokitno
Slavsk
Ghikhov
Rylsk
Pinsk
Mozir
Putivl
Sudja
Oboyan
Warsaw
Siedlce
Biala
Brest Litovsk
Chernigof
Konotop
Sumy
Ovruch
Nezhin
Romny
Lebedin
Bielgorod
Radom
Ivangorod
Lublin
Kovel
Lokhvitsa
Achtyrka
Kharkof
Kielce
Sandomierz
Zamosk
Lutzk
Rovno
Novgrad Volynsk
Ostrog
Rodomisl
Kief
Mirgorod
Zhitomir
Perejaslav
Poltava
Rzeszow
Jaroslaw
Konstantinov
Berditchef
Machnovka
Skvira
Boguslaf
Cherkasi
Tarnow
Przemysl
Sambor
Lemberg (Lwow)
Tarnopol
Proskurof
Letitchev
Vinnitsa
Svenigorodka
Kremenchug
Novomoskovsk
Stryj
Uman
Guisin
Novomirgorod
Zinoviev
Alexandria
Verkhodnieprovsk
Ekaterinoslaf
Kesmark
Presov
Stanislau
Bratzlav
Kamenetz Podolsk
Mohilef
Jampol
Olgopol
Bobrinetz
Oliviopol
Nikopol
Uzhorod (Kaschau)
Kolomea
Cernauti Czernowitz
Balta
Munkacevo
Szigel
Ananayef
Miskolcz
Botuchany
Beltsi
Debreczin
Oradia Mare (Grosswardein)
Bistritz
Jassy
Roman
Chisinau (Kishenef)
Bender
Tiraspol
Nikolaief
Otchakov
Cherson
Berislave
Aleshki
Genitchi
Kinburn
Odessa
Perekop
Cluj (Klausenburg)
Maros Vasarhely
Berlad
Akkerman
Szeged Szegedin
Mako
Arad
Alba Iulia (Karlsburg)
Focsani (Fokchany)
Bolgrad
Ismail
Eupatoria
Karasubasar
Simferopol
Temisoara (Temesvar)
Sibiu (Hermanstadt)
Brasov (Kronstadt)
Galatz
Braila
Baktchi Serai
Sevastopol
Balaklava
Livadia
Buzeu
Rimnik
Pitesti
Ployesti
BUKHAREST
Belgrade
Slatina
Constanta (Kustendji)
Mangalia
Crajova
Giurgevo
Silistria
Turtukai
Kalafat
Vidin
Rustchuk
Nish (Nissa)
Pleven (Plevna)
Sistova
Rasgrad
Shumen (Shumla)
Varna
Kruchevatz
Pirot
Tirnovo
Lescovatz
Novibazar
SOFIA
Sliven (Slivno)
Burghas
Mitrovitza
Pristina
Vranya
Stara Zagora (Eski Sagra)
Ineboli
Amasera
Prisrend
Plovdiv (Philippopolis)
Uskup
Kirk Kilissia
Midia
Riva
Sinerif
Kandra
Eregli
Kuprili
Adrianople
Demotika
Zafaranboli
Adabazar
Ismid
Khandek
Skutari
Gebizeh
San Stefano
Rodosto
Ochrida
Bitolia (Monastir)
Seres
Drama
Enos
Mekri
ALBANIA
Duna
Dvina R.
Niemen R.
Memel
Pregel R.
Lyck
Bug
Pripet R.
Goryn R.
Styr R.
Sluteh R.
Uborť R.
Beresina
Dnieper
Desna
Seim
Sula
Psel R.
Vorskla
Oka R.
Ugra R.
Moskwa
Volga
Lovat
Vistula
San R.
Dniester R.
Pruth R.
Sereth R.
Bistritza
Maros
Aluta
Schyl
Arjish
Danube
Tisza
Koros R.
Szamos
Morava
Timok
Isker R.
Vit R.
Jantra R.
Struma
Mesta Su
Maritsa
Tunja
Vardar
Alma R.

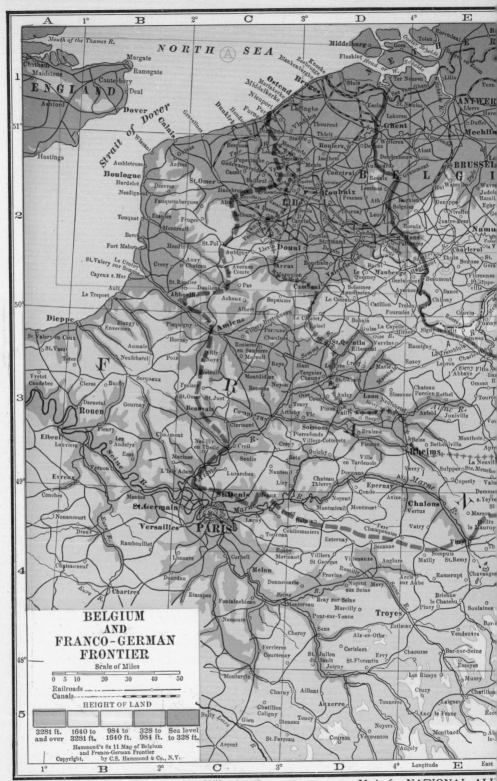

BELGIUM
AND
FRANCO-GERMAN
FRONTIER

Scale of Miles

0 5 10   20   30   40   50

Railroads ....
Canals .... ---- .... ----

HEIGHT OF LAND

| 3281 ft. and over | 1640 to 3281 ft. | 984 to 1640 ft. | 328 to 984 ft. | Sea level to 328 ft. |

Hammond's 8x11 Map of Belgium
and Franco-German Frontier
Copyright,   by C.S. Hammond & Co., N.Y.

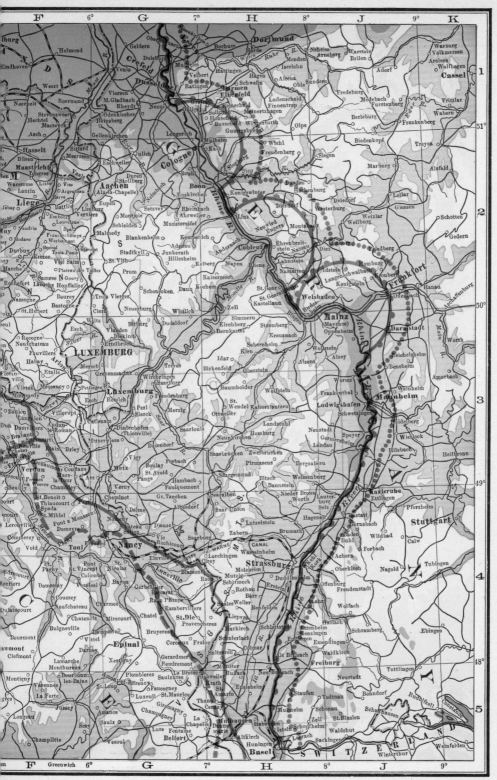

LIMIT OF ALLIED OCCUPATION ●━━●━━●
LIMIT OF NEUTRAL ZONE ●●●●●●●●●

LOWLANDS
OF
NORTHERN FRANCE
AND
BELGIUM
SCALE OF MILES

0   5   10   15

Railroads..............................
Canals..................................
Forts....................................
Fortresses..............................

HEIGHT OF LAND

656 feet and over
328 to 656 feet
164 to 328 "
0 to 164 "
Below Sea Level

Hammond's 8 x 11 Map of Northern France
Copyright by C.S.Hammond &Co,

ARMISTICE LINE NOV. 11th. 1918
FARTHEST GERMAN ADVANCE 1914
FARTHEST ALLIED ADVANCE TO
                    MARCH 1918
GERMAN ADVANCE 1918

N O R
S E

ENGLAND

Margate
Birchington
Herne Bay
Whitstable   Sarre
Faversham   Minster   Ramsgate
    Boughton   Sturry
Chilhamo   Canterbury   Wingham   Sandwich
    Chartham   Bridge
         Barham   Eastry
Ashford   Shoulden   Deal
    Smeeth   Walmer
Walmer   Lydden
Ruckinge   Shornchiffe   Ewell   DOVER
    Hythe   Sandgate   FOLKESTONE
    Dymchurch
New Romney
Littlestone
Lydd
Dungeness

STRAIT OF DOVER

E N G L I S H

C H A N N E L

Paris Plage
Touquet
Cucq
Merlimont
Berck
La Plage
Waben
Fort Mahon
Quend le Jeune
St.Quentin en Tourmont
le Hourdel
Nouveau Brighton
St.Valery sur Somme
Cayeux sur Mer
Lanchères

DUNKIRK
St.Pol
Gravelines   Loon-Plage   Ft.Castelna
Oye   Ft.Franca
Marck   St.Folquin   Bourbourg   Steene
CALAIS   Nieulay   Coppenax
Sangatte   Les Attaques   St.Pierre-Brouck   Bissex
Escalles   Audruicq   Zeggers Capp
Wissant   Watten   Ochtez
Le Gris-Nez   Gulnes   Ardres   Noordpe
Cape Gris-Nez   Leubringhen   Landrethon   Zuyt
Audresselles   Marquise   Lieques   Nordausques   Ft.de la Bar
Ambleteuse   Moulle   Ft.aux Mo
Wimereux   Wimille   Colembert   Journy   Ft.des 4 Moulins
        Longueville   ST.OMER
BOULOGNE   Coulomby   Lumbres   Pihem
Le Porte   Hardelot   River   Witte
Wirwignes   Desvres   Vismes   Thérouanne   Lis
Condette   Samer   Campagne-les-Boulonnais
Nesdigneu   Rumilly   Fauquembergues   St.Hi
Nesles   Zoteux   Enquin   Auchy
Dannes   Frencq   Hucqueliers   Radinghem   Westrehem
Camiers   Maninghem   Quilen   643   Lisbourg   Flori
Etaples   Fruges   Heuchin
Neuville   Ruisseauville   Azincourt   Be
Montreuil   Beaurainville   Blangy   Anuin   Valhues
Brimeux   Fequemicourt   Wavrans   Bryas
Wailly   Campagne-les-Hesdin   Magni
    Lépine   Hesdin   Le Parcq   St.Pol   Richou
Nampont St.Martin   Wail   Herlin-le-Sec   Averd
Douriez   Galametz   Buneville   Sibiville
Vron   Régnauville   River Nunco   Bouber
Dompierre   Labroy   le Boisle   Erin
Bernoy   Crécy   Froyelles   Willencourt   Bonfières   Grand F
Rue   en Ponthieu   Auxi le Château   Noeux
Forest Abbaye   Canchy   Hiermonto   Bealcourt   Bouquemaisonc
Noyelles sur Mer   Yvrench   Conteville   Mézerelles   Neuvillette
Hautvillers   Occoches   Frohen le Grande
Boismont   Grouch
Beaumetz   Us

Made for NATIONAL ALUMNI   M A

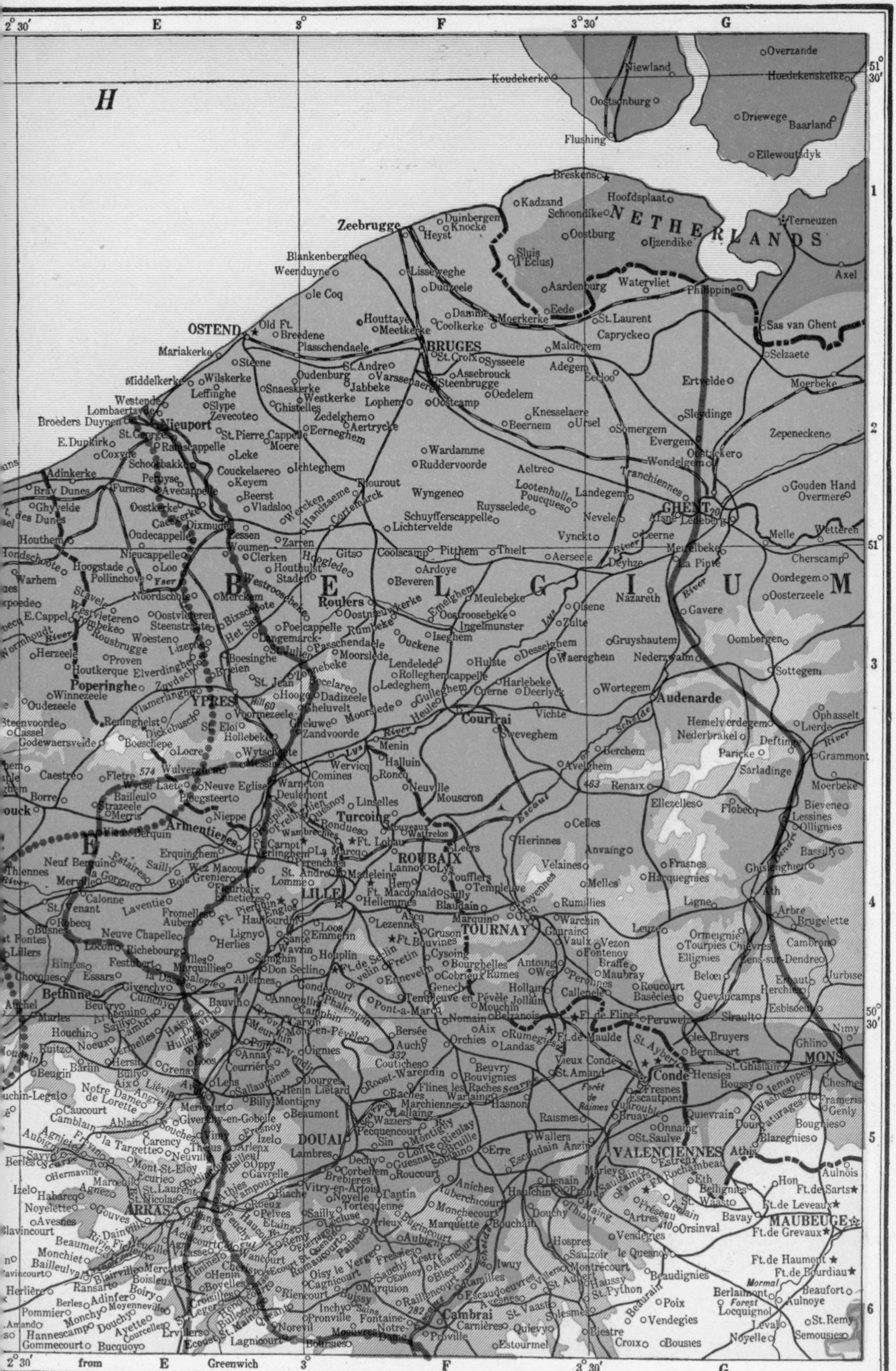

2° 30′
E
3°
F
3° 30′
G
H
51° 30′
1
2
51°
3
4
50° 30′
5
6
NETHERLANDS
BELGIUM
Overzande
Hoedekenskerke
Koudekerke
Niewland
Oostsonburg
Driewege
Baarland
Flushing
Ellewoutsdyk
Breskens
Kadzand
Hoofdsplaat
Schoondike
Terneuzen
Zeebrugge
Duinbergen
Knocke
Heyst
Oostburg
Ijzendike
Sluis (l'Eclus)
Blankenberghe
Weenduyne
Lisseweghe
Dudzeele
Aardenburg
Watervliet
Philippine
Axel
le Coq
Houttaye
Meetkerke
Damme
Coolkerke
Moerkerke
Eede
St. Laurent
Caprycke
Sas van Ghent
OSTEND
Old Ft.
Breedene
Plasschendaele
BRUGES
St. Croix
Sysseele
Maldegem
Adegem
Eecloo
Selzaete
Mariakerke
Steene
St. Andre
Oudenburg
Varssenaere
Assebrouck
Steenbrugge
Ertvelde
Moerbeke
Middelkerke
Wilskerke
Leffinghe
Snaeskerke
Jabbeke
Westkerke
Lophem
Oostcamp
Oedelem
Westende
Lombaertzyde
Slype
Zevecote
Ghistelles
Zedelghem
Aertrycke
Knesselaere
Ursel
Sleydinge
Broeders Duynen
Nieuport
St. Georges
St. Pierre Cappelle
Moere
Eerneghem
Beernem
Somergem
Zepenecken
E. Dunkirk
Ramscappelle
Coxyde
Leke
Schoorbakke
Wardamme
Ruddervoorde
Evergem
Oostacker
Wondelgem
Adinkerke
Pervyse
Couckelaere
Keyem
Ichteghem
Aeltre
Tranchiennes
Bray Dunes
Furnes
Avecappelle
Beerst
Vladsloo
Thourout
Wyngene
Lootenhulle
Poucques
Landegem
Gouden Hand
Overmere
Ghyvelde
Oostkerke
Caeskerke
Werken
Handzaeme
Cortemarck
Ruysselede
GHENT
Afsne
Ledeberg
Houthem
Oudecappelle
Dixmude
Eessen
Schuyfferscappelle
Lichtervelde
Vynckt
Nevele
Leerne
Melle
Wetteren
Woumen
Zarren
Nieucappelle
Clerken
Hondschoote
Gits
Coolscamp
Pitthem
Thielt
Aerseele
Deynze
Meulebeke
La Pinte
Cherscamp
Hoogstade
Loo
Houthulst
Hooglede
Ardoye
Oordegem
Warhem
Pollinchove
Yser
Staden
Westroosebeke
Beveren
Oosterzeele
Noordschoote
Merckem
Roulers
Meulebeke
Olsene
Nazareth
Gavere
E. Cappel
Westvleteren
Oostvleteren
Bixschoote
Oostnieuwkerke
Emelghem
Oostroosebeke
Zulte
Crombeke
Steenstraate
Het Sas
Poelcappelle
Rumbeke
Ingelmunster
Rousbrugge
Woesten
Langemarck
Passchendaele
Ouckene
Iseghem
Desselghem
Gruyshautem
Oombergen
Herzeele
Lizerne
St. Julien
Moorslede
Nederzwalm
Proven
Boesinghe
Zonnebeke
Lendelede
Hulste
Waereghem
Houtkerque
Elverdinghe
Brielen
Rolleghemcappelle
Harlebeke
Sottegem
Poperinghe
Zuydschoote
St. Jean
Becelaere
Ledeghem
Deerlyck
Wortegem
Winnezeele
Vlamertinghe
Hooge
Dadizeele
Gulleghem
Cuerne
Oudezeele
YPRES
Hill 60
Gheluvelt
Moorslede
Heule
Audenarde
Reninghelst
Voormezeele
Courtrai
Vichte
Ophasselt
Steenvoorde
Dickebusch
St. Eloi
Gheluwe
Schelde
Hemelverdegem
Lierde
Cassel
Hollebeke
Zandvoorde
Sweveghem
Nederbrakel
Godewaersvelde
Boeschepe
Menin
Deftinge
Locre
Wytschaete
Lys
River
Paricke
Grammont
Berchem
Caestre
Wulverghem
Messines
Wervicq
Halluin
Avelghem
Sarladinge
Fletre
Wytse Laete
Neuve Eglise
Comines
Roncq
Renaix
Moerbeke
Borre
Bailleul
Ploegsteert
Warneton
Deulemont
Linselles
Neuville
Mouscron
Ellezelles
Flobecq
Bievene
Strazeele
Frelinghien
Quesnoy
Lessines
Meteren
Merris
Nieppe
Turcoing
Escaut
Celles
Ollignies
Armentieres
Bondues
Wattrelos
Bac St. Maur
Herinnes
Dendre
Estaires
Erquinghem
Ft. Carnot
Ft. Lobau
Leers
Anvaing
Bassilly
Neuf Berquin
La Gorgue
Sailly
Verlinghem
Wambrechies
La Marcq
ROUBAIX
Velaines
Frasnes
Merville
Laventie
Bois Grenier
Wez Macquart
Perenchies
St. Andre
Lannoy
Lys
Toufflers
Templeuve
Melles
Hacquegnies
Ghislenghien
Calonne
Fleurbaix
Lomme
Madeleine
Hem
Rumillies
Ligne
Ath
St. Venant
Fromelles
Ennetieres
Ft. Pierrebin
Englos
LILLE
Ft. Macdonald
Hellemmes
Sailly
Blaudain
Froyennes
Orcq
Warchin
Arbre
Brugelette
Robecq
Aubers
Haubourdin
Lezennes
Ascq
Marquain
TOURNAY
Gaurain
Leuze
Ormeignie
Busnes
Neuve Chapelle
Lignv
Loos
Emmerin
Gruson
Ft. Bouvines
Vaulx
Vezon
Tourpies
Chievres
Cambron
Lillers
Herlies
Santes
Wavrin
Houplin
Cysoing
Fontenoy
Ellignies
Lens-sur-Dendre
Richebourg
Festubert
Illes
Marquillies
Sainghin
Don Seclin
Ft. de Seclin
Fretin
Bourghelles
Antoing
Braffe
Maubray
Beloeil
Hinges
Essars
La Bassee
Salome
Allennes
Ennevelin
Rumes
Wez
Roucourt
Basecles
Quevaucamps
Erbaut
Chocques
Givenchy
Gondecourt
Cobrieux
Genech
Peronnes
Hollain
Jollain
Herchies
Jurbise
Bethune
Cuinchy
Bauvin
Annoeullin
Phalempin
Templeuve en Pevele
Mouchin
Callenelle
Esbisoeul
Annezin
Beuvry
Carvin
Pont-a-Marcq
Bercanois
Ft. de Flines
Peruwelz
Sirault
Annequin
Auchel
Marles
Sailly
Cambrin
Haisnes
Douvrin
Wingles
Mons-en-Pevele
Nomain
Aix
Rumegies
Ft. de Maulde
Les Bruyers
Nimy
Houchin
Noeux
Vermelles
Hulluch
Meurchin
Pont-a-Vendin
Bersee
Orchies
Landas
Bernissart
Ghlin
Ruitz
Annay
Oignies
Auchy
Vieux Conde
St. Aybert
MONS
Grenay
Loos
Courrieres
Coutiches
Beuvry
St. Amand
Conde
Hensies
St. Ghislain
Beugin
Barlin
Hersin
Bully
Lens
Sallaumines
Dourges
Henin Lietard
Roost-Warendin
Bouvignies
Flines les Raches
Scarpe
Foret de Raimes
Fresnes
Escautpont
Boussy
Jemappes
Chesmes
Notre Dame de Lorette
Aix
Angres
Lievin
Mericourt
Billy-Montigny
Raches
Marchiennes
Wallers
Hasnon
Quarouble
Quievrain
Wasmes
Frameries
Genly
Caucourt
Ablain
Souchez
Givenchy-en-Gobelle
Beaumont
Lallaing
Waziers
Raismes
Bruay
Onnaing
Dour
Bougnies
Camblain
Carency
Thelus
Vimy
Fresnoy
Izel
Pecquencourt
Montigny
Rieulay
Bruille
Valenciennes
St. Saulve
Blaregnies
Aubigny
Villers
la Targette
Neuville
Arleux
DOUAI
Sin
Lambres
Guesnain
Loffre
Somain
Erre
Escaudain
Anzin
VALENCIENNES
Estreux
Athis
Aulnois
Savy
Acq
Mont-St-Eloy
Ecurie
Oppy
Gavrelle
Dechy
Roucourt
Marly
Rochambeau
Hon
Ft. de Sarts
Hermaville
Maroeuil
Roclincourt
Izelo
Habarcq
Agnez
St. Laurent
St. Nicolas
Athies
Fampoux
Corbehem
Brebieres
Vitry-en-Artois
Aniches
Denain
Prouvy
Famars
Eth
Bellignies
Ft. de Leveau
Noyelette
ARRAS
Biache
Noyelle
Cantin
Auberchicourt
Haulchin
Thiant
Maing
Preseau
St. Waast
Jenlain
Bavay
Avesnes
Gouves
Roeux
Pelves
Tortequenne
Douchy
Artres
Orsinval
MAUBEUGE
Blavincourt
Beaumetz
Dainville
Feuchy
Etaing
Sailly
Lecluse
Arleux
Bugnicourt
Monchecourt
Marquette
Bouchain
Vendegies
Ft. de Grevaux
Fichel
Neuville
Achicourt
Wancourt
Remy
Ecourt St. Quentin
Aubigny
Fressies
Abancourt
Hospres
Sauzoir
le Quesnoy
Monchiet
Blairville
Mercatel
Henin
Cherisy
Rumaucourt
Palluel
Oisy le Verger
Sauchy Lestre
Epinoy
Blecourt
Iwuy
Montrecourt
Ft. de Haumont
Ft. de Bourdiau
Bailleulval
Ransart
Boiry
Boyelles
Croisilles
Bullecourt
Riencourt
Cagnicourt
Marquion
Raillencourt
Ramillies
Villers
Haussy
Beaudignies
Berlaimont
Mormal Forest
Beaufort
Herliere
Adinfer
Moyenneville
Quéant
Inchy
Buissy
Sains
Escaudoeuvres
Avesnes
St. Aubert
St. Python
Beaurain
Poix
Locquignol
Aulnoye
Pommier
Monchy
Douchy
Ayette
Ecoust
Noreuil
Pronville
Fontaine-Notre-Dame
Cambrai
St. Vaast
Solesmes
Vendegies
Levalo
St. Remy
Hannescamp
Courcelles
Ervillers
St. Mein
Lagnicourt
Bourlon
Moeuvres
Proville
Carnieres
Quievy
Beaurepaire
Noyelle
Semousies
Gommecourt
Bucquoy
Estourmel
Croix
Bousies
from
Greenwich

A"

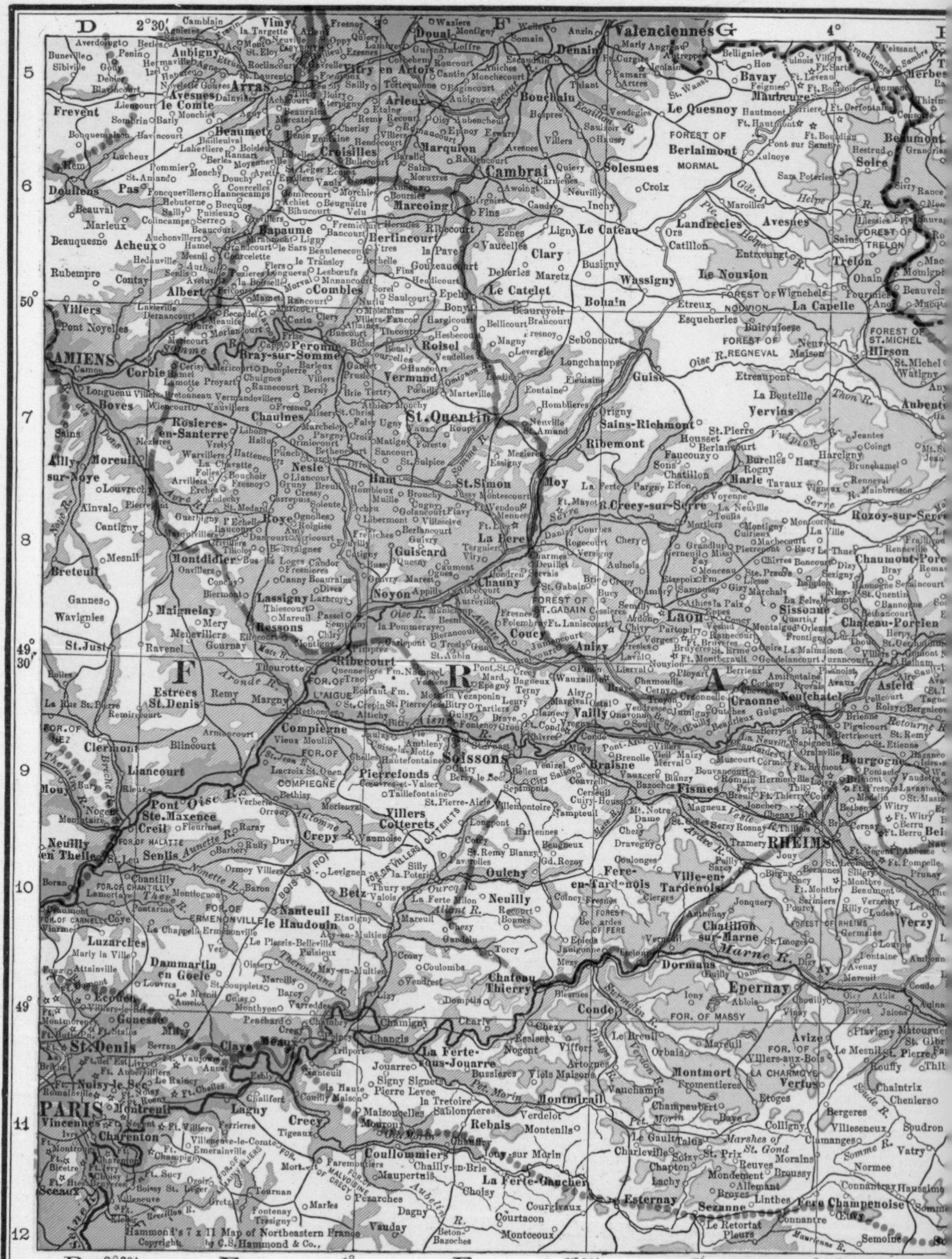

Valenciennes
Douai
Arras
Cambrai
Bapaume
Albert
AMIENS
Peronne
St. Quentin
Le Cateau
Landrecies
Avesnes
Maubeuge
Le Quesnoy
FOREST OF MORMAL
Guise
Hirson
Vervins
Laon
La Fere
Ham
Nesle
Roye
Montdidier
Noyon
Chauny
Coucy
Soissons
Compiegne
FOR. OF COMPIEGNE
Villers Cotterets
FOR. OF VILLERS COTTERETS
Senlis
Creil
Chantilly
Clermont
Beauvais
Braisne
Fismes
RHEIMS
Craonne
Neufchatel
Sissonne
Chateau-Porcien
Rethel
Chateau Thierry
Dormans
Epernay
Montmirail
La Ferte-sous-Jouarre
Meaux
Coulommiers
La Ferte-Gaucher
Esternay
Sezanne
Fere Champenoise
Marshes of St. Gond
St. Denis
PARIS
Vincennes
Charenton
Sceaux
Aisne R.
Marne R.
Oise R.
Somme R.
Ourcq R.
Hammond's 7 x 11 Map of Northeastern France
Copyright by C.S. Hammond & Co.,
D 2°30′ E 3° F 3°30′ G 4° Longitude H

ARMISTICE LINE NOV. 11th 1918

FARTHEST GERMAN ADVANCE 1914

Made for NATIONAL ALUMNI

MA

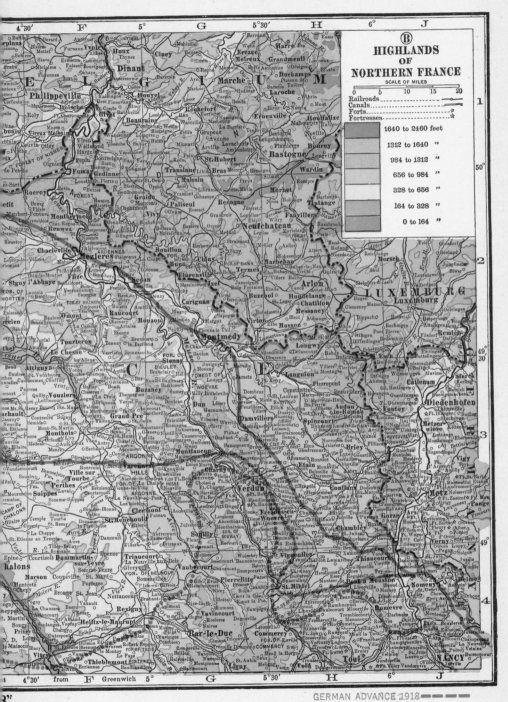

HIGHLANDS OF NORTHERN FRANCE

SCALE OF MILES

0   5   10   15   20

Railroads ....
Canals ....
Forts ....
Fortresses ....

1640 to 2460 feet
1312 to 1640 "
984 to 1312 "
656 to 984 "
328 to 656 "
164 to 328 "
0 to 164 "

GERMAN ADVANCE 1918

FARTHEST ALLIED ADVANCE TO MARCH 1918

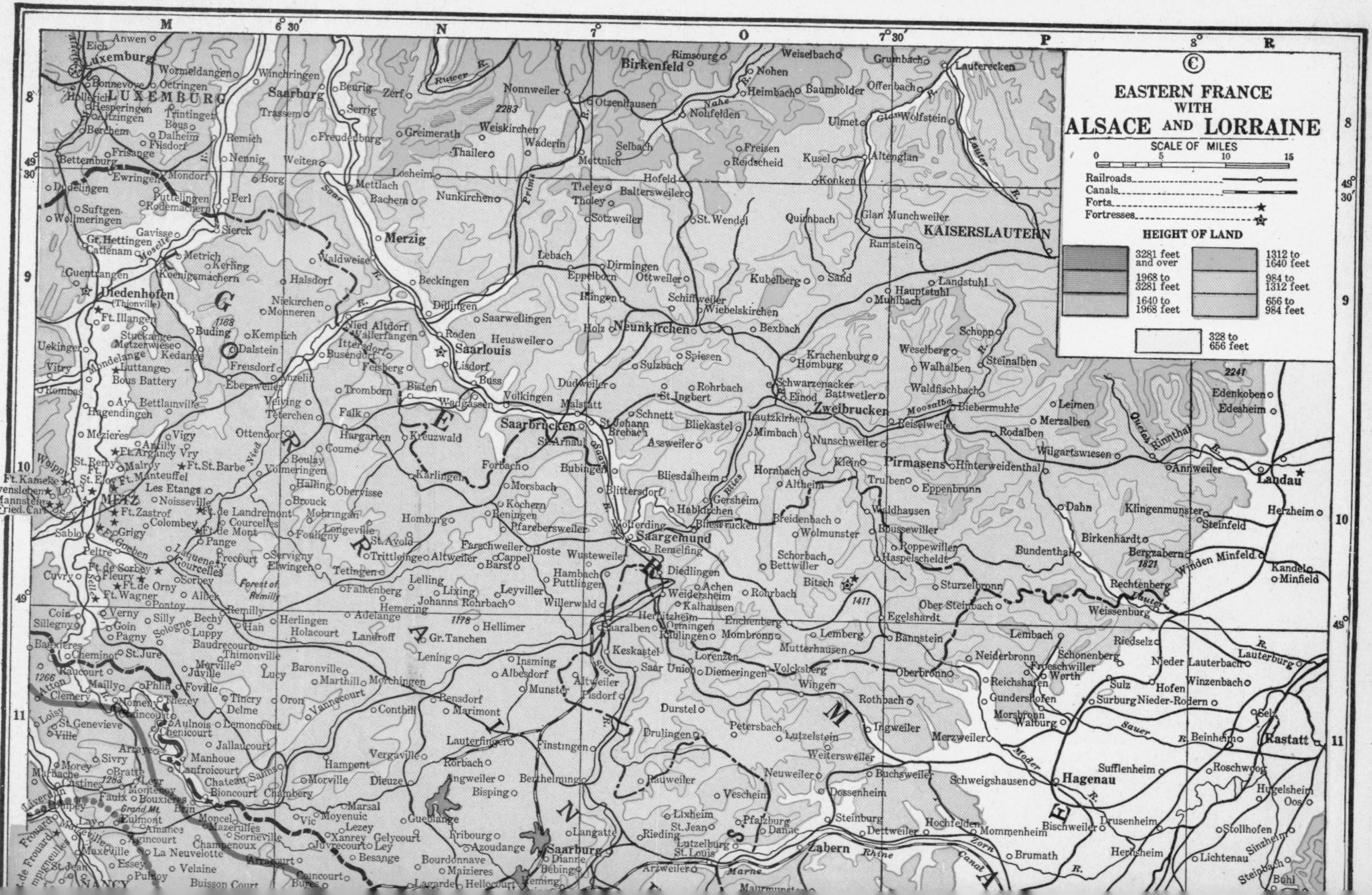
EASTERN FRANCE WITH ALSACE AND LORRAINE
SCALE OF MILES
0 5 10 15
Railroads
Canals
Forts
Fortresses
HEIGHT OF LAND
3281 feet and over
1968 to 3281 feet
1640 to 1968 feet
1312 to 1640 feet
984 to 1312 feet
656 to 984 feet
328 to 656 feet
LUXEMBURG
Luxemburg
Diedenhofen (Thionville)
Metz
Saarburg
Merzig
Saarlouis
Saarbrucken
Neunkirchen
Birkenfeld
KAISERSLAUTERN
Zweibrucken
Pirmasens
Landau
Saargemund
Bitsch
Weissenburg
Hagenau
Rastatt
Zabern
Saarburg
Nancy
LORRAINE
ALSACE

MAP

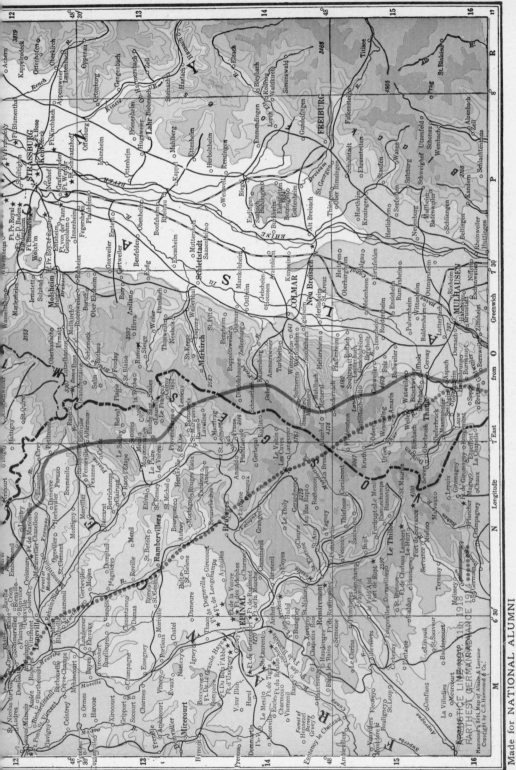

"C"

Made for NATIONAL ALUMNI

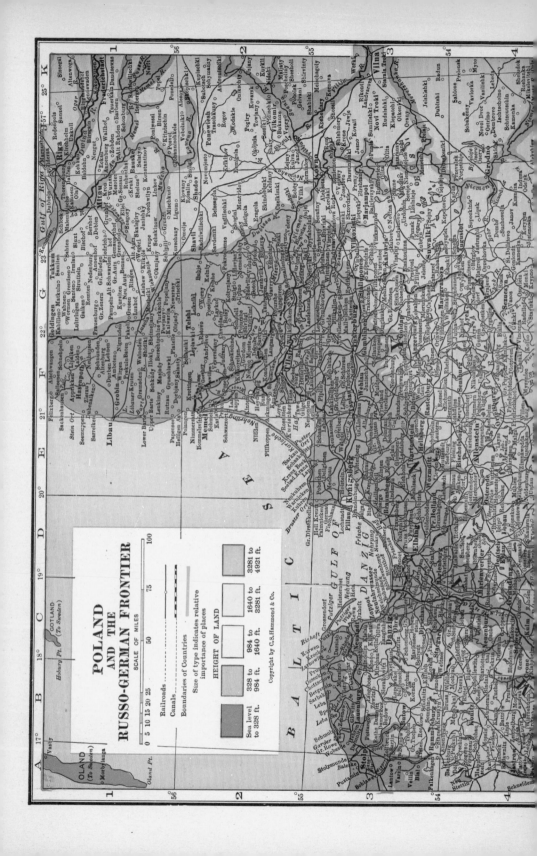

POLAND
AND THE
RUSSO-GERMAN FRONTIER

SCALE OF MILES

Copyright by C.S.Hammond & Co.

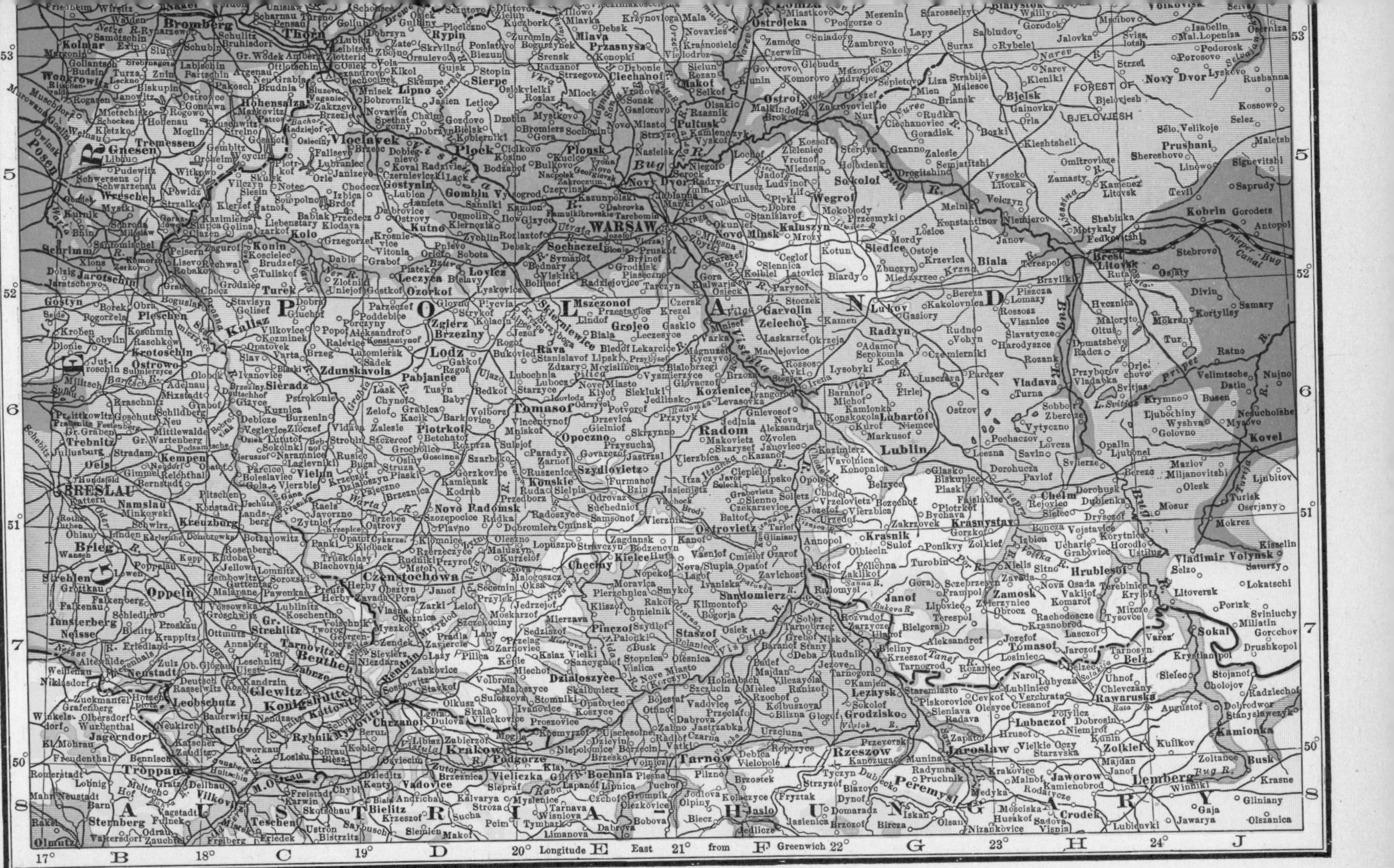
P O L A N D
A U S T R I A - H U N G A R Y
G E R
Bromberg
Thorn
Posen
Gnesen
Hohensalza
Vloclavek
Plock
Lipno
Mlava
Przasnysz
Ostroleka
Lomza
Bjelsk
FOREST OF BJELOVJESH
Novy Dvor
Prushani
Kobrin
Brest Litovsk
Pultusk
Ciechanof
Plonsk
WARSAW
Sochaczef
Siedlce
Sokolof
Vegrof
Biala
Lukov
Radzyn
Vladava
Kovel
Lodz
Zgierz
Brzeziny
Skierniewice
Rava
Grojec
Garvolin
Lublin
Lubartof
Chelm
Krasnystaw
Hrublesof
Zamosk
Vladimir Volynsk
Kalisz
Turek
Kolo
Konin
Kutno
Leczyca
Lovicz
Pabjanice
Piotrkof
Tomasof
Radom
Kozienice
Opoczno
Konskie
Szydlovietz
Kielce
Checiny
Sandomierz
Ostrovietz
Novo Radomsk
Czenstochowa
Sieradz
Zdunskavola
Vielun
Kempen
Ostrovo
BRESLAU
Oppeln
Brieg
Kreuzburg
Beuthen
Gleiwitz
Konigshutte
Kattowitz
Krakow
Podgorze
Tarnow
Rzeszow
Jaroslaw
Peremysl
Lemberg
Rawaruska
Zolkief
Jaworow
Troppau
Teschen
Bielitz
Sokal
Bug R.
Vistula
Narev R.
Pripet
Dnieper - Bug Canal
Warta
Oder
17°
18°
19°
20° Longitude East 21° from Greenwich 22°
23°
24°
53
52
51
50
5
6
7
8
B
C
D
E
F
G
H
J
Made for NATIONAL ALUMNI

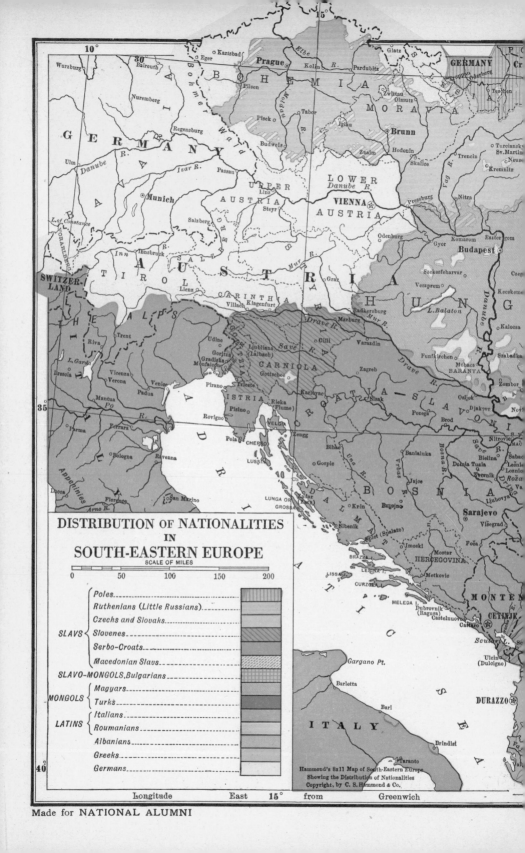

DISTRIBUTION OF NATIONALITIES
IN
SOUTH-EASTERN EUROPE

SCALE OF MILES

| 0 | 50 | 100 | 150 | 200 |

	Poles
	Ruthenians (Little Russians)
	Czechs and Slovaks
SLAVS	Slovenes
	Serbo-Croats
	Macedonian Slavs
SLAVO-MONGOLS	Bulgarians
MONGOLS	Magyars
	Turks
LATINS	Italians
	Roumanians
	Albanians
	Greeks
	Germans

Hammond's 8x11 Map of South-Eastern Europe
Showing the Distribution of Nationalities
Copyright, by C. S. Hammond & Co.

Longitude   East   15°   from   Greenwich

Made for NATIONAL ALUMNI

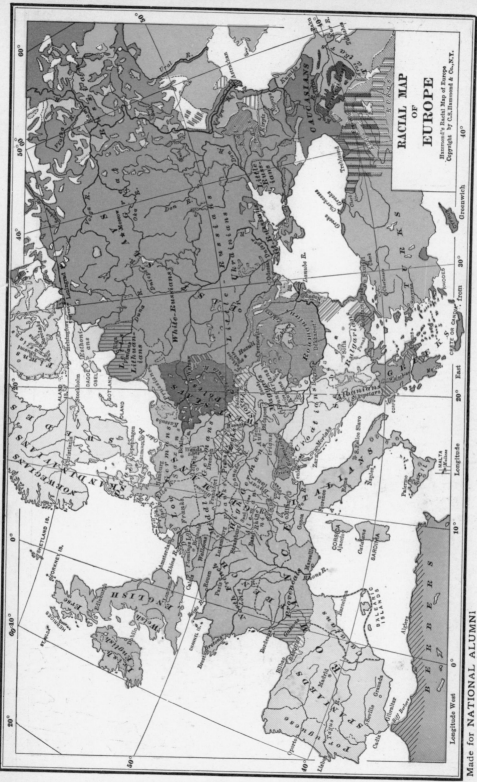

RACIAL MAP
OF
EUROPE

Hammond's Racial Map of Europe
Copyright by C.S.Hammond & Co.,N.Y.

Made for NATIONAL ALUMNI

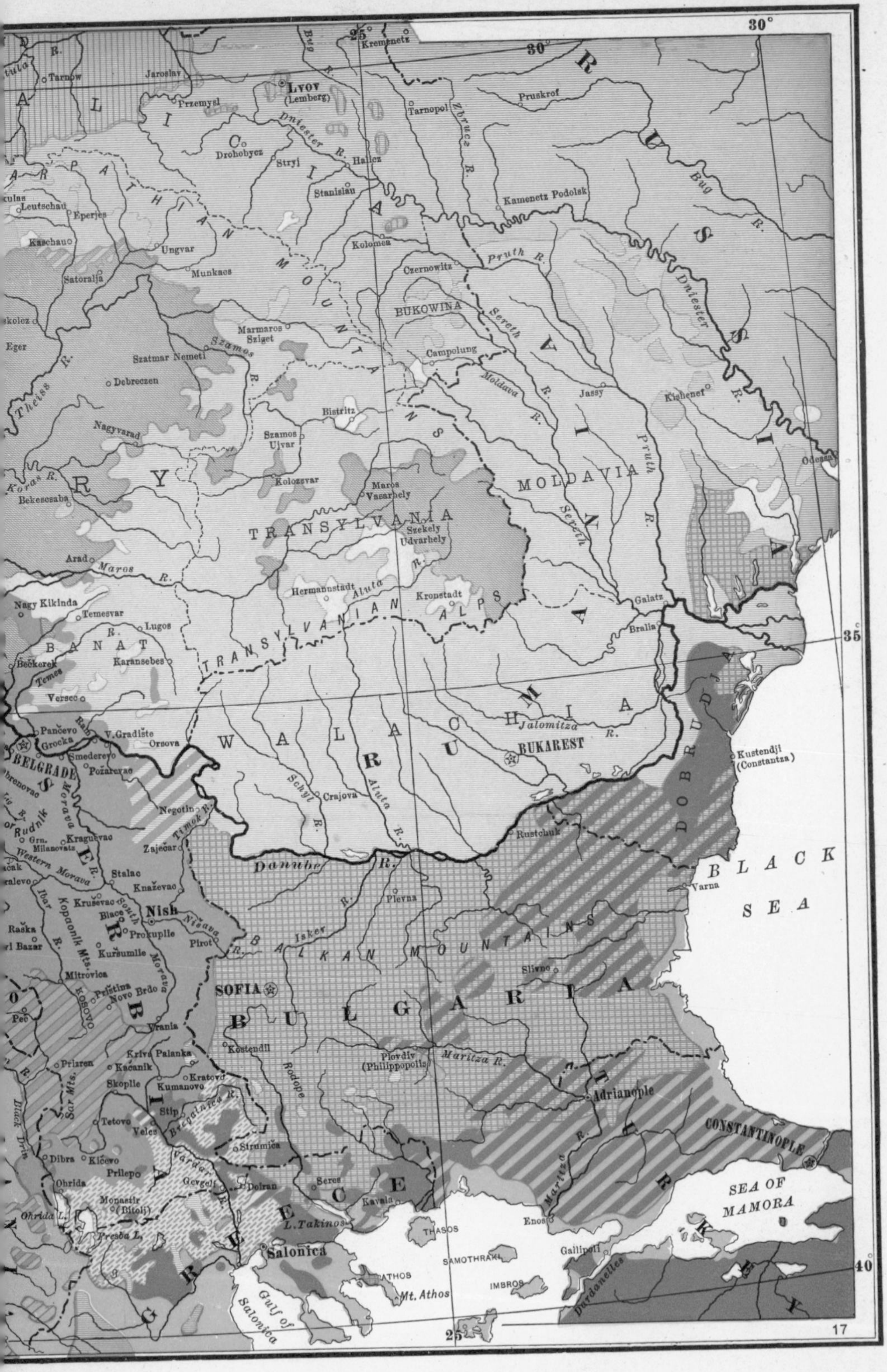

RUSSIA
BESSARABIA
GALICIA
CARPATHIAN MOUNTAINS
HUNGARY
TRANSYLVANIA
TRANSYLVANIAN ALPS
BUKOWINA
MOLDAVIA
WALLACHIA
RUMANIA
DOBRUDJA
BANAT
SERBIA
BULGARIA
BALKAN MOUNTAINS
GREECE
TURKEY
BLACK SEA
SEA OF MAMORA
Gulf of Salonica
Lvov (Lemberg)
Kremenetz
Tarnow
Jaroslav
Przemysl
Drohobycz
Stryj
Halicz
Stanislau
Kolomea
Czernowitz
Tarnopol
Pruskrof
Kamenetz Podolsk
Leutschau
Eperjes
Kaschau
Ungvar
Munkacs
Satoralja
Eger
Marmaros Sziget
Szatmar Nemeti
Debreczen
Nagyvarad
Bekescsaba
Arad
Szamos Ujvar
Kolozsvar
Bistritz
Campolung
Jassy
Kishenef
Odessa
Maros Vasarhely
Szekely Udvarhely
Hermannstadt
Kronstadt
Galatz
Braila
Nagy Kikinda
Temesvar
Lugos
Karansebes
Beckerek
Versec
Pančevo
Grocka
V. Gradište
Orsova
BELGRADE
Smederevo
Požarevac
Obrenovac
Negotin
Kragujevac
Grn. Milanovatz
Zaječar
Stalac
Knaževac
Kruševac
Nish
Blace
Prokuplje
Pirot
Kuršumlie
Mitrovica
Priština
Novo Brdo
Vrania
Peć
Prizren
Kriva Palanka
Kačanik
Kratovo
Skoplje
Kumanovo
Štip
Tetovo
Veles
Strumica
Dibra
Kičevo
Prilep
Ohrida
Gevgeli
Doiran
Monastir (Bitolj)
Salonica
Seres
Kavala
Craiova
BUKAREST
Rustchuk
Kustendji (Constantza)
Varna
Plevna
SOFIA
Kostendil
Slivno
Plovdiv (Philippopolis)
Adrianople
CONSTANTINOPLE
Enos
Gallipoli
THASOS
SAMOTHRAKI
IMBROS
ATHOS
Mt. Athos
Danube R.
Dniester R.
Bug R.
Zbrucz R.
Pruth R.
Sereth R.
Moldava R.
Theiss R.
Szamos R.
Maros R.
Koros R.
Temes R.
Aluta R.
Schyl R.
Jalomitza R.
Timok R.
Morava R.
Western Morava R.
South Morava
Ibar R.
Nišava R.
Isker R.
Maritza R.
Rodope
Vardar R.
Bregalnica R.
Black Drin
Sar Mts.
Kopaonik Mts.
Rudnik
KOSOVO
Ohrida L.
Presba L.
L. Takinos
Dardanelles
25
30
30°
35
40
17